THE ECONOMY OF PROMISES

The Economy of Promises

Trust, Power, and Credit in America

Bruce G. Carruthers

PRINCETON UNIVERSITY PRESS

PRINCETON AND OXFORD

Published by Princeton University Press
41 William Street, Princeton, New Jersey 08540
99 Banbury Road, Oxford OX2 6JX

press.princeton.edu

All Rights Reserved
ISBN: 978-0-691-23538-7
ISBN (e-book): 978-0-691-23621-6

British Library Cataloging-in-Publication Data is available

Editorial: Meagan Levinson and Jacqueline Delaney
Production Editorial: Jenny Wolkowicki
Jacket design: Karl Spurzem
Production: Erin Suydam
Publicity: James Schneider and Kathryn Stevens

This book has been composed in Adobe Text Pro

Printed on acid-free paper. ∞

Printed in the United States of America

10 9 8 7 6 5 4 3 2 1

CONTENTS

ACKNOWLEDGMENTS

It will surprise no one that in taking so long to write a book about promises and credit, I have made many promises and accumulated many debts. Long before this project started, my academic career began because two professors at Simon Fraser University showed me what curiosity looked like and encouraged me to follow suit: many decades later I am still grateful to Paul Heyer and Anthony Wilden for setting an example. Working with William Leiss, William D. Richards Jr., Dallas W. Smythe, and M. A. Stephens further enriched my undergraduate experience, although I doubt I did much for them. Curiosity then carried me away from communications theory and semiotics and toward economic sociology, and eventually to this book. I spent 2006–7 at the Radcliffe Institute for Advanced Study, then directed by the outstanding Drew Faust, where I began to think seriously about this project. The late Judy Vichnaic helped make it a very special experience indeed. Then in 2013–14, I visited the Wissenschaftskolleg zu Berlin and wish to thank the former rector Luca Giuliani and institute staff for ensuring a memorable and fruitful year. I especially thank the other Wiko fellows whose world-class expertise reminded me why it is such a pleasure to hang with very smart and talented people. Thanks to a Cary and Ann Maguire Fellowship from the Kluge Center, I spent the summer of 2016 at the incomparable Library of Congress, tracking down sources and following clues that led through the library's rich collections. The Kluge staff ensured a most productive stay and granted me the able research assistance of Rachel Linton, then a Georgetown undergraduate. I was able to work on this book again in 2018–19 during a wonderful year in Uppsala spent at the Swedish Collegium for Advanced Study. I thank Christina Garsten, the current Principal, and Bjorn Wittrock, the former Principal, and all of the staff for their warm support, as well as my fellow Fellows, who provided unending intellectual stimulation and great fun. Many different academic audiences have heard parts of the argument, and have offered useful feedback and encouragement, but my academic home for the past thirty years has been the Sociology

Department at Northwestern University. Many fine colleagues have come and gone, but what never leaves is a robust ethos of civility embraced by a diverse community of researchers and a commitment to rigorous social scientific inquiry pursued in many ways. Among this group, some heroically played multiple roles, and so I must acknowledge that Carol Heimer and Art Stinchcombe were simultaneously colleagues, friends, neighbors, and cofounders of the Lochinvar Society. I appreciate how much those who share my end of the hallway have indulged me in conversation over many years: Mary Pattillo, Steve Epstein, Laura Beth Nielsen, and Ann Orloff are particularly tolerant interlocutors, although proximity to my office made it hard for them to escape. I have also enjoyed years of stimulation thanks to the Comparative-Historical Social Science workshop, with usual suspects who included Jim Mahoney, Ann Orloff, Monica Prasad, and Tony Chen. I owe a particular debt of gratitude to Timothy Guinnane and Monica Prasad, who both read the entire manuscript and provided detailed comments and terrific suggestions during a global pandemic. Had we been alive during the Black Death, I suspect they would have quickly responded to my draft illuminated manuscripts and, inter alia, corrected the Latin and kindly explained where I misunderstood Aristotle. I also appreciate the comments I received from two anonymous reviewers for the press, and I have tried to honor their many good suggestions. Of course, they bear no responsibility for my errors. My editor from Princeton University Press, Meagan Levinson, was a distinct pleasure to work with, and I appreciate Jenn Backer's very capable copyediting. Thanks to Julia Braham for help with the index. For some key cites on the history of black-owned banks, I thank Geoff Clark, and I must thank Howard Bodenhorn for steering me to Geoff Clark. For specific advice on flow-of-funds data, I thank Bill English, and also thank Tim Guinnane (again) for pointing me in the direction of Bill. Rachel Weber's willingness to share her knowledge of commercial real estate was a great help. And I learned a lot about the history of credit rating by collaborating with my former graduate student Barry Cohen.

Life experience brings both good and bad. The bad has been easier to bear, and the good sweeter to enjoy, because I shared it with others. My generous friend Kevin Williams kept me abreast of the Canadian publishing industry and provided tremendous help during some tough times. Karin Konstantynowicz has always been a great sounding board and ensured that my knowledge of BC politics didn't become too out of date. I collected more friends after my Canadian days, mostly in pairs it seems. The following helped make life fun, and when it wasn't fun, made it rewarding: Jim Kerr and Eileen Finan, Ed Amenta and Francesca Polletta, Ken Alder and Bronwyn Rae, Wendy Wall and Jules Law, Frank Dobbin and Michele Lamont, Bernie Reilly and Jennifer Chisholm, Steve Epstein and Hector Carrillo. And there are many others, I am happy to say. My academic life is always made better because of non-academics, and I particularly thank the Gentlemen's Book Club, which for years has forced me to read novels, and then to hear what smart, thoughtful people have to say about what we've read.

My late brother-in-law Cliff Doerksen enriched life with his wit, knowledge of music and film, and acclaimed study of mince pie. My dear and accomplished sister Elspeth Carruthers is my oldest friend, and I cannot remember a time when she wasn't an important part of my life. And I'll thank Billy Carruthers just for becoming his own wonderful self. My late parents, Janet Wilson Greenhow and Bruce Magoffin Carruthers, always were supportive, in their ways, even if they didn't know what academia was all about. Fortunately I have an aunt, Mary Carruthers, who knows it well and whose academic career offers a model for how to succeed through thick and thin. To marry a person is to inherit their family, and I won the lottery with my in-laws Mark Espeland and Anne Mitchell, and their amazing spouses Anne Boyle and John R. Mitchell. Sadly, John passed away as this book went to press, and I'll sorely miss putting a copy in his hands. I have been truly blessed with two wonderful children, Samuel Nelson Espeland Carruthers and Esther Jane Carruthers Espeland, whose adventures and accomplishments always fill me with love and pride (and occasional anxiety). And finally, and most especially, there is my spouse and love, colleague, friend, trusted critic, sometime coauthor, always co-parent, co-conspirator, and fellow traveler, Wendy Nelson Espeland, whom I cannot thank enough. Our life together continues, and I am grateful from the bottom of my heart.

THE ECONOMY OF PROMISES

1

Introduction

Wealth, in a commercial age, is made up largely of promises.
—ROSCOE POUND, 1945

A promise is a simple thing. It expresses an intention about the future. If I promise you today to meet you for lunch tomorrow, it means that today I intend to have lunch with you the next day, and I communicate my intention by making an explicit promise. To *promise* is to say more than just *maybe* or *perhaps* I'll have lunch with you; it is to offer a sincere assurance that we'll have lunch together; it is to say that I will try hard to show up. And our lunch plans are typically embedded in a social relationship: we may be friends, family, or colleagues, and so it makes sense that we would have a meal together. Ideally, the person making a promise genuinely means to fulfill it, has the capacity to fulfill it, and fully understands what they are committing to do. Ideally, the person to whom the promise is made also has full understanding of this intention about the future and finds it credible. And, ideally, promises made are promises kept.

People make lots of promises about matters great and small. They organize their social lives by making promises to have lunch, to meet at the movies, or to go to a party. At work, they promise to deliver a report by the end of the week. In business, people make promises about deliveries and payments. A parent promises children that they can play computer games, but only after they have finished their homework. An author promises to submit the final version of her book manuscript by a certain date. Important social occasions and rituals are marked by promises: an oath promising to

1

tell the truth precedes testimony in a court of law; those who enter into high political office first make a solemn pledge; priests utter a sacred vow when they are ordained into the Dominican or Franciscan religious orders; and to gain access to Oxford University's venerable Bodleian Library a reader must promise "not to bring into the Library, or kindle therein, any fire or flame." A wedding vow is a special kind of promise that simultaneously transforms the legal and social status of two people from "unmarried" to "married." A contract is a very general type of legal commitment, built around promises to perform certain actions that together will constitute a transaction. People make promises when they want to shape the future, and when they want to fashion their own and others' expectations about the future.[1] Prediction and enactment go together.

What exactly is a promise? According to philosopher John Searle (1976) it is a type of illocutionary speech act,[2] specifically a "commissive." The point of a commissive is to commit the speaker to a future course of action. Promises express the promisor's intention to bring words and deeds together by performing actions that comply with the promise.[3] It isn't sufficient that a person secretly intends to do something; rather, they must express that intention in a way that is legible to others.[4] And those who believe someone else's promise will adjust their expectations and actions accordingly. Of course, not all promises are credible. How do we know that a promisor will keep their promise? A promise to pay money embodied in a formal loan agreement clearly relies on extralinguistic institutions (i.e., law and courts) to help make the promise binding and credible. If someone fails to keep such a promise, the lender has legal recourse. But such recourse involves making the best of a bad situation that the lender surely wishes to avoid in the first place: it is generally better to lend to someone who keeps their promise than it is to have to sue someone who broke their promise.[5] And people can make promises and come to agreements without relying on formal contracts or legal sanctions.[6] Whether formal or not, a key issue for a promise concerns whether the promise seems believable. In the extreme, someone who promises the impossible, or something too good to be true, should not be believed.

Aside from its legal status, a promise also possesses a certain moral sanctity: it is right and proper to keep one's promises; an individual who does so will be praised as "trustworthy" or as someone whose "word is their bond." Keeping promises is generally a good thing, especially when they concern debts.[7] This doesn't mean that people always keep their promises, of course, but it does bestow honor and status on those who do and dishonor upon those who don't. And this moral valence has a halo effect in the sense that keeping promises in one realm of life can raise one's status in others. Trustworthiness, that is, the propensity to keep one's promises, is often considered to be a durable personality trait that will be manifested in many different life situations. Witnessed in one context, it can be generalized to others. But, as economist Timothy Guinnane (2005) points out, trustworthiness has become increasingly dependent on *institutions* (that, e.g., enforce contracts, record credit histories, and undergird loan collateral) rather than just *personalities*.[8] The growth of the economy of promises depended much more on institutional development than on the improved moral fiber of ordinary Americans, and this institutional scaffolding has come from both public and private sources.

Credible promises have limits. Some are dictated by physical reality: one cannot credibly promise to travel faster than the speed of light, for example.[9] Such limits don't change much over time. Other limits are set by legal reality, and these can change in important ways. For example, borrowers can't use property they don't own as collateral for a loan, and I cannot use my own body as collateral because I cannot transfer ownership of it to someone else. More generally, if economic rights are legally uncertain, they cannot function effectively as collateral. The water rights attached to land were highly valuable in the arid West but didn't possess enough legal clarity for lenders.[10] Usury laws, which cap the interest rate charged for a loan, impose a different kind of legal constraint: if the statutory limit were set at 8 percent, then a borrower couldn't legally promise to pay more than that amount.[11]

This book is about the modern history of a particularly important kind of economic promise: the commitment to pay a monetary debt.[12] Such promises undergird the credit that animates modern economies. Indeed, today we have a credit economy, an economy of promises. For example, a person buying a new car could pay cash, but more often they borrow money to purchase the car. In this way, one transaction (to purchase the car) becomes two (obtain a loan, then purchase the car). The lender provides money in exchange for the borrower's promise to repay the loan in a certain manner (perhaps making monthly payments that start next month and continue for four years). And by making a promise that the lender finds credible, the borrower can then use the borrowed funds to purchase a car. There is no need for the buyer to wait until she has saved enough money to cover the full cost. To the extent that they rely on credit, consumers make many promises, and those who sell to consumers receive many promises.

Just as businesses extend credit to their retail customers, and so accept their promises, businesses usually obtain trade credit from their own suppliers. Firms rarely pay cash for their goods and raw materials. Instead, they receive the goods and then have a conventional period of time (perhaps sixty days) in which to pay for them. In effect, they have borrowed from their own suppliers, and have given in exchange a promise to pay the money within sixty days. A supplier that finds its customers' promises to be credible will happily ship them goods and extend them credit, and suppliers know that giving credit is often necessary to make a sale. To the extent that they rely on credit (both giving and receiving), business also make and receive many promises. To give a sense of the sheer volume, consider that in 2019 U.S. corporations borrowed about $1.75 trillion by issuing bonds, while in the same year U.S. households had $4.18 trillion worth of outstanding consumer debt.[13] That is a lot of promises. And all of them were directed toward the enactment of an imagined future in which money ebbs and flows, economic transactions occur, and promises are fulfilled.[14] Credit brings this imagined future into the present.

The U.S. economy has always depended on credit and promises.[15] Since before the nation's founding, there was never enough hard currency to cover all the transactions that people wanted to execute, and barter wouldn't work except on a small scale. Whether money consisted of gold or silver coins, private banknotes, government-issued greenbacks, scrip, or anything else, cash was scarce and so of necessity people depended on credit. For trade over anything but short distances, payment by cash was impractical even if it was available. And of course people borrowed for many reasons. In an agrarian economy, farmers needed credit to purchase land,[16] and they had to buy seed and equipment in the spring but couldn't sell their crops until the fall harvest. So they borrowed from their suppliers on an annual basis. In turn, the country stores supplying farmers had to wait till the fall to be paid and so couldn't pay their own bills until then. They borrowed as well from wholesalers and suppliers. And then, wholesalers and suppliers borrowed from banks. Thus, a national rhythm of credit followed the annual cycle of planting, growth, and harvest. But if credit was necessary, it was also understood to be a dangerous necessity. Handled well, the household, farm, or business could thrive, obtaining and extending credit when needed, making payments as promised. But if credit were managed poorly, or if the borrower just had some bad luck, credit problems could drive people and businesses into bankruptcy.[17] Troubled debtors were beholden to their creditors as they struggled to meet their obligations and keep their promises. And insolvency had a worrisome tendency to spread as the failure of one debtor threatened to pull down others. In a financial panic, cases of bankruptcy could multiply like an infectious disease.

Today, credit is more important than ever. Millions of households and businesses are knit together in a complex tangle of transactions, giving and receiving promises even though they are mostly strangers to each other. How is this possible? How can the economy function on the basis of promises among anonymous individuals? The mystery deepens if we appreciate the materiality of modern economic success and its embarrassment of riches. As compared to the past, today's households enjoy vast quantities of durable goods, living in large residences and consuming energy and objects at an unprecedented (and unsustainable) pace. But the tangible circulation and consumption of physical goods depends on the less obvious circulation of intangible promises. Indeed, the stages of a typical life course are now organized around credit: many people take out student loans to go to college; in or out of college, they obtain credit cards and by using them begin to build a credit record; they finance their first new car purchase with a loan; when they buy their first home, they usually take out a mortgage; if they start a small business, it will often involve loans from family. The debts from one stage of life affect someone's ability to move on to the next stage.[18] Someone short of cash and between paychecks obtains a short-term high-interest "payday" loan, or pawns a valuable object at a pawnshop. If they already own a home and need additional cash, they can take out a home equity loan. Unexpected medical expenses often put people into debt. To be fully an adult is to have experienced various forms of indebtedness, but it is not simply a matter of individual choice. Indeed, two of the types of debt just mentioned are actively supported by government policy: most student loans are guaranteed by the federal government, which encourages lenders to lend, and the interest paid on home mortgages receives favorable tax treatment, which encourages borrowers to borrow. Over their life course, individuals often begin to borrow in early adulthood, accumulate assets during their peak earning years, and in retirement live off those assets.

This spread of indebtedness throughout society is concerning: debts are burdensome and surely it is better to avoid them. Perhaps there are promises that people shouldn't make. Polonius famously advised his son to "neither a borrower nor a lender be," that is, to avoid credit altogether! But access to credit can help households and businesses remain afloat by enabling them to make necessary purchases or survive a current shortfall, and the ability to obtain a home mortgage on good terms helped many households accumulate wealth and enjoy upward mobility. Some have even argued that expanded access to credit among middle- and working-class households helped compensate for the recent stagnation in incomes and dramatic growth in inequality, relieving political pressure for redistributive public policies.[19] The entire housing industry depends heavily upon credit, as does the automobile industry. Small and medium-sized firms are particularly reliant on bank loans and trade credit for their financing needs. Large American corporations raise long-term capital by issuing bonds, and they obtain short-term capital by issuing commercial paper or taking out bank loans. Sovereign governments, from local municipalities up to the federal government, are continuously borrowing to finance their operations. Credit circulates in many forms among many parties, and the recent process of "financialization"[20] means that firms and households have become increasingly embedded in an expanding network of financial relationships and obligations.

Financialization entails issuing and accepting financial promises. Why make promises? Debtors borrow because they need money now and can credibly promise to repay it in the future. Debt is useful to the debtor: consumers can borrow to purchase a home or a new car; they can finance a college education or cover medical expenses. Businesses similarly use debt to finance an investment, to pay for supplies or inventory. Some businesses (e.g., private equity groups) are notorious for their reliance on debt and for maximizing leverage. A few more statistics illustrate the magnitude of the economy of promises:[21] in 2020, nonfinancial corporate businesses had $7.26 trillion in outstanding debt securities (bonds) and $3.89 trillion in loans. Among individuals in 2020, there was $10.94 trillion worth of residential home mortgages. Many households and businesses have gone into debt, made promises, and become more financialized. Although they have made this choice, circumstances can tip the scales and favor debt. Government tax policy, for example, gives favorable treatment to mortgage interest payments by households and rewards debt over equity as a way to raise business capital. So the growth in financial leverage hasn't happened spontaneously.

People make promises for lots of reasons, but why accept them? Mostly, people believe a promise when it seems credible and they trust the promisor. My friends show up for lunch because they believe me when I promise to show up for lunch, at the appointed time and place. They find my promise credible, despite the fact that it isn't legally binding, and they adjust their expectations accordingly. More generally, if I and my friends find each other's promises to be credible, if we trust each other, then we can coordinate our future activities in advantageous ways. We can organize our futures together. The same holds true for the economic promises that undergird credit. Generally, lenders will lend if they trust the borrower, if they believe the promises that the borrower has made to them. With credible promises, consumers can obtain the money they need to buy cars, homes, and other durable goods, and those who sell to them enjoy their business. Businesses can purchase what they need from their suppliers, and the latter can sell more goods. Firms can obtain the financing they require to obtain working capital or make long-term investments. And the overall economy can operate at a much higher level than would be possible if everyone had to pay cash up front for every transaction. The fact that firms regularly borrow shows that it is not only individuals who make credible promises but also organizations. Credit isn't just personal. And one of the real accomplishments of the modern credit economy has been to get people to trust others they don't know personally.

Formality can make promises more credible. It is one thing to casually mention a vague plan to repay a debt, but it is quite another to write such a promise on a piece of paper that is signed, dated, and witnessed and uses legally binding language. A formal promise, one that conforms with legal standards, allows the parties to the promise to invoke the coercive power of the law to enforce that promise. It is not, of course, that people do not trust those who make informal promises. Indeed, for some, their word is their bond and nothing more is required. However, other things being equal, a formal legal promise carries more weight, and its breach entails more consequence. Such promises are taken more seriously, and how such promises are encoded in law greatly affects their value and efficacy.[22]

Sadly, people do not always keep their promises. Some prove to be untrustworthy, even if someone else trusted them. Some borrowers default on their loans, because of either choice or necessity, and so the lender suffers. Broken promises often lead to a kind of "postmortem" examination where people try to figure what went wrong: Was it due to unforeseen circumstances that made repayment impossible? Was it because someone chose to break their promise? The answer, which isn't always obvious, sets the stage for the next time that an individual makes a promise and affects whether others will believe them then. And because social life usually involves a succession of promises, rather than "one-shot deals," it is frequently possible to assess someone's current pledge against the backdrop of their own past promises. Promisors develop reputations, both good and bad, and however much promises are about the future, they are rooted in the past.

What happens when people break their promises and fail to pay their debts? The question of "whom to trust" is always posed against the backdrop of how to deal with broken promises and the associated non-payments, defaults, and insolvencies. Failure is one of the distinguishing features of a market economy, and the framework for it is set by bankruptcy law.[23] Certainly failure was a common experience in the business community.[24] Although those making or receiving promises can adjust for this unfortunate possibility, matters are not entirely up to them. Government policy sets the terms for what happens when people break their promises. As organizations that specialize in making loans, banks are forced by bank regulators to "recognize" broken promises and make financial provision for them.[25] Otherwise, lenders might be tempted to pretend that all is well with their clients, even if it isn't. Unpaid creditors have the right to sue the debtor in court, to garnish wages, or to repossess collateral. Personal and corporate bankruptcy rules determine the treatment of insolvent borrowers, how and when their assets are to be distributed among creditors, and whether a firm is reorganized or simply liquidated.[26] However, these rules don't apply when the borrower is itself a sovereign power. If a state government defaults on its debts, sovereign immunity complicates the situation and outcomes that would occur in the case of a private corporation, like closure and liquidation, don't happen. The states of Louisiana and Mississippi stopped payment on their debts in the 1840s, for example, but they didn't close down.

Failure sometimes stems from a debtor's temptation to over-promise. But frequently, failure follows from misfortune or bad luck: crops fail, people lose their jobs, families face unexpected medical expenses, unanticipated disasters occur. Going into debt is a convenient way to smooth household consumption in the face of variable income or unforeseen problems, to keep a troubled business afloat by borrowing from Peter in order to pay Paul, or to increase a firm's rate of profit by maximizing "leverage" through the issuance of debt rather than equity.[27] But even when it is taken on for good reasons, debt can become an overwhelming burden and debtors consequently break their promises. Lenders tend not to believe all the promises they hear, and their level of skepticism is conditioned, in part, on what might happen if those they trusted fail.

In general, there is no simple solution to the problem of broken promises. To *trust* everyone, to believe all promises, is to invite inevitable disappointment and loss. It is to be utterly naive. But to *distrust* everyone, to doubt all promises, is to enter a world of unsustainable caution, suspicion, and even paranoia. Universal mistrust of all by all will bring the economy to a halt.[28] Less dramatically, a bank loan officer who never makes a loan is soon out of a job.[29] The key question is: whom to trust?[30] How best to tell the difference between those who will, and those who won't, keep their promises? In the case of credit, answering this question means telling the difference between those who are creditworthy and those who are not. It means forecasting the willingness and ability of a specific debtor to repay a particular debt sometime in the future. This is no simple task, but it is inescapable.

Lenders who accept promises can make two kinds of mistakes. First, they might trust someone who is untrustworthy and subsequently breaks their promise. This mistake has clear consequences: when a borrower defaults, the lender doesn't receive the money owed them. In the extreme case, the lender loses all their money. A second mistake involves not trusting someone who really is trustworthy. An opportunity is lost, but its magnitude is rarely obvious and it can seem purely hypothetical. The asymmetry between these two types of mistakes gives one greater salience than the other. To trust an untrustworthy borrower unambiguously means lost money, but to distrust a trustworthy borrower produces a less drastic outcome. This makes it easy to err on the side of caution and not lend to a creditworthy individual, even though the possibility of making the second kind of mistake remains real.

Today, many economic assets consist of nothing but promises. The long-term promise that a homeowner makes to repay a mortgage sits as an asset on the lending bank's balance sheet. The promises that customers make in order to receive goods from a supplier constitute another asset, the supplier's "accounts receivable." People who are extremely rich possess lots of intangible assets, with portfolios filled with corporate bonds and other financial promises. Unlike older forms of wealth (e.g., land, cattle, gold bars), promises are intangible. Their value does not reside in their material characteristics. In fact, physically they may be no more than words on a page or entries in an electronic database. But despite this immateriality, today they possess great economic value, and to be wealthy is to have accumulated a lot of promises. As of April 2019, the total value of commercial and industrial loans made by U.S. commercial banks equaled more than $2.3 trillion, and the total of all motor vehicle loans was worth over $1.1 trillion. At the same time, all outstanding one-to-four family residential mortgages were together worth over $10.8 trillion,[31] and the most exotic promises, financial derivatives, were also worth trillions.[32] These staggering figures bear out Roscoe Pound's observation and underscore that promises constitute the intangible substance and value of the modern economy.

As financial promises, loans link together two distinctive groups, the lenders and the borrowers. Their ties to each other, and their interdependent roles, last so long as the debt remains outstanding. Much social science has been devoted to the analysis of other important economic distinctions including, for example, those between employers and employees, producers and consumers, blue-collar workers and white-collar workers, workers and capitalists, or owners and non-owners. The difference between debtors and creditors overlays and complicates these other, much studied, distinctions.[33] And it offers complications of its own because, among other things, debtors can also be creditors, operating on both sides at the same time. People give and receive promises simultaneously, and so have contradictory interests.

The key question in an economy of promises is about "whom to trust." It is the starting point of this book. Asking and answering this question occurs daily and pervasively, and has been going on for as long as people have borrowed money. How people have understood trustworthiness, how they assess it in others, and in what ways they have sought to signal their own trustworthiness have all evolved in important and surprising ways. What made an individual look like a good borrower in 1821 (high moral character) is not the same as in 2021 (high FICO score). A dispersed, localized, and informal evaluative process has become much more centralized, nationalized, formalized, and calculative. Instead of being judged by local lenders, who might also be neighbors, kin, or coreligionists, debtors are now continuously monitored by a small number of large credit rating agencies that unobtrusively accumulate "big data" and calculate precise scores.[34] This evolution undergirds the growth of the modern credit economy in the United States and its singular dependence on promises. Rather than rely on their own personal judgments, lenders increasingly used an extensive informational apparatus that identified borrowers, measured their financial means, tracked their credit record over time, and summarized their trustworthiness in a single number, scale, or rating. These new institutions shaped credit in the United States, but some have gained even greater global significance.[35] Rationalization, formalization, and quantification all suggest greater neutrality and objectivity.[36] But we will learn otherwise. Participants in the credit economy have also benefited from the development of a commercial legal framework that has made it easier to make legally binding promises and enforce debts. Furthermore, as lenders fine-tuned the terms under which they extended credit to consumers, some of them realized that it could be more profitable to lend to persons who did not fully repay their debts on time and who, in effect, bent but didn't break their own promises.[37] And the determination of trustworthiness remains subject to social influences favoring those who are similar and familiar over those who are not. As a rule, people tend to trust and affiliate with those who are like themselves.[38]

By studying how credit grew, this book helps us understand trust. We learn that trust is as much a product of institutions and social networks as it is about personalities and moral fiber. This means that the particularities of institutional history matter, especially when arrangements get "locked" into place. We will appreciate that claims about the contemporary decline of trust, or its disappearance in national politics, need to be tempered by the reality that our economy of promises couldn't function without a great deal of trust. But we must also discard some of the naively "solidaristic" and harmonious connotations of trust. Credit, promises, and trust are suffused with power, shaped by conflict, and riven with inequality.

During a financial crisis, many promises are disbelieved. Only the most credible promises (e.g., those issued by the national government or a central bank) become acceptable as market actors hunt for liquidity and rush to convert their assets into cash.[39] When failure becomes widespread during a severe depression, so many people break their promises that political pressure builds for the government to intervene.[40] Pervasive economic hardship suggests that many people may have broken their promises through no fault of their own. What to do with mass insolvency when it is obvious that a large proportion of the bankrupt were just unlucky rather than culpable? Sometimes governments try to support the ability of troubled debtors to make new and more credible promises, and so get credit flowing again. For example, during the 1930s the federal government created a variety of programs to help make homeowners' promises to repay their mortgages more trustworthy, and so encouraged more lending. Similarly, in the nineteenth century some states retroactively modified promises and set a moratorium on the ability of lenders to foreclose or seize collateral. And although the U.S. Constitution provides for a bankruptcy law, throughout the nineteenth century new federal bankruptcy statutes were repeatedly passed following an economic crisis in order to provide general relief to debtors, only to be repealed when creditor interests reasserted themselves.[41] Consequently, for substantial periods there was no federal bankruptcy statute in effect. Such episodes brought to the surface the deep connections between economy, law, and the polity, and reflected the ebb and flow of debtor interests in politics.

Financial promises are broadly affected by economic cycles. During an expansion, credit is cheap, speculative bubbles develop, and too many promises are issued and accepted. By contrast, a sharp downturn undermines the ability of debtors to keep their promises and often prompts some kind of policy intervention.[42] In periods of severe deflation, the burden on debtors intensifies because they repay their debts with money that is worth more (because overall prices declined). The converse situation involves inflation, where creditors suffer because the repayments they receive are worth less (because prices increased). Since loans are denominated in legal tender, a change in the general value of money means that a dollar loaned at one point won't have the same purchasing power as a dollar repaid later. Lenders and borrowers who perfectly anticipate inflation, or deflation, can simply adjust the terms of their debt contract. If inflation is a problem, for example, lenders can raise the nominal interest rate they charge and shorten the maturity of the loans they make. Or they can include an index clause that tracks changing costs[43] or a "gold clause" that requires payment in precious metal rather than currency. But mostly, lenders and borrowers don't perfectly anticipate the future, and the value of their obligations can be affected in unexpected ways. In periods of hyperinflation, the problem of trust becomes compounded by another: can one trust money?

The Premises of Promises

People are free to make their own promises, but not under circumstances of their own choosing.[44] If they want their promises to be legally binding, the menu of choices becomes limited. And some parties have the power to insist that promises comply with particular standards. Various government regulations have limited the kinds of promises that people could make. For example, the Uniform Small Loan Laws passed by many states in the early twentieth century set interest rates for small loans and required that lenders be transparent about loan terms so that borrowers could fully understand the promises they made (i.e., no hidden fees or misleading interest rates). At the federal level, the Equal Credit Opportunity Act tried to ensure that lenders treated promisors equally, regardless of whether they were male or female, black or white, old or young. Yet, legal rules sometimes induced creative circumvention. For example, adding "fees" to a transaction can raise the cost of a loan without breaching statutory interest rate caps. And federalism in America posed the problem of legal pluralism: much commercial law is state law, and hence varies from one state to the next. A loan provision that was legally binding in New York State may not have been legal in California, which obviously created difficulties if a New York creditor wanted to lend to a California debtor.[45]

Promises can be vague and informal or specific and formal. People are free to make vague promises, but their options are constrained if they want their promises to be formally recognized. This variation affects the understandings of both promisor and others of what exactly the promisor has committed to do. Context resolves some although not all ambiguity,[46] but vague promises can lead to divergent understandings of what the promise really meant. They can produce disputes about whether the promisor has truly "kept her word." However, vagueness can also be useful by providing flexibility to a commitment that can then be adapted to unforeseen conditions. Imprecision, in other words, isn't always a problem. Consider two promises: "I promise to help you move" and "I promise to arrive at your apartment next Saturday at 9 A.M. and until 5 P.M. I shall pack boxes with household items, load them into the truck, drive the truck to the new location, and help unload the truck." The first is a vague and succinct promise, and obviously there are many ways to be of help on moving day. A promisor who performs any one of them can claim to have kept their promise. The second is a lengthier and more specific promise, and it would be relatively easy to determine if the promisor had kept her word (did she actually show up at 9 A.M.?). However, the second promise possesses less flexibility and may not be as adaptable to changed circumstances. For example, if the move has to be delayed until Sunday because of bad weather, showing up as promised on Saturday won't help.[47]

Legally binding promises are formal promises. But not everyone is qualified to make such a promise. To be sure that something which looks like a promise is authentic, it is necessary to consider whether the promisor can really issue such a promise (i.e., that they are recognized as a bona fide promise-maker).[48] To promise is to commit to perform certain actions, and not everyone is deemed responsible for their own behavior or able to make future commitments on their own behalf. If a promise is a formal expression of an intention, then the legal status of a promise depends on the status of the promisor. An "IOU" note written by a five-year-old child isn't taken seriously. Similarly, a person who is insane, mentally "unsound," or experiencing acute dementia isn't legally held to account for their actions, including their promises. Matters become more complicated when persons aren't just making promises for themselves but on behalf of someone or something else. They must be authorized to act as a representative, trustee, agent, or fiduciary so that the promises they make bind whomever they represent.

Promises also vary in their uniformity, and there is a difference between standardized and idiosyncratic promises.[49] The provisions of a "bespoke" promise can reflect the specific concerns of the individuals making and receiving the promise, and they express whatever distinctive bargain the lender and borrower have struck. Such uniqueness can make the promise valuable to both sides, precisely because it exactly reflects their goals and circumstances. Yet it can be harder to judge the credibility of a unique promise because one has to consider the likelihood of performance in light of an idiosyncratic situation about which information may be scarce: there is no baseline of past experience to draw upon. But people can make more standardized promises, too, and these are easier to assess. Since they conform to a standard, they involve elements that have been seen before, that are based on a template, and whose implications in a variety of settings are well-known. Standardized promises can be judged in light of past experience with similar or identical promises. They are comparable. This difference matters because many economic promises have become increasingly standardized and then used at scale. Consider the widespread use of standard-form contracts in consumer finance, for credit cards. They usually come from the creditor side, and so the agreements are set by the credit card company on a take-it-or-leave-it basis. The two parties do not actually bargain over the terms of their deal. Frequently, cardholders don't even read the agreement (which consists of many pages of legal boilerplate) and so are not fully aware of the promise they have consented to make. In effect, such individuals make promises whose terms are set by the recipient of the promise and are not entirely understood by the promisor.

With standardized promises, one key issue concerns the standards themselves. Who sets them? Who writes the boilerplate? With considerable legal resources and ample experience in consumer finance, big credit card companies can set terms that favor creditors over debtors, and cardholders have little chance to remedy the situation except by shopping around for a better deal or forgoing credit cards altogether. But standards are sometimes set by third parties that neither borrow nor lend. In the 1930s, for example, the Federal Housing Administration (FHA) set uniform standards for home mortgage loans that soon were adopted by both lenders and borrowers. Such mortgages were said to be FHA-conforming, and could be insured by the federal government. In the 1960s and 1970s, the U.S. government passed several laws aimed at reducing racial and gender-based discrimination in credit markets, and these also helped standardize bank lending procedures and documentation. And recently the Consumer Finance Protection Bureau devised simple standardized loan agreements so that both the consumer borrower and the sophisticated corporate lender can understand the terms and conditions of the loan. Third parties, like the government, can also set standards that prohibit certain kinds of promises. Where applicable, usury laws typically set a cap on the interest rate that a lender can charge, and therefore the borrower cannot make a legally binding promise to pay more. Exemption laws can prevent lenders from using certain kinds of property as collateral.[50]

Debts can also arise without prior consent or explicit promises. In such cases, no lender has assessed the borrower's willingness and ability to repay. Someone who fails to pay their federal income taxes, for example, has turned the federal government into a creditor, although the government didn't agree to do so. Instead, the taxpayer decided not to meet their tax obligations. Situations involving involuntary creditors, in other words, do not depend on the prior acceptance of promises. A bank that loaned money to an insolvent firm is a creditor, as are the firm's unpaid employees. But the latter are involuntary creditors who didn't agree to lend their employer money. Rather, they were simply not paid the wages owed them.[51] Similarly, if that insolvent firm also produced environmental impacts that cause long-term harm, then those affected in the future will be owed compensation even though they didn't consent to become creditors. Or if fees, surcharges, or fines were imposed on someone convicted of a crime, they become an involuntary debtor to the state.[52] Nevertheless, involuntary debts constitute only a small proportion of total financial obligations.[53]

Impersonal Promises

My discussion has thus far focused on promises as acts of individual persons. But many promises are impersonal in the sense that they are being issued by institutions rather than individuals: corporations, governments, nonprofits, nongovernment organizations, special purpose entities, and so forth. After states passed general laws of incorporation during the nineteenth century, the number and size of corporations grew dramatically, and they were granted the status of legal personhood. Entire sectors of the economy became dominated by large organizations that acted as both borrowers and lenders. Increasingly, the individuals who issued promises did so on behalf of an organization, and it was the organization that became obliged by the promise. If a firm borrows money from a bank, for example, the CEO or CFO signs the contract. But the promise binds the firm, not the person. And if the loan requires collateral, it is the firm's assets that secure the loan, not those of the individual.

When an organization makes a promise, it is no simple matter to determine its "intention" or "willingness" to repay. A corporation may have legal personhood, but that doesn't make it a person. Yet, legally an organization can be as bound by its obligations as is a natural person. Impersonal promises are promises nevertheless. In an economy where single-owner proprietorships have been displaced by large corporations, and where special purpose entities[54] are routinely created as part of financial engineering, impersonal trust is an important issue. Over the last two centuries, one of the biggest changes in the credit system has been that those issuing financial promises have shifted from real persons to fictive individuals: organizations of one sort or another. Who makes promises and is obligated by them has changed.

I have introduced promises in simple terms, but the history of credit in the United States reveals that people devised ways to put promises together, to build compound and collective promises. Simple promises can function like building blocks to construct more complicated promises. One example comes from a common method used to bolster the creditworthiness of an individual borrower: have another person act as guarantor or cosignor. If the debtor fails to repay, the guarantor promises to do so. In this way two promises, the original promise of the borrower and the conditional promise of the guarantor, are linked together, and it makes the lender more willing to lend. A person can also compound their own promises, as when a borrower uses collateral to secure a loan. The borrower's original promise is reinforced by an additional promise to hand over collateral in the event of non-payment. Modern lenders often require a borrower to insure the asset that serves as collateral for a loan (e.g., someone who gets a mortgage must insure their home). In this way, the original promise to repay the loan is accepted by the lender conditional on other promises regarding collateral and insurance.

Recently, through a process called "securitization,"[55] investment banks and others have taken many fairly simple promises, like home mortgages, and combined them to produce complex structured financial instruments like CDOs (collateralized debt obligations) and RMBSs (residential mortgage-backed securities).[56] And while the underlying assets, such as home mortgages, obligate individuals, the new instruments obligate impersonal legal entities like special purpose entities or special investment vehicles. Such aggregations created new possibilities for the assessment of promises. It was one thing to judge the credibility of an individual's promise to pay, and quite another to assess an entire pool of mortgages involving many such promises and structured in a specific fashion. Rather than gauge the particulars of a person's character, credit record, and situation, lenders have used increasingly sophisticated statistical approaches. They need not worry so much about whether a single person will repay their loan but instead focus on the average rate of repayment among a group of borrowers, on the desirability of a diverse portfolio of underlying loans to ensure uncorrelated risks, and on hard-to-calculate conditional probabilities. To accomplish this, lenders shifted away from qualitative judgments about the trustworthiness of individual people, assessments that often focused on character and personal reputation, toward more standardized and numerically based evaluations of groups of borrowers. Quantification made it easier to aggregate judgments and put together pools of promises. Indeed, the quantification of trust is one of the most important developments that has occurred, and reflected a trend occurring in other areas of commerce (e.g., insurance) and public policy (e.g., cost-benefit analysis).[57]

When formulated, a financial promise joins two parties: the promisor and the promisee. The legal system acts as third-party enforcer for legal promises. But the promise need not bind those same two parties until it is fully realized, because some promises are able to circulate. Although the promise was originally made by the borrower to the lender, the latter can sometimes pass the obligation on to someone else, usually by selling it, transferring it, or having it "discounted."[58] When this happens, and the promisor acts to satisfy their obligation, payment won't go to the person who originally loaned them the money. Instead, it will go to whoever possesses the promise at maturity, and the current possessor's right to enforce the promise is as strong in law as was that of the original promisee. This ability to circulate gives mobility to promises, and concerns their "negotiability."[59] It allows the original lenders to recover their capital well before the debt fully matures and severs the long-term tie that joined the original parties to a long-term debt.[60] It also creates the possibility of a secondary market for promises (where promises can be priced, among other things) and dislodges promises from the dyadic context of the originating lender and borrower. This change can greatly enlarge the number of creditors who, in effect, are willing to lend, but by making the role of creditor a more generalized and anonymous one, it loses some of the advantages that come from durable social relationships. Instead of owing money to a particular person, the debtor owes money to whoever holds the promissory note on the day it comes due (or, if it is an "on demand" note, whenever the holder presents it for payment). And that person could be a complete stranger. The advantage to knowing one's creditor, or having a personal relationship with them, becomes apparent when problems arise. Should the debtor be unable to pay the debt, a prior social connection with the creditor can help facilitate the negotiations or adjustments needed to keep the debtor current. Obligations can be restructured if the original terms prove too onerous and the debtor is threatened with insolvency, but those negotiations may be more difficult to bring to an amicable resolution when conducted with strangers.

Interdependence

Promises create interdependencies among people, and are themselves interdependent. The most obvious interdependence arises directly between debtors and creditors: at one point, the debtor depends on the creditor (as a source of funding), and then later the creditor depends on the debtor to repay. The borrower is beholden to the lender and is only released from their obligation upon full repayment. Recent evidence suggests that for individuals, being a debtor is a stressful and burdensome situation,[61] and so dependency can be both an economic and personal problem. Whether on balance these interdependences are good or bad isn't always clear. The recent push for greater "financial inclusion" is motivated by the belief that giving poor people increased access to credit will make their lives better.[62] But the push against "predatory lending" reflects recognition that some forms of credit are harmful, even if borrowers "choose" to borrow. Some criticize the recent increase in household indebtedness and conclude that "consumer debt has stripped working people of their wealth and contributed to ever-widening inequality" (Ott and Hyman 2013: 29).

Interdependence grows when individuals make and accept promises at the same time. They are debtors to some and creditors to others, embedded in a complex network of multiple obligations. This means that their ability to keep their own promises often depends on whether others keep their promises to them. If a company's customers don't pay their bills, then the company has a harder time servicing its own bank loan. These complex and indirect interdependencies are one reason why problems can cascade quickly through a network of credit relationships: a firm's insolvency will hurt its creditors, its creditors' creditors, and eventually its creditors' creditors' creditors. In this way, failure becomes infectious.[63] A financially troubled firm often has to protect itself by vigorously pursuing those who owe it money while at the same deferring payment to its creditors, in an attempt to buy time and preserve liquidity. The relationship between assets and liabilities isn't something that just sits on a balance sheet but rather is a tension enacted in real time by firms that are trying to survive. As debtors approach insolvency, new interdependencies arise among the creditors: if a debtor repays one, there is less money available to repay the others. Conflicting interests put creditors in a zero-sum game with each other and can set off a "rush to the assets."

This balancing act is particularly acute for the lending institutions that specialize in promises, that is, banks. A financial institution that takes deposits and makes loans has to balance the promises it makes to some with the promises it receives from others. And it isn't simply a matter of equalizing assets with liabilities, for the liabilities are frequently short-term while the assets are long-term. There is, in other words, a maturity mismatch. Many nineteenth-century banking crises were sparked by worries among depositors that their bank couldn't keep its own promises and let them withdraw their money on demand. And as depositors lined up to claim their cash, banks could not retrieve the money they had loaned out to borrowers. Bank runs spread easily and could engulf solvent but illiquid institutions.[64] Recently, banks that relied on "wholesale funding" in repo markets performed a different balancing act, but one that left them similarly vulnerable.[65]

Credit-induced interdependencies pose a particular challenge because however well a creditor can evaluate and manage its debtors, it is difficult to deal with its debtors' debtors, whose indirect influence may nevertheless be significant. Trust is imperfectly transitive in that even if I trust someone (and lend them money), I cannot necessarily trust those that they trust (i.e., the people to whom they loaned money), although my fate depends on my debtors' debtors.[66] Information about such persons is harder to obtain and necessarily indirect, and the channels of influence are weak. The uncertainty is greater, and the vulnerabilities more difficult to gauge. One of the biggest changes in the credit system concerns how borrowers become "legible" to those with no direct connection to them or prior knowledge about them, often through quantitative measurements and ratings.

Interdependence among creditors means they try to learn about rival claims for the simple fact that prior debts diminish creditworthiness. How to learn if someone already owes money?[67] How to know if a property is already mortgaged? Thanks to public registration systems it is possible to learn if an asset being offered as collateral has any prior liens against it, a fact that will interest a lender as prior liens typically have seniority. Other interdependencies arise from the fact that creditors often compete with each other, and this influences their willingness to lend and on what terms. Suppliers compete for customers, and generous credit terms are often part of the deal. Similarly, bankers compete for creditworthy customers. This means that although the decision to lend is made with a primary focus on the borrower's situation, lenders keep an eye on what their peers are doing as well.

The interdependencies created by promises do not necessarily provoke conflict, pitting debtor against creditor; nor do they always set rival claimants on a debtor against each other, where one's gain is the other's loss. In fact, promises can create a community of interest between the borrower and a lender. As a loan matures and until it is fully repaid, the lender has a genuine interest in the willingness and ability of the borrower to repay. Banks want their customers to succeed and repay their debts, and generally borrowers gain the support of their lenders. A particularly striking example occurred during the American Civil War, at a time when the political survival of the United States was in doubt. The secretary of the treasury explicitly noted that borrowing money helped to both fund the Northern war effort and create a financial constituency with an interest in the success of the Union. As creditors, Northern bondholders became strong supporters of the government to which they loaned money as their political loyalties were bolstered by financial ties.[68] Creating common interests was a great idea, but as with so many other good ideas, this one occurred in antiquity to a Greek, Eumenes, who protected himself in Alexander the Great's army by borrowing money from his enemies.[69] However much they disliked him, they needed to keep him alive.

Recognizing and managing the interdependencies that emerge from complex networks of promises remains a challenge. One partial solution concerns those who have claims on the same debtor. Conflict arises because a debtor who repays one creditor may not be able to repay another, a trade-off that becomes especially acute when debtors run short of money. But if creditors can be rank-ordered so that some *must* be paid before others, the conflict is resolved.[70] And, indeed, seniority does exactly this by creating a priority ordering among competing claimants. By statute or contract, senior creditors gain access to a debtor's assets before junior creditors. Secured creditors, who have collateral, can seize a debtor's assets before unsecured creditors. Another interdependence applies to those who are simultaneously debtors and creditors, lending to some while borrowing from others. They can get squeezed if their own debts come due but their debtors are slow to pay. This vulnerability persists especially if the debts owed them have long-term maturities. If they can transfer or sell these assets, however, then the problem can be avoided. A wholesaler that can sell off its "accounts receivable" will transfer the credit risk associated with the debts its customers owe it, in exchange for cash that it can then use to settle its own obligations. When a bank "securitizes" its portfolio of home mortgages, it can accomplish something similar: the risk that people will fail to make their mortgage payments is transferred elsewhere. And some financial securities, like bonds, are negotiable securities, which makes them easy to sell.

Whom to Trust?

To lend money involves a practical question of trust. It requires that the lender believe that a debtor will keep their promises and repay their debts. But it is unrealistic to suppose that everyone does so, or that everyone should be trusted. A banker who trusts everyone will not last long. How do lenders decide whom to trust? How have they differentiated between the trustworthy and the untrustworthy? However much one might debate the general meaning of trust, much rests on the ability to make this practical distinction repeatedly, on a large scale and in a timely manner.

The question of whom to trust is an old one, but it is answered in new ways. In general, information is key. Lenders gather information about borrowers in order to learn who is, and who is not, trustworthy; they make predictions about that person's future actions. Sometimes the information is about personal character. If a lender knows enough about someone's personality, then they can decide whether that person is trustworthy. Frequently, such personal information circulates through social networks. A lender might learn about a borrower because they are directly acquainted, because they have mutual friends, or because they belong to the same group. Such informal means of information gathering work well on a small scale, in communities where social networks knit the population together, and where people know each other's "business." But they work less well on a mass scale, where lenders and borrowers are numerous, anonymous, geographically mobile, and socially disconnected from each other.

The modern credit economy operates on a mass scale, and although there are pockets bound together by social networks and face-to-face interactions, information about whom to trust generally has to be obtained through other means. A college student needing short-term cash can borrow from their parents, but to finance higher education today students usually require much more than what their families can muster. Today's lenders depend on a set of *institutions* that acquire, process, and distribute large volumes of formal information about individual and organizational borrowers, on a mass scale, and use that information to evaluate promises. These institutions emerged over the course of the nineteenth and twentieth centuries and have become critical to the operation of today's credit markets.

The shift toward formalized quantitative information about the trustworthiness of borrowers started with the establishment of mercantile agencies in the 1840s. The first such agency was founded by Lewis Tappan, a failed businessman who learned the hard way about the importance of good credit information, but other competing agencies soon appeared.[71] These for-profit establishments focused primarily on the problem of unsecured trade credit, extended from suppliers to their business customers. Relying on a growing network of correspondents and branch offices, they gathered information about individual businesses, organized and processed it, and then sold credit ratings and reports to their customers. In effect, they commodified credit information and helped suppliers deal with increasing numbers of anonymous customers. With the rapid development of the U.S. economy, this business expanded so that more and more firms were rated and the leading mercantile agencies (notably Dun's, and Bradstreet's) expanded across the country. Soon it was possible for a New York City wholesaler to learn about the creditworthiness of a firm in Peoria, Illinois, even if the wholesaler knew no one in Peoria nor had ever been there. Peoria may have been entirely outside the wholesaler's social networks, but it was not beyond the reach of the mercantile agency. The commercial success of these mercantile agencies in helping decide whom to trust inspired others, and consulting their information became a routine part of business practice.

Some rating agencies operated in the realm of high finance, classifying long-term bonds and helping to allocate capital for investment. Since 1909, agencies like Moody's gathered information about railroads, utility companies, corporations, state governments, municipalities, and even sovereign nations and issued ratings using a scale that has become familiar around the world. In effect, they tried to do for long-term bonds what the mercantile agencies had done for trade credit. Like the mercantile agencies, the bond raters initially adopted a "user pays" business model: they created information about debtors and then sold it to the investors who, presumably, used it to improve their own financial decisions. Many decades later, they switched to the "issuer pays" model. The most highly rated bonds, issued by the most trustworthy borrowers, are classified "Aaa" by Moody's. The next highest category of bonds are given the "Aa1" rating. Far below, the "Caa2" rating is given to so-called "junk bonds," which in the opinion of Moody's are speculative and subject to very high credit risk.[72] Devised in the early twentieth century, this rating system was applied at the end of the century to the new financial instruments created through securitization and other types of financial engineering: mortgage-backed securities, asset-backed securities, collateralized debt obligations, and so on. One of the chief goals of this financial engineering was to create as many "Aaa"-rated securities as possible out of the underlying assets, because such a rating signaled to investors that a financial promise was as safe and trustworthy as could be.

A different group of rating agencies developed ways to evaluate individual borrowers in the context of consumer debt. Many local credit agencies operated in the nineteenth and twentieth centuries to help local merchants keep track of their customers, but in the 1950s, Fair, Isaac and Company created the FICO score, a numerical rating applied to individuals.[73] Today, rating agencies like TransUnion, Experian, and Equifax compile vast data sets with information on roughly two hundred million U.S. consumers, with the highest scores given to the most creditworthy individuals.[74] Lenders almost never possess direct knowledge of the personalities and character of consumers; instead they use the consumer's credit score when deciding whether to make a loan, or how to price it.

This new way to answer the question of whom to trust has become widespread, in part because it is so portable. The credit ratings applied to long-term bonds and the credit scores for individual borrowers were first created to help lenders make good choices, but people discovered other uses for them. Both in the United States and abroad, for example, financial regulatory agencies use bond ratings in their prudential regulations and to set bank capital requirements.[75] Insurance companies and employers have used consumers' credit scores in their product pricing and hiring decisions. Mortgage lenders use FICO scores to determine an applicant's eligibility for a loan. Landlords use ratings to review applications for rental housing.[76] And in the financial derivatives markets, ratings are used to measure counterparty risk and set collateral.[77] Under the Trump administration, the Department of Homeland Security even used low credit scores as grounds to reject a non-citizen's application for admission to the United States.[78] How ratings and scores are calculated remains a proprietary mystery, but this type of information can easily be incorporated into algorithmic decision making about credit. Starting in the 1990s, for example, Fannie Mae (also known as the Federal National Mortgage Association) developed its own "Desktop Underwriter" software to automate the underwriting process for residential home mortgages. And consumers can now go to an internet website, enter personal identifying information and submit an application, and then receive a loan decision almost instantly: there is no friendly loan officer at the other end, only computer code. Credit ratings have greatly benefited from improvements in technology that have made it easier and cheaper to acquire, store, and process large amounts of information. And that has made ratings ever more fateful.

A debtor's future ability-to-pay weighs heavily on the minds of creditors, and this too can be estimated numerically. For individuals, employment status mattered a great deal: did the borrower have a steady job and reliable income?

The standardization of employment relations and the spread of wage labor made these questions easier to answer. The market value of assets owned by the debtor is another feature that can usually be measured: valuable assets can serve as collateral. Prior indebtedness is important, too: does the individual have other financial obligations that claim some of their earnings? For firms, the development of standardized accounting techniques provided quantitative measures of financial performance and made it possible to assess the ability of a business to service its debts. Audited balance sheets and profit-and-loss statements helped lenders judge the financial condition of a debtor firm, as well as make projections about its future status. For the largest publicly traded corporations, New Deal–era reforms played an important role in mandating the disclosure of standardized financial information.

The rise of credit rating and scoring fundamentally reshaped how people answered the question of whom to trust and how they evaluated financial promises. Today, credit has little to do with someone's inner personal character, except insofar as this is manifested in large, proprietary data sets and reflected in quantitative scores. Small worlds of local knowledge and qualitative judgments set in a context of close social networks have become broader landscapes with large-scale quantitative measurements and formal calculations, increasingly shaped and dissected by computer algorithms. In the past, successive generations of information technology supported the circulation of credit information. Thus, the national postal system, the telegraph, and later telephone systems all helped transmit growing volumes of information about credit.[79] Today, big data, artificial intelligence, and machine learning are refashioning the allocation of credit, and the role of human judgment will undoubtedly diminish.[80] But this is not entirely new, for the nineteenth century witnessed the first steps in the quantification of trustworthiness, and the ledgers of the original mercantile agencies stored large amounts of information in paper format.[81]

How to Do Other Things with Promises

The creation of a financial obligation means that someone lends to another person in exchange for a promise of future repayment. Promises are used by borrowers to secure resources, and that is the usage of primary interest here. But financial promises can be adapted to a variety of purposes, both good and bad. Credit involves differentiating between the trustworthy and the untrustworthy, but frequently differentiation turned into discrimination, and credit became an instrument for social inequity. Various forms of lending discrimination have plagued credit markets,[82] and in the 1960s and 1970s political groups mobilized to ensure that racial minorities and women could enjoy equal access to credit.[83]

Beyond simple profit, promises can be used by lenders to achieve various ends. For example, loans are a staple of public policy, offered by governments to direct resources toward favored economic sectors and recipients. A public loan program may offer below-market interest rates as a way to encourage borrowers to make promises they can more easily keep. Governments have used loans as an instrument of foreign policy, providing resources on favorable terms to clients they wish to support. Governments have also steered loans and loan guarantees to privileged domestic constituents. Consider how many countries support their agricultural sector with loans and credits, and note how much the U.S. government has sustained the housing market through various lending programs.[84] And if support doesn't come from a loan program, it can come from a loan guarantee program, where the government or some other agency guarantees repayment so that lenders will lend without worry. Governments can encourage specific types of loans by granting the income generated by the loan favorable tax treatment: giving bonds "tax-exempt" status is one way to encourage investors to buy them. Or it might subsidize certain types of loans, making them cheaper for borrowers and thus increasing loan activity. Finally, governments can directly bolster their own fiscal position by requiring, or encouraging, others to lend to them. For example, domestic banks have been "encouraged" to purchase federal or state bonds, and so in effect to lend to the government.

Some scholars have given pride of place to credit as a type of post-Keynesian economic policy.[85] In the heyday of Keynesian economics after World War II, the U.S. government used fiscal and monetary tools to intervene in the economy, maintain aggregate demand, and smooth out business cycles. But Keynesian policy lost its standing in the "stagflation" era of the 1970s, to be replaced by monetarist and later neo-liberal policies. At roughly the same time, the postwar wage growth enjoyed by U.S. workers ground to a halt, and income inequality began to increase. If the federal government became more cautious about using public policy to maintain wage growth and boost the economy, as prescribed by Keynes, it nevertheless encouraged the expansion of private credit so that people with stagnant incomes could still enjoy a high standard of living, buying houses and purchasing durable goods.[86] Private promises could serve a public purpose.

Nongovernment lenders also use loans as a type of support. When loan transactions are embedded in social networks, family members sometimes lend to their relatives not simply because they think it profitable but as an expression of support and familial solidarity. Family loans may be zero interest, and of indefinite maturity. Family members have often acted as loan guarantors, for similar reasons. Less amicably, loans can also be used to subordinate other persons. If the terms are especially onerous, or if the balance of power strongly favors lenders, then a loan can become an instrument of domination. "Debt peonage" arose when lenders kept borrowers in a state of durable indebtedness and subordination, using debt to maintain social hierarchies and as a means of control. Although different from outright slavery, debt peonage gave lenders a great deal of power and an interest in insuring that debtors never fully repaid their debts.

On the debtor side, the example of Eumenes illustrates that sometimes borrowing isn't just about the money. Debtors may seek loans not because they need additional resources but because they want supporters and constituents. To be sure, debtors are often beholden to their creditors, but there are circumstances where the balance shifts and the creditors become supporters of the debtor, if only because their financial interests become aligned. Bankers have long known about this danger, and admonished themselves not to lend too much to a single customer, lest they be in thrall to the debtor. To paraphrase John Maynard Keynes: "If I owe my bank $1,000 and can't repay, then I'm in trouble. But if I owe my bank $1,000,000,000 and can't repay, then my bank is in trouble." In effect, promisees can be captured by the promisor.

Promises and Power

It is tempting to view a financial promise as something like a partnership between equals: one person consents to make a promise, and the other agrees to receive it. But promises involve power and inequality in at least three important ways. First, and most obviously, power inheres within credit relationships. A debtor depends on their creditor and so the latter has power over them; debtors are beholden to creditors. This imbalance has been noted for centuries and commentators continue to affirm it.[87] Yet power within the debtor-creditor relationship isn't static, and it shifts and can even flip. Sometimes debtors dominate their creditors, as clever Eumenes recognized several millennia ago, and as too-big-to-fail banks realized more recently. At some point, creditors become so vulnerable to debtors that they lose their leverage. So as much as power exists within credit, one shouldn't assume that debtors are always subordinate.

Second, access to credit is itself a form of empowerment: it grants purchasing power to a debtor who otherwise wouldn't have it. Advocates for "financial inclusion" or the "democratization of finance" stress this because they recognize that people who are denied the ability to borrow face diminished life chances. Debt can help people solve their problems. Of course, the degree of empowerment varies. But in many lives there come moments when timely access to borrowed money would make the difference between failure and success.

The third way that power arises is less visible than the first two and operates in the background. This concerns the power to constitute credit relationships as such, to set their forms and preconditions, and to create the infrastructure that upholds credit.[88] As lenders wonder which borrowers are creditworthy, the ability to define creditworthiness per se involves power. And as we shall see, this type of background power is currently shifting and cohering as a new privately owned informational apparatus bases the terms of creditworthiness on pervasive quantitative information about debtors. Personal qualities are turned into abstract quantities, and the latter are aggregated and analyzed in an increasingly centralized fashion by algorithms. The computational formula that generates a credit score weights some factors more than others, and includes some pieces of information while leaving others out, but it constitutes a practical definition of creditworthiness that is given widespread effect. By that formula, some debtors will look good and others will not. Similarly, the ability to set the overall terms of credit represents a form of power. Currently, the Federal Reserve uses open market operations and other policy instruments to set interest rates and determine the price of credit, and it is guided by the twin goals of price stability and economic growth. Low interest rates, and expectations about future interest rates, make all forms of credit cheaper, and the volume of promises and activity grows. High interest rates make promises dear, and so their volume shrinks. But the Fed was established in 1913, roughly at the halfway point of this story, and it took decades for it to create and then utilize its power over domestic credit markets.

Book Outline

The United States has always had an economy based on promises, but the manner in which questions about trust and trustworthiness have been posed and answered has changed in important ways. This evolution and expansion undergirded the rise of the modern credit economy, but it wasn't a smooth ride forward. Financial crises signaled the widespread collapse of promises and a collective disbelief in their credibility. Frequently, these collapses motivated public and private attempts to build new institutional scaffolding in support of promises: the 1837 crisis prompted the development of credit ratings; the depression of the 1890s justified passage of a permanent bankruptcy law; the 1907 crisis led to the establishment of the Federal Reserve System; and the Great Depression led to a multitude of public policies in support of financial promises. At various points, political groups believed the financial system to be deeply unfair, systematically privileging some over others. During the 1880s and 1890s, agrarian groups and populists attacked a monetary and banking system that failed to give them adequate credit. During the 1960s and 1970s, women and minorities criticized a discriminatory financial system that denied them full access to consumer and mortgage credit. In this book, I will describe the changes that have occurred, spell out their implications, and explain their significance. I have organized my analysis around different types of credit, offering a roughly chronological discussion of each in turn. I make no attempt to be exhaustive, and so there are types of credit that I overlook and historical details that I omit. I offer an interpretive essay rather than an encyclopedia of the history of credit.

Chapter 2 presents a fuller treatment of the relationship between credit and trust, defining trust and discussing the critical elements of the trust problem. It will identify some key analytical threads to follow in subsequent chapters. In chapter 3 I turn to trade credit and the invention of credit reporting and rating. Trade credit concerns short-term unsecured loans between suppliers and customers, and it sustains the supply chains upon which commerce depends. It also prompted the creation of credit rating in the middle of the nineteenth century. Chapter 4 discusses banks, which have always been foremost lending institutions. How banks operate as creditors is especially revealing given that lending is their specialty. Despite the recent emergence of a "shadow" banking system, for most of the last two centuries banks have been the primary creditor group. In chapter 5, I examine the other side of debt and focus on consumer borrowers. Many commentators have noted that the United States developed a "mass consumer" society, and it turns out that "mass credit" undergirded mass consumption. Inventing new ways to lend to growing numbers of individuals has been an important part of the development of the modern credit economy, and consumers are increasingly assessed using ratings and scores. Chapter 6 considers corporate debtors, and how it is that for-profit firms have been able to borrow. Long-term borrowing by corporations is usually done through the issuance of bonds, and so this chapter also addresses the continued expansion of credit ratings and bond ratings in new debt markets. In chapter 7, I focus on one especially consequential form of borrowing: mortgages. A mortgage is simply a loan secured by real estate, but because of the significance of homeownership in the landscape of American society, and because where a family lives matters so much for things like education, employment, and economic opportunity, it is important to understand the history of this particular type of promise and how it has been shaped by public policy. Chapter 8 deals with broken promises. However much goodwill and optimistic expectations surround the making of promises, there are many disappointments. Debtors sometimes fail to fulfill their end of the bargain, and this is common enough that those who deal with promises must make provision. Lenders try to avoid this situation, of course, but when it arises what happens? The last empirical chapter deals with a unique class of borrowers: sovereign governments. Promises are made, enforced, and broken within a framework of rules that are set by government, so how do these rules apply when governments borrow? Sovereign immunity means that the enforcement of sovereign debts poses particular challenges and that the methods applied to ordinary debtors don't necessarily work. Ranging from school districts and municipalities to state and federal government, sovereign borrowers issue many promises to fund public policy. What role do public promises play?

Promises always join two sides at a minimum, the promisor and promisee, but in practice they invariably bring together many more. The dyadic promise often functions as a convenient fiction, for as financial promises are compounded, complicated, circulated, and multiplied, they create more complex communities of interdependence. These are not so easy to govern using bilateral instruments like contracts.[89] And so other modes of public and private governance have come to play a role in managing the networks of interest created by credit. These shape credit in distinctive ways and help explain why change was so uneven across the different forms of credit.

Financial promises organize modern economic life. They can form a bridge between the present and the future, and a link between debtors and creditors. Promises are ubiquitous, and although some of them are never fully realized, they generally have worked well enough to sustain a system of credit that fuels the economy. When promises are broken on too great a scale, however, the results are spectacularly bad: financial panics, economic recessions, and even depressions. But if promises are hard to live with, they are impossible to live without. Pervasive distrust is no way to run an economy. The core elements of a promise are quite simple, but the growth of today's credit economy bore witness to the multiplication and increasing elaboration of promises. Promises-to-pay are now compounded, pooled and sliced, securitized, bought and sold. As in the past, the credibility of promises is carefully examined and evaluated. But unlike in the past, that assessment today occurs on a mass scale and is increasingly cast in the form of ratings, scores, and numbers. It is no longer a matter of looking someone in the eye and judging their character through a firm handshake. Quantification now plays a crucial role in the allocation of credit, and evaluation depends on an elaborate institutional apparatus that operates in the background: weighing, measuring, enumerating, and calculating.

2

Trust and Credit

An economy of promises consists of transactions that unfold over time. Sometimes they take a simple form, as when one person borrows now and promises to repay next month. Or both sides can agree to do something in the future (deliver goods next week, receive payment in sixty days). Promises can also be extremely complicated and can even be constructed out of other promises, as illustrated by financial instruments like residential mortgage-backed securities (RMBSs), based on underlying residential mortgages. Whether complex or simple, the issuance of a promise means that one or both of the parties to the transaction carry an obligation into the future, and the key question is: will they fulfill that obligation. Will they keep their promise? And does the other party *trust* them to keep that promise?

"Trust" is a dangerous but intriguing concept to work with. On the one hand, so many social processes and interactions seem to involve trust that onc is clearly dealing with a very important feature of human social life and behavior. On the other hand, precisely because so many social processes and interactions concern trust, it threatens to become an all-encompassing concept that applies always and everywhere, and thus dissolves into vacuity. This tension is reflected in the vastness and variability of the literature on trust. Many virtues of trust have been identified. Trust "lubricates" economies, reduces transaction costs, and undergirds effective institutions,[1] and so the loss of trust is economically harmful.[2] Furthermore, trust facilitates both cooperation and production, it enables communication, ameliorates uncertainty, improves resource management, and may even help produce better health outcomes.[3] Trust appears to benefit society in many different ways, although some scholars question whether it is always necessary for all types of cooperation.[4] The creation of trust is more mysterious, and is attributed variously to national culture, aristocratic social arrangements, repeated interactions, dense social networks, third-party enforcement, or the importance of reputations.[5] Some have made sweeping claims about national differences in trust. Japan and Germany, according to Fukuyama (1995), enjoy high levels of trust, whereas Italy does not. Within modern Italy, Putnam (1993) asserted, the north possesses more "social capital" and consequently more trust than does the south. Others claim that trust can change over time, rising or falling depending on how members of a society perceive major social institutions or each other (Paxton 2005).

Given this conceptual range, I choose not to define trust so broadly as to encompass all the ways this term is used. Rather, my interest in trust stems from its connection with credit, and therefore I adopt a more specific meaning. As I conceive it, trust exists between individuals (including fictive individuals, like corporations), but not between individuals and things. I am therefore not interested in the kind of trust that applies when someone says: "I trust the sun will rise tomorrow" or "I trust that my car will not break down." Instead, I follow Cook, Hardin, and Levi (2005) in proposing that if person A trusts another person B, then A proceeds with the expectation that B is going to act in a certain way or do certain things. A trusts B to do X, where X is some particular action. I also set aside notions of trust that are global or unconditional, so I do not consider someone who trusts everyone under all circumstances about everything (indeed, I am not sure such people even exist). Thus, trust is relational and conditional. In its basic form, trust obtains between people and involves specific circumstances and actions.

Trust becomes a problem for person A when B's behavior affects A, and when A is not sure what B will do. Trust therefore matters in situations that involve both vulnerability and uncertainty.[6] B's actions affect A, but A doesn't know what B will do, even when B has made a promise. So A faces the question: does she trust B? Person A may try to mitigate the problem by addressing one or both of these two features: she may try to reduce her vulnerability to B, or she may try to reduce her uncertainty about what B will do. She can find ways to protect her interests by reducing her dependence on, or exposure to, B's actions. She may also gather additional information to predict better how B will act, or try to influence how B will act. A will ascertain B's future ability and willingness to do X. As we will see in later chapters, in dealing with vulnerability and uncertainty, lenders frequently rely on social institutions and third parties. People in A's situation seldom fend for themselves.

It is important to recognize the difference between trust and trustworthiness. Trust concerns A's expectations about whether B will do X. Trustworthiness concerns whether B will in fact do X. Given that A trusts B to do X, if B performs X then B has proven to be trustworthy. Not everyone who is trusted is trustworthy, and not everyone who is distrusted is in fact untrustworthy. In the relation between A and B, trust concerns what A does, while trustworthiness depends on what B does. Life would be simple indeed if people were either trustworthy or not, and everyone trusted the trustworthy and distrusted the untrustworthy. With the difference between trust and trustworthiness in mind, we can briefly consider one particular connection between the two. If A trusts B, does this by itself make B more trustworthy?[7] Does trust generate trustworthiness? If so, a small initial act of trust might set off a virtuous circle in which both trust and trustworthiness grow. Or, conversely, initial distrust might engender subsequent untrustworthiness, and so a vicious circle unfolds.[8]

Suppose that A trusts B, and that B trusts C. What are the implications? Some *social* relations possess formal properties that can have *social* implications. For example, a relation might be transitive, symmetric, or reflexive. A transitive relation means that if A relates to B, and B relates to C, then A relates to C. One example of this concerns friendship: if A is friends with B, and B is friends with C, does this mean that A is friends with C? In fact, friendship is often (although not completely) transitive: the friend of a friend is often a friend.[9] In the case of trust, transitivity would mean that if A trusts B,[10] and B trusts C, then A would trust C. In other words, if someone trusted someone else, then the former would also trust those that the latter trust. If transitivity holds for these sorts of relationships, then trust would radiate out through social networks. A symmetric relation means that if A relates to B, then B relates to A, and vice versa. For trust, symmetry would mean that if A trusts B, then B trusts A. Symmetry would mean that trust was always mutual and bilateral, not a one-sided matter. Finally, reflexive relations are ones where A relates to A. In other words, A trusts A.

Whether trust relations possess the features of transitivity, symmetry, and reflexivity remains to be seen. At this point, however, it seems plausible to suppose that mostly people trust themselves (and hence that trust is reflexive)[11] and that through a general norm of reciprocity they tend to trust those who trust them back (symmetry). Furthermore, if trust is embedded in particular kinds of social relations (e.g., if friendship or kinship generates trust), then the transitivity of those relations can support the transitivity of trust. If A is a friend of B, and B is a friend of C, then often A is also a friend of C. Friendship is the kind of social relation that supports trust, so the transitivity of friendship could engender a transitivity of trust. However, this transitivity would undoubtedly decay beyond a certain distance. That is, if A trusted B, B trusted C, and C trusted D, then A is more likely to trust C, and B is more likely to trust D. But transitivity seems less likely between A and D. Were trust relations to possess all three of these features, trust would constitute an equivalence relation that could induce a division of social groups into mutually exclusive subgroups in which members of each group trusted each other and no group member trusted anyone from a different group. Under these circumstances, trust relations would be divisive (between groups) and solidary (within groups) at the same time. Generally, evidence suggests that people tend to trust others who are members of the same social group, and hence who are like themselves.[12] And when people live in small communities where folks know each other, the transitivity of trust suggests that its overall level would be relatively high. But one of the key challenges in relation to credit stemmed from the fact that economic transactions increasingly occurred between people who were not members of the same community: how could complete strangers learn to trust each other?

Consider the situation where A and B are weighing an exchange where A lends money to B at one point in time, and later on B will repay a slightly larger sum. A is wondering whether or not to trust B. The problem, in simple terms, is that there are two kinds of would-be borrowers, the trustworthy and the untrustworthy. And although lenders want very much to distinguish between them, the differences are not always apparent (except in retrospect). Unlike lenders, borrowers may know whether or not they are really trustworthy, but they cannot easily or credibly convey to lenders what they know about themselves. This fundamental asymmetry of information (as economists put it) pervades credit relations.[13]

In economics, the canonical example of information asymmetry comes from the "market for lemons." Akerloff (1970) showed how the market for used cars is affected by the fact that sellers of used cars know much more about the true quality of the car than do buyers (in particular, whether a used car is really a lemon). And the most obvious way to redress this imbalance, namely having the seller communicate information about quality to the buyer, doesn't work because the buyer knows the seller has an incentive to exaggerate. Thus, claims made by the seller are not credible, even when true. Similarly, in credit markets borrowers know much more about their true creditworthiness than do lenders, although creditworthiness is something lenders want very much to know about. And borrowers cannot simply tell lenders how creditworthy they are because they have a credibility problem. Borrowers can assure the lender that they will indeed repay the loan but are greeted with skepticism.

Lending involves the two features identified by Carol Heimer (1999) as characteristic of trust situations: vulnerability and uncertainty. The lender is vulnerable to the borrower depending on the size and duration of the loan. And since repayment comes in the future, the lender cannot be sure what the borrower is going to do after the loan is made. In deciding whether to trust, would-be lenders address these two features and try either to make themselves less vulnerable or to gather more information about the future actions of the debtor, or both. There are several directions in which to pursue these strategies. Lenders have reduced their vulnerability to debtors, and managed their uncertainties, in different ways, depending on legal and institutional environments, social networks, business practices, social norms, and other factors. Today's bankers, for example, can rely on a commercial legal code to help enforce formal loan contracts and can turn to bankruptcy law if the debtor becomes insolvent.[14] In the past, legal systems were less dependable and so lenders had to enforce agreements in other ways.[15] In seeking information to reduce uncertainty, today's creditors can use many sources, including credit ratings, balance sheets, filings with the Securities and Exchange Commission (SEC), and various other kinds of financial numbers to learn how able a debtor will be to repay a loan. In the past, such systematic quantitative information about debtors didn't exist and so lenders sought information about borrowers from other informal sources.[16]

In later chapters, I am going to discuss in detail how people managed trust problems for particular kinds of credit, and how their solutions evolved over time, but for now I offer a general overview. The beginning point for a creditor involves an examination of the authenticity of a promise. Is what appears to be a promise actually a bona fide promise? One doesn't want to accept a promise that was made ironically or as a joke. And was it actually issued by the party who will be bound by the promise, as opposed to someone else? How can someone's identity be determined?[17] Authentication is an important first step in the evaluation of trustworthiness. Since the worth or significance of a promise depends on who is making it, it is critical to connect specific promises with the person or organization issuing the promise. Anonymous promises (i.e., that might be made by anyone) are of dubious value, and the problem is non-trivial when promises circulate widely and are passed onto third parties.

Authentication varies by the medium in which the promise is made. With the addition of certain formal features, a verbal expression can be turned into a solemn oath. When promises are made on paper, a signature becomes critical. The person making the promise signs the paper (so it becomes legally binding), and perhaps there are witnesses to the promise who also sign in order to attest to its authenticity. As a centuries-old practice of authentication, the signature functions because it has been deemed unique to an individual (although vulnerable to forgery). But there are other authentication strategies for written promises, such as the use of special materials (e.g., high-quality banknote paper), iconography (engraved images), or registration (keeping a separate record of the promise). In addition, one has to be sure that the person making the promise is someone who can make such promises (i.e., they aren't a legal minor, they are the appropriate corporate officer, etc.) and that they intended to make such a promise (i.e., it wasn't an accident). Finally, one has to determine who the promise is being made to, or to whom the obligation is being extended. Promises can be made to a specific individual (e.g., the lender) or someone non-specific (bearer, assignee, etc.). Registration puts a record of a promise into the hands of a third party (e.g., a public authority), in addition to whatever record the two parties to the transaction possess.[18] Duplicate and triplicate copies can be checked against each other to ensure authenticity.

Assume that a promise to repay money has been issued and authenticated, that is, it is a "real" promise made by a qualified person. The question remains: should the lender trust? There are many ways to deal with this question, and all of them have influenced the extension of credit, depending on context and time period. I outline them here, but we will discuss them all in subsequent chapters.

1. Personal qualities of the debtor. For a long time, creditors have focused on the personal or psychological character of the debtor as the key to trustworthiness, assuming that some people keep their promises better than others. In chapter 5, we will see how this has shaped credit for individuals and consumers. As one commentator put it: "the rock bottom foundation upon which the whole system of credit is based is character" (Skinner 1904: 91).[19] Debtors with sufficient moral fiber will always try to repay their loans, and like other personality traits this is deemed to be a durable propensity: over time and in different situations, persons of good character will reliably keep their promises. Thus, information about character allows the lender to have a better sense about how the borrower will behave in the future. The problem for lenders is how to discern persons with true integrity, and how to separate them from the others. This can be an especially vexing problem because people who wish to borrow will all try to appear trustworthy, even if they are not. A variety of heuristics and rules of thumb have been used over the years (claiming, e.g., that merchants with well-organized account books are more trustworthy, that married men are more trustworthy than single men, that trustworthy people will look you straight in the eye and provide a firm handshake, that homeowners are more trustworthy than renters, etc.).

Such heuristics can unfairly disadvantage some people. Research on racial and gender discrimination in modern credit markets, for example, has outlined how biased attributions of trustworthiness can shape discretionary decision making to favor some groups over others. Such biases can function like self-fulfilling prophesies.[20] More generally, discrimination benefits some (members of the in-group) and disadvantages others (members of the out-group) and is motivated by the tendency to view members of one's own group as having better character. However, the importance of personal character diminishes (although not entirely) as credit becomes more anonymous and as people rely on new sources of information. For example, credit card offers are made to millions of people each year in the United States, and obviously the issuers are not personally acquainted with the credit card holders.[21] And even before credit cards, creditors operating in large cities had less opportunity to get to know debtors personally and so had to figure out how to extend credit on the basis of other criteria.[22]

2. Informal social relationships between debtor and creditor. Sometimes, debtors and creditors know each other. Stable, long-term social relationships between the two, such as friendship, kinship, or being neighbors, can render a debtor more trustworthy in the eyes of a creditor, especially if the relationship involves strong normative obligations. Furthermore, the prospect of a relationship that will continue into the future has significance. Such social ties are more important in smaller, stable communities, and were reflected in early patterns of bank lending (chapter 4) and in the extension of credit to individuals (chapter 5). High levels of social and geographic mobility increase the chances that people will have to deal with others with whom they have a weak social relationship, or none at all.

People are more likely to trust their siblings and good friends than complete strangers. Social relationships have this effect on trust for two reasons.

First, they make available all kinds of "inside" information: people who are closely connected generally know a lot about each other and so there is less uncertainty about future behavior.[23] Second, relationships involve ongoing obligations that allow the lender to shape the borrower's future behavior. This means that outside the confines of the loan transaction per se, the debtor and creditor have various informal obligations to each other that build on their past and extend into the future. Such mutual dependencies and opportunities make the debtor vulnerable to the creditor and give creditors the chance to sanction the debtor informally in case of non-payment. A debtor who refuses to repay can be punished by a creditor who withdraws from the relationship (e.g., ends the friendship) or who uses common social ties to sanction the debtor (e.g., spread gossip about the debtor's reputation within a circle of friends). The historical importance of informal relations is obvious from the simple fact that in the past so much credit flowed through family and friendship networks,[24] and frequently business, family, political, and religious ties overlapped a great deal.[25] Meech (1923: 53) suggests that personal relations were very important in enabling U.S. firms in the early twentieth century to float their commercial paper on the open market, and also that informal relations made it easier for a debtor to renegotiate terms if they got into trouble.[26] Research on the importance of social ties follows Mark Granovetter's famous article on embeddedness (1985) and documents how informal relationships influence contemporary bank lending to midsize and small firms.[27] Yet, as we will see, the *relative* importance of informal social ties has diminished.

3. Formal-contractual relationships between debtor and creditor. Debtors and creditors can be connected formally as well as informally. The formality of contracts offers specificity about expectations with respect to who will do what and when, and greater enforceability for the provisions of the agreement. Contracts can also calibrate the balance of power between the two parties and determine the durability of their connection. With reliable commercial laws, loan contracts can help make the debtor repay, prevent debtors from undermining their own ability to repay, and reduce the cost to the creditor of debtor default.[28] A loan agreement can also require debtors to provide information to creditors, so they are updated about the ability of the borrower to repay (e.g., corporate debtors may have to submit an audited balance sheet on a quarterly basis). We think of contracts as largely private arrangements between freely consenting parties, but in fact governments sometimes regulate debtor-creditor contracts in order to protect one party (usually the borrower) from exploitative transactions.[29] The terms of certain types of loan contracts may be constrained (e.g., usury laws that set interest rates) or require use of standardized terms and conditions (e.g., average percentage rate [APR] for the interest charged).

Formal loan agreements may identify collateral so that, in the event of default, the creditor can seize an asset belonging to the debtor. Mortgage loans secured by real estate have played an enormous role in housing markets and the geography of American society, as chapter 7 will discuss. Alternatively, the legal title to an asset may not be transferred to the buyer/borrower until the loan is completely repaid (as in hire-purchase agreements or installment loans). Secured transactions are among the oldest and most common ways for creditors to reduce their vulnerability, and they depend on the debtor having clear title over whatever property serves as collateral (and things get complicated if debtors use the same property as collateral for multiple debts). This means that changes in property rights can change collateral. After the Civil War, for example, ex-slaves could no longer function as collateral for loans to former slave owners, and so cotton plantation owners had to secure loans in some other fashion.[30] Under traditional common law, married women had no independent legal personality and therefore could not own property. Not until married women's property rights laws were passed during the nineteenth century could they borrow using proper collateral.[31]

Chapter 3 will say more on this topic, but one of the most important features of debt contracts concerns whether or not they are negotiable. In Common Law, this feature developed during the early eighteenth century and had important practical implications because it gave liquidity to debts.[32] It allowed people to exchange debts, trade them, pass them on, and use them in effect like money, knowing that they were still legally enforceable by subsequent bearers. Formal negotiability (and similar qualities like assignability, alienability, and transferability) means that debts do not necessarily bind the same two persons, debtor and the creditor, in a connection that lasts until the debt is fully extinguished. The original creditor can transfer the debt to a third party, to whom the debtor will be equally obliged, and therefore step out of the relationship and recover their money. If, for example, A lends money to B, and B signs a promissory note "to A or bearer," then A can transfer the note to someone else, C, who as bearer will still have a valid claim over B. Thus, creditors can "exit" the relationship, for a price. Negotiability means that debtors need not know their creditors. It also means that A can use B's note to satisfy A's own debts to others (thus,

B's promissory note functions like money). Finally, negotiability alters the original trust problem: A may have decided that B is trustworthy enough to borrow money, but when A tries to transfer B's note to C, C now has to consider B's trustworthiness. Negotiability lifts trust and trustworthiness out of a specific debtor-creditor relationship and gives obligations greater generality and mobility. It also creates the possibility of a market for debt, and a market for trust.

The impact and evolution of formal law have been researched mostly by legal and economic historians, as well as law-and-economics scholars. Comparative work on the reliability and efficiency of the legal system argues that good laws enhance financial development, which then translates into higher rates of economic growth.[33] This research suggests that legal progress allows people to write "better" loan contracts that are more reliably enforced and that this encourages lending. But formal contracts have limits, and sometimes they can be supplemented or complemented by the social relationships discussed in item 2 above.[34] Furthermore, when credit transactions cross jurisdictional boundaries, legal pluralism can add significant uncertainty: when a New York supplier provides credit to a customer in California, which state law applies? For all the attractions of making specific and binding agreements, businesspeople sometimes transact without signing a formal agreement.

4. Debtors' social networks. Debtors and creditors have a connection to each other, but they are also both embedded in larger and more encompassing social networks. These affect how people behave in their roles as debtors and creditors. Some types of networks constrain debtor behavior in ways that influence creditworthiness, depending on what position the debtor occupies in the larger network. For example, a debtor who enjoys high social status within a community may suffer if she defaults on a debt and this becomes widely known—her high status and sterling reputation function as hostages, and fear of losing them will encourage her fidelity. But her status exists only by virtue of her place within a social network or community.

Sometimes borrowers deliberately join social networks that involve collective liability for debts, as in many micro-credit arrangements. Analyses of the Grameen Bank, rotating credit associations, Hebrew Free Loan Societies, credit unions, and similar arrangements reflect this aspect.[35] In addition, certain kinds of third-party relationships insert debtors into webs of incoming obligations that bolster their creditworthiness. For example, someone with a wealthy family or rich friends has connections to people who can act as loan guarantors. At the same time, someone with outgoing obligations may behave more responsibly and be perceived to be a better risk (witness the belief that married men with children were more trustworthy than single men).[36] Outside of the specific debtor-creditor dyad, social obligations both to and from the debtor can affect creditworthiness and perceptions of creditworthiness.

5. Financial characteristics of the debtor. This feature concerns the future capacity of the debtor to repay the loan and depends on creditors' ability to measure that capacity. Will the debtor have sufficient financial resources to service the loan? The expansion of consumer credit in the twentieth century was helped by the standardization of employment relations and income reporting, which made it easier to know how much a particular individual earned and whether their income would continue into the future. A person with a permanent job has a more stable income than someone with only a temporary job and will be regarded as more creditworthy. And the necessity to pay income taxes imposed on wage earners standardized ways to calculate annual personal income and created a convenient benchmark measure of income. Furthermore, as more households use financial services, their assets, liabilities, and income streams become measurable. For example, a loan applicant can report the balances in their savings and checking accounts, and thus document their ability to service a loan. But if they save money by putting it in a mattress or burying it in the backyard, it is harder for others to gauge.

How well creditors can determine the financial situation of a debtor firm has changed enormously with increased financial information. Today, filing and disclosure requirements imposed by regulatory bodies like the SEC, the development of generally accepted accounting principles (GAAP), and the availability of trained professional accountants and auditors ensure a high volume of standardized financial information about many firms. In some cases, this can even allow a potential creditor to look "upstream" of the debtor, to the debtor's debtors, and estimate how likely it is that the debtor will be repaid and able to service its own debts (e.g., assessing nonperforming loans or accounts receivable). Furthermore, information about a particular firm can now be set into a wider context of information about industry conditions, markets, business cycles, and overall economic trends.

During the nineteenth century and earlier, individual and corporate debtors were largely opaque. Firms kept information to themselves and sometimes wouldn't even inform their own shareholders about how well they were doing. Eventually, disclosure requirements were set by regulatory agencies but also by private bodies like the New York Stock Exchange.[37] Chapter 3 details how much new information was created and sold privately by credit rating agencies like Dun and Bradstreet for small business, and later by Standard and Poor's and Moody's for corporate bonds and other tradeable securities.[38] Lenders have also demanded more information directly from debtors, requiring them, for example, to file financial statements as a condition of getting a loan.[39] Various ways were invented to ensure that potential creditors could determine how much debt a borrower is currently carrying (via, e.g., public registration requirements for liens and secured transactions). There is much more quantitative information available than in the past, although it doesn't ensure complete transparency. Sociological studies of accounting acknowledge the biases of quantitative information, as well as the professional interests of accountants, so this information cannot be said to be straightforwardly "objective."[40] And corporate accounting scandals (e.g., Enron, WorldCom) remind us that quantitative information can be manipulated and corrupted to a considerable extent.

The financial situation of debtors is affected by the totality of their liabilities. That is, a creditor wishes to know if a prospective debtor has other obligations to other creditors. The creditor will also want to know the nature and magnitude of those debts since they would compete with the creditor's own claims on the borrower's debt-servicing capacity. When there are competing claims, which one has priority? This important question is often settled through legal rules that govern seniority: secured creditors have priority over unsecured creditors and can simply seize their collateral to satisfy the debt. However, in many jurisdictions secured loans come with filing requirements so that a lien or similar device gets publicly registered. This means that all potential lenders can know if there are other lenders whose claims will have higher priority. When a debtor gets into financial trouble, seniority becomes critical.

In making these determinations about borrowers, lenders rely on their own direct sources of information, and they often look to information provided by third parties (such as rating agencies), but they sometimes also pay attention to peer behavior. That is, one heuristic for making decisions is to rely on what others are doing and make inferences from their actions. Colloquially, this pattern is sometimes called "herding." For example, if one bank is lending money to a business, another bank may take that fact by itself as a positive sign and conclude that the business must be creditworthy. Peer behavior can be informative.

6. Goals of the debtor and creditor. What are the intentions of the lender in making the loan, and what does the debtor intend to do with the money? These affect not only information and its interpretation but also the significance of vulnerabilities that emerge from a transaction. Is the loan a narrowly economic transaction or does it involve extra-economic values and considerations? If, for example, a creditor wants to lend money as a gift or as part of a philanthropic gesture, then repayment isn't such a problem, and neither is the trustworthiness of the debtor (in the sense of whether they repay).[41] Research on the social meaning of money shows that money can be a surprisingly useful vehicle for the expression of cultural meanings and distinctions, and thus its deployment through a loan can accommodate many non-economic goals.[42]

Loans can also be bundled with other economic transactions and used to pursue a broader set of goals. Lenders are often more willing to extend credit when loans are used to facilitate a sale, as with installment loans for durable goods.[43] Many discovered that consumers purchase goods more frequently if the seller also provides credit to finance the purchase, and this realization helped create modern consumer society. Indeed, conflict between sales departments and credit departments within the same firm was not uncommon as salesmen pressed for the extension of credit to customers that the credit department deemed marginally creditworthy.[44] Sometimes creditors served higher-level goals like economic development. For example, many state-chartered insurance companies were required in the nineteenth century to invest their money in government securities, municipal bonds, farm mortgages, or whatever suited the political goals of the state government that granted the charters.[45] By law, certain goals were thrust upon a particular set of creditors, in exchange for the right to incorporate and operate. Finally, lenders may lend simply to conceal failure. Sometimes financial institutions extend new loans to hide the fact that a borrower couldn't repay their old loans and that the bank didn't want to recognize the loss. This is typically done by extending or "rolling over" loans in order to disguise their nonperforming status.

Those who borrow money seek to boost their current purchasing power and are willing to forgo future resources (when repayment occurs) in order to do so. But the specific reasons why a debtor sought a loan also matter, particularly when those goals bear on the ability or willingness of the debtor to repay.[46] Traditionally, banks were much more willing to lend money to fund business activity rather than personal consumption. Someone who intended to earn a profit seemed a better risk than someone who simply wanted to consume more. However, even as non-business personal lending expanded, lenders continued to track the borrower's goals. Consider that mortgage lenders assessed an individual borrower's desire to provide a home for their family in deciding whether to lend.[47] The concern about goals shaped the decision about whether to lend but also the terms of the loan. Given that money is fungible, lenders sometimes use the loan contract to tie the hands of the borrower and restrict use of the loan to particular purposes.[48]

7. General remedies for debtor default. Outside of the specific contractual agreement between debtor and creditor, modern market economies provide a legal framework for debtor insolvency. Chapter 8 addresses what happens when the creditor lends to a debtor who fails. How are the losses distributed among a firm's stakeholders or an individual's claimants? These rules are normally set forth in bankruptcy or insolvency laws, but they are also conditioned by laws of incorporation that granted limited liability to certain kinds of firms.[49] Early rules did little more than coerce debtors by putting them into prison until they (or their families) repaid their debts.[50] During the nineteenth century a series of federal bankruptcy laws were passed and then repealed in the United States, often in response to economic crises that created large numbers of troubled debtors. Modern bankruptcy laws can vary from creditor-friendly (making it easy for lenders to extract their money from the insolvent borrower) to debtor-friendly (allowing debtors to discharge their debts, exempt property from seizure, and get a "fresh start"). When applied to firms, bankruptcy law can privilege liquidation, where insolvent firms are simply shut down and all the assets handed over to the creditors, over reorganization, where firms are allowed to restructure debts, lower costs, and get another chance to succeed.[51] Bankruptcy law affects debtor-creditor relationships by setting the rules for economic failure: what happens when the debtor is unable to repay? Depending on the rules, firms have been able to make bankruptcy part of business strategy,[52] and individual bankruptcies have functioned like a safety net for financially troubled households.[53] Corporate bankruptcy law has become more consequential as deregulation and privatization moved more economic assets into competitive markets and subjected them to harder budget constraints.[54]

8. Creditor diversification. Whether a creditor lends to a particular debtor depends on the merits of the loan, but it can also depend on how that loan fits into a larger portfolio of loans. On a stand-alone basis, a loan may look like a profitable investment, but put into the context of the lender's other financial relationships, it may not make good sense. Diversification into uncorrelated risks is now a rigorous investment strategy, but as chapter 4 reveals, for some time bank lenders have appreciated the value of "not putting all their eggs into one basket." A rational investor worries about risk and rate of return, and diversification is one way to manage risk. Modern creditors can also utilize credit insurance (discussed in chapter 3), a product unavailable in the early nineteenth century, to reduce their vulnerability to a particular debtor. Furthermore, under certain circumstances, the problem of the trustworthiness of particular debtors can be mitigated by pooling large numbers of similar debtors together and then estimating statistically the general likelihood of default within a pool of loans, as well as the variance (and covariance). The creditor no longer worries so much about a specific debtor but rather wants to know the average rate of loss in the larger pool of loans and then simply charges enough interest to cover such losses (securitization of home mortgages in the secondary mortgage market does this). This shift from individual loans to loan pools depends on prior standardization, quantification, and the deployment of actuarial methods that create and exploit new types of information.[55]

9. Intermediaries between debtor and creditor. Sometimes the *indirect* connections between debtors and creditors matter as much as their *direct* connections. Those who are positioned between the two parties can act like intermediaries, providing credible and confidential information to both sides, vouchsafing a debtor's reliability, and generally acting like an economic matchmaker. The importance of investment banks for modern corporate bond and stock issues suggests that in some instances, intermediaries play a critical role signaling which debtors are trustworthy and whose promises should be trusted.[56] Research on brokerage, network structure, and intercorporate networks has explored some of these issues, illustrating not only what brokers can do for those they connect together but also why someone might act as a broker.[57]

10. Overall monetary environment. Since debts are eventually to be repaid in money, the status of the monetary system has a significant effect on debtor-creditor relations. Whether to trust a debtor can be influenced by whether one can trust the legal tender that such a debtor would use to repay a loan.[58] Dramatic changes in overall price levels or widespread uncertainty about the value of money can so favor debtors (in the case of inflation) or creditors (deflation) as to affect the overall willingness of people to undertake loan transactions.[59] In an inflationary environment, lenders might try to reduce their vulnerability by insisting on higher interest rates (to adjust for the erosion of the value of currency) or shorter loan maturities, denominating the loan in some other more stable currency or medium of exchange, or even including an index clause in the loan contract. Inflation rates have waxed and waned throughout U.S. history, but the U.S. monetary system itself changed during the Civil War, with the formation of the National Banking System, and again with the establishment of the Federal Reserve System. Before the Civil War, for example, individual banks issued their own paper banknotes, which then circulated along with the notes of all other banks. The real value of a banknote depended not only on the nominal sum printed on the piece of paper but also on the solvency of the issuing bank.[60] Since much less was known about the solvency of small out-of-state banks than about local institutions, such non-standardized and heterogeneous money made it hard for those receiving cash to know what it was they were getting, and it complicated the trust problem faced by lenders. Distinguishing between authentic banknotes and counterfeit notes was also a substantial challenge, and so people worried whether cash was genuine.[61] Then, during the Civil War, the United States went off the gold standard and didn't return to convertibility until later, and only after such intense political controversy as to worsen monetary uncertainties.[62] So for a time, even banknotes issued by fully solvent banks were not convertible into specie. And not until the Federal Reserve System was established in 1913 did the United States have a central bank charged with managing the monetary system in order to avoid or ameliorate financial crises.

These ten factors are not equally important in all instances. But each affected either knowledge or vulnerability and so could influence a lender's willingness to accept another's promise. From the creditor's standpoint, it is obviously best when all the factors line up the same way and make lending an easy decision: an instance where the debtor is of good character, signs a formal contract, has a strong informal relationship with the creditor, and would harm their reputation in the event of default. And a situation where none of these things were true would offer similar clarity. Matters are rarely so simple, however. Often some aspects signal a higher level of trustworthiness while others indicate less, giving the creditor a mixed picture. Whatever overall assessment the creditor makes, the creditor can refuse to make a loan, or can adjust the terms of the loan to reflect the overall level of trust. In the latter case, a skeptical lender might shorten the maturity of the loan, charge a higher interest rate, make a smaller loan, and insist on collateral.

The ten factors don't operate independently. For instance, attempts to enhance trustworthiness along one dimension can worsen it along another. Consider that a creditor who insists on a formal loan contract may actually undercut his or her personal relationship with the debtor (in rather the same way that a prenuptial agreement can take the bloom off a romance) and so inadvertently reduce the overall level of trust. An informal social relationship can also be threatened if a lender too aggressively interrogates the details of a debtor's finances (imagine insisting on an audited financial statement before lending money to a friend). Furthermore, informal social relationships can strengthen a debtor's obligation to repay the loan, but equally they can increase a creditor's obligation to lend in the first place (and in the event of debtor insolvency, strengthen the obligation to forgive or roll over the delinquent debt). Such interdependencies create complex trade-offs.

Those who deal in credit frequently try to exploit multiple factors at the same time. In addition to learning about someone's character, a potential creditor might sign a formal contract, obtain a lien, and try to learn about a debtor's reputation from others. They might also try to complicate a transaction in ways that enhance its value (e.g., lending to someone who will then use the money to make a purchase from the lender, as in the case of retail credit). But the effect is not simply additive or linear, for information about creditworthiness that one receives via one signal must be *interpreted* in the context of all the other signals. The assessment of creditworthiness involved a type of *practical hermeneutics*, and only in specific cases was information combined in a simple or mechanical fashion (e.g., credit scoring).

Lenders have devised various heuristics to deal with some of these aspects of lending. For business credit, one of the best-known involved the so-called "Three Cs": character, capacity, capital.[63] This heuristic gave lenders a simple recipe that enabled them to focus on three key facts and ignore other complications. For individual credit, occupation, gender, and marital status functioned as rough measures of creditworthiness.[64] However, such rules of thumb only offer guides for decision making, and the interdependencies among the factors can sometimes be almost intractable.

Change meant that one basis for trust might displace other bases. In eighteenth-century New York, development of a more functional legal system meant that courts, commercial law, and formal contracts substituted for personal relationships in the extension of credit.[65] Of course, personal relationships still made a difference, but they were no longer critical, and the generality of law, in contrast to the particularity of social ties, allowed for a more expansive development of credit. During the nineteenth century,

American local and regional markets became integrated at a national level, and along with long-distance trade came national credit information (supplied by credit reporting firms like R. G. Dun) and the development of laws that enforced the property rights involved with commercial paper and other forms of negotiable instruments.[66] These formal means allowed for more anonymous borrowing and made it easier for people to lend to strangers, outside of their circle of personal relationships. Credit reporting and rating have developed considerably since then and are now widely used around the globe to facilitate trade among strangers.[67] After the Civil War, domestic currency became much more standardized and so postbellum credit relationships were less affected by concerns about the uneven value of paper currency. Lenders could more dependably trust the money they were repaid.

Credit pervades the modern economy, but it is not akin to an "oil" that uniformly lubricates all economic transactions. Rather, it is unevenly distributed and can be free-flowing in some regions of the economy and more "viscous" in others. In subsequent chapters, I will address some of the more important varieties of credit and show how trade credit (the short-term unsecured credit that a supplier or manufacturer typically extends to its customers) differed from bank credit, which differed in turn from consumer credit, which differed again from home mortgage lending. Each institutional setting involved a different balance among the various factors. In some cases, lending was deeply affected by public policy and political priorities. For example, starting in the 1930s a number of new policy measures encouraged the flow of money into home mortgages, resuscitated the housing market, and helped reshape the geography of American society.[68] These included providing credit insurance for home mortgages, setting underwriting standards, providing housing loans, and establishing a secondary market for mortgages, and involved a number of public agencies like the FHA (Federal Housing Administration), FNMA (Federal National Mortgage Association, aka "Fannie Mae"), and the VA (Veterans Administration). In a different sector of the financial system, New Deal regulations created the SEC (Securities and Exchange Commission) and required publicly traded companies to provide standardized and detailed financial information to the public. And well before the New Deal, federal government programs were steering credit to farmers and strengthening their position as borrowers.[69]

The changes that have transformed the problem of trust posed in credit markets do not reflect the unfolding of some master process like *modernization*, nor do they express single imperatives like *rationality* or *efficiency*. The causes of change are not solely technological, economic, social, or political. This is a complex story involving unintended consequences. The fundamental elements of trust may be simple (vulnerability, uncertainty), but their manifestation is multifaceted and evolving. However, there has been a long-term shift away from personal bases for trust to more impersonal bases. In 1800, trust and creditworthiness grew out of direct knowledge of someone's personal character or direct connection through personal or familial relations. By 1950, these personal bases had been supplemented, and even eclipsed, by impersonal institutions that created trust by providing information or reducing the vulnerability of creditors. And today, "big data" makes the allocation of credit dependent on pervasive information routinely harvested from people's on- and off-line lives. The overall effect has been to sustain an economy that, to a remarkable degree, relies on promises.

3

Trade Credit and the Invention of Ratings

Trade credit is one of the oldest and most important forms of credit and has underpinned market exchange for many centuries. It stems from transactions between suppliers and their business customers, in both international and domestic trade. Suppose in 1840 a New York City wholesale dry goods supplier had a customer in Buffalo, New York. This customer would typically be a merchant or store owner who acquired goods from suppliers and manufacturers and resold them to local customers. Usually, the merchant-customer acquired goods from the wholesaler on credit, on a buy-now-pay-later basis. The duration of the loan was determined by the gap between when the goods were shipped and when they were paid for. In effect, the merchant-customer would have an open account with the wholesaler. Such customers might have to pay within a month, or ninety days, or eight months (the exact duration depended on circumstances and convention). But credit was expected, and indeed wholesalers would lose business if they insisted on cash transactions only. Coins and paper currency were in scarce supply, and before the Civil War, people were bedeviled by the non-uniformity of U.S. currency.[1]

With trade credit, two distinct transactions were in effect bundled together, a sale and a loan, with the latter making the former possible. A successful commercial relationship could generate a stream of such pairings. To compensate for deferred payment, the supplier might charge a higher price for credit than for cash sales (or find some other way to reward customers who paid cash), or they might simply raise overall prices. Trade credit was typically short-term and unsecured. That is, maturities were measured in days rather than years and the supplier-lender did not go through the legalities of negotiating a formal loan agreement and securing a lien over the goods shipped or in some other fashion obtaining a security interest in the customer's assets. Collateral was uncommon, and even if there was a lien, enforcement was difficult as a practical matter (especially across state lines).[2] Instead, the supplier simply shipped the goods and hoped that turnover of the customer's inventory would generate enough cash to ensure repayment. Since merchants often extended credit to their own retail customers, their success necessitated a careful balancing act: securing credit from suppliers while extending it to customers, and ensuring that the latter paid reliably enough so that suppliers could be satisfied. Retailers operated within a web of cross-cutting credit obligations, seeking profit while trying to remain solvent.

Nineteenth-century trade credit started as book credit. The terms and amount of the debt were recorded in the supplier's books, and nowhere else.[3] There was no signed contract, promissory note, purchase order, or written IOU issued by the customer. The supplier hopefully knew something about the customer, perhaps on the basis of their reputation or prior dealings, and was willing to ship the goods. Suppliers had few options for reducing their vulnerability, but they often started out by making only small consignments (to see how the customer behaved), and they could always sanction a problematic customer by refusing further business.

Three major changes marked the expansion of trade credit. First came the development of credit rating agencies. These organizations emerged in the 1840s and 1850s and helped suppliers and wholesalers assess the creditworthiness of potential customers. After all, since sales depended on trade credit, it was always tempting to give credit in order to increase sales. Credit rating agencies provided systematic information about the creditworthiness of many small firms and facilitated long-distance trade among strangers. A high rating meant that a firm was considered a good risk. These rating agencies were able to commodify valuable information about other firms and sell it on a large scale. As we will see in subsequent chapters, the methods devised by credit raters proved to be very influential and spread from trade credit to bank credit and eventually to bond ratings. Today, various rating agencies play a key role in the governance of global and domestic capital flows.

The second major change in trade credit came later in the nineteenth century. Larger and better-known firms were able to secure short-term credit by issuing unsecured, negotiable promissory notes that came to be known as "commercial paper." These were sold in order to raise working capital, finance inventory, and otherwise help with the firm's short-term needs. Rather than have a debt sitting on the books of a particular supplier, well-known firms could take advantage of liquid capital markets to issue promises to whoever was willing to make a short-term loan. For investors, commercial paper had the attractive feature of being negotiable, which meant that holders of the paper could recover their money by passing it on to someone else, rather than waiting for the borrower to repay. In effect, customer firms could finance purchases by borrowing from a much wider group of lenders than just their own suppliers. And this new method was also available to the supplier firms, who could issue commercial paper to help cover the loans they had to extend to their own customers. Supplier firms were also able to take advantage of newly emerging "factors" or "sales finance companies," who would acquire the supplier's accounts receivable (i.e., the short-term loans made to customers) in exchange for cash up front. Thanks to factoring, a supplier didn't even have to wait sixty days for the money due from a sale.

A third development, perhaps not as dramatic as the other two, also altered the financial vulnerability of trade creditors. At the end of the nineteenth century, a market for credit insurance emerged.[4] By purchasing credit insurance, creditors could protect themselves from excessive losses due to debtor default. As with other forms of insurance, this provided a way for creditors to pool their risks so that no single insured creditor would have to bear the full brunt of a customer's non-payment. But the pricing of credit insurance was built upon the system of credit ratings, further amplifying the importance of the latter.

Together, these three changes significantly altered the economic situation for domestic trade relations in the United States. Credit ratings provided useful information about hundreds of thousands of firms and made it easier for a supplier to learn something about a potential customer who was otherwise a complete stranger. Credit ratings addressed the trust problem for trade credit by providing a new type of information to reduce uncertainty. The other big change, which I call the "mobilization of debt," allowed obligations to circulate, and this enabled trade creditors to manage their level of vulnerability either by going into debt themselves (by issuing their own commercial paper) or by using a factor to transform debts due to them into cash. Either way, they reduced the need for collateral as a way to reduce vulnerability. By turning to third parties, creditors inadvertently changed the assessment of creditworthiness from a largely private and idiosyncratic process (one particular creditor evaluating a particular debtor) into something more public and collective. For example, in extending credit to a customer, suppliers had to decide for themselves how creditworthy the customer seemed. But whether or not the supplier could "sell" its accounts receivable to a factor, and at what price, depended on how creditworthy the entire roster of customers seemed to the factor, who wasn't a party to the original debt transaction. As debts circulated, multiple and repeated assessments of creditworthiness had to be made, and a "market" emerged as arbiter. The original financial relationship between debtor and creditor, embedded in whatever social ties joined them, became a formalized and alienable commodity.[5] The final development involved a different set of third parties, credit insurers, who in exchange for premiums agreed to compensate an insured creditor in the event of debtor non-payment, thus reducing a creditor's vulnerability. Like the credit raters, credit insurers had to devise some kind of an estimate of the risk involved in a credit transaction, and to calculate "normal" losses in an industry, in order to price their services.

The importance of credit for commerce also increased as the volume, frequency, and geographic reach of credit grew. Merchants, traders, and other businesspeople needed both to obtain credit and to extend it. Thus, they were simultaneously debtors and creditors, and operated within a web of debt relationships. The vulnerability and interdependence that credit created meant that credit was always a worrisome problem. Even when merchants managed their own situation well, if debtor-customers were too slow to pay then the merchant would soon become hard-pressed to repay their own suppliers on time. Problems were contagious, and insolvency and illiquidity had an unfortunate tendency to spread through the credit network. Someone's situation could be seriously damaged by the actions of a debtor's debtor (or someone at further remove). However hard it was to manage a business and to negotiate directly with customers and supplier firms, it was virtually impossible to monitor or control the indirect connections. As Edward Balleisen notes, by various estimates the proportion of business ventures that failed during the 1840s and 1850s was somewhere between 40 and 50 percent,[6] so it was highly unlikely that firms could escape the effects of the failure of others, even if they themselves did not collapse. As trade expanded over greater distances and encompassed more firms, and as the limits of traditional information gathering became more evident, each individual firm gained more exposure to market-based risks whose dispersion and complexity also grew. The intractability of credit is one reason why U.S. court caseloads were for so long dominated by debt-related lawsuits.[7] When caught between rocks and hard places, businesspeople would eventually resort to formal legal proceedings after exhausting other avenues (reminding, pleading, threatening, imploring, etc.). And particularly for out-of-state creditors, collection of debts remained a very serious problem.[8] For them, especially, it was critical to avoid credit problems in the first place.

Trade Credit in the Nineteenth Century

Domestic trade in early America was hampered by the difficulty of transporting commodities over long distances. To ship goods was a protracted and expensive undertaking, especially over land and before the widespread development of railroads. In 1800, for example, it took roughly forty-two days to get from New York City to the place on the southern shores of Lake Michigan that eventually became Chicago. By 1857, however, travel time had dropped to two days.[9] Similarly, in 1800 the cost per ton-mile for freight was about thirty cents by wagon. In 1857 the cost per ton-mile for freight via railroad was about one-tenth that amount.[10] Commercial rhythms were set by the largely agrarian economy and so the ebb and flow of goods followed the planting and harvest seasons. Farmers invested in seed and equipment in the spring but had to wait until the fall harvest to repay their suppliers. This annual pattern cascaded through the economy, from the farmers to the retail merchants, to wholesalers and then to suppliers and manufacturers. It also flowed through the financial and banking system as overall credit conditions tightened and loosened over the course of the year. Credit flowed out to the farmers in the spring, and repayments flowed back in the fall.

In his study of western Massachusetts in the late eighteenth and early nineteenth centuries, Clark (1990: 29–30) pointed out that the New England rural economy centered on domestic production. Small family farms consumed most of what they produced and functioned in a way that was largely independent of the market. Rural households undertook in-kind exchange locally, and swapped labor services, with their relatives and neighbors, but these informal exchanges and social favors rarely produced legal debts or formal obligations. Local trade was governed by a collective ethos of mutual support, reciprocity, and neighborliness, which made it unlikely that people would turn to formal-legal means to enforce their claims.[11] Shaped by communal norms, no strict "bottom line" logic applied. Put another way, households in colonial New England operated in two modes at the same time: monetary and non-monetary.[12]

In this early period, non-local trade worked differently. It possessed a stronger "for-profit" orientation, entailed monetary valuation of transactions, and involved fewer farmers and more merchants and traders. For one thing, there was no communitarian ethos or system of generalized reciprocity, and so people were more insistent on establishing and protecting their formal claims.[13] Trade credit still relied on open accounts and informal social networks, although formal debt instruments (like promissory notes or bills of exchange) were also used.[14] For open accounts, also known as "book debts," the debt was evidenced by an entry in the creditor's account book and possessed less formality than a promissory note.[15] Such debts were difficult if not impossible to transfer and so an obligation remained in the hands of the original creditor until it was finally extinguished. Such assets wouldn't circulate. Since it was difficult to learn much about potential trading partners at a distance, people usually worked through preexisting social and business networks. Business customers who sought credit often undertook annual or semi-annual buying trips to a major city (e.g., New York or New Orleans) to visit their suppliers in person. There, face-to-face, buyer and seller could size each other up as potential debtor and creditor, and negotiate. Orders were placed, goods shipped, and payment would be due after a conventional period like sixty days, ninety days, six months, and so forth. If the customer was a country store in a largely agricultural region of the country, suppliers might have to wait until after the fall harvest to get their payment as the store itself would not be paid in cash for its own sales to retail customers. Credit flowed (roughly) east to west and south in the spring, and repayment would surge back in the fall.[16]

Over time, the balance between local and distant trade shifted as trade with distant strangers grew and as monetized transactions replaced in-kind exchange. Formal credit relations within the New England rural economy "thickened" with this changing balance.[17] Other regions of the country were less dominated by independent subsistence farmers and more fully integrated into world markets, particularly those areas that produced commodities like sugar, cotton, or tobacco.[18] Production of cash crops thoroughly joined regional economies in the southern and central Atlantic regions to credit networks that extended overseas, usually to England.

Tobacco production in the Chesapeake Bay area, for example, linked large Maryland planters to Scottish merchants who provided the necessary credit and purchased the resulting tobacco products.[19] Merchants were willing to extend long-distance credit to tobacco farmers because they knew that it financed a valuable cash crop that could be readily sold. Credit multiplied as large planters were able, in turn, to lend to other local residents in the region. These long-distance links made planters vulnerable to credit conditions on the other side of the Atlantic, a situation over which they had no control. Thus, for example, as credit tightened in Britain in the early 1760s, planters were hard-pressed to pay their debts to overseas merchants and in turn had to squeeze their own debtors.[20] Across the Atlantic there was no community-based ethos to soften the constraints imposed by tight credit.[21] In the American South, sugar and cotton producers were similarly dependent on credit, and similarly linked to export markets. Cotton and sugar "factors" worked closely with producers, extending credit, purchasing their product, and helping market it.[22] Thus, the plantations that used slave-based production could finance their operations.

The ability of cotton and sugar production to attract so much credit was due, in large part, to the fact that these were high-demand cash crops that reliably generated the income needed to repay loans made in support of their cultivation. Lenders evaluated individual borrowers, to be sure, but they were also mindful of overall market conditions. Production of all these cash crops (sugar, tobacco, cotton) involved substantial amounts of credit that was typically extended through networks of ongoing personal and business relationships. Through these connections, creditors gathered information about the personal character and financial situation of borrowers and could make their credit decisions accordingly. However, heavy reliance on social networks raised a number of characteristic difficulties. One was that the obligations that accompany close personal or family ties are invariably mutual. When a debtor is also a cousin (or nephew, uncle, etc.), the kinship tie can certainly enhance the debtor's willingness to repay. But it may also strengthen the creditor's obligation to be "flexible" or "understanding" when the debtor is for some reason unable to repay. A social connection is not a one-sided resource. Use of networks also made creditors beholden to the peculiarities of family structure or friendship groupings. One cannot simply invent additional cousins and siblings, even if it may be convenient to do so. Other non-kin ties, like friendship, can be cultivated deliberately, but these take time and resources to develop. Social networks often leave large "blank areas" where no prior connections exist to be deployed.[23]

The shift away from independent subsistence farming into specialized production for markets, and the increase in urban populations, led in the latter part of the nineteenth century to a growing retail sector and a more elaborate distribution system for foodstuffs, household items, dry goods, and ready-to-wear clothing. This trade increasingly linked producers and manufacturers in the major cities of the East, like New York, Boston, and Philadelphia, with consumers and customers in cities and towns in the South and Midwest. Continued immigration and population growth increased the number of strangers with whom a supplier had no prior connection. Consumers in both rural and urban areas relied on country stores, general stores, dry goods shops, and eventually department stores to obtain the items they needed to maintain their households.[24] Continuing earlier trends, the number of employees working in retail grew from 196,000 in 1869 to 1,132,000 in 1899, only thirty years later.[25] Over this same period, the total value of manufactured food items increased from $673 million to $1.96 billion, the value of clothing produced went from $229 million to $743 million, and total durable goods production increased from $263 million to $634 million.[26] Since the U.S. population went from 38.9 million to 78.4 million at the same time (roughly doubling), and the percent of the population living in urban areas increased from 25.7 to 39.8 percent (it had already gone from 6.1 percent in 1800 to 15.4 percent in 1850), increases in commodity production partly reflected a shift toward purchasing consumption goods for the household instead of producing them within the household. The growth in market-based urban consumer demand created a complicated credit network linking retailers, wholesalers, suppliers, manufacturers, importers, jobbers, factors, warehouses, and distributors.[27]

Mercantile credit was usually unsecured, so creditors had no collateral to seize in the event of default.[28] Without collateral it was hard to remedy mistakes after the fact. Furthermore, the provision of credit was an important means for firms to attract and hold on to their customers, and so to simply withhold it in order to minimize losses was not a viable option. In the matter of trade credit, it was hard to reduce one's vulnerability to zero: credit and sales were too closely linked. As one newspaper article put it: "A man cannot know everybody, and yet, in most cases, he has got to be ready to deal with everybody if he would not fall hopelessly behind in the commercial race."[29] With the geographical expansion and intensification of interregional trade, merchants and suppliers found that reliance on their own direct business ties and social networks as a way to manage trust problems became increasingly inadequate. There were simply too many customers that the seller had never heard of before or who were outside the seller's social networks. And as more trade crossed state lines, it became harder to enforce debts in court.[30] So the twin problems of uncertainty and vulnerability grew worse.

Credit Reporting

One new and uniquely American source of information appeared in the wake of the financial crisis of 1837: credit reporting.[31] Instead of continuing to rely on their own informal sources of information about the creditworthiness of others, merchants could now turn to a third party, a "mercantile agency," whose business it was to provide independent and encompassing assessments of the creditworthiness of other firms.

The Mercantile Agency (later known as R. G. Dun) was founded in 1841 by Lewis Tappan, a prominent textile merchant and ardent abolitionist who had failed in the panic of 1837. According to Rowena Olegario (2006: 40), the idea of a credit agency was already "in the air," but it was Tappan who brought this idea firmly into reality.[32] Organizationally, Tappan established a central office (in New York City, close to his clients) and attached to this a network of independent confidential correspondents, distributed across the country, who provided information about the firms in their local vicinity.[33] William Armstrong gave a thumbnail summary: "Lewis Tappan . . . applied himself to the establishment of a commercial agency, the object of which is, to ascertain, by means of agents throughout the country, the character and standing of the merchants in the different towns, so that when the New York dealers receive applications for goods from traders at a distance, they have only to refer to Mr. Tappan to ascertain their degree of trustworthiness."[34] Using the well-functioning national postal system, correspondents mailed information about firms to the head office.[35] This information was transcribed and edited, and then turned into credit reports that could be sold to anyone with an interest in a particular firm. At first, clients had to visit the Agency's office in person in order to obtain information about a potential customer, receiving it via a verbal report. Since both Tappan and his customers were based in New York City, a personal visit was no obstacle. As of August 1841, Tappan had acquired 133 subscribers to his new service, mostly in the dry goods business.[36]

Although many organizations could be interested in someone's ability to pay their debts (e.g., banks, insurance companies, employers, etc.), rating agencies served the mercantile community first and concentrated on trade credit. In an early advertisement, Tappan attracted customers by giving them the chance to assess for free the information his firm would provide: "Any merchant, who wishes to test the value of the information can do so gratuitously. No better way has been thought of than for such to bring a list of the bad debts they have made since the establishment of the Agency in

1841, and ascertain how the debtors stood on the books of the Agency when the goods were sold to them."[37] Merchants would see that their bad debts were foreshadowed by the information the Agency would have provided to them, had they the wisdom to subscribe to the service. Later that year, Tappan again appealed to potential customers: "For the information of those who are not acquainted with the object of the Mercantile Agency, it may be stated that it is to procure accurate information, in a legitimate way, about standing, responsibility, &c. of country merchants, and keep it constantly revised for the benefit of the Merchants in this city who subscribe to the Agency."[38] Agency information would be as timely as it was accurate.

The *Merchants' Magazine and Commercial Review* of January 1851 (p. 46) stated that the overall purpose of the new credit rating system was to "uphold, extend, and render safe and profitable to all concerned, the great credit system, on which our country had thrived." More specifically, however:

> It was mainly intended as an aid to the Jobber. His customers, scattered over many States, were periodically visiting him for the purpose of renewing their stock of goods; generally cancelling, in whole, or in part, previous obligations, while they contracted new ones. The intelligent jobber would necessarily need to be informed, on the opening of a new account, respecting the then circumstances of his customer. From year to year, he would desire to be freshly advised of the good or ill success attending him. Information of this character can, in general, be satisfactorily obtained only at the home of the trader. Hence, the main object with the agency is, to furnish THE HOME STANDING of a merchant obtained from intelligent and reliable sources, THERE [original emphasis].

Later on, as we will see, credit ratings were used to serve a broader set of constituents, including banks and insurance companies, and the rating format spread to other kinds of debts and debtors.

The identity of sources was kept confidential. Indeed, the Agency went to some length to keep them secret, believing that secrecy was important for the accuracy of the information they provided. For example, correspondents' letters were destroyed after being transcribed into the Agency's ledgers.[39] But the Agency had to rely on people who were knowledgeable about local businesses and business dealings, and this meant mostly using local attorneys (it also used postmasters, sheriffs, bank cashiers, and merchants).[40] According to the *Bankers' Magazine and Statistical Register* of January 1858 (p. 546), correspondents were selected "for their integrity, long residence in the county, general acquaintance, business experience and judgment. Their duties are to advise the Agency promptly, by letter or telegraph, of every change affecting the standing or responsibility of traders; to notify it of suits, protests, mortgages, losses by fire, endorsements, or otherwise; to answer all special inquiries addressed to them by any of the associate offices; and to revise before each trade season, or oftener if required, the previous reports of every trader in the county, noting any change for the better or worse."

Building up the network of correspondents was key to enlarging the scope of the firm and enhancing the value of the information it provided to subscribers. In 1846, the Agency had 679 correspondents around the country, and by 1851 there were some 2,000 (correspondents were less numerous in Southern states because of Tappan's strong and public support for abolition).[41] Correspondents were not directly employed by the Agency, but it struck an informal deal with them: in exchange for information, the Agency would steer collection work to correspondents. Since the Agency's clients were often out-of-state creditors, and since non-payments, defaults, and insolvencies were common, clients often turned to the Agency for suggestions about local attorneys to use for debt collection.[42] But this quid pro quo arrangement was not entirely satisfactory, for it gave the Agency little control over what information it received and when, and correspondents weren't exclusive in providing information. Eventually, agencies employed their own reporters who would operate from a growing network of branch offices.[43] The ability of these networks to gather information on a national scale was such that later in the nineteenth century the life insurance companies also sought out credit reporters as a source to obtain individual data about health risks.[44]

Credit rating was an idea whose time had clearly come, and soon the Agency attracted competitors like Bradstreet's (established in 1849). The absence of nationally branched banks undoubtedly played a role in creating an opening for the mercantile agencies: had they existed, such banks could have used their own internal systems to acquire and circulate information about creditworthiness. As it was, many states only allowed unit banks or severely restricted the number of branches.[45] Competition prompted innovation and emulation, and credit raters rivaled each other in breadth of coverage and the type of information provided. Bradstreet's began to issue reference books, that is, compilations of summary assessments of the creditworthiness of thousands of firms published in book format, and its success with this format encouraged the Mercantile Agency to follow suit in 1859. No longer would subscribers have to go in person to the head office in New

York City to learn about the creditworthiness of potential customers: they simply consulted the reference books they received in the mail. These books were published with increasing frequency until 1873 when the Agency was issuing its books four times a year. Reference books would focus on a city or region, listed firms alphabetically (by the last name of the proprietor), giving their street address and line of business (dry goods, stationary, printer, tailor, saloon, etc.), and then evaluated the firm's creditworthiness by classifying it into a set of ordered categories along one or two dimensions.[46] A key that explained the meaning of the rating categories accompanied the reference book, as part of the introductory material. The category systems changed over time and varied from agency to agency. In 1860, Bradstreet's used a single dimension that ranked firms from "AA" at the top to "E" at the bottom.[47] Rating systems later became two-dimensional and in 1880, for example, the Mercantile Agency measured pecuniary strength (a measure of net worth) using an ordinal scale that estimated the capital in the firm, ranging from A+ ($1,000,000 or more) down to K (less than $2,000). General credit was also measured with ordered categories, from A1 ("unlimited"), through 1, 1½ ("high"), 2 and 2½ ("good"), down to 3 and 3½ ("fair").[48] Sometimes, firms were listed but given no rating (either for pecuniary strength or general credit, or both). In this case, the accompanying key stated: "The absence of a Rating indicates those whose business and investments render it difficult to rate satisfactorily to ourselves. We therefore prefer, in justice to these, to give the detailed reports on record at our Offices." In other words, no rating was given when the Agency possessed information that it could not, or would not, translate into its own rating categories.[49]

Thanks to the mercantile agencies, a subscriber could easily consult a reference book to get quick information about the creditworthiness of a particular firm. Highly rated firms were obviously better risks for trade credit than low-rated firms, and the informational value of the subscription increased as coverage widened and became more timely. Armed with credit ratings, a firm could try to avoid making the big mistake of lending to a debtor who subsequently defaulted: "Our mercantile agencies, however, at this point, have, in hundreds of instances, made revelations to our merchants in time to save them from many a heavy blow."[50] Systematic information made it easy to make comparisons, to decide which firms were similar, and which were different, and whose promises could be trusted.

Although ratings were intended to add transparency to credit relations, the process of evaluating a particular firm and classifying it into the Agency's category system was itself opaque. The Agency gathered large amounts of information about firms from multiple sources possessing varying degrees of credibility. Some of what it learned verged on gossip and hearsay, much of it was conflicting or ambiguous, and most of it was qualitative. Across different firms, input information was unsystematic and arrived at the headquarters at uneven intervals: sometimes the Agency knew a lot (as measured by the size of the entry in the ledgers and how often information was updated) and sometimes it knew only a little. It might seek information directly from a firm (by having personnel try to obtain a statement from the firm's proprietor), but it also frequently used indirect sources (industry "insiders," local notables, Agency subscribers, the local business community, etc.). And for a long time, whatever financial information an agency could obtain was undisciplined by credible accounting standards or rules.[51] No regulations required firms to construct a balance sheet, disclose financial records, or even calculate income in a systematic fashion.[52]

There are indications of what rating agencies wanted from their correspondents and reporters, but for a long time the agencies were not very specific about what informational "inputs" were to be used in the rating process. One letter of instruction sent out to Bradstreet's correspondents in 1869 states:

> If there are any dealers who have recently come into your midst of whom little is known, please state where they were previously located (after giving us such information as you can), that we may obtain the full particulars from that place. 1) Give length of time in business. 2) Amount of own capital in business. 3) Amount of net worth, after deducting all liabilities of every nature. 4) Of what is estimated wealth composed? (Viz.: Real estate less incumbrances, capital in business, personal property, which includes bonds and mortgages, stocks, notes, etc., etc.) 5) Character? Good, fair, poor. 6) Habits? Good, medium, poor. 7) Business Qualifications? Very good, good, medium, poor. 8) Prospects of success? Good, fair, medium, poor. 9) Succeeded whom? If any person or firm, state whom. 10) Give individual names of partners, with age.[53]

Mercantile Agency ledger entries reveal an ongoing interest in rough "balance sheets" for firms, a listing of assets and liabilities together with an estimate of their value. But in the absence of generally accepted accounting rules, or professional accountants, such estimates were crude and unsystematic. Overall, the creation of ratings in the nineteenth century did not involve a systematic process through which specified pieces of information were gathered and combined, and then transformed into standardized ratings in an algorithmic fashion.[54] The process was both irregular and opaque.

Information received from correspondents and reporters was transferred into the proprietary ledgers. Ledger entries were frequently narrational in recording small stories about what had reportedly happened to a firm. For example, a man called J. W. Finerty was in the furniture business in Illinois, and the Mercantile Agency ledger entry from December 20, 1855, noted that Finerty "has been doing bus[iness] for one Mitchell who failed in NY City & sent his goods here. F[inerty] has helped him to smuggle his effects— from Easter crs. [creditors]—F[inerty] was a journeyman cabinet maker, without a $ in the world. They are now beginning to quarrel, the result will be a scramble & failure (unless I am mistaken)."[55] A year and a half later, Finerty had formed a partnership with a Mr. Liebenstein, as upholsterers and cabinet makers: "Have done little bus[iness] this past winter & spring & yet have retained their position pretty well. L a saving Hebrew. F a rough and ready Irishman who wd be v. likely to blunder if left to himself but with his partner they get along admirably & doubtless mkg a little. Means lim[ited] by shd thk them safe."[56] The ethnic stereotyping revealed in these passages was common. And although there were few businesses owned or operated by African Americans, when they were registered in Agency ledgers, the racial identity of the proprietor was carefully noted.[57]

Regardless of the unevenness and inconsistency of the raw evidence, all rated firms listed in the reference books were placed into the same classification scheme of ordered categories. The coding process through which qualitative information was combined, summarized, and put into the schema was itself unclear: there were no explicit instructions to guide Agency personnel about how to process or encode the information they acquired. In fact, it wasn't until 1894 that the Agency produced its first manual of instructions for branch managers.[58] Despite this general opacity, several features of the process are apparent. First, the complexity and multidimensionality of information was greatly reduced. Credit raters received many different kinds of information about firms, but their published ratings provided highly simplified "bottom-line" summaries. So the process necessarily involved a substantial reduction of information. Second, ambiguities, inconsistencies, and contradictions disappeared. In the ledgers, some facts indicated greater creditworthiness while others signaled less. Some information was explicitly disbelieved by the rating agency personnel (or at least the records document their skepticism). But the published rating placed a firm into a single unambiguous category of creditworthiness and invited comparison with other classified firms.[59] Ratings appeared much tidier than the messy information that supported them. Third, credit raters knew that creditworthiness depended on social relationships, and the ledgers frequently distinguished between "strangers" and the "friends" of a debtor firm. If a firm got into financial difficulty or became insolvent, friends could expect to be repaid before strangers, and hence their claims were in effect stronger. So the same firm might be creditworthy in relation to "friends" but not in relation to "strangers." However, the published ratings made no such distinction and treated creditworthiness as if it were a feature of the debtor and not dependent on the strength of the creditor's relationship to the debtor. Finally, ledger entries always recounted the provenance of information and whether it came from reliable sources, including from the rated firm itself. In the latter case, ledger entries often reflected an understanding by the agency that soliciting information directly from a firm could set off a reactive process in which firms deliberately tried to look good. Ledger entries took note of what proprietors said about their own firm, and then judged whether the claims were believable or not and whether proprietors embellished their situation. As ratings gained in importance, as more and more subscribers used them to make credit decisions, the incentive for rated firms to make themselves "look good" in the eyes of the agency increased. But the ratings published in the reference books made no mention of the variable reliability of sources, nor of reactivity. These messy complications were kept in the background and out of sight.

As a client of the Agency, a wholesaler in New York City could consult the rating books to get a summary assessment of a prospective or current customer and then decide to ship the goods, or not, depending on the rating. Clients could also solicit credit reports, which gave a fuller account of a rated firm. In order to control access to the information contained in the reference books, the Agency required its subscribers to return their old books before they could receive their new copies, a process that eventually happened four times a year. Needless to say, this made it hard for clients to accumulate information on creditworthiness over time or to assess systematically the accuracy of the ratings. In general, mercantile agencies were deeply concerned about the possibility of plagiarism and devised various ways to protect their intellectual property, including recourse to lawsuits.[60] For example, in its 1875 reference book Bradstreet's agency made clear to its subscribers that its books were merely loaned, not sold, to them, that subscribers were not to share the information with anyone else, and that subscribers could not obtain information from the agency on behalf of anyone else.

The process of collecting and combining information about rated firms may have been obscure, but many commentators believed that mercantile agencies were forced to seek the truth. They were in the business of selling information, after all, and if their "product" was flawed, then buyers would cease to pay for it. The complexities were well recognized: "Their true and only interest is, to get as near as possible to the truth in every report. The least deviation on either side from this standard, may have, nay must have an unfavorable influence upon their own prosperity. If they report a man too favorably, and the subscriber, thus induced to trust him, loses his debt, they are blamed. If they report him too unfavorable, and the subscriber thereby loses a good paying customer, they are equally blamed. In fact, the entire success of the system depends upon the general truthfulness and justice of their records—upon having every report they give out verified by the results to which it leads."[61]

The growth of the credit rating industry unfolded in several ways. Most obviously, the number of firms being rated grew enormously. The Mercantile Agency's reference books of 1859 listed about 20,000 firms. By 1868 the reference books covered some 400,000 firms,[62] and at the end of the nineteenth century the Agency was rating over one million firms on a truly panoptic scale.[63] To accomplish this vast increase in the volume of information, the Agency grew in size, opening branch offices around the United States (Boston in 1843, Philadelphia in 1845, and so on) and even in foreign countries like Canada and the United Kingdom (offices in London and Montreal opened in 1857). By 1916, it had branch offices in places like Bilbao (Spain), Moose Jaw (Canada), Perth (Australia), Cape Town (South Africa), and Buenos Aires (see Dun 1916). It also shifted from reliance on independent correspondents to reporters who worked directly for the Agency, out of one of the branch offices. There is little information on exactly how many clients subscribed to the credit rating service, but Olegario (2006: 161) states that the Agency had about 20,000 clients in the mid-1870s and that this number doubled over the next decade. Given how much their clients wished to avoid lending to firms that failed, the agencies became deeply interested in failure. The rating agencies tracked overall commercial failures (even when there was no federal bankruptcy law), and their figures were reported in publications like *Dun's Review* and frequently reproduced in other newspapers, nationally and internationally.[64] Given the successful growth of the credit rating industry, it seems clear that there was robust demand for the ratings and other information that it produced and sold.

In addition to correspondents and reporters, credit raters increasingly depended on the firms themselves to provide information about their own financial circumstances. These were termed "statements," and credit agencies often solicited them, although they didn't always receive or believe them. The unwillingness of a firm to provide a statement was itself deemed significant,[65] but not every statement was trustworthy. As an exercise in measurement, the solicitation of a statement was a reflexive process: those who were being measured knew they were being measured, and knew that the measurement was consequential (a good rating was helpful, a poor rating was not). So the process of measurement itself affected that which it measured (hence, reflexivity). We shouldn't be surprised if firms were tempted to offer flattering statements that made themselves "look good," nor that rating agencies sometimes took such statements with many grains of salt and were well aware of these complications.[66] Reflexivity aside, there was no accounting profession, independent auditors, or even accounting principles to standardize the financial information contained in such statements.

Rating along two dimensions became the industry norm in the postbellum period, and of these two "pecuniary strength" (termed "net worth" today) seemed the easiest to measure.[67] But even the best estimates of pecuniary strength involved a significant degree of uncertainty. For example, in assessing the worth of Mandel Brothers in 1876 (a Chicago dry goods firm), the Mercantile Agency contacted the firm's banker and recorded in the ledger that he was "an extra cautious man of ripe experience and one who possesses our confidence thinks it will be safe to believe them worth over 125m$ [i.e., $125,000]."[68] In this instance, the Agency's assessment of pecuniary strength was based on someone's opinion, albeit that of an educated and cautious individual. The second dimension, "general credit," lacked even the specificity of pecuniary strength and was measured using a cruder set of categories. So despite the scale of information gathering, and notwithstanding the claims made by the rating agencies, much uncertainty remained. Consider the case of Donald Gordon, a dry goods dealer in Rochester, New York, whose failure in December 1883 came as a great surprise to his creditors in New York City. Although he was well-known to the mercantile agencies, he did not make a statement to them and so his actual creditworthiness remained a matter for conjecture.[69]

As credit ratings increased in importance, they became more problematic for those who were rated, and more contestable. A good rating helped firms get better access to credit, whereas a low rating made life difficult. Firms receiving low ratings had little recourse and sometimes threatened legal action. In fact, credit rating agencies were justifiably concerned about the possibility of litigation from several directions. To put it simply, credit raters could make two kinds of mistakes: they could give a good rating to a firm that wasn't creditworthy, or they could give a poor rating to a firm that was in fact creditworthy. In the first instance, a client who extended credit to an untrustworthy debtor on the basis of the high rating, only to have the debtor default, could well blame the misleadingly high credit rating and seek satisfaction in court. This kind of mistake could produce highly visible consequences that prompted legal action. In one example, the firm of Crew, Levick & Co. sued Bradstreet's to recover damages from allegedly false information. Crew, Levick had obtained a credit report from Bradstreet's about another firm, and on the basis of that report extended credit, which they were subsequently unable to recover.[70] Unfortunately for the plaintiff, the judge ruled in favor of Bradstreet's.[71]

In the second type of mistake, firms that received erroneously low ratings knew they would have difficulty obtaining credit and could suffer from the credit agency's critical judgment. They too might seek legal redress on the grounds that their business problems were actually caused by the agency's mistakenly low rating. For instance, in Louisville, Kentucky, Augustus Bieher sued R. G. Dun for damage to his credit and reputation on the grounds that Dun falsely reported to its clients that he had defaulted on a prior debt.[72] In St. Louis, Mr. Mellier took Bradstreet's to court, arguing that its erroneously low rating of his firm had injured his standing and damaged his credit.[73] There were many lawsuits in state courts, but the case of *Beardsley v. Tappan* went all the way to the U.S. Supreme Court before the court ruled in favor of Tappan.[74] Firms that declined to extend credit to a truly creditworthy customer, because of the low rating, suffered from a lost opportunity, but such mistakes had lower salience and seldom prompted legal action.

These legal questions remained unsettled for many decades.[75] Determining the extent of liability for mistakes forced the courts to consider new legal questions, and every state had its own rules and precedents for issues like slander and libel. Furthermore, it wasn't entirely clear what constituted a "mistake," in the case of credit rating. These legal uncertainties put credit raters on the horns of a dilemma.[76] On the one hand, they wanted to assure clients of the value of the information they were selling. Thus, credit raters repeatedly explained how useful ratings could be for managing credit.[77] Dun publicly invited potential subscribers "to do an inspection of our facilities, and an examination of the fullness and completeness of our system for the protection of all who have occasion to grant a credit."[78] And not only did both major rating agencies regularly compile and publish aggregate failure statistics (which were reproduced widely),[79] but in some of its published tabulations Bradstreet's classified business failures so that its readers could see that very few failed firms had been given the highest rating and that most of the failed firms had been given only a "moderate" or "fair" rating, or even no rating at all.[80] Since highly rated firms seldom failed, subscribers could follow the ratings to avoid lending to firms likely to fail. Indeed, Bradstreet's was publicly congratulated for providing such prescient information.[81] Business failure of a debtor was an outcome of deep interest to agency subscribers, and so the agencies were careful to track such events.[82] On the other hand, the agencies could not be too explicit about what ratings would do, or assert that ratings were completely reliable, for this would expose them to the accusation that they made false and self-serving statements. Audiences were invited to draw out the implied relationship between ratings and failure mentioned above, but the agencies did not explicitly do so themselves. Credit agencies walked this fine line by being emphatic but vague about the value of credit ratings.

Agencies went to some lengths to keep a suitable legal distance from the information they provided. Dun employees were instructed to mind the language they used when writing reports for clients: "When reports are cautionary, it is unsafe to say 'We advise caution,' or 'We believe they are in trouble;' the words 'Caution is deemed expedient,' or 'Trouble is reported,' should be used. Let it be borne in mind that it is never the opinion of the Agency, which is being given, the word 'We' must therefore never be used in any report" (Dun 1918: 26). In addition to adopting the passive voice when they wrote, employees were also instructed that they were not in the business of giving advice for which they or Dun could be held accountable: "The business of the Agency is to give the facts, figures and opinions obtained by its reporters. It is not within its province to give advice to anybody. The words 'advise' or 'recommend' are objectionable. In giving unfavorable credit comments, it is proper to say 'the trade,' or 'those consulted, do not consider the account desirable.' It is improper to say 'Credit is not advised' or 'recommended,' or in any way to convey the slightest inference that the language used comes direct from the Agency instead of from those consulted" (Dun 1918: 9). And, of course, agencies added protective language to the standard contracts they signed with their clients.

Despite taking such measures, agencies worried about lawsuits. One typical example concerned a suit filed against Dun & Co. by the Bank of Birmingham, Alabama, which on the basis of a favorable Dun report had given credit to one W. A. Kitts of Oswego, New York, and suffered losses.[83] An unhappy Dun client had relied on Dun's ratings and come to grief. Another example concerned S. F. Gilman of Omaha, who used a Dun rating to extend trade credit to a Kansas firm that subsequently defaulted. Gilman sought damages from Dun because the "excellent" rating it gave to the Kansas firm proved to be so misleading.[84] And rated firms sued as well. Another typical example involved James L. Oswald from Allendale, South Carolina, who sued Bradstreet's because, he claimed, it had issued a mistakenly negative report about him and consequently damaged his prospects: no one would give him trade credit.[85] Similarly, Mrs. Fannie Behrens of Chicago sued Dun in the amount of $10,000 for issuing a false report about her and hurting her credit.[86] The agencies forum-shopped as a way to minimize their legal risks, believing that they fared somewhat better in federal than in state courts, and better in northeastern states than in the South or West.[87] When necessary, they also tried to settle out of court and avoid setting unfavorable precedents. And in addition to facing lawsuits from clients and firms they rated, rival mercantile agencies sued each other for violation of copyright protection, arguing that their intellectual property had been pirated by the competition.

As the nineteenth century progressed, and despite worrisome litigation, credit ratings became more widespread and were increasingly regarded as legitimate encapsulations of a debtor's true creditworthiness. By 1860, mainstream business opinion generally held that the ratings were truly useful. For example, one article states: "The usefulness of the Agency is unquestionable. Without it, the credit system, in a country like ours, with vast distances between seller and buyer, would make mercantile pursuits the most uncertain of all. Its principal advantages are as follows: It points out to the city merchant solvent, prudent, and thriving customers; cautions him against the doubtful; and apprises him promptly of changes which make it proper to press the collection of his claims. . . . It makes the solvent and punctual trader known in every city, giving him credit."[88] By the late 1880s, opinion far from the mercantile heart of New York City posited: "The mercantile agency system is an indispensable adjunct to business. All modern business is so largely done on credit that a proper rating by an impartial person is eminently to be desired, not only by the seller, but by the honorable purchaser."[89] And by the beginning of the twentieth century, a credit expert declared that "it [the credit agency] is the most indispensable, the oftenest used and the most versatile tool with which the credit man is equipped."[90] Credit rating had become part of the fabric of American commercial life.

The development and evident usefulness of credit rating brought it to new audiences.[91] As we will see in the next chapter, banks began to use credit ratings as a kind of "early indicator" of the creditworthiness of bank loan applicants. In an article offering advice to bankers, Oscar Newfang recommended that "in the first place, he [the banker] learns all that he can about the business record of the borrower, in order to see whether he has always been honorable in his dealings in the past. For this purpose the reports of the two leading mercantile agencies [i.e., Bradstreet's and R. G. Dun] are invaluable."[92] At the end of the nineteenth century, as U.S. banks became more systematic in making loans, and as they organized separate credit departments, they incorporated credit ratings into the information they gathered about customers and borrowers.[93] Credit insurance companies, which like banks are centrally concerned with the management of risk, also began to use the credit ratings created by mercantile agencies in their risk assessments.[94] Additionally, credit rating as a method was emulated and applied to corporations and long-term debt, particularly the use of ordered categories (with alphanumerical labels) to represent creditworthiness. Railway bond raters (like John Moody) essentially adopted the method developed by the mercantile agencies and eventually applied it to all manner of corporate securities and bonds issued by a variety of borrowers. From its very local origins in facilitating trade credit issued by New York City suppliers, credit rating spread widely as a way to deal with the uncertainties of credit.[95]

Ratings for general mercantile credit operated for many decades as a duopoly of R. G. Dun and Bradstreet's, until the two firms merged in 1933 to form Dun and Bradstreet, a firm that continues today to provide credit information about small businesses. Other smaller rating agencies had a specific geographical focus (e.g., providing ratings for the city of Cleveland), while some specialized in a particular industry (e.g., furniture manufacturers). For broad spectrum ratings across industries and around the United States and abroad, however, people had to look to Dun or Bradstreet's. The extension of trade credit among businesses during the 1950s continued to depend heavily on the ratings generated by Dun and Bradstreet.[96] And, according to Seiden (1964: 71–73), the validity of Dun and Bradstreet's ratings was demonstrated first by their use by credit insurers (like the American Credit-Indemnity Company) to price their risks and by the loan loss experience of the Reconstruction Finance Corporation (one of many New Deal institutions).

For all their limitations, credit ratings offered summary information about creditworthiness that enabled merchants to transact with a much wider circle of customers than had hitherto seemed possible. Merchants could trade far beyond their social networks, and at much greater distances. And eventually, they were able to trade overseas with the information that Dun provided through its global network of branch offices. But if this was such an advantageous innovation, why did it not appear in the other parts of the world that had long faced similar problems of credit and creditworthiness? Various commentators sought to explain why credit rating developed in the United States and not elsewhere. Bryan, for example, thought it was a combination of geography and ancestry: trade in Europe occurred over shorter distances and between family firms that had been dealing with each other for multiple generations, so it was easier to obtain credible information via social networks.[97] European firms had their own credit problems to manage, and sought information to help resolve them, but traditionally they didn't get it from something like a mercantile agency. In France, for example, notaries possessed a great deal of credit-relevant information but notarial offices didn't expand onto the same scale as the rating agencies.[98]

Promissory Notes and Commercial Paper

If credit ratings helped creditors deal with uncertainty, the growing use of commercial paper for the short-term financing of large firms helped address the problem of vulnerability. Early on, informal book debt was commonly used to document trade credit, but it suffered the deficiency of being hard to transfer. That is, the obligation was recorded in the ledgers of the creditor and remained on the creditor's balance sheet until it was satisfied. Only when the debt generated a stream of cash repayments could the creditor use this asset to satisfy his or her own debts. And the pattern of cash flow depended on the maturity of the debt. The debt itself simply couldn't be transferred to anyone else: it was an illiquid asset. But if the debtor/customer gave the creditor/seller an unsecured promissory note (e.g., $1,000 due in 60 days), and if the legal system was one that recognized negotiability, then creditors could endorse the note and pass it on to someone else, in satisfaction of their own obligations. The new holder of the note would have as strong a claim over the debtor as the original creditor possessed. Unlike book debt, transferable debt gave the original creditor an early exit option, a way to recover the loan well in advance of its full maturity. And if the note passed through several sets of hands, then a debtor could end up repaying money to a complete stranger in another part of the country.[99] Of course, this would only work if the person to whom the endorsed paper was transferred thought the original debtor sufficiently creditworthy. In other words, for the debt to arise in the first place, the creditor had to trust the debtor. But for the debt to be transferred, someone else had to deem the debtor sufficiently trustworthy (and would price the debt accordingly). For a market in commercial paper to function in a significant way, many others (not just one or two) had to share judgments on the creditworthiness of the issuer and find a way to enact those judgments.

The growing use of written debt instruments in place of book debt produced more mobility and liquidity for trade credit. It gave creditors the opportunity to use the debts owed them as a kind of quasi-money that they could, in turn, use to satisfy their own obligations. If lending to someone meant that the creditor had a potential trust problem, here was a chance to shift that problem onto someone else, for a price. Commercial paper widened the community of evaluation so that the acceptability of a debtor's paper depended not only on what the initial creditor thought but also on what the creditor's creditors thought, or anyone else who might accept paper instruments. Whatever the direct creditor thought, for commercial paper to possess liquidity it mattered how the creditor's creditors regarded the debtor's creditworthiness. But commercial paper could never fully function like money because it lacked money's anonymity, uniformity, and legal tender status: a single dollar's worth of legal tender is exactly the same as any other dollar and can always be used to satisfy an obligation, whereas commercial paper depended on the issuer and wasn't legal tender. But the overall shift from book debt to paper debt was significant, as Bruce Mann observes: "The assignability of notes and bonds severed the connection between debts and their underlying social relations, thereby making possible a transformation in the relations between debtors and creditors."[100]

The basic mechanics of commercial paper were fairly straightforward. Instead of receiving sixty days' worth of book credit from a supplier, the customer/debtor paid for goods with a short-term unsecured promissory note. As a negotiable security, a promissory note could pass from firm to firm, and the second (or third) holder would have as strong a claim as did the original creditor. In the case of one-name paper, only the original issuer was responsible for repaying the debt when it became due. In the case of two-name paper, both the issuer and the cosigner were responsible (with the cosigner acting as guarantor in case the issuer failed to pay). Would-be receivers of this paper had to ask themselves how creditworthy they deemed the issuer, in the case of single-name paper, or the issuer and cosigner, in the case of two-name paper. And clearly, one big difference between one and two-name paper was that ceteris paribus the latter was regarded as a safer investment (since two people or firms were responsible for repayment, not just one).

"Negotiability" is an important legal feature that helps impart mobility to financial promises: it allows creditors to pass the promises they have received from debtors on to someone else. But negotiability was nevertheless not fully recognized in the common law tradition before the seventeenth century.[101] Under common law, a debt was a *chose in action*, and as such reflected a personal relationship between individuals: only the original creditor could enforce a debt in court, and thus the obligation the debtor had to the creditor could not be transferred to someone else. On the matter of assignability, the law distinguished between bills of exchange and promissory notes in a manner that was problematic. But these complications were lifted at the end of the seventeenth century, and negotiability received statutory recognition with passage of the Promissory Notes Act of 1704 by Parliament.[102] Despite this positive development, and the fact that the United States inherited Britain's common law tradition, within the United States there remained considerable legal variation on the matter of negotiable paper before the promulgation of a model Negotiable Instruments Law. As Beutel argues (1940), negotiability in general was transplanted from England to the American colonies, but significant differences existed between the states.[103] For example, Oregon and Nevada did not require that a promissory note always be in writing, and the exact liability of the drawer of a note also varied.[104] So long as the state laws governing negotiability were not standardized, the circulation of commercial paper across states lines would obviously be complicated by legal pluralism. Indeed, one of the first acts of the National Conference of Commissioners on Uniform State Laws (NCCUSL), a body created by the American Bar Association at the end of the nineteenth century to standardize state law, was to propose in 1896 a Uniform Negotiable Instruments Act and to urge its passage by state legislatures.[105] However, these complications constrained but did not extinguish the circulation of financial promises like commercial paper.

At the end of the nineteenth century, specialized bill brokers acted as market makers for the commercial paper market. That is, they bought and sold commercial paper as their chief activity, and so gave liquidity to the market. Chicago offers one example: thanks to the growth of commodities markets in grain, timber, pork, and beef, Chicago commodity suppliers often received a massive infusion of promissory notes from their eastern customers. Dry goods wholesalers also received commercial paper during the fall and winter selling seasons. By the 1880s, specialist firms had been established in the city, dealing in commercial paper.[106] This commercial paper was largely unsecured and single-name, but thanks to the brokers it became highly liquid and so could be bought or sold at a moment's notice. The market price given to commercial paper served as a public signal for collective beliefs about the creditworthiness of a particular issuer. Furthermore, with a developed market it became possible for reputable firms to issue commercial paper directly to the market rather than specifically as payment to suppliers: in effect they could borrow from the market. Their ability to do this depended, of course, on their own financial condition but also on their relationship to the commercial paper houses.[107] Personal ties between firm executives and the head of a commercial paper brokerage made it easier for firms to borrow this way. Later on, as large corporations began to issue commercial paper to meet their short-term financing needs, debtors could place their paper directly, without using a broker or other intermediary. For example, the General Motors Acceptance Corporation (GMAC, the financing arm of General Motors) initiated direct placement in 1920,[108] and other large firms followed suit. The biggest firms could rely on their reputation to attract buyers of their paper, but eventually the rating agencies provided ratings akin to the ones they issued for bonds. Moody's, for example, began to rate corporate commercial paper in the early 1970s, following the crisis in the commercial paper market caused by the failure of Penn Central Railroad.[109]

Banks were frequent investors in commercial paper, buying it from bill brokerages. Banks were reluctant to invest in long-term commercial loans, but they would purchase the short-term commercial paper that business transactions generated and so in effect provide working capital to firms.[110] Such paper, known then as "real bills," occupied a special place in nineteenth- and early twentieth-century banking theory. In a nutshell: "The traditional real bills doctrine held that the monetary liabilities of the banking system should ideally be backed by holdings of short-term, self-liquidating commercial bills."[111] This doctrine was both normative and descriptive, articulating what banks should and did do (more or less).[112] It meant that banks were supposed to take the money they received from depositors (a liability) and invest it in commercial paper (an asset). Demand deposits could be withdrawn at short notice, and in order for the maturity of assets to match those of liabilities, the money had to be put into short-term loans. Since commercial paper was typically paid off in sixty or ninety days, the bank could be sure that its money wasn't locked up for too long, and there was no obligation to renew the loan. If there was an immediate need for liquidity, the bank could try to sell off its "real bills." Furthermore, acquiring commercial paper gave banks a chance to diversify their investments across a variety of industries and companies.[113] Finally, according to the real bills doctrine, investment in real bills imparted an "elastic" quality to the domestic money supply (which expanded and contracted with the agricultural cycle of planting and harvesting).

The real bills doctrine guided private banks, but it also figured centrally in the design of the policy instruments of the Federal Reserve System.[114] The key one at first was the "discount window," the primary means for the Federal Reserve System to inject liquidity into financial markets by discounting the "real bills" held by member banks. Emergency liquidity was widely perceived as the solution to recurrent financial crises (occurring in, e.g., 1884, 1893, and 1907) that had afflicted the U.S. economy, and the discount window would give banks the means to acquire liquidity from the new central bank. As the lender of last resort, the Fed could accept promises that others would no longer take. By setting standards for what kind of commercial paper was eligible for discount at the window, the Federal Reserve Banks privileged some kinds of paper and indirectly regulated the commercial paper market. In particular, Federal Reserve standards put pressure on member banks to obtain financial statements from the private companies that issued commercial paper to ensure their eligibility for discount.[115] This increased the amount of information available about commercial paper issuers. Eligibility standards also reinforced the use of credit ratings. An early New York Federal Reserve Bank circular addressed the topic of eligible paper, outlining what member bank assets could be brought to the Fed discount window for rediscounting, and revealed that mercantile agency credit ratings factored into the determination of eligibility.[116]

Another arrangement developed that was functionally similar to the use of commercial paper. This involved the sale or assignment by a firm of its accounts receivable (money owed to it) to a discount house, finance company, or commercial acceptance trust.[117] The motivation for the firm to do this was similar to that for accepting negotiable promissory notes from a debtor: the firm could liquidate debts owed it and before maturity turn them into ready money.[118] The purchaser or recipient of the accounts receivable typically relied on the usual credit rating agencies (Dun, Bradstreet) to determine the creditworthiness of both the firm and those who owed it money, and the purchaser would itself depend on a bank for its own financing.[119] This arrangement developed just before World War I and became particularly important in the automobile industry, where dealers would acquire cars from manufacturers on credit and then sell them to consumers on credit.[120] As we shall see in the chapter on consumer credit, installment loans became very important for the consumption of durable goods like automobiles (and pianos, sewing machines, etc.), and installment lenders often tried to liquidate their accounts receivable.[121]

The commercial paper market grew during the latter nineteenth century and early twentieth century to the point where it became an important part of the landscape for business credit.[122] Its depth and liquidity provided a new option for the management of trade credit. Indeed, just after World War I the total amount of commercial paper outstanding in 1919 was $1.186 billion.[123] Thereafter the total outstanding value varied depending on the overall economy and short-term borrowing needs of large firms. Borrowing firms could either issue paper on the market to finance their short-term needs for working capital or give negotiable notes to their supplier/creditors who could in turn use the commercial paper market to rediscount their customer's notes. Either way, the vitality of this credit market allowed lenders to reduce their financial vulnerability to their customer/debtors by selling the obligations they acquired to someone else.[124] However, it changed the question of trust. No longer was it sufficient that a particular creditor found a particular debtor trustworthy, for in order to transfer that debtor's obligation to a third party, others would have to assess the trustworthiness of the debtor and deem it adequate. The original creditor's positive judgment was no longer sufficient.

Credit Insurance

Carefully discriminating among would-be debtors is one way to deal with credit ex ante: figure out who is least likely to repay and avoid them, or at least price the loan accordingly. But despite the best efforts of creditors, some debtors don't repay. How might creditors manage the problem ex post? Insurance is one institution that deals with risk. And since the development of insurance in the early modern era, a growing number of different risks have been mitigated with life insurance, maritime insurance, flood insurance, fire insurance, and so on. At the end of the nineteenth century, credit risks joined the list and became insurable because of the development of credit insurance. Purchasing such insurance quickly became a routine option for suppliers/creditors.[125] Three companies started to write credit insurance policies in the United States: the American Credit-Indemnity Company (founded in 1893),[126] the Ocean Accident and Guarantee Corporation, and the London Guarantee and Accident Co., starting in 1895 and 1905, respectively.[127] These policies were sold only to wholesalers, manufacturers, and jobbers (but not retailers) and were intended to protect them from the possibility that one of their business customers would be unable to repay the money that had been loaned to them.[128] In other words, credit insurance served exactly those types of businesses that were also using credit ratings. Credit insurance did not compensate the creditor for the entire value of the loan, only the excess above "normal loss," and with a co-insurance provision as well. But it was touted as akin to collateral for a bank: a measure intended to deal with a bad situation after the fact.[129] Furthermore, only certain accounts could be insured, and then only up to a fixed maximum. Credit insurance contracts specified a limited set of debtor conditions that triggered payment, including bankruptcy, assignment, compromise, and attachment.[130]

Although insurance has been around for centuries (particularly maritime and fire), credit insurance in the United States was spurred by the passage in 1898 of a new Bankruptcy Act.[131] As I will discuss in chapter 8, there was no federal bankruptcy law for much of the nineteenth century. Instead, debtors and creditors had to rely on a patchwork of state laws to manage the legal aspects of insolvency and non-payment. Only after the new federal law gave sufficiently constant and stable meaning to the term "bankrupt" across all U.S. states could insurance companies use the event of bankruptcy as the key triggering contingency in an insurance contract.[132] They could insure against an adverse event once the definition of that event was clear.

Credit insurance offered a way to mitigate the possibility of lending to an insolvent debtor, but once established, it was also touted on the grounds that it served more than just narrow private interests. Some commentators noted that financial panics were ignited and fueled by a collective sense of unease, a general lack of confidence, which could be ameliorated by credit insurance. "Experts have held that panics would be entirely eliminated if a sufficient line of credit insurance were carried by manufacturers and jobbers."[133] Commercial failures often cascaded through the credit network as the financial shock of losses spread to the failed firm's creditors, and then the creditor's creditors, and so on, but "credit insurance universally prevalent would certainly prevent this."[134]

In addition to its reliance on federal bankruptcy law, credit insurance also depended on the rating system that had been developed for trade credit. Buried within the details of the insurance contract lay the credit ratings created by Dun and Bradstreet.[135] Indeed, one account suggested that credit insurance succeeded only because it used credit ratings.[136] If a firm wanted to purchase credit insurance, it could only insure those accounts it had with customers who possessed "preferred" credit ratings. The insurance company set an internal threshold that separated "preferred" from "inferior," but it was the rating agencies who determined the specific ratings given to the insured's customers. In addition, maximum payout limits were set using the credit ratings.[137] Thus, the importance of credit ratings amplified as they were incorporated into the "machinery" of credit insurance.[138] And those ratings were still in use more than half a century later.[139]

The use of insurance shifted the logic of assessing creditworthiness. Because insurance combines risks among the insured and across their trading partners, it became less critical for wholesalers and suppliers to discern the precise creditworthiness of each single customer, at least in so far as they might lead to excessive losses. Rather, by paying for insurance they could use the actuarially based calculations of the insurance industry, plus the risk assessments of credit raters, to estimate the overall likelihood of default over a pool of customers (grouped by credit rating) and then pay a premium sufficient to cover expected losses. Creditworthiness and trustworthiness as characteristics possessed by singular debtors mattered somewhat less (of course, creditors were still concerned because credit insurance compensated for excess losses, not total losses). What became more important was the ability to estimate average creditworthiness (and trustworthiness) across groups of debtors, and this could only happen once insolvency had become a comparable, measurable, and determinate legal outcome.[140] And even if access to insurance meant that suppliers didn't directly have to rely so much on credit information, credit ratings continued to matter indirectly because they shaped how insurance companies measured credit risk and priced their policies.

Conclusion

Trade credit is closely linked to the basic mechanics of a market economy. People and firms transact goods, but frequently there is a gap between receipt of the goods and payment for them. The gap can occur for many reasons, but when payment happens after the goods are supplied, it is bridged by trade credit.[141] In extending credit, even for as short a period as thirty days, the creditor has to wonder about the debtor's creditworthiness and the credibility of their promises. The answer to this question was originally provided by direct knowledge of the debtor's character and reputation, through ongoing transactions, or through mutual involvement in overlapping social networks. Trade credit was also tempered by adherence to a communitarian ethos that sustained local trade and involved relatively informal means for documenting indebtedness. But as trade expanded over the course of the nineteenth century, the numbers of trading partners and the average distance over which trade extended grew. Furthermore, traders necessarily became enmeshed in extensive credit networks that exposed them to distant and hard-to-control risks, and so the twin problems of uncertainty and vulnerability grew worse. To refuse credit and transact strictly on a cash basis was virtually impossible. Trade credit was as inescapable as it was problematic.

New methods for gathering information about trading partners developed, and creditors found ways to protect themselves financially. The financial crisis of 1837, and his own business failure, prompted Lewis Tappan to try to resolve some of the uncertainties faced by merchants. The opportunity to do so was inadvertently created, in part, by the peculiarities of the U.S. banking system. Unlike countries such as Canada, where a small number of large banks maintained branches across the entire country, in the United States most banks were small and locally based, frequently having a single branch.[142] There were no multibranch bank networks with internal information systems to help a supplier in New York City determine the creditworthiness of a customer in Iowa City or Seattle. Instead, it was the rating agencies that developed national networks to collect information at the local level and distribute it widely, with small banks among their best customers.[143] And after passage of the Bankruptcy Act of 1898, insolvency became a sufficiently well-defined legal event that insurance companies could calculate baseline probabilities and make debtor default an insurable risk. For trade credit, these two innovations were produced by market-based organizations: credit ratings sold to clients by firms like Dun and Bradstreet's, and the provision of credit insurance as a new business product.[144] The development of negotiability also created new possibilities, although it entailed more basic legal changes that involved courts and legislatures: a firm could use the obligations of its debtors to satisfy its own obligations and "exit" early from a relationship with a debtor.

These changes didn't happen independently. The credit rating system, for example, was absorbed into the inner workings of credit insurance. And the mobility of debt made possible by negotiability and the emergence of commercial paper markets often put debts into the hands of distant creditors, whose inability to use physical or social proximity, or a bank network, to gain information about debtors helped drive the demand for credit ratings. The effect was simultaneously to expand trade credit and to alter how it worked. It became a more distant, formalized, and anonymous undertaking. Gauging credit and evaluating creditworthiness involved a seemingly more rational calculus that used the standardized credit ratings produced by credit raters, balanced against actuarially calculated default risks that credit insurers fashioned. And yet, however precise and systematic credit ratings appeared to be, the raw information out of which ratings were fashioned was anything but. Gossip, rumor, reputational hearsay, and self-reports were in abundance and even the "hardest" financial information was produced without the rigor of accounting standards or professional accountants. Not until well after the establishment of the credit rating industry was there a functioning infrastructure to produce "hard" financial numbers.

4

Bank Lending

In business, as in everything else, character counts. The merchant whose life is clean and open and above board can say with Sir Galahad:

My strength is as the strength of ten,

Because my heart is pure.

—*THE YOUTH'S COMPANION*, JUNE 27, 1901, P. 330

Modern credit often involves banks. These are, after all, the primary institutions that specialize in credit. Modern commercial banks take deposits and make loans, acting as financial intermediaries between savers and borrowers, and managing the maturity mismatch between their short-term liabilities (deposits) and their long-term assets (loans). Within the bank, it is the job of bank loan officers to lend to the creditworthy, to reject unworthy applicants, and to differentiate between them over and over again. On the lending side, banks have become well versed in the practice of evaluating the promises that borrowers make. In rationing out credit, decision makers in banks rely on the vast accumulations of stored information that characterize financial institutions.[1] Sometimes the information is stored in files, and some of it in bankers' heads, but the necessity of information is inescapable, and its accumulation inexorable: "he [the banker] will find himself utterly unable to proceed in the way of making profit, without an adequate stock of information."[2] Taking deposits is an easier matter, and banks don't have to be as picky about whom they deal with.[3] Before the establishment of deposit insurance, it was the depositors who tried to be picky.

In the past, American banks undertook activities quite different from their modern functions of taking deposits and making loans. In fact, there were periods when the survival of banks depended on activities like issuing banknotes or rediscounting commercial paper. But generally, banks have been in the business of evaluating others' promises, and so they embody a specialized organizational nexus of trust. Additionally, however, banks issued banknotes and took deposits and so made their own promises that their notes were redeemable into specie or payment on demand. Banknote users found these promises more or less credible, depending on the solvency and reputation of the particular bank. When banks themselves were distrusted, either because note holders worried that banknotes could not be converted into specie or because customers worried that they wouldn't be able to access their deposits, bank runs occurred. And if this distrust spread to other institutions, a full-fledged financial panic could ensue.

Banks did not pursue these financial activities on their own or without public oversight. Particularly during the antebellum period when establishment of a bank required a special charter granted by the state legislature, banks were created through quid pro quo deals harnessed to the economic aspirations of state government or to its fiscal needs. The United States in the early nineteenth century was a land-rich and capital-poor country, and so state governments had a keen sense that banks were needed for economic growth.[4] A growing market economy required financial services. In exchange for the privilege of incorporation, banks were sometimes directed by the state or federal government to make particular kinds of investments, and taxes on banks could make a substantial contribution to public revenues.[5] But despite their perceived role in economic development, banks were politically controversial because they embodied new forms of wealth whose legitimacy seemed problematic in comparison to the tangible land that traditionally undergirded yeoman farmers. Furthermore, acts of incorporation bestowed special monopoly powers on a well-connected few. So banks were perceived to serve a controversial mixture of public purpose and private privilege. And one consequence of special acts of incorporation was that only a few banks could be established. Each deal had to work its way through the political process and compete for limited legislative attention.

Later on, banks were transformed by the Civil War legislation that established the National Banking System, by the equally consequential establishment of the Federal Reserve System in the early twentieth century, and by New Deal reforms. In the late nineteenth and early twentieth centuries, populist farm and labor groups were highly critical of banks, and their opposition shaped the design of the Federal Reserve System and the politics of New

Deal financial reforms.[6] People needed money to borrow but resented the power that creditors possessed over debtors. As compared to the banking systems of many other countries, in the United States small unit banks were remarkably commonplace. States shifted to general laws of incorporation to make it easier to establish banks, and set low capital standards.[7] Many states also restricted or prohibited branch banking, insisting that banks could only operate in a few locations and curtailing competition between them.[8] As populations grew in the South, Midwest, and West, they were frequently served by these marginal financial institutions. Small, poorly capitalized local banks feared market competition from bigger banks, but their political clout with state government helped protect them.[9]

As we will see, methods of bank lending evolved over time and varied across different regions of the United States. How were borrowers' promises evaluated? Antebellum New England banks often relied heavily on the social networks of their directors and managers to find suitable debtors. "Insider" networks were so important to these banks that they almost seemed to be practicing a nineteenth-century version of "crony capitalism." Western, Southern, and mid-Atlantic banks also used their social networks, albeit to a lesser extent. Banks everywhere invested in short-term commercial paper known as "real bills," although not exclusively.[10] The "real bills doctrine" stipulated that commercial banks *should* invest in real bills, and *only* in real bills, but there was variable compliance with the doctrine. Banks developed separate credit departments at the end of the nineteenth century to help manage credit more systematically, and in so doing borrowed techniques from the mercantile agencies that had been evaluating credit since the 1840s. In the early twentieth century, the "real bills doctrine" helped shape the institutional architecture and policy instruments of the new Federal Reserve System. And later in the twentieth century banks shifted from business credit to individual credit, making personal loans to individuals to fund consumption rather than just business loans to firms to fund production and sales. Personal loans became smaller, more numerous, and less often secured by tangible assets. Instead, an individual's future income became the basis for a personal loan.

Nineteenth-Century Banking

In the early nineteenth century, banks were very special organizations. To be legally established, a bank needed a specific charter granted by a state legislature.[11] In other words, citizens were not free to found a bank simply because they wished to (unlike their freedom to start a farm or open a store).

Furthermore, there were no general laws of incorporation that would allow virtually anyone to pay the fee, file the paperwork, and set up a bank.[12] Rather, bank promoters had to get state politicians to pass a specific law to establish a specific bank. Consequently, there were not many banks and each one underwent a very political birth. Since the rules varied from state to state, the process of founding a bank differed across the country.

Following the rapid expansion of the U.S. population and economy, the number of state banks grew from only 28 in 1800, to 327 in 1820, and 1,562 in 1860.[13] Part of this increase was driven by the overall growth of the United States, but it also reflected the shift to "free banking."[14] Starting with states like Michigan (in 1837) and New York and Georgia (in 1838), the process of founding a bank changed. No longer did bankers have to get a special law passed by the state legislature. Instead, individuals could establish a bank simply by fulfilling some bureaucratic procedures and complying with capital, reserve, and note issue requirements.[15] To create a bank was no longer a privilege reserved for those with special political access, and consequently the number of banks grew rapidly.[16] Since banks were understood to support economic development because they provided financial services, the change was deemed a good thing. But even so, banks were occasionally encumbered with requirements concerning their lending and investment activity: they might have to invest a certain proportion of their capital in state bonds, or farm mortgages, and so on. The requirements varied from one state to the other,[17] and by setting lower standards a given state could attract new banks that would provide financial services to a growing population. Population growth, economic growth, and growing numbers of banks all spurred each other on.[18] But of course weaker standards produced banks that would more easily fail.[19]

Although most banks were chartered by the states, two notable exceptions received federal charters: the First Bank of the United States, which operated from 1791 to 1811, and the Second Bank of the United States, operating from 1817 to 1836. These two institutions were founded and dissolved in political controversy about the power of the federal government and the constitutionality of banks, and their operations were troubled by worries about monopoly power.[20] While in existence, however, they provided valuable financial services to the young federal government, facilitated interregional payments (in part because they had branches in multiple locations), influenced the actions and profitability of private banks, and issued banknotes whose value was nearly uniform across the country.[21] Following the Second Bank's demise in 1836, it was not until the establishment of the

Federal Reserve System in 1913 that the United States again had a public national banking institution.

In 1860 on the eve of the Civil War, there were 1,562 state banks, possessing almost $1 billion in assets. Such banks issued banknotes, which then circulated as currency, and they discounted promissory notes, bills of exchange, and other commercial paper, in effect giving cash to businesses in exchange for promises made to them. With so many banks issuing currency, it was hard to determine what banknotes were really worth, or whether or not they were counterfeit. Notes were all denominated in dollars, but the real value of a banknote depended on the financial condition of the issuing bank, which was not easy to determine. This led to publications like *Bicknell's Counterfeit Detector and Bank Note List*, published twice a month in Philadelphia, which listed written descriptions of counterfeit notes and summarized the value of banknotes (whether at par or discounted).

The uneven development of the financial system is reflected in the amount of bank money per capita in different states and regions. In New England in 1820, there was $7.14 bank money per capita, while in the middle Atlantic (New York, New Jersey, Pennsylvania, Maryland, Delaware, and D.C.) there was only $2.16. By 1850, New England had $15.99 in bank money per capita, the middle Atlantic enjoyed $15.46, while the south Atlantic (Virginia down to Florida) had only $10.00 per capita. Bank money was even scarcer in the Midwest, with Indiana and Wisconsin enjoying only $3.91 and $3.24 per capita, respectively, in 1850.[22] Bank money per capita was clearly rising, but there were durable regional variations in the provision of banks and bank services, and these figured in political conflicts over banking and finance. In 1825, for example, there were 159 state-chartered banks in New England, 122 in the mid-Atlantic region, but only 32 in the South and 17 in the West.[23] People in the South and West particularly resented the dominant position occupied by eastern banks, especially those from New York City.

Banks extended more credit through discounting than they did through direct loans.[24] They did so by acquiring the short-term commercial paper discussed in chapter 3, roughly in accordance with the real bills doctrine. Such paper was either single-name (a basic promissory note that obliged the issuer to pay a sum by a designated date and was typically given by a business customer to a supplier as payment for a transaction) or double-name (where the note was signed by the issuer and then endorsed by the recipient, obligating them both). Banks preferred double-name paper since it offered more security by being backed by the creditworthiness of two parties rather than just one.[25] In regions dominated by export cash crops (e.g., cotton in the deep South or tobacco in the south Atlantic), much of the paper financed commodity production and distribution: plantations borrowed to fund their own springtime planting activities or that of their tenants. Intermediaries borrowed to finance sales and distribution. In these instances, specialized financial networks revolved around export commodity production, and the credit linkages extended from cultivators in the rural United States to textile manufacturers and tobacco importers in Britain.[26]

Depending on their charter, state banks were also required to make certain investments to bolster the local economy.[27] Property and plantation banks in the South, for example, had to provide mortgages to farmers and planters. In other places, newly chartered banks had to invest in canals and so underwrite infrastructural developments. More often, however, banks had to invest in government bonds and in effect lend to the state government. These ties between banks and states were reciprocated in states where the state government owned stock in the banks.[28]

Patterns of bank investment varied by region. In New England, which had a relatively large number of banks early on, the characteristic pattern has been named "insider lending."[29] Branch banking was prohibited in New England, so each bank operated in a specific location. Most of their funds came from shareholders rather than deposits. Since banks didn't lend to individuals as consumers, and since credit was largely extended in the form of discounts, banks would rediscount commercial paper brought to them by local businessmen. Normally, such credit was extended to bank directors, the relatives of bank directors, or to persons with some direct personal connection to the bank directors.[30] There was little "arm's-length" lending, but at the time this wasn't regarded as corrupt or illegitimate. It was how banks in New England usually did business. Shareholders who invested in a bank expected that their money would eventually go into the network of business activities that were personally linked to the bank directors. The "insider" status meant that banks knew a good deal about the people they gave credit to, and social relationships gave a bank extralegal means to enforce agreements and ensure that credit recipients met their obligations.[31] Since credible information about arm's-length borrowers was hard to obtain, and since legal enforcement of debt contracts was expensive and time-consuming, lending through social networks made some sense.

Further south, lending patterns in the mid-Atlantic region depended less on the use of bank directors as a social network hub for lending, and so there was less insider lending.[32] Furthermore, banks in New York, Pennsylvania, and New Jersey tended to be larger than the ones in New England,

and this made it hard for a small group of bank directors to dominate credit operations: large banks had too much capital to lend and directors' networks were too limited to funnel it all.[33] For example, the Black River Bank in Watertown, New York, was owned and controlled by Loveland Paddock and his two sons. And yet, in 1855 the bank made 2,674 loans to 978 different borrowers, most of whom were either merchants or manufacturers.[34] Such a wide dispersion of loans across so many debtors would not happen if the Black River Bank had confined its lending to the kin and close friends of the Paddock family.

Gibbons (1858) portrayed the internal deliberations that shaped a bank's discount decisions. Merchants brought the commercial paper they had been given by their own customers to a bank for rediscount, and the bank had to decide what paper to accept and how much to accept. The bank board of directors met with the bank president and cashier, and discussed the notes brought to the bank for discounting (Gibbons 1858: 26). The board paid particular attention to the reputation and circumstances of those named in the note (as either issuer or endorser), and, in Gibbons's example, the bank's rule was to accept only two-name paper. Perceived problems with drinking or gambling were sufficient to make someone's paper ineligible, and the group referred to independent credit evaluations done by mercantile agencies like R. G. Dun.[35] The directors also depended on their prior experience with a particular customer when considering a new request.

Banks were sufficiently scarce in the American South and West that state governments often took an active role in founding and capitalizing them, frequently setting weak standards that made banks easier to establish but more vulnerable in a crisis. Branch banking was legal in a few states, and this feature helped banks diversify their loans and survive episodic financial crises.[36] Nevertheless, credit and banknotes were scarce outside of the Northeast, and the U.S. banking system was characterized by large numbers of small, unit banks.[37] In rural areas, it was particularly hard to conform to the real bills doctrine and restrict credit to merchants, if only because the mercantile community was so small and soon saturated with credit. Thus, rural banks often loaned to farmers and planters.[38]

Like other businesses, banks were frequently embedded in networks of voluntary organizational affiliations. Through the nineteenth century, but especially after the Civil War, a number of large-scale voluntary organizations were founded and spread across the country, involving thousands of members in local chapters that were part of a national organization.[39] Membership in fraternal groups like the Independent Order of Odd Fellows, the Freemasons, the YMCA, the Knights of Pythias, and various temperance organizations gave an individual access to a national network of co-members and often provided the basis for various service and mutual-assistance measures. Smart local bankers knew that membership was an important step to building social connections that could be very useful in soliciting business and gathering information. They also believed that membership signaled good character and could help ensure the trustworthiness of a borrower. These organizations were usually segregated along racial (e.g., the Farmer's Alliance vs. the Colored Farmer's Alliance), religious (e.g., the Knights of Columbus for Catholics), ethnic and gender lines (witness the YMCA vs. YWCA), but nevertheless they gave members useful links that went beyond family, kinship, or neighborhood.[40]

National Banking System

The Civil War administered a giant economic shock to the American banking system. Suddenly, trade and credit links between the North and South were cut off, and many Northern merchants and suppliers were left with uncollectible debts. Both North and South went off the gold standard. In addition, economic resources were mobilized to serve the two war efforts, and the combatants had to raise money to cover vastly expanded military expenses. Since banks had previously been harnessed to public projects, it was easy to conceive of using them to support public borrowing for the war. The outcome obviously had very different effects in the North and South. The defeat of the South heavily damaged the Southern economy and banking system. Confederate currency and bonds became worthless at war's end, rendering many Southern banks insolvent.[41] The abolition of slavery liberated the former slaves and erased much of the "wealth" formerly possessed by Southern planters, making them less creditworthy as borrowers.

During the war, the Union government created the National Banking System. One measure established a new system of federally chartered banks whose banknotes were backed by government bonds. Thus, to issue banknotes these new banks had to purchase government bonds and in effect lend to the Northern government. Financial support for the government was one goal of the new banking system,[42] but another was to standardize the domestic currency.[43] The Union government later put a tax on the banknotes of state-chartered banks in order to make federal charters even more attractive, and consequently the number of state banks declined sharply from 1,466 in 1863 to 297 in 1866 (many state banks reincorporated as national banks).[44] The

National Banking Act of 1864 created the Office of the Comptroller of the Currency, which offered regulatory oversight. National banks were subject to capital and reserve requirements and restricted from investing in mortgages, and branch banking was prohibited.[45] National banks had higher capital requirements than most state banks, and so they were both harder to establish and less likely to fail.[46] These requirements helped standardize the value of the notes issued by banks and created a more uniform national currency. The standardization of paper money radically reduced the variability of banknotes because their real value no longer rested on the idiosyncratic solvency of the issuing bank: all national banknotes were backed by government bonds. The use of banknote detectors declined because people no longer had to worry so much about whether they could "trust" a particular banknote.

National bank requirements were harder to meet in the more capital-poor parts of the country, particularly the South and West. Hence, the geographic distribution of national banks strongly favored the East and Northeast, bolstering complaints about the inadequacy of banking and financial services and unavailability of currency in some regions of the United States.[47] National banks earned money from note issue, from their investments in government bonds and commercial paper, from bank loans, and also from bankers' balances. The latter were monies they kept on deposit with correspondent banks, used to facilitate clearing operations but which also earned interest and could count toward a bank's reserve requirements. As many have noted, correspondent banking arrangements meant that money "pyramided" in New York, designated the central reserve city.[48] There funds were often invested in stocks, via "call loans," and so linked the banking system with the speculative instabilities of the stock exchange.[49]

Like their predecessors, national banks in the latter nineteenth century invested in commercial paper and real bills. In 1895, for example, about 60 percent of national bank loan portfolios consisted of either two-name or one-name unsecured time loans, and 0 percent was in mortgages.[50] The restrictions against investment in mortgages by national banks created opportunities for other kinds of financial institutions and encouraged creativity by some national banks in rural areas. Keehn and Smiley (1977) discuss a number of ways that national banks could invest in mortgages, although their ability to do so was constrained by law. As discussed later in chapter 7, starting in the 1830s, special building and loan societies (precursors to "thrifts" and "savings-and-loans") were founded to help members of the working class purchase homes. The goals of these non-bank financial institutions were both economic (encourage homeownership) and moral (encourage responsible behavior), but such organizations could go where banks either could not go, because of regulation, or would not go.[51]

Like other nineteenth-century social institutions, banks were racially segregated. Especially in the South, where most African Americans lived after the Civil War, discriminatory enforcement of the color line made it hard for African American households and businesses to obtain financial services from white-owned banks.[52] Founded in 1865, the Freedman's Savings Bank represented the major effort by the Republican-led federal government to provide banking services to former slaves.[53] Initially created so that African American soldiers in the Union Army could deposit their pay, the bank first established branches in locations with high concentrations of black troops (with its headquarters in New York City): Norfolk, Washington, and Richmond. But additional branches were quickly established in cities with large black civilian populations, including Baltimore, New Orleans, and Charleston. Eventually, the bank had 34 branches, 32 in the South.[54] By 1870, this bank offered financial services to roughly 12 percent of the entire Southern black population, including savings accounts, mortgages, and loans.[55] Like other federally chartered banks, it was required to invest in federal government bonds, a conservative and safe asset. But other investments were more speculative, the bank was badly and sometimes corruptly run, and it suffered political resistance from white politicians.[56] Following the financial crisis of 1873, and despite the last-minute efforts of Frederick Douglass, the bank failed in 1874, and in the absence of deposit insurance it paid out only fifty cents on the dollar to depositors.[57] Its failure tarnished the image of banks among African Americans,[58] but even so, as a brief instance of financial inclusion, it had positive effects for those able to use its services.[59]

The failure of the Freedman's Bank and continued discrimination from white-owned banks meant that the African American community had to pool its capital and establish its own banks, much as it established other mutual-aid institutions like fraternal orders, insurance companies, and funeral homes. In fact, mutual-aid organizations were often instrumental in founding black-owned banks.[60] Reporting in 1907, the Capital City Savings Bank of Little Rock, Arkansas, stated: "We are lending money to the Negro men of the city; we are securing them credit and accommodation with wholesale houses which they never enjoyed before. We are redeeming homes for many Negroes who, in a measure, had lost them" (DuBois 1907: 149).[61] Early black-owned banks were small and focused on taking deposits, lending on real estate, and servicing their sponsors (e.g., church congregations or fraternal organizations), but they generally didn't do much commercial lending.[62] Despite recurrent efforts, the number of such banks remained small and so even after the end of official segregation, the African American community remained relatively "unbanked" and forced to obtain financial services from non-bank providers like payday lenders, check-cashing stations, and pawnshops.[63]

The Development of Credit Evaluation Capacity

The methods used by banks to manage loans, set policy for discounting, and analyze creditworthiness began to change at the end of the nineteenth century. To varying degrees, banks had previously relied upon the narrow social networks of their boards of directors (in the case of strict "insider lending"), broader social networks, membership in formal voluntary associations, general reputations about a borrower's character, and other informal methods.[64] Banknote detectors helped banks evaluate each other's notes, and the perceived value of commercial paper depended directly on the reputation of the issuer. But banks began to systematize their lending by emulating the mercantile credit rating agencies in two ways, and eventually "insider lending" came to be viewed as a suspect practice.[65] First, banks directly consulted credit ratings to evaluate their own borrowers: "The reports of the principal commercial agencies are always on hand and almost hourly referred to" (Carroll 1895: 122).[66] Their use of these ratings was undoubtedly encouraged by the fact that ratings largely determined whether firms extended short-term trade credit, and the real bills and commercial paper that banks discounted concerned short-term trade credit.[67] Banks would also use the special reports that mercantile agencies could produce about a particular company.[68] In so doing, banks recognized the importance of ratings, as well as the fact that bank loans were more likely to be repaid by a firm if all others doing business with that same firm deemed it creditworthy.

Even more significant than using credit ratings, banks began to copy how credit raters assembled information to calculate credit ratings. At the end of the nineteenth century, banks started to construct their own specialized credit departments and, like the credit raters, to gather, preserve, and organize systematic information relevant to creditworthiness.[69] As Kniffen said in 1915: "Twenty years ago, the credit department was unknown, but to-day it is part of the organization of every well-managed bank."[70] The influence of trade credit on bank credit seemed direct: "Mercantile credit work is the father of bank credit work, which has developed from it only within recent years" (Steiner 1924: 712). One commentator suggested that banks were pushed in this direction by a financial crisis that demonstrated the importance of prudent credit policy: "The panic of 1894 showed the necessity for revising credit department methods and banks followed the example of mercantile houses in the establishment of such departments" (Gehrken 1922: 261).[71] Whatever the proximate cause, banks recognized the need to gather their own information and to use it more systematically: "One very necessary adjunct to the discounting department, especially in a large and busy bank, is a credit or information department, for it is exceedingly important, particularly when loaning upon the ordinary single-named time paper, that the standing of the proposed borrower be known. . . . The use of commercial agency reports will be found useful in a measure, and special reports from these agencies can be obtained, but not always as quickly as needed. Here is where the need of a credit-department is to be found" (*Bankers' Magazine*, February 1900, p. 248).[72] The credit reports produced by Bradstreet's and R. G. Dun were useful to banks, but of course they were not fully adequate and so banks would gather additional information.[73] According to Steiner (1923: 443), separate credit departments were established first among large New York City banks,[74] then among banks in Philadelphia and Boston, and only later did the innovation spread south and west through the banking community.[75]

The need for greater organizational capacity to manage information eventually became urgent.[76] For example, readers were told in no uncertain terms that "if there is no systematic credit department in connection with the discount desk, one should be organized at once" (*Bankers' Magazine*, November 1897, p. 691) and that "every bank should have a well-organized and thoroughly equipped credit department" (Cannon 1893: 535). Another commentator noted that banks trailed mercantile houses with respect to credit methods: "There is not a large mercantile house of any consequence to day in the United States, that has not a thoroughly equipped credit department, in charge of a competent man; and yet, strange to say, the number of credit departments in banks throughout the United States can be counted almost upon the fingers of your two hands" (*Bankers' Magazine*, March 1898, p. 580). The nature of the change was also apparent: banks would have to invest personnel and equipment in the specialized task of gathering, preserving, and organizing information. They would have to create forms and files, storing information so that it could be retrieved in a timely manner and generally shedding previous informality: "The personal factor in banking has gradually diminished in force, and of necessity it has been replaced by system and method with more or less of mechanical appliances which were not in the least required under conditions formerly prevailing" (*Bankers'*

Magazine, March 1898, p. 374).[77] This shift from informal personal judgments based on qualitative information to bureaucratic decisions based on explicit ratings and systematic credit information was justified using the language of science: "Thus the banker finds that much of the intimate touch is lost, and that consequently it is more difficult than formerly to estimate the personal side of the risk, which has made it necessary to base opinions largely upon a scientific investigation of the history of the management, and upon an intensive analysis of the financial records of the borrowing individual, firm or corporation" (Miller 1927: 4).[78]

The material basis for this expanded information-processing capacity was not glamorous. Banking publications of the period contained numerous discussions of filing systems, forms, filing cabinets, clerks, carbon paper, and paperwork.[79] Doubtless the newly invented typewriter was a welcome addition to the office equipment necessary to manage all the paperwork. But the central importance of the credit file within this expanded information system underscores that these changes made bank credit more bureaucratic.[80] Institutional records supplanted personal recollections, and paper forms provided a template for the systematic collection and organization of particular kinds of information. The proverbial forms-in-triplicate offered a level of redundancy that frail human memories could not sustain.[81] Just as files, filing cabinets, and paperwork supported the complex information flows that were necessary for internal coordination within large-scale industrial corporations,[82] new information technology made specialized bank credit departments possible.

Once established, a credit department would accumulate "accurate information regarding the financial responsibility and integrity of persons, firms and corporations, systematically recorded so that it can be brought into immediate use" (Puyans 1936: 498). But in order to organize, preserve, and interpret information about debtors, banks had to acquire it in the first place. And one of the best places to get it was from the debtors themselves.[83] The problem, however, was that firms were generally reluctant to make financial information available to outsiders, and so getting formal financial statements directly from them proved to be a big challenge. Additionally, firms had an incentive to mislead or at least to make themselves look good in order to qualify for credit.[84]

For decades, the mercantile agencies had struggled to obtain credible information directly from the firms they rated, usually in the form of a financial statement (which resembled a balance sheet, listing assets and liabilities), and their efforts produced mixed results.[85] Prendergast (1906: 199) claimed that in 1902 about 37 percent of the ratings produced by credit rating agencies were based on information provided by the rated firms themselves. Since mercantile agencies didn't directly lend money to anyone, it was easier for them to ask intrusive questions about private financial matters, even if firms didn't answer. By contrast, the banks generally did not, perhaps for fear of offending customers whose goodwill would be undermined by explicit probes into their private affairs.[86] Banks relied on informal and relationally based sources of information to learn what they could about debtors. Furthermore, in the absence of generally accepted accounting standards, it was difficult to know exactly what information to solicit, how it was calculated, and how to make such information comparable enough to be able to make comparisons across firms.[87] Even the basic accounting rules for valuing assets had not been worked out.[88]

By the end of the nineteenth century, however, banks were making concerted efforts to obtain more financial information directly from their borrowers and customers,[89] and the practice spread.[90] Banks tried to systematize such statements by developing a standard template form (a "blank") that all banks would administer to their borrowers. For example, the New York State Bankers' Association first devised standard blank forms and recommended these to member banks, and then the American Bankers' Association followed suit.[91]

Two other devices were considered particularly effective ways to enhance the accuracy and credibility of financial statements. The first involved having the statement signed by the proprietor, president, or appropriate corporate officer.[92] A signature meant that someone personally connected with the firm vouched for the veracity of the statement, and under some conditions this could make the signatory legally liable.[93] For example, states considered laws prohibiting the submission of false statements,[94] and Congress passed a law making it illegal to send false signed statements through the U.S. mail.[95] Another device involved independent audits. Having a third-party examine and certify a financial statement, and offer some assurance about its accuracy, could also help establish the statement's credibility.[96] Recourse to such a third party, who would be some kind of accountant, nevertheless raised problems about how auditors figured into the conflicting interests of the firms issuing statements and the audiences reading them.[97]

Firm-issued financial statements went from being exceptions to the rule to being the rule. Before long, failing to get a statement was itself a significant fact: "The absence of any statement should be the first danger sign for the bank credit man" (Wall 1919: 57).[98] Assuming that a lender obtained a credible, certified financial statement from a borrower, key information would be of particular interest. Whether they discounted commercial paper or made a loan, banks had shorter time horizons than the investors who purchased bonds or shares. So banks were particularly interested in information that shed light on the borrower's short-term situation. A typical balance sheet categorized, valued, and summed the assets and liabilities of the firm. Bankers were therefore interested in the firm's *current* assets and liabilities. Current assets are those which can be realized immediately or in a relatively short period of time—they are the most liquid of the firm's assets. These included cash, notes and accounts receivable, and merchandise or inventory.[99] Current liabilities included accounts or notes payable, that is, short-term promises. Bankers focused on the current ratio, current assets divided by current liabilities, and as a rule of thumb wanted it to be at least 2 to 1.[100] Meeting this threshold signaled to a bank that a firm would likely be able to meet its short-term liabilities and thus was creditworthy in the short term.[101] They would also compare a firm's balance sheets from different points in time in order to discern trends.[102]

Government and Financial Information

In trying to extract more information from firms, banks were inadvertently assisted by the newly established Federal Reserve System, with its discount facility. Following the 1907 banking crisis, the Federal Reserve System was originally intended to solve the problem of an "inelastic currency." When needed, member banks could obtain additional liquidity by bringing their commercial paper to one of the Federal Reserve banks and exchanging it for cash. Only commercial paper or "real bills" of a certain quality were eligible for rediscounting by Federal Reserve banks, and to qualify member banks had to obtain financial information from the firms issuing the notes. The Federal Reserve Board issued Circular No. 13, stipulating that borrowers' financial statements had to be certified by a public accountant.[103] This regulation prompted strong complaints from banks, who regarded it as impractical given the current state of accounting practice, and so the Fed compromised by issuing a new Circular in 1915 that exempted loans worth less than $2,500 from such regulations.[104] Nevertheless, the Federal Reserve's discount policy strongly encouraged banks to get more detailed information about their client firms. In fact, one banker pointedly recommended that when banks solicited financial statements from businesses, they enclose an informational pamphlet that explained the eligibility requirements for commercial paper rediscounted by Federal Reserve banks.[105]

Other types of policy also prompted the creation of more standardized accounting information. In regulated industries like utilities, railways, and insurance, regulatory agencies often imposed financial reporting requirements and allowed industry to set prices so as to obtain a "fair rate of return."[106] Such a standard of "fairness" made no sense unless there was a systematic way to calculate profits, investments, and the rate of return, and the formulae with which to estimate these values were usually set by the regulatory agency.[107] The imposition of a federal income tax also helped standardize the reporting of financial information for both individuals and corporations because it defined "taxable income" in a way that was valid across the country.[108] Standardization of financial terms made it easier to obtain information.

These new regulatory interventions necessitated the calculation of new types of financial information, but they also energized the accounting professionals who were more than bookkeepers and whose expertise lay in the creation, management, and interpretation of financial information. As Miranti (1986) argued, the establishment of the Federal Reserve Board in 1913, and the Federal Trade Commission in 1914, created regulatory opportunities for the accounting profession. Within a short period, accountancy acquired many of the key features of a profession that sustain expertise (including state licensure, specialized training, and a professional association), although the process of profession building was deeply conflicted. And that expertise was deployed to help create standards for financial statements.[109] The establishment of the Securities and Exchange Commission (SEC) during the New Deal offered another regulatory opportunity to create even more standardized financial information about large, publicly traded corporations and to require the involvement of the accounting profession in the creation of that information. Thus, through a number of critical episodes, the accountancy profession was inserted into a vastly expanded process in which otherwise reluctant firms provided standardized financial information to a set of audiences.[110] Many of these episodes were shaped by changes in government fiscal, economic, or regulatory policy, but private regulations also played a role.[111] And whether intended or not, the outcome was a much richer set of financial information about potential debtors.

Credit Men and the Three Cs

In addition to accountants, the "credit men" (as they were then called) also had professional aspirations. As one commentator put it: "The art of successfully extending credit is crystallizing into a profession" (Hunter

1914: 1). The National Association of Credit Men (NACM, later called the National Association of Credit Managers) was organized in 1896 out of a set of city-level groups of credit personnel, during a decade of depressed economic conditions that brought home the problem of credit gone awry.[112] The NACM took positions on a number of important issues of the day, being publicly in favor of a new national bankruptcy law (the Bankruptcy Act of 1898 was the first permanent bankruptcy law for the United States), criticizing the mercantile agencies, eventually commenting on Federal Reserve System policy, and urging greater use of financial statements.[113] The NACM gave consideration to how credit worked in other countries in order to draw lessons for the United States.[114] It urged the credit rating agencies to indicate when their ratings were based on a statement from the rated firm, although Dun and Bradstreet refused to do so.[115] Credit men didn't secure state licensure (one of the key features of a profession), but they formed a national organization and possessed specialized skills that (they argued) qualified them for their work. For decades, the NACM continued to provide its expert advice on a number of financial and credit issues and promoted its members as specialists in the evaluation of trustworthiness.

Despite greater use of credit ratings, the development of an organizational apparatus to manage information by credit departments, greater reliance on financial statements, and increased involvement of professionals (like accountants) and quasi-professionals (credit men), the process of assessing creditworthiness did not yet become completely mechanical or algorithmic. However much banks tried to systematize their procedures and use formal documents and quantitative information, loan officers still had to exercise considerable discretion. "No definition or standard can be so precise or exact as to eliminate the necessity of the exercise of judgment in its application, and in no field of endeavor is there greater need for such exercise as in that of banking" (Coman 1904: 328). Among other things, lenders continued to evaluate individuals who wanted to borrow, without being able to rely on simple numbers: "Bankers . . . always have a regard to the moral character of the party with whom they deal; they inquire whether he be honest or tricky, industrious or idle, prudent or speculative, thrifty or prodigal" (*Bankers' Magazine and Statistical Register*, July 1884, p. 34). Judgment among bankers was informed by various rules of thumb and heuristics, the most prominent of which was the "Three Cs."

The "Three Cs" offered a shorthand mnemonic device indicating the factors that lenders were supposed to weigh in making their decisions: capacity, capital, and character. "And in determining the borrower's responsibility it is generally agreed by bankers that the three primary essentials are: Character, Capacity, and Capital."[116] By the early twentieth century, virtually all bank handbooks and textbooks mentioned the "Three Cs," making it a standard part of a banker's tool kit.[117] Indeed, this heuristic seemed to possess universal value: "The three 'C's'—character, capital, and capacity—apply with equal force in Chicago and Chile, in Denver and Denmark, in Buffalo and Bombay."[118] As more financial information became available, capacity and capital became easier to estimate. Character, however, remained elusive: "Character is difficult to appraise. No precise unit of measurement exists. It is intangible and may easily be simulated. The credit man seeks to appraise character, yet in practice usually investigates reputation. Yet the two are distinct. Character lies within the man himself, while reputation exists in the minds of others."[119]

The opacity of personal character is one reason why lenders were urged to learn as much as they could about a borrower: "I do not believe in delving too deeply into a man's private affairs, but where it can be done, it is well to observe his domestic relations. If he is a man of domestic habits and enjoys pleasant home life, he is the more apt to be successful in business, other things being equal."[120] Any chance to glimpse into a borrower's inner life was a chance worth taking. Character was a psychological composite of several traits, so its examination was multistranded: "The first point to engage his [the lender's] attention will be the character of the applicant for credit. His veracity, sobriety, general personal integrity and mode of life, in and out of business."[121] Kniffen (1911: 421) asserted that "character means more than mere honesty. It means habits, companionships, past record, antecedents." And although character was understood to be an individual feature, it seemed clear that groups of individuals (particularly the executives who managed a firm) also possessed character that had to be judged.[122]

The evaluation of character was something that could not rely on paper files and organizational records alone. In this respect, personal contact between the lender and the would-be borrower was deemed critical. Such contact could be required as part of the loan application process, but it could also happen more casually, when both banker and customer interacted as members of a church congregation or fraternal society. Borrowers had to be looked in the eye, sized up in person, the firmness of their grip tested, their honesty judged, and so on. "But the finer degrees of character such as perseverance, thrift, ingenuity—as well as weakness and purpose—may be appraised more accurately by word of mouth, the handshake, or a friendly moment with the applicant" (Haines 1936b: 539). Unstated was the fact that in a segregated society, informal contacts were organized along racial lines and they seldom included women. And even as the importance and volume of formal written information increased, some things could best be discerned face-to-face: "One of the prime requisites [of a loan officer] is development of the ability to read character. Often the first interview will settle a credit problem regardless of the existence of vast amounts of financial information."[123] However encompassing and precise financial statements became, some things could only be gauged through direct personal contact.

Although all three factors mattered, character seemed to be first among equals. "Character is ordinarily regarded as foremost among the essentials of a good credit risk. The banker cannot take the honesty of the applicant for credit for granted. Yet it is this part of the risk—the moral risk—which is the most difficult to appraise."[124] Without character, banks shouldn't lend.[125] In importance, capacity came in a close second to character: will future earnings be sufficient to service the loan? Capacity was easier to measure: "The most valuable index for measuring this element of the credit risk is the detailed operating statement showing the profits or losses over a period of years."[126] The last factor was capital: what is the value of the assets committed by the borrower? "The third element in the credit risk which requires investigation is capital or collateral. The prospective borrower's capital is the ultimate measure of the collateral he can offer, whether it is specifically pledged or not" (Munn 1923: 501–2).[127]

Using this simple mnemonic, bankers tried to assess a business borrower's willingness and ability to repay a loan.[128] Its application encouraged them to use a full range of information, starting with the social network–based sources that influenced traditional insider lending (e.g., friendship and kinship-based connections) and including their own personal knowledge of the borrower. It also prompted reliance on the newer and more formal information that accumulated in the files of a bank's credit department: records of prior loans and bill payment history, balance sheets, tangible assets, liens and other legal encumbrances, credit ratings, and so forth. The latter category of information made it possible to increase the overall volume of lending activity, to a level that would have completely overwhelmed the limited memories and finite social networks of individual bankers, and to lend to borrowers at such social and geographic distances from the lender that they were effectively strangers.[129]

Other Lending Strategies

The three Cs summarized the complexities of creditworthiness and helped focus the minds of bankers on three things that really mattered. The third "C," capital, pointed to a common strategy for successful bank lending. Discounting commercial paper, the dominant mode of credit extension by banks in the nineteenth century, essentially involved unsecured lending. To be sure, a promissory note obliged the original issuer and subsequent endorsers, but it was fundamentally a simple promise. And the fact that such notes tended to be for relatively short periods of time (thirty days, sixty days, etc.) meant that lenders didn't have to make long-term predictions about a borrower's future. But even if the lender had no legal claim over collateral, a healthy measure of capital made it more likely that the debtor could repay.

Acquisition of more information about a debtor was one way to manage credit, but securing the loan with collateral was another. That is, a lender could acquire a property interest in some asset of the borrower, so that the asset could be seized in the event of debtor default. Such security is the hallmark of mortgages, where a loan is secured by real estate. The existence of collateral allows lenders to protect themselves in the event of debtor default, and so minimize their losses. Collateral isn't the same as capital: it is an asset that the lender can actually seize, if need be.

Secured lending works only when the bank can be sure that the borrower has clear title to specific and identifiable collateral, when the value of the collateral is estimable, stable, and sufficient to cover the sum owed, when the underlying asset is "recoverable," and when it can legally be subject to a lien.[130] Lenders prefer collateral that can easily be resold.[131] Thus, early on, loans were secured by land, crops, and durable goods (through chattel mortgages on objects like automobiles, pianos, harvesters, and sewing machines). Later, loans could be secured by intangible forms of property like shares, bonds, commercial paper, or accounts receivable as these kinds of assets became more widely held or could be encumbered by a lien.[132] Westerfield (1932) documents a shift in commercial bank loan portfolios during the 1920s toward secured lending and points out that the collateral underpinning that change generally consisted of financial assets. Lenders want to be sure that the borrower actually owns the particular asset that is being offered as collateral (which is why clear title matters) and that property rights are freely transferable.[133] Lenders also want to ensure that the value of the collateral will be maintained for the duration of the loan.

Thus, for example, mortgage lenders often insisted that borrowers obtain fire insurance for their home, or a firm making an auto loan required that the borrower insure their automobile.[134] Finally, since creditors can possess multiple competing claims over the same assets, lenders are very interested in seniority. Other things being equal, secured lenders always prefer to have senior rather than junior status since that gives them first claim on the assets, but all such claimants will want to know if the collateral is already encumbered or not.[135]

Under the right conditions, lenders can collateralize their loans. Because security involves another layer of legal formalities and transaction costs (beyond the basic loan contract), not all lenders deem it worthwhile. But for those who do obtain security, it can substantially reduce vulnerability to debtor default, and hence make the lender more willing to lend. Better collateral reduces the need for information, and the possibility of losing a valuable asset also gives the borrower an additional incentive to keep up payments and avoid foreclosure.[136] However, if the value of collateral falls substantially below the value of the loan (as happened in 2008 when U.S. home values collapsed and many mortgaged homeowners were "under water"), debtors may decide to stop their loan payments and simply let the creditor foreclose on the property.

Another strategy that became important among bankers involved diversification. Today, investors embrace highly developed statistical rationales for portfolio diversification and use quantitative measures to guide them (e.g., the beta coefficient).[137] Diversification of a lending portfolio involves trying to avoid highly correlated risks (e.g., don't lend only to firms in a particular industry, or in a specific geographic region, or lend too much to a single firm). Early twentieth-century bankers did not have a formalized theory to guide them, but they possessed folk wisdom about "not putting too many eggs in one basket." In discounting commercial paper, for example, bankers had an opportunity to spread their risks around by ensuring that they acquired the paper of firms in a variety of different industries. Prudential bank regulations often set a cap on how much a bank could lend to a single customer and so prevented banks from becoming too reliant on the solvency of a single debtor. There were limits on diversification, however, given that branch banking was prohibited in many states, and unit banks (especially those in smaller or rural communities) inevitably did a lot of local lending. Lacking the ability to diversify geographically, non-branched banks were highly vulnerable to local economic conditions, and more prone to failure.[138]

Early motivations for loan diversification were less informed by a sense that uncorrelated risks would reduce the overall variance of a bank's loan portfolio than by a concern over the balance of power between lenders and borrowers. In an article on "practical banking" the *Bankers' Magazine* (August 1884, p. 113) advised its readers: "Distribute your loans rather than concentrate them in a few hands. Large loans to a single individual or firm, although some times proper and necessary, are generally injudicious and frequently unsafe. Large borrowers are apt to control the bank, and when this is the relation between a bank and its customers, it is not difficult to decide which in the end will suffer." People usually thought that lenders had total power over borrowers, but bankers knew it could be otherwise. Later on, readers were warned that "more than one bank has been wrecked by the unwise plan of 'putting too many eggs into one basket'" (*Bankers' Magazine*, June 1901, p. 815). The eggs-in-a-basket message was repeated in an article that went on to declare: "Investment nowadays is coming to be a science, and one of its principles which is coming to be more and more clearly defined is that of diversification" (*Bankers' Magazine*, March 1910, p. 449).[139] By the 1920s, the statistical aspects of diversification were becoming clearer, although the exact details were not. One article favoring diversification argued that investment in a variety of securities enabled the "law of averages" to operate and so protect the portfolio.[140]

Diversification shifted the focus away from single loans to the entire loan portfolio. An individual loan could go sour, but so long as the bank was sufficiently diversified, and so long as its margins were high enough to cover average losses, it wouldn't suffer overly much. The focus on diversification changed how banks could think about their risks, from a consideration of each loan on a case-by-case basis to something more akin to how insurance companies considered their risks, viewing them all together and subject to actuarial calculation. A single loan that might not make sense on a stand-alone basis could be a good idea as one part of a broader portfolio. Chapter 7 will discuss how this "actuarial logic" came to full fruition in the area of home mortgage lending.[141] When loan amounts were especially large, banks also hedged their risks through syndicated lending. This involved having a group of banks participate in a loan, where each participant took on only a portion of the total loan amount. Loan syndicates typically were organized by a lead bank, which undertook the bulk of the loan negotiation and assessment process and which consequently received the bulk of the fees, with other banks acting as passive partners.

Investment Banking

As U.S. financial markets developed, corporations and governments established ways to raise capital or borrow money long-term. Traditionally, they did this by issuing financial securities like stocks and bonds, where these could be traded on secondary markets like the New York Stock Exchange. Stocks or shares involved an ownership interest and were used by for-profit corporations to raise capital: shareholders owned a piece of the company, depending on how many shares they held. By contrast, bonds did not involve ownership rights and were issued by both corporations and governments to borrow long-term. Bondholders were entitled to interest payments, but had no control rights. Governments and organizations seldom marketed their securities directly to buyers; usually, they used the services of what we now call an investment bank. For much of the nineteenth century, it was primarily the job of intermediaries to place U.S. securities in European financial markets, usually London. But as New York City gained importance, securities were floated and traded there as well.[142] Stock and bond issues involved large sums, and to ensure their success the lead bank often assembled a syndicate of banks, with each taking responsibility for placing a portion of the securities with investors in exchange for a share of the profits. Investment banking depended on personalities, relationships, and private information.[143] J. P. Morgan, for example, headed an eponymous bank and used his elaborate network of personal ties with other bankers, corporate leaders, and political elites to do his investment banking work.[144] After the Glass-Steagall Act of 1933, investment banks in the United States had to separate from commercial banks and so the two types of institutions became distinct. Not until deregulation in the 1990s, and the repeal of Glass-Steagall in 1999, were commercial and investment banking functions performed by the same banks.

Personal Loans

For a long time U.S. commercial banks loaned to businesses by discounting their bills and commercial paper. Banks left personal credit for individuals to retailers, department stores, general stores, durable goods manufacturers, and, for lower-income households, loan sharks and pawnshops (see chapter 5). As one textbook put it: "The earning capacity of an individual is not a proper basis for credit, for it may cease at any moment."[145] Credit for individuals was "consumptive credit," whereas credit for businesses was "trading credit" (Kniffen 1915: 393).[146] In assessing creditworthiness in the former case, lenders would probably only see one of the three "Cs," namely character. When lending to business, lenders expected to consider all three.[147]

Of course, by lending to businesses, U.S. commercial banks sometimes in effect loaned indirectly to individuals. For example, a bank that loaned money to an automobile dealership that in turn made loans to its customers so they could purchase cars on an installment plan was lending to car buyers, one step removed. Or if a bank loaned money to a consumer finance company that made small loans to individuals, the bank was indirectly lending to consumers. Such indirect connections were common within credit networks. But not until the late 1920s did commercial banks begin to lend directly to individuals. In part, this was because of their reluctance to make "consumption" loans, and it was also because consumer or personal loans tended to be relatively small (which meant that the "overhead" cost was relatively high). But with growing numbers of salaried employees in the U.S. economy, other financial institutions had already demonstrated that small personal loans could be profitable, and so banks finally entered the market. Full-time employment offered stable future earnings that gave lenders some assurance that the loan could be repaid.

Commercial bank lending to individuals began very publicly when the First National City Bank of New York (predecessor of today's Citigroup), then the largest bank in the United States, announced in May 1928 that it would open a personal loan department at one of its Manhattan branches and make available to salaried workers loans worth between $50 and $1,000 for up to one year (loans had to be cosigned by two other "responsible" persons). The new loan department was an instant success, with roughly 500 applicants seeking personal loans on the first day of operation.[148] Within a week, the Bank of the United States opened its own personal loan department, and other banks followed as well.[149] And within a month, National City Bank opened personal loan departments in all of its branches in Manhattan, the Bronx, and Brooklyn.

Beyond the attraction of profitable opportunities, New York banks were encouraged by New York State Attorney General Albert Ottinger, who was then leading a very public campaign against loan sharks and who wanted to increase alternative sources for small loans.[150] This gave welcome political support to the banks. After a year, the program was judged a great triumph: National City Bank loaned more than $16 million to over 51,000 persons in small loans that averaged about $320 in value.[151] Thereafter, as the stock market crash was followed by a deepening economic depression, and ordinary business lending dried up, many commercial banks continued to expand their small loan business in order to generate earnings.[152] Changes in bank regulations in a number of states allowed other banks to start making personal loans as well,[153] and personal loan departments became a national phenomenon.[154] As we will see in chapter 5, personal loans coming from banks joined the funds coming from other lending institutions (credit unions, industrial banks, personal finance companies, installment loans, etc.) to help lay the foundation for a credit-based consumer society.

Personal lending involved much smaller sums and larger numbers of borrowers, and it worked differently than business lending. Most obviously, an operating business generates cash revenue that can service a loan, whereas ordinary people have only their salaries. Business borrowing will fund economically productive activity, whereas personal borrowing typically funds some form of consumption, asset purchase, or debt consolidation. Personal loans were often called "character loans" because there was no capacity, collateral, or capital involved. The borrower's future earnings were the only basis for repayment, so it was particularly important for lenders to confirm the borrower's employment status and salary.[155] To enhance the likelihood of repayment, it was standard practice for lenders to get at least two cosigners ("co-makers") for the loan, whose own creditworthiness would bolster the borrower's. Lenders could also practice a modest version of diversification by ensuring that the borrower and co-makers weren't all employed by the same firm.[156]

Trusting the Banks

By the middle of the 1930s, commercial banks updated their lending practices by developing a small loan business, by diversifying their loan portfolios, by collateralizing more of the loans they made, and by creating and staffing a professional credit department. A number of these developments were reinforced by the growing involvement, and competence, of the accounting profession, as well as quasi-professional groups like the National Association of Credit Men and the Commercial Law League (comprised of lawyers who specialized in debt collection and bankruptcy). All these changes would, in some manner, help banks make better decisions about whom to trust. They also helped banks survive a trying decade in which banks failed by the thousands.[157] Among the most vulnerable banks were the small, state-chartered, unit country banks whose assets were hit hard by the depression in American agriculture, whose ability to diversify outside of the local economy had been limited, who were vulnerable to bank runs, and who generally had little organizational capacity to evaluate creditworthiness.[158]

The issue of trust cut two ways for banks. Banks were more likely to avoid failure if they figured out how to separate trustworthy from untrustworthy borrowers, but success also depended on whether they themselves could seem trustworthy, especially to their depositors. Trust mattered on both the asset and liability side of the balance sheet. Much of the capital raised by twentieth-century commercial banks came from their depositors, not their investors (or shareholders). And so banks remained vulnerable to depositors who lost their confidence in their bank and rushed to withdraw their money en masse. In case of widespread withdrawals or actual loan losses, only a thin cushion of capital stood between the bank and failure. Banks faced a maturity mismatch between their long-term assets and their short-term liabilities, and if enough people demanded their deposits back quickly enough, a bank might be hard-pressed to repay them all in cash (recall Jimmy Stewart's famous speech to his depositors in the movie *It's a Wonderful Life*). Depositors' worries about bank liquidity could soon become self-fulfilling prophesies that would infect one bank after the next. The macroeconomic consequences of major bank panics could be severe.[159]

Fears about bank insolvency were exacerbated by the fact that branch banking was a rarity in the United States: national banks were prohibited from having multiple branches, and most states prohibited it as well. In 1910, only nine states allowed statewide bank branching.[160] As a comparison with the Canadian bank system makes clear, extensive branching could give to banks a size, geographic spread, and financial robustness that greatly enhanced their chances of survival.[161] Between 1920 and 1926, 3,063 U.S. banks failed, as compared to one Canadian bank over the same period.[162] Canada's national banking system was comprised of a small number of large multibranch banks. Political concern about bank failures, and how quickly they could wipe out the hard-earned savings of small depositors, prompted establishment of the U.S. Postal Savings system.[163] Created in 1911 after the 1907 financial crisis, postal savings accounts offered a safe place for farmers and workers to deposit their money, even in parts of the country ill-served by regular banks. Although long opposed by the banking community, this system survived until 1966, when it was liquidated by Congress.[164]

Until the Great Depression, the danger of bank runs was real because depositors didn't trust their own banks, or were worried that others would distrust their banks. So many U.S. banks failed or were threatened with insolvency that in the early 1930s the federal government created a new system of federal deposit insurance to help reduce depositors' fears about the trust-worthiness of their bank.[165] A number of the states that prohibited branch banking had experimented with deposit insurance to bolster their banking systems, but these had all been costly failures.[166] The Federal Deposit Insurance Corporation (FDIC) was established as a temporary measure by the Glass-Steagall Act in 1933, and then put on a permanent basis by the Banking Act of 1935. Initially, individual deposits were insured up to $2,500, but the maximum was soon raised to $5,000. Henceforth individual depositors did not have to rush to their banks and withdraw their funds at the first sign of trouble, and the measure greatly strengthened the smaller, single-unit banks.[167] Nationally chartered banks belonging to the Federal Reserve System were automatically enrolled in FDIC, as were state-chartered Federal Reserve member banks. Many non-member state banks enrolled in FDIC, but a number stayed out. Although coverage was not universal, FDIC in combination with its partner organization FSLIC (Federal Savings and Loan Insurance Corporation, established in 1934) applied an insurance arrangement to make most banks and savings-and-loans seem trustworthy to their depositors, making credible the promise that demand deposits were truly available on demand. The number of FDIC-insured banks that closed down was roughly 60–70 per year in the late 1930s and then declined so that after World War II only a handful were closed annually.[168]

In addition to short-term measures like "bank holidays,"[169] the banking crisis of the early New Deal changed other types of bank regulation. Whether they were chartered at the state or federal level, banks were subject to regulatory oversight. A state or federal bank "examiner" would visit the bank, study its balance sheet, assess its assets and liabilities, and identify problems that needed solving. In the worst case, the examiner might determine that the bank was insolvent and needed to be closed. In the early stages of the Great Depression, so many banks failed so quickly that politicians and regulators sought multiple ways to bolster the financial sector. One involved a change in how federal bank examiners valued bank assets. This seemingly obscure change in accounting rules proved to be unexpectedly consequential in the long run.

Many banks invested in bonds, which were regarded to be conservative investments, and so their balance sheets were damaged when bond prices collapsed. Federal bank examiners traditionally valued bank bond portfolios using their current market price: bonds were "marked to market." But in 1931, the Comptroller of the Currency issued a new rule for bond valuation. Henceforth, bond ratings issued by rating agencies like Moody's or Standard and Poor's (S&P) would be incorporated into valuation rules so that only low-rated bonds would be "marked to market." Highly rated bonds, that is, those that were in the top four bond rating categories as determined by the rating agencies, could be valued at their historic cost.[170] Since bond prices had declined, their value when purchased was higher than their current price, so the Comptroller allowed examiners to act as if bank bond portfolios were worth more than current market prices indicated. In effect, this new rule offered an important measure of regulatory forbearance. State bank regulators followed the Comptroller's new policy,[171] and in 1938 the National Association of Supervisors of State Banks affirmed the use of bond ratings in state regulations, with the highest-rated bonds (i.e., those with "AAA," "Aa," "A," or "Baa" ratings) being valued at their historic cost.[172] The Comptroller's decision set a strong precedent, and bond ratings issued by Moody's, S&P, or Fitch were henceforth incorporated into many other financial regulations.[173]

Legislation passed during the Great Depression dramatically altered the regulatory setting for banks. After World War II, the Federal Reserve Board assumed a much more active role in national macroeconomic policymaking and replaced the discount window with open market operations as the chief policy instrument. Individual bank depositors were now protected by deposit insurance, and so the necessity for them to "trust" their bank diminished. Federal housing policy helped change and expand mortgage lending so that more people could purchase their own homes. The Glass-Steagall Act split off commercial banks from investment banks. Operating under this new regulatory framework, however, commercial banks still had to figure out whom to trust. And banks expanded beyond their traditional focus on business credit to include consumer credit, so they were concerned about the trustworthiness of both firms and individuals.

Within this new framework, commercial banks offered expanded credit to fuel the postwar economic boom. Unlike during the 1919–20 period, when bank lending focused chiefly on commercial loans, lending after World War II spread in many directions: commerce, agriculture, consumers, real estate, and securities.[174] Businesses borrowed to help fund rapidly growing production of durable goods.[175] Investment in consumer and personal loans amplified lending trends begun in the 1930s that were temporarily suspended by wartime anti-consumption measures. And starting after the war, real estate loans from commercial banks increased sharply, and climbed steadily through the 1950s.[176] These more extensive lending activities were managed by banks whose capacity for credit evaluation had been greatly expanded by their own specialized credit departments and which built on information provided by rating agencies. Furthermore, thanks to New Deal disclosure requirements imposed on publicly traded corporations and enforced by the SEC, much more standardized financial information about firms was available than before. Banks could exploit a growing volume of quantitative information about borrowers.

Quantification and Business Lending

Bank lending to small and medium-sized businesses always combined personal judgment with numerical measurement. The president of a small local bank or the loan officer of a large bank would approve a loan only after considering both the personal character of the business owner and numerical evidence gleaned from a balance sheet. This combination of "hard" and "soft" information was encompassed by the "Three Cs" rule for lending. Since small businesses were relatively opaque to outsiders, the access to information possessed by a local bank could be a real advantage: lender and borrower had a direct personal relationship, and both were embedded in the same social networks. Something akin to the "insider lending" pattern identified for the nineteenth century by Lamoreaux (1994) persisted well into the twentieth century. However, the importance of "relationship lending" varied depending on the size of the two parties. Using evidence from the late twentieth century, researchers emphasize how little financial information exists about small businesses, and what there is often flows privately through the particular relationship that a small business establishes with its bank.[177] The two sides build up a degree of trust that facilitates mutual disclosure and learning, and this positively affects the availability and pricing of credit. Furthermore, small local banks were more likely to use "soft" information, whereas bigger banks relied more on standardized information obtained from financial statements.[178] As the number of independent banks declined in the United States at the end of the twentieth century, and as banks merged and consolidated, some of the special abilities of small banks to tap local information channels may have been lost.

Bank lending changed not simply because there were fewer small banks but also because banks continued to formalize and quantify how they measured credit risk. In particular, during the 1990s many large banks began to develop their own internal credit risk rating methods for business borrowers.[179] These new metrics sometimes estimated the likelihood of borrower default but also the expected losses. With small businesses in particular, it was not difficult to extend the scoring methods developed for consumer credit (discussed in chapter 5) to businesses whose finances were almost indistinguishable from those of the owner/proprietor. If business loans were numerous enough and homogeneous enough to be pooled together and considered as a group, they could be subject to quantitative statistical analysis. In addition, banks started to securitize categories of loans and to shift them off their own balance sheets.

The use of credit scoring seems to be associated with a small but significant increase in lending activity to small businesses, although the effect is complicated.[180] As with the bond rating agencies, a bank's internal credit rating system placed a borrower into an ordered category system. Having more categories meant greater granularity and subtler distinctions but also made the rating system more expensive to maintain. Unlike the ratings generated by bond rating agencies, or Dun and Bradstreet, these ratings were not made public. Instead, they were used for internal purposes, including measurement of the overall risk profile of a bank's loan portfolio, loan origination, loan loss reserves, loan monitoring, and employee compensation.[181] Their internal use did not protect them from conflicts of interest, however. In many settings, bank loan officers (or "relationship managers") usually help set ratings. When their compensation is set using "risk-adjusted rate of return" measures, these loan officers can have an interest in underestimating risks.

Once sufficiently widespread, bank credit scores for businesses could be used for external purposes as well. In particular, these scores entered into the securitization process and regulatory bank capital standards. Credit scores calculated by a bank provided quantitative measures of risk for its assets and so when banks securitized loans (e.g., creating a "collateralized loan obligation" or CLO) they had a convenient metric with which to estimate financial performance and default risk, even for complex securitizations. Credit scores thus played a role in disintermediation and in the shift in bank business models from originate-to-hold to originate-to-distribute.[182] Scored and measured, aggregated and analyzed, illiquid loans could be turned into marketable securities, and banks could reduce their required capital reserves by moving assets off their balance sheets.

Internal scoring also became important for the Basel II bank capital standards, published in 2004 by the Basel Committee on Banking Supervision on behalf of the G-10 countries. This international financial standard has gone through different versions (Basel I, II, and III), but the point has always been to set standards for the amount of capital that a bank must possess, as a function of its assets. Capital gives a bank the ability to withstand losses without becoming insolvent, and thus imparts stability to the financial system.

Well-capitalized banks are stronger banks. But bank managers will be tempted to minimize regulatory capital as a way to leverage higher profits. A capital standard provides a "floor" below which a bank cannot go. The importance of the Basel standard reflects the shift of bank regulation from the national to the international level and the fact that many financial institutions now operate at a global level.[183] Originally, regulations were set by the jurisdiction in which a bank was domiciled: an Illinois-chartered bank was subject to Illinois regulations; a federally chartered bank was overseen by the Office of the Comptroller of the Currency, and later on by the Federal Reserve Board or FDIC. But as banking globalized, as banks assembled assets and liabilities across different countries and multiple jurisdictions, some measure of coordination became necessary if regulations were to be effective. Financial regulators in the United States were particularly motivated by the experience of the Mexican Debt Crisis of the early 1980s, which severely threatened a number of very large U.S. banks with substantial Mexican exposures, and by a rising tide of bank failures.[184] But to raise capital standards unilaterally would have put U.S. banks at a competitive disadvantage in relation to foreign banks subject to less onerous requirements. Multilateral standards solved this problem by ensuring that all the international banks from all the major financial centers had to comply with the same standard at roughly the same time.

Setting minimal capital requirements was a traditional way to ensure bank soundness: it kept the bank afloat if too many of the promises it had accepted went awry. In the Basel era, the level of capital required depended on the amount, type, and riskiness of the assets that the bank possessed. Riskier assets required more capital. According to the Basel I standard, set in 1987, banks had to possess capital equal to 8 percent of their risk-weighted assets, where assets that were considered "riskless" (e.g., cash and bullion) were given a 0 percent risk weight. Riskier assets were given a higher weight and so required more capital. But banks subject to this standard soon figured out ways to evade it (via "regulatory arbitrage"). For example, Basel I encouraged banks to reduce their capital requirements by using "off balance sheet" vehicles to pursue risky investments or through the securitization of bank assets.[185] The Asian Financial Crisis demonstrated the continuing importance of institutional financial stability, so Basel I was updated.[186]

The Basel II standard, set in 2004, provided a menu of possibilities for banks, allowed for more complicated risk weights, and in particular allowed banks to use either external ratings (issued by agencies like Moody's or Standard and Poor's) or internal ratings (created by the bank itself) in setting risk weights.[187] While the Basel Committee on Banking Supervision offered some oversight about what constituted a viable internal rating system, banks nevertheless enjoyed considerable leeway over how to model risks and how to aggregate them up to the portfolio level.[188] The new capital standard was designed to encourage banks to develop their own internal rating systems, on the grounds that these improved private risk management and lessened reliance on regulators. However, the limits of these internal systems, even the most sophisticated, became abundantly clear in 2008. Financial institutions were hit hard by price drops, market shifts, and default rates that, according to their own models, were extraordinarily improbable (so-called "tail events" or "black swans"). This led to some soul searching about overconfidence in quantitative models and the inadequacies of various modeling strategies.

Politics and Banking

After the disastrous wave of failures in the early 1930s, New Deal regulations helped stabilize banks and other financial institutions, and for several decades the number of failures was very low. Depositors could trust that their money was safe in a bank, and most banks operated in a relatively stable market environment. Yet the civil rights movement posed again the issue of economic inequality between white and black Americans, whether the banking system played a role in creating inequality, and whether it could help solve the problem. African Americans in urban areas remained underserved by banks and other financial institutions, and people considered again the role that black-owned banks might play in solving the problem. During the 1960s and in response to a combination of government encouragement, political pressure, and black economic nationalism, the number of black-owned banks grew from eleven in 1963 to twenty-two in 1969.[189] Despite doubling in number, such banks remained a tiny proportion of the overall population of commercial banks, and they tended to be small, undercapitalized, and unprofitable. More such banks were founded during the 1970s, but a high proportion of them failed and they were either closed down or merged with white-owned banks. Despite early hopes, they did not serve as powerful engines of economic development in black communities.[190] Racial wealth and income inequality endured, and urban blacks continued to have to use non-banks for many of their financial services. Federal legislation like the Community Reinvestment Act of 1977 and the Home Mortgage Disclosure Act of 1975 tried to change the behavior of white-owned banks, but as chapter 7's discussion of mortgage lending discrimination will show, the results were unimpressive. Minority exclusion from credit continued.[191]

A different kind of politics led to deregulation of the financial sector. Starting in the 1980s a number of key New Deal provisions were relaxed or repealed. For example, Regulation Q, instituted in 1933, prohibited interest payments on checking accounts and capped the interest that could be paid on savings accounts. As market interest rates rose during the 1970s, this created severe difficulties for banks and savings-and-loans since depositors looked elsewhere for a better rate of return, sometimes putting money into a NOW or money market account.[192] And so depository institutions started to lose their depositors. For institutions locked into long-term assets like home mortgages, the financial pressure became intense. The result was that starting with the 1980 Depository Institutions Deregulation and Monetary Control Act, interest rate regulations were weakened. But this was only the beginning of much broader deregulatory changes. The separation between commercial and investment banking weakened and disappeared with the full repeal of the Glass-Steagall Act in 1999. Banks increasingly were able to offer a full range of financial services, far beyond taking deposits and making loans. Branch banking and interstate banking became common as restrictions on branch banking were relaxed or removed entirely, and a long series of mergers and acquisitions produced some truly large banks while at the same time many small community banks disappeared.[193] The unregulated status of the growing over-the-counter (OTC) derivatives market was affirmed with ever greater conviction, and so core actors in that market, the big dealer-banks, could act without fear of regulatory oversight.[194] And a large and largely unregulated "shadow banking" system developed to mobilize and invest savings, performing many banking functions and transacting with banks, but without official status as a bank. As Matthias Thiemann shows in the case of the asset-backed commercial paper market, securitization was one of the signature activities performed by "shadow banks" as they evaded official oversight, building up unregulated risks that unraveled in 2008.[195]

Conclusion

Banks play a central role in the economy of promises. This is chiefly because they specialize in the evaluation and acceptance of borrowers' promises. How they do so, and to whom they do so, has evolved in significant ways. But the credit they extend supports business activity, public policy, and consumer spending, and so banks have been and continue to be key organizations within the U.S. financial system.

Banks are creatures of law that enable economic activity and contribute to domestic economic development.[196] In general terms, they intermediate between savers and borrowers. Early on, state-chartered private banks were often encumbered with financial obligations that were intended to help grow the state economy: they were required to make certain kinds of loans to support certain kinds of activity. States encouraged the founding of banks in newly settled regions by setting low standards and restricting competition among them, even though this produced weakly capitalized banks that were especially vulnerable in a crisis. But despite these deficiencies, the financial services they provided were too useful. The system of national banks created during the Civil War was directly tied to the success of the Union government in its military struggle with the South. And later, the Federal Reserve System was established in the wake of the 1907 crisis to help stabilize the financial system and mitigate the financial panics that dogged the U.S. economy.[197] For their entire history, U.S. banks have rarely acted as purely private parties: they have always engaged public policy and political purpose.

Making loans involved accepting promises and granting purchasing power to debtors. Banks specialized in judging the creditworthiness of borrowers and in assessing the promises they made. From a very local starting point, banks scaled up their operations and so accumulated a great deal of formal and informal information about borrowers. Early on, they necessarily relied on informal information obtained through personal contacts and social networks. But starting in the late nineteenth century, they began to supplement this with formal information that exploited the newly created credit rating system, the spread of standardized financial and accounting measures, and the ability to track an individual's credit history. Judgments about the trustworthiness of a borrower expanded beyond character to include balance sheets, profit-and-loss statements, earnings, and bounced checks. Some of the informal information dissipated, however, as deregulation set off waves of consolidations and mergers, forging large banking systems out of small networks and individual banks. The latter were repositories for local knowledge about local communities and got lost as they were integrated into the large-scale information systems that large banks necessarily relied upon.[198] And as banks embraced securitization, they shifted from an "originate-to-hold" to an "originate-to-distribute" business model, earning short-term profits from fees generated via high-volume securitizations and becoming less concerned about long-term earnings from the interest that performing loans paid.[199]

5

Individual and Consumer Credit

Much of the development of credit in the United States since the nineteenth century has involved the expansion of individual or consumer credit. Businesses have always been embedded in credit networks, borrowing from some while lending to others. But households faced their own credit constraints and increasingly individuals are making promises that others can accept or reject. The growth of household credit, and the role it played in the development of a mass consumer economy, constituted an important part of the economy of promises. If a platinum Visa card symbolizes contemporary consumerism, however, credit for households long preceded the invention of the credit card or other modern forms of credit. Going into debt has been familiar to ordinary people for centuries.

Debt used to bear a particular cultural stigma. In the late eighteenth and early nineteenth centuries, to be indebted was a type of subservience and was sometimes likened to slavery.[1] Debts undermined the independence of farmers and workers and threatened their social status. Extreme indebtedness could put someone in a position of debt servitude, utterly beholden to a creditor. Indebtedness also signaled a person's failure to uphold key values of thrift and self-control. Someone who spent beyond their means lacked personal discipline and self-restraint. So debt was something to be avoided, if possible, and otherwise to be minimized. Debts were variably problematic, however, depending on their purpose. Debts accumulated for productive activity (investing in a business or farm) could be acceptable under certain circumstances, whereas debts taken on simply to fund "unproductive" personal consumption were not.

Despite being heavily stigmatized at the outset, the extent and diversity of household debt grew over time. In different ways and for different purposes, lenders devised new methods to provide credit to individuals, and people found new reasons to borrow. Debt shed some of its problematic cultural baggage. Since there were so many more families than corporations or firms, consumer credit has generally involved larger numbers of smaller loans than business credit. This has meant that the cost and effort of making a loan to an individual are generally higher in proportion to the total value of the loan than for business loans. Since the profit earned on a loan traditionally depends on the size of the principal, small personal loans are therefore relatively expensive to make as compared to large business loans. The incentive to make high-volume consumer credit feasible meant that lenders particularly welcomed the invention of consumer credit scoring, automated underwriting, the application of statistical methods to credit assessment, or other innovations that routinized and simplified the loan process. The quantification of credit has become particularly advanced for consumers, to the point where most adults living in the United States have their own FICO score and a credit history tracked by one or more of the major credit reporting agencies, TransUnion, Experian, or Equifax. Furthermore, consumer credit has typically paired an experienced lender possessing a large loan portfolio with a much less knowledgeable borrower who lacks experience in how such transactions unfold. Legally, the loan contract presumes that the two sides are equals, but in reality they are not.

In the early nineteenth century, most U.S. households were units of consumption and production. Especially in the rural areas where most people lived, a farm household produced a variety of agricultural products, consumed some of them directly, and sold or exchanged the balance. Many of the inputs required for production were obtained on the market (e.g., seed, fertilizer, tools, and machinery). Cash crops like cotton or tobacco were almost exclusively produced for the market. Rural households were not completely self-sufficient on the consumption side, either, and so they purchased foodstuffs, dry goods, clothing, and home furnishings. And the uneven flow of income and expenditure followed a seasonal rhythm: springtime meant buying seed and fertilizer, but not until the fall harvest could the crops be sold for cash. Consumption, by contrast, happened year-round. Farm families would typically borrow in the spring and repay their debts in the fall. In a good year, they might have some savings left over, while in a bad year they could accumulate debts that rolled over into the next crop season. By the mid-twentieth century, however, most U.S. households no longer lived in rural or farming areas, and they were no longer units of production. Rather, adult members of the household worked full-time as employees; by spending their wages they acquired the goods and services necessary to support themselves and their families.

To sustain themselves as units of social reproduction,[2] households have to reconcile earnings and expenditures. Household resource inflows have to match or exceed the outflows, with the latter dependent on the size and composition of the household. Wages, unfortunately, can be highly variable in the short run. People are hired and fired, promoted and demoted, depending on the local labor market. Their hours-worked may vary from week to week, or they may shift between temporary, part-time, and permanent full-time positions. Some part of their earnings might be stable (an annual salary) and another part variable (a bonus). Or if they work on commission, their income is entirely variable. By contrast, household spending tends to be relatively stable. Family members need to eat and be housed and clothed, and except for unexpected expenses driven by things like illness, most spending is predictable.[3] And aside from changes caused by births, deaths, and weddings, household membership also tends to be fairly stable.[4] Over a year, a family of four generally remains a family of four. Variable income combined with stable spending means that the two will often not equal each other. In the happy event that income exceeds spending, the household can save. And indeed, over a lifetime individuals may try to save while they are working so that they can build up savings for their retirement or to make major purchases.[5] But what happens when income drops below spending? Either the household uses accumulated savings to cover the shortfall or it borrows to make up the difference. Tapping into savings can bridge a temporary deficit, but eventually the savings run out.

Not all households are equally exposed to income variation. For households dependent on market wages, the proverbial "good steady job" meant relatively stable income over long periods of time. Temporary, seasonal, contingent, interim, "freelance," or otherwise irregular work, on the other hand, often produced highly unpredictable earnings.[6] Some households have a single wage earner; some have more than one. The chances that household income varies in ways that produce unexpected shortfalls depend very much on job quality: marginal or low-income work puts people at greater risk of having to borrow. And their low earnings give them less margin for error. Public policy can stabilize incomes if, for example, a government offers unemployment benefits to maintain income even when a wage earner becomes unemployed. But for much of American history there were no such programs, nor have they fully replaced wages lost due to unemployment, and they only covered limited periods of unemployment. This has meant that many Americans have had to look to credit markets, prior savings, or their social networks as ways to maintain consumption and support their households.

Banks were relative latecomers to consumer finance (see chapter 4). During the nineteenth century and well into the twentieth, banks didn't make direct personal loans.[7] An individual might borrow from a bank to fund their business enterprise but not to pay for their personal or household consumption. Business loans were considered "productive," while personal loans were not. So for many decades the story of consumer finance did not directly involve banks. Other organizations and institutions loaned to households and individuals.

One of the earliest forms of household credit was also one of the most informal: store or book credit. This was credit extended directly from a store to its customers, or from a merchant to their clients, and it allowed buyers to acquire goods from a specific supplier, giving a promise instead of cash at the time of purchase and paying later.[8] Households needed goods for both production and consumption, so the items purchased on credit might include agricultural supplies and dry goods (clothing, household items, etc.) or foodstuffs. Book credit didn't involve banks, promissory notes, or formal contracts.[9] The store owner tracked the debt as a running balance kept in a ledger book or in his or her head. And credit was extended not necessarily because a customer was insolvent or experiencing financial difficulties but rather because cash in general was scarce, and cash incomes highly irregular. Credit was a necessary part of doing business, and although merchants could deny credit to some, they couldn't deny credit to all and still have customers. For example, a detailed look at the books of a store in West Feliciana Parish in Louisiana during the 1850s shows that credit sales consistently outpaced cash sales through all four seasons of the year, even as sales ebbed and flowed.[10]

Book credit usually flowed between members of the same local community, and social norms governed its extension and acceptance.[11] Obligations would be settled intermittently, perhaps in goods or services rather than in cash, and in light of the personal circumstances of the debtor as well as the social tie between debtor and creditor. Embedded in the same social networks, people knew a great deal about each other and social reputations, whether for honesty, dishonesty, forbearance, or severity, were easily circulated. Membership in a particular religious group could be taken as a significant marker of trustworthiness.[12] Personal character was the lens through which lenders perceived creditworthiness.[13] These social patterns applied even for debts that weren't settled in an orderly fashion. Mann's study (1987: 17) found that 90 percent of the disputes over book debt in colonial Connecticut were between people in the same county, and about 60 percent involved people from the same town. Such debts were non-assignable (unlike negotiable securities) and therefore so long as they were outstanding, they bound together the same debtor and the creditor. Unlike a bond or a promissory note, a creditor could not transfer the debt to someone else. In this way, credit relations added to the tapestry of social ties that bound communities together. But such ties could be positive or negative. Some were solidaristic and brought people together, but others separated them. Race, for example, divided communities and those cleavages manifested in the extension of credit. In places like Texas and Oklahoma, stores carefully tracked the racial identities of their customers, noting in their ledgers who was black and which customers were members of Native American tribes.[14]

Similar credit arrangements were common in the postbellum South, although the social consequences were different. As in other regions, Southern store merchants regularly extended credit to local farming households, which had to await cash earned from the fall harvest to pay their debts.[15] If the debtor couldn't fully repay, the debt might be "rolled over" and accumulate over multiple years. Merchants often obtained a lien over the farmer's crop to collateralize the loan. Many Southern states passed crop lien laws in order to facilitate lending and help plantation owners obtain credit, but one effect was to encourage cultivation of cash crops like cotton, which could easily be used as collateral.[16] Furthermore, control over credit gave rural merchants a great deal of power over local debtors, and the interest rates they charged were high enough that compounded debts were hard to escape.[17] Southern landlords used credit relations as a way to maintain power over the sharecroppers who rented their land, including former slaves and their descendants.[18]

In the postbellum South, debt resubordinated people. Combined with vagrancy laws, penal codes, the convict lease system, crop liens, and criminalization of breach of contract, debt peonage laws enabled Southern white elites to keep newly freed ex-slaves, and their descendants, in virtual servitude.[19] In this context, credit was not an empowering way for borrowers to manage their own consumption or to protect their families from volatile earnings. It offered none of the benefits of "financial inclusion" but rather enacted a form of dependency. Debt servitude clearly subordinated borrowers to lenders. Debt peonage also occurred in the Southwest, in regions that were formerly part of Spanish Mexico. Slavery and involuntary servitude were abolished by the Thirteenth Amendment to the U.S. Constitution, and the Peonage Act of 1867 was intended to end debt peonage, but the coercive use of debt to subordinate domestic populations continued for decades.[20]

Despite the use of credit as an instrument of social control in the postbellum South, in other situations it served largely commercial purposes. Throughout all regions of the United States, and well into the twentieth century, stores continued to supply book credit directly to their customers.[21] From the standpoint of the retailer, the extension of credit was necessary to sell goods and as such was a common business practice. Knapp's study of retail credit in Nebraska in the early 1920s found that more than half of purchases made at furniture, grocery, hardware, and clothing stores were done on credit.[22] To insist on cash for every transaction would have excluded many customers and cut into sales. A merchant had to monitor retail credit carefully, however, so as not to become overextended: bad debts could accumulate and overwhelm the business. The big department stores and department store chains that developed in the late nineteenth century (e.g., Marshall Field's, Sears, Penney's, Macy's) also extended credit to selected customers,[23] but to do so on a national scale required a high level of formality. Such organizations solicited financial information and kept systematic credit files on their customers. Mail-order mass retailers like Spiegel's also used credit to fuel their sales of household and other goods to a national customer base.[24] For convenience, some stores began to issue to their most creditworthy customers a physical card that the customer would present when making a purchase. And so, the charge card was born.

Retailers and Department Stores

General stores provided credit to individual buyers in rural areas, while in the cities and suburbs, specialized retailers, department stores, and mail-order firms serviced consumers. They faced the same constraint: it was hard to succeed in retail and not give credit to customers.[25] Success meant more customers, and soon the numbers of people, their payment histories and financial circumstances, became far more than a single person could remember. Hence, the birth of specialized credit departments and retail credit reporting agencies in the late nineteenth century. The latter typically focused on a particular city or specialized in a specific trade, and they gathered two kinds of information about individuals, negative and positive.[26] Negative information recorded bankruptcies, insolvencies, bounced checks, defaults, failures, late payments, and so on. From a creditor's standpoint, these events were not equally serious (bankruptcy was much worse than just a late payment), but their occurrence always diminished the standing of a potential borrower. Positive information, by contrast, recorded accomplishments like debts fully repaid and on time, checks that cleared, positive bank balances, stable employment, and so on. These all signaled that a potential borrower was a good risk. Individual credit agencies accumulated such information and provided it to local merchants, either in a comprehensive reference book or as individual reports. Most agencies were run on a for-profit basis, so they sold information to their clients, but some agencies were organized on a cooperative basis and provided information as a service to member retailers from the local business community.[27] Either way, clients or member firms were expected to provide ledger information about their own customers, as input for individual credit records, so that agencies could pool the accumulated experience of multiple retailers about an individual.

Although they started out as local operations primarily serving local retailers, credit agencies and their employees were quick to form alliances and create national organizations, including the National Association of Credit Men (founded in 1896), the National Association of Retail Credit Agencies (1906), and the Retail Credit Men's National Association (1912).[28] These organizations helped institutionalize credit rating on a national scale, diffusing methods and practices. The expansion of interregional commerce encouraged the formation of partnerships between agencies in different parts of the country. Through a process of expansion and acquisition, a small number of them eventually grew to become some of today's dominant agencies.[29]

Credit agencies, like the mercantile agencies that focused on small businesses, were in the information business. The volume of data they accumulated went far beyond the capabilities of human memory, and so their core assets consisted of files. The completeness and timeliness of credit file information were critical to the success of an agency. The organization of the files and the speed with which information could be retrieved mattered a great deal, and as one specialist put it: "The credit department cannot have too much information."[30] Credit agencies, like banks, utilized state-of-the-art information technology, which in the late nineteenth century consisted of vertical files, filing cabinets, index cards, memos, reports, standardized forms, copies in triplicate, typewriters, and carbon paper.[31] This informational apparatus was deployed to estimate an individual borrower's willingness and ability to repay a debt. And here, as in so many other types of credit, personal character was the critical feature.[32] Since agencies seldom had personal knowledge of the borrower, they relied on a number of other sources who might, including bankers, merchants, and attorneys. Some key facts could signal character: homeownership, marital status (married men were deemed more creditworthy than single men), occupation (college professors and schoolteachers were more reliable), and job tenure.[33]

   Credit departments, like credit agencies, accumulated and managed information. But they did so only for the firm of which they were a part, typically a department store, mail-order seller, or other large retailer. They often subscribed to the services of credit agencies and accessed various outside sources of information.[34] Spiegel's, a large mail-order firm that had to process thousands of orders in a short amount of time, did its initial credit assessment on the basis of only five variables: order size, occupation, marital status, race, and customer location.[35] Primarily, credit departments used their own customer files, tracking each buyer for how reliably they paid their bills and managed the credit extended to them. Like credit agencies, credit departments embraced the latest information management systems, built around paper files stored in filing cabinets. In tracking creditworthiness, credit departments sometimes disagreed with the sales department, which always understood that the generous extension of credit was good for sales and customer relations, even if it did risk lending to a person who defaulted.[36] Customers who paid cash could easily switch from one store to another, but credit bound the customer to a particular seller.[37] Furthermore, firms prioritized customers who were creditworthy but who seldom used credit: such persons offered a profitable opportunity and in targeting them retailers learned how to extend credit to people who didn't necessarily want it.[38]

The Installment Plan

Another important form of credit emerged after the middle of the nineteenth century, associated with the sale of durable manufactured goods. These were large, expensive items that ordinarily would require a household to accumulate a substantial sum in order to make a purchase. The necessity for families to save first in order to buy later delayed sales and might even curtail them. It isn't clear where the idea originated, but installment loans enabled sellers to extend credit to buyers, in effect earmarking a loan for one specific purchase. The borrower could use the money only to acquire a durable good from the supplier. The earliest goods sold on installment plans included Singer Sewing machines, agricultural machinery, pianos, and encyclopedias.[39] Later, installment plans were used to sell household appliances like washing machines, radios, refrigerators, and so on. Sellers set the terms of the transaction on a take-it-or-leave-it basis in a standardized contract (sometimes called a "conditional sales contract"). Although details varied, the basic plan required the purchaser to make an initial "down payment" and then to make a series of payments at regular intervals to cover the balance. The purchaser took possession right after the down payment and so could use the item even before it was fully paid for. In other words, the buyer could act like an owner of an asset, even before establishing title over the property. The balance due on the loan was a form of credit extended from the seller to the buyer.

Installment loans were advantageous to lenders in a number of respects. Most obviously, installment loans promoted sales of large, expensive goods.[40] A consumer who couldn't afford an item would be loaned the money to make the purchase, and such credit boosted sales. Second, the commodity sold served as collateral for the loan. Should the purchaser fail to make a payment, the seller could repossess the item and the buyer would lose whatever money he or she had already paid.[41] Since installment credit didn't conform to the traditional definition of a loan, it wasn't subject to usury laws and so the interest rate could easily exceed the legal maximum. In fact, it was easy to disguise the full cost of an installment purchase, so consumers often didn't know the real price.[42] With installment loans, consumers often consented to opaque arrangements and in effect made promises that they didn't fully understand. These arrangements were highly formalized, involving written agreements and standardized contracts, and sellers did not require detailed knowledge of the buyer's personality or character. If the lender deemed a particular buyer to be a greater credit risk, or if the value of the good depreciated rapidly after purchase, the size of the initial down payment could simply be adjusted upward.[43] For purchasers, the attractions of the installment arrangement were obvious: buy now and pay later. There was no need for deferred gratification.

In the early twentieth century, installment lending played a key role in making the automobile a mass consumer item and eventually in refiguring the landscape of American society. With the automobile as the primary mode of transportation, networks of roads and highways expanded, urban regions "suburbanized," and a new way of life, built around the car, became possible. At first, cars were luxury items that required assiduous savings if an average family were to buy one in cash. Saving was a hurdle that many could not surmount. Automobile dealers quickly realized that financing sales via credit would enable more families to afford a car, and so the industry embraced installment loans. The transition was dramatic: before 1913 most cars were purchased with cash, but by 1920 almost two-thirds of new car sales were financed with credit.[44] Indeed, overall installment lending in the United States came to be dominated by the auto industry. By 1929, over half of all installment loans involved car dealers.[45] And at the same time, 64 percent of all new and used car sales were made on installment plans.[46] This system of credit helped turn the automobile from a luxury good enjoyed by only a few into a mass-produced and mass-consumed good that was a part of almost every household. The proportion of families owning cars increased from about 1 percent in 1910 to 60 percent by 1930.[47] It also helped turn the automobile industry into one of the cornerstones of America's industrial economy.

Although they increased sales, installment loans nevertheless put automobile dealers on the horns of a dilemma. In the 1920s and 1930s the typical maturity for a car loan was twelve or eighteen months.[48] Lending to large numbers of customers tied up substantial amounts of capital for at least a year, and since dealers had to pay for the cars they received from car manufacturers (which were not equipped themselves to sell to dealers on credit), dealers were in a financial bind. Car dealerships were not like banks, able to use deposits to make loans: instead, they had to lend, but couldn't borrow. What emerged was a complex system involving another specialized firm, the sales finance company, which helped to finance both the automobile inventories held by dealers and the installment loans used by consumers to purchase automobiles.[49] Sales finance companies like the Commercial Credit Company and CIT Financial Corporation began their operations in the 1910s as the car market expanded and grew to dominate the industry. They would purchase installment loans (or "paper") from the dealers, providing cash in exchange for the right to the revenue stream generated by the car loan repayments. Dealers could sell on credit, buyers could buy on credit, and the total volume of car sales grew. Before long, General Motors established its own sales financing operation, the General Motors Acceptance Corporation (GMAC).

Sales finance companies spread beyond the automobile industry, although that remained a center of their activity. During the 1920s, they became involved in other installment lending activities, applying methods perfected for cars to the sale of radios, refrigerators, washing machines, home furnaces, and other durable goods for the household. They even moved out of consumer lending and helped finance the sale of capital goods to businesses.[50] In every instance, they enabled lenders to offer more credit by "buying" loans from the lenders, and having the same effect as when a contemporary bank "securitizes" its loans.[51] Mass consumption became a possibility thanks to installment loans funded by sales finance companies. Outside of installment credit for consumers, a similar system developed to fund business inventory and receivables.[52]

The emergence of sales finance companies weakened the links between consumer debtors and creditors. Rather than receiving credit directly from a local business owner, someone from the borrower's own community, loans were designed, extended, and managed by bureaucratic financing organizations with no personal connection to the debtor. Installment loans were also relatively standardized, offered to borrowers on a take-it-or-leave-it basis and not negotiated individually. These "arm's-length" arrangements made it harder to adjust the initial terms or to be subsequently flexible and offer forbearance should the debtor get into financial trouble. But they were readily scalable. When a sales finance firm became involved, the originating creditor would be replaced by some other entity, to whom the debtor was obliged. Availability of installment loans encouraged households to go into debt because they made it easy to buy desirable consumer goods, and the periodic payments that such loans required dovetailed with a population increasingly dependent on wage labor as its primary source of income. Permanent full-time employees who received regular wages could reliably service their debts, and so employment status augmented personal character as the basis for a loan. In fact, some installment loan contracts used the borrower's future wages as security for the loan. In a "wage assignment" arrangement, the lender had priority access to the borrower's wages, no matter what other household needs might apply. These and other aspects of installment loans were abused by some lenders and prompted calls for regulation to protect borrowers.[53]

Finance companies continue to play an important role in consumer finance.[54] At the end of 2015, they were the third largest institutional providers of consumer credit, after banks and the federal government. It is now a highly concentrated industry with a small number of large firms accounting for most of the activity, and such firms continue to specialize in specific types of credit: car loans, non-vehicle consumer loans, real estate, or business credit.[55] Since they are not banks, finance companies do not take deposits as a way to raise funds. Instead, in addition to their own equity they rely on nonrecourse borrowing (relying on loans secured with collateral) and issuance of notes, bonds, and debentures. And they generally either finance consumer purchases or make direct loans to consumers.

Cash Loans

This type of credit best exemplifies what we ordinarily think of as a "loan" and gives the borrower the unrestrained purchasing power of legal tender: money that can be spent however the borrower chooses. Unlike installment loans or store credit, which involve loans that are specifically devoted to a consumer purchase, cash is open-ended. Because cash represents *generalized* purchasing power, after the loan is made the lender has little control over how the borrower uses the money. While sellers were willing to fund sales to consumers, profiting from both the sale and interest on the loan, cash loans to individuals were slower to develop.

Whereas store credit often had a predictable yearly pattern (farmers borrowed in the spring to repay in the fall, or people borrowed to fund Christmas gifts and repaid in the new year), the need for cash might arise unexpectedly.[56] A child fell seriously ill and so the family faced unusual medical expenses. A parent died and so the children had to deal with funeral expenses. Or a wage earner was laid off from work, or worked fewer hours than usual, and so the family's income was interrupted. Of course, some people had insurance to deal with such risks, but in the nineteenth century and well into the twentieth, most people lacked private insurance, public insurance schemes didn't exist, and some risks were not yet insurable. Households and families had to deal with unpleasant surprises on their own, and in the absence of savings, the obvious solution was to borrow.

The pawnshop was one traditional source of cash, operating for many centuries in different countries and provoking little political concern in the United States. A person who owned a valuable object could use it to secure a short-term cash loan, allowing the pawnbroker to keep the object until the loan was repaid. Only some kinds of objects were suitable in the eyes of the pawnbroker: if the borrower failed to repay, the "pawn" functioned as collateral and so would be sold by the broker to recover the value of the loan.[57] Hence, the object had to be something with an easily estimated market value. The size of the loan varied with the local market value of the pawn, as judged by the lender, and typical objects included jewelry, silverplate, anything made of precious metal, musical instruments, tools, and so on.[58]

The borrower continued to own the object but had to forgo possession until the loan was fully repaid. While loss of use was a disadvantage, pawnshops could be a source of quick cash and borrowing this way involved minimal formalities.[59] A borrower in greater need could increase the size of the loan simply by pawning a more valuable object, or if facing a recurrent need for cash, could pawn the same object several times. In addition, the lender only had to estimate the worth of the pawned object; it was not necessary to assess the creditworthiness of the borrower.[60] If the borrower didn't repay the loan as and when due, the lender kept the pawn.[61]

Some specialized financial institutions serviced particular ethnic groups. Only members of the group were eligible to borrow, but for those who could, these offered timely money to deal with a problem. For example, starting in the 1880s Hebrew Free Loan Societies were established in a number of U.S. cities, founded by Jewish immigrant groups.[62] These operated well into the twentieth century, and until other sources for personal credit developed, loan societies were a significant source of cash.[63] The funds could be used for commercial purposes (to start a small business) or to deal with personal emergencies. In New York City, the loan society required that the loan be endorsed by a sponsor, who was responsible for the loan if the borrower failed to repay.[64] Other groups made use of informal financial institutions like rotating credit associations, where small sums were regularly pooled together within a group and the resulting lump sum given to one of the members.[65] Pooling continued until every member had enjoyed their turn receiving the lump sum. These institutions used preexisting ethnic and religious social bonds to render more credible the promises that group members made. Through such vehicles, group members loaned money to each other. Some informal activities also functioned like financial institutions, although that was not the intention. Illegal gambling (the "numbers racket"), for example, effectively mobilized and pooled savings within the black community.[66]

Pawnshops and ethnic institutions could help, but households that needed cash loans in short order mostly lacked good alternatives at the end of the nineteenth century. Pawnshops required that the borrower surrender a valuable object, and many poor households had nothing worth pawning. And ethnically based arrangements were only available to people with the right ethnicity. One unfortunate alternative was the "loan shark." Loan sharks operated illegally and coercively, charging interest rates far in excess of statutory limits. But for people in dire straits, there was nowhere else to turn, and the high interest rates frequently trapped debtors into a situation

that only got worse. Once publicly identified, the "problem" of loan sharking prompted a general political conversation about the situation of wage
earners in America and whether public policy could protect workers as borrowers from predatory lenders.[67] The policy debate prompted a variety of
legal and institutional innovations.

Loan sharking came into the national public eye in the early twentieth
century, was extensively discussed in newspaper articles and social science
journals, and was roundly condemned by policy advocates.[68] Although most
states had usury laws that set interest rate limits, enforcement was a problem
and the laws proved easy to evade. Lenders could attach fees, discount their
loans, bundle loans with other transactions, or find other ways to boost the
cost of a loan well beyond any statutory limit. Although distressed borrowers
were willing (if not eager) to pay the high interest rates a loan shark charged,
these rates were widely viewed as exploitative and illegitimate. The imbalance of power between lender and borrower seemed especially extreme.
Loan sharks preyed on the ignorance of borrowers, who failed to understand the onerous terms they consented to, and repayment was frequently
enforced by threats of violence.[69] Loan sharks gained additional leverage
over borrowers because, in this period, many big employers would dismiss
an employee that they knew to be borrowing from a loan shark. Railroad
workers were identified as being particularly vulnerable to loan sharks, in
part because they were paid a regular wage.[70] Loan sharks would frequently
insist on a wage assignment as security for the loan, allowing them to siphon
repayments directly from the borrower's salary.[71] Loan sharks were classic
examples of "predatory lending."

Political opposition to loan sharking coalesced around the Russell Sage
Foundation (RSF), a newly established organization based in New York City
that used "scientific philanthropy" to address social problems. For various
reasons, the RSF decided to focus on the problem of credit for poor people,
using loan sharks as a convenient target.[72] Given the ineffectiveness of usury
laws, the RSF's strategy was to encourage legitimate lenders to enter the
market for small cash loans and drive out the loan sharks. The demand side
of the market would undoubtedly persist because poor people would always
have need for emergency loans, but the RSF's reformers thought they could
induce change on the supply side. Early on, the RSF supported remedial loan
societies and the establishment of credit unions, but before long it settled
on the Uniform Small Loan Law (USLL) as the chief instrument for helping
small loan borrowers. The goal of this law was to regulate small loans (worth
$300 or less) in such a way as to encourage the entry of legitimate lenders into

the market and so push out the loan sharks. The RSF designed a model law that it updated repeatedly, fine-tuning the law on the basis of experience, and urged states around the country to adopt it. By 1930 over two-thirds of the states had passed the USLL.[73] The law allowed lenders to charge a monthly interest rate that compounded to a 42 percent annual rate, but it prohibited additional fees and mandated transparent and standardized loan terms: the borrower would really know what he or she was getting into. In other words, the promises that small loan borrowers could make under the auspices of the USLL would be standardized and simplified to prevent predatory outcomes and render them more transparent to borrowers. The USLL also required that lenders be licensed and bonded, and subject to inspection.

While it is hard to know how much the USLL directly improved the conditions of small loan borrowers, at the same time a new group of legitimate lenders entered the market and expanded their operations.[74] Known as personal finance companies, or sometimes as "industrial lenders,"[75] these lenders formed an industry group, the American Association of Personal Finance Companies, which worked with the RSF to lobby state governors and legislators to pass the USLL. They supported the USLL because it allowed them to lend at high interest rates, well above the caps set by extant usury laws,[76] but without enduring the dishonor of loan sharking. Personal finance companies, most prominently the Household Finance Corporation,[77] soon provided a substantial amount of small loan credit to U.S. families.[78]

Loans from personal finance companies often involved "chattel mortgages." That is, to reduce the vulnerability of the lender the loan was secured by personal property of the borrower deemed suitable to function as collateral. This was often a large piece of furniture or a piano, and it could both motivate the debtor to repay and compensate the creditor if he or she didn't repay.[79] However, unlike with pawnshops, this property remained in the possession of its owner,[80] and unlike with installment loans, credit didn't necessarily fund a specific purchase. Personal finance companies might also obtain a "wage assignment," giving them the contractual right to garnish the debtor's wages.[81] In deciding whether to make a loan, the lender would assess the value of the proffered collateral but also the character and familial situation of the borrower, as well as his or her income and employment status.[82]

Remedial loans were another strategy supported, for a time, by the RSF.[83] These consisted of small loans made at below-market rates by a charitable organization. There were a handful of such lenders, with the most prominent being the Provident Loan Society of New York. Founded in 1894, this institution functioned like a charitable pawnshop: it made small loans to customers on the basis of articles they pledged, at interest rates half those charged by for-profit pawnshops. In its first two years of operation, the Provident Loan Society made over 63,000 loans at 1 percent per month, with the average loan being for $18.50.[84] No one expected that this institution could by itself satisfy all the demand for small loans, because it clearly didn't have the financial capacity. Rather, the hope was that by offering a more competitive interest rate it could force other pawnshops to lower their interest rates.[85] However, remedial lenders were too small and few to have a significant impact.

Credit unions were a cooperative nonprofit financial institution that originated in Germany in the nineteenth century and was "imported" into the United States via Quebec, Canada.[86] The model credit union was usually based on a common employer, either a large private firm or public sector organization,[87] and people were eligible to participate because of their common employment status. A credit union pooled the savings of its members, and then made loans to its members, using its knowledge of their personality, earnings, and financial situation to determine who was creditworthy and to ensure repayment. The membership owned the credit union. In other words, credit unions were built on top of preexisting social groupings, among people united by work and community.[88] Through the organizational vehicle of the credit union, group members issued promises to each other.

The RSF was an early supporter of credit unions but it decided to focus on the USLL. In part, this was because a different philanthropic foundation, Edward Filene's Twentieth Century Fund, endorsed credit unions and provided vigorous support for many decades.[89] Credit unions were an organizational form new to the United States that required enabling legislation at the state level, and so a great deal of energy was devoted to getting states to pass the necessary laws. By the mid-1930s, the Credit Union National Association had sponsored credit union bills that passed in forty states.[90] And in 1934, Congress passed a law allowing for the federal chartering of credit unions. By 1938–39, there were around 8,500 credit union offices nationwide, and credit unions loaned out $279 million in 1939.[91] The number of state and federal credit unions grew steadily and by the mid-1950s there were roughly 8,000 of each, with a total of around 8 million members.[92]

Credit unions gave their members encouragement to save but also met their demands for cash loans. Froman (1935: 293) noted that the four most common reasons why people borrowed from their credit union were to pay for medical and family expenses, to purchase coal for heating, and to buy clothing. As compared to other small lenders, credit unions were cheap, charging lower interest rates than the others. However, loans were only available to members and membership was largely restricted to the employees of large organizations. By design, credit unions could never be more than a partial solution to the problem of credit for poor people.

Many of these alternative arrangements emerged to meet the demand for loans because commercial banks traditionally did not make small personal loans. Rather, they made short-term loans to business. In fact, before 1925 fewer than one hundred U.S. banks even had personal loan departments.[93] During the 1920s, however, some banks recognized the growth in consumer lending, realized that there were profits to be made in small non-business loans, and opened personal loan departments. Such loans were made without collateral, and on the basis of the applicant's income. Once a leading bank like the National City Bank of New York successfully adopted this innovation in 1928, others followed.[94] The demand for personal loans far exceeded the bank's expectations and it quickly expanded its own capacity to make such loans.[95] Banks were further encouraged when New Deal institutions like the Federal Housing Administration began to insure home improvement loans so that banks would make loans to homeowners beyond the mortgages used to purchase a house.[96]

Commercial banks relied on many of the same criteria that other small loan lenders used in deciding whom to trust. But commercial banks, as deposit-taking institutions, had much more money to lend out than any of the others. And if the borrower was already a depositor with the lending bank, the bank possessed a good deal of detailed and confidential information about the borrower's personal finances. Furthermore, banks had a substantial preexisting infrastructure (including trained personnel, offices, files, etc.) that could be repurposed to support small loans. It became clear that borrowers sought small loans from banks for many of the same reasons why they borrowed from personal finance companies and credit unions: to consolidate older debts, to deal with unexpected medical expenses, to compensate for interrupted income, and so on.[97] Even though they developed their own credit files about individuals, banks often consulted with local credit bureaus, which tracked the payment history of individuals (rather than small businesses) and sold their information to subscribers.[98] As mentioned earlier in this chapter, local bureaus emerged at the end of the nineteenth century and were mostly established by the mercantile community of a particular city, who cooperated by pooling credit information about their customers.[99]

As their numbers proliferated, credit bureaus formed national associations so that information could be shared between cities as well as within them.[100]

The procedure used by commercial banks to make a loan differed from that of the other large-scale small loan lenders. Most significantly, banks seldom collateralized personal loans or put a lien on the debtor's property.[101] For one thing, many of the tangible assets that best secure a loan might already be collateralized by someone else.[102] Instead, banks would typically insist on one or two other persons as endorsers, guarantors, or "co-makers," who would be held responsible if the original debtor defaulted.[103] In this way, bank lenders made use of the borrower's own social networks to reinforce the borrower's promises. But the primary source for repayment remained the borrower's personal income. Therefore, after establishing an applicant's personal identity, banks went to considerable lengths to confirm the applicant's employment status, job tenure, salary, and occupation.[104] The prevailing "employment at will" standard meant that future employment was never guaranteed, even for those who held a job for a long time. But lenders could still tell the difference between stable and unstable employment. Banks also learned to manage their borrowers after making the loan: providing timely reminders, making repayment easy, and acting quickly if a borrower fell behind.

Despite the hard times of the Great Depression, and subsequent wartime dislocations, commercial banks continued to expand into personal lending. Their growing involvement offered an important point of leverage for the federal government as it intervened in consumer credit markets. Unlike the USLL, which imposed state-level regulation of small loans, Regulation W was imposed by the Federal Reserve in September 1941 to control consumer credit. It targeted installment credit in order to curtail consumer demand and dampen inflation, and when implemented it substantially reduced the volume of installment lending between 1941 and 1943.[105] But this federal regulation of consumer promises ceased once the war was over, and thereafter the situation for banks returned to "normal."[106] Later, however, other federal regulations were imposed to enhance transparency and fairness in lending.[107] One key to the success of commercial banks involved treating the extension of personal loans as akin to the mass production of a standardized good: the development of large-scale, low-cost organizational routines and paperwork helped reduce costs and made "mass finance" a viable activity.[108] Banks soon eclipsed other lenders, although they never entirely displaced them. Personal finance companies, pawnshops, credit unions, and so on continued to provide small cash loans to some households.

Credit Cards

Much of the credit that mid-twentieth-century households received was earmarked: people received long-term loans so they could buy a house, or they were given shorter-term credit so they could buy a car or refrigerator, or they borrowed to make purchases from a specific retailer. Not only did this arrangement give lenders a good reason to lend, but it also frequently meant that borrowers possessed a tangible asset that could function as collateral. The possibility of losing the collateral motivated borrowers to keep their promises, and seizure of collateral would help compensate the lenders if borrowers failed to keep their promises. And such credit was temporally bounded as well: once one transaction was completed, an individual seeking subsequent credit would have to be evaluated all over again, although a successful series of such transactions created a "good" credit record. Despite these constraints, borrowing to buy became more common, and the experience on both sides helped lay the foundation for a broader consumer economy. Cash loans, by contrast, were for smaller amounts and didn't involve such earmarking: the borrower acquired unfettered purchasing power. But both kinds of loans, the earmarked and the unearmarked, obligated borrowers to a regular schedule of repayments over a period of time (twelve months, eighteen months, five years, etc.). This arrangement dovetailed with the spread of regular full-time employment among working individuals. The typical male head of an American household was someone who earned a salary, paid out in regular amounts (either weekly or monthly) by their employer. This predictable income stream could then be used to service debt, synchronizing household outflows of money with the cash inflows.

The private obligations that arose from consumer credit were subject to public regulation, for a variety of reasons. Widespread credit raised aggregate consumption, and so during World War II concerns about price inflation led the U.S. federal government to curtail credit in order to reduce consumption. Before the war, however, the federal government sought to encourage economic activity and so it offered loan guarantees for certain types of credit, especially in the domestic housing market. Other regulations addressed the asymmetry of debt contracts, but not the asymmetry so familiar to economists. What mattered was not that borrowers knew more about their willingness and ability to repay than did lenders but rather that lenders understood much better than borrowers the contractual terms and conditions of the loan. Borrowers needed to be protected from abusive and predatory lenders who might deceive their customers about the true cost of a loan or take advantage of their inexperience.[109]

The next major change in household credit came after World War II and involved the development of revolving credit. Credit cards emerged first in the travel and entertainment industry to facilitate high-income cardholders' patronage of fine restaurants. But they broadened to the point where credit cards could be used to pay for a wide range of goods and services, as more and more businesses accepted them for payment. In other words, credit cards didn't tie credit to a specific transaction. They offered credit that could be used, at the discretion of the cardholder and up to their credit limit, to cover transactions with any merchant who accepted the card. From the standpoint of the borrower they had the same open-ended quality as cash. Furthermore, borrowers didn't have to pay off their entire balance at the end of the month; they only had to make the minimum required payment. Credit card usage also broadened in the sense that cards spread downward from high-income households to middle- and then eventually to lower-income households.[110] As higher-income families became saturated with credit cards, issuers could only find additional market share by going further down in the income distribution and giving credit to households who, by traditional criteria, seemed less creditworthy. To make this possible, the kind of information formerly gathered by local credit bureaus had to be integrated and expanded on a national scale, and so the spread of credit cards in the United States was entwined with the emergence of credit scoring.

Municipal credit bureaus had existed since the late 1860s and provided a platform for sharing information about local individuals among local merchants.[111] Sometimes they focused on a specific industry. For example, in 1904 the Atlanta Retail Grocers and Butchers Association established a credit bureau so that members could access credit information about their customers,[112] while in 1917 the New York City paint, oil, and varnish industry created a similar facility for its members.[113] The Alfred Best Company, based in New York and Chicago, published ratings for the insurance industry, and even the sheet music industry organized to gather retail credit information.[114] Frequently, credit bureaus concentrated on a particular community. The Credit Rating Association of Minneapolis, for example, was organized in 1888 to provide credit information about individuals and small businesses in Minneapolis to its subscribers. Its 1919 volume contained almost 1,500 pages of information, with persons and businesses rated and listed alphabetically by name, and with a simple rating key included.[115] Over time, local credit bureaus affiliated with national organizations like the Associated Credit

Bureaus of America (ACB) or its predecessor, the National Association of Mercantile Agencies, in order to pool information across a broader area. By 1927, 800 local credit agencies were members of the ACB, and membership doubled again between then and 1955.[116] They typically gathered credit information from their individual members or subscribers, pooled and organized that information, and then made it available to those same members or subscribers.[117]

In the early twentieth century, some mass retailers and department store chains like Sears, Roebuck & Co. began to issue store credit cards to selected customers. As a convenience, creditworthy customers could settle their account monthly and avoid having to pay cash for each of their purchases at Sears. The innovation caught on, and soon credit via store cards was a virtual necessity if a mass retailer wanted to attract customers.[118] Some hotels and oil companies similarly gave cards to customers who were permitted to make purchases on credit.[119] Department stores kept records on each customer's account and so could track a particular person's purchasing and payment history. But like many other retail lenders they also relied on outside credit bureaus for additional credit information.[120] This form of store credit was somewhere between a classic installment loan, which could only be used to purchase a specific item, and a cash loan, which could be used for any purpose. Store credit cards could be used to purchase items sold by the store. Similarly, oil companies issued cards so that their customers could easily purchase fuel at a gas station. By comparison with mass retailers, local stores were much less able to offer similar levels of credit to their customers.[121]

What became the first general-purpose payment card, Diner's Club, appeared in the early 1950s so that well-off patrons of fine restaurants in New York City could dispense with cash when they dined out. Starting from this exclusive market niche, the arrangement spread and so before the end of the 1950s the Diner's Club card was accepted in restaurants and other retail establishments all over the United States.[122] Credit cards were a vehicle that allowed small local merchants to offer the convenience of credit to their customers and better compete with the large department stores.[123] A number of rival products were soon launched, including credit cards from Bank of America, American Express, and Hilton Hotels. Card issuers earned money by charging both the merchants from whom cardholders made purchases and the cardholders themselves (usually, via an annual fee). But all of these credit cards faced the same initial problem. In order to get people to hold a particular card, there had to be enough merchants who accepted it in lieu of cash so that a cardholder could get enough use of the card to justify paying the annual fee. And in order to get merchants to accept a card, there had to be enough customers who wanted to use it to justify the cost. But in the beginning, there were neither merchants nor customers: each side could only be recruited by the expectation that there were or soon would be enough parties on the other side of the transaction to make adoption worthwhile. In practice, credit card companies started by issuing cards to many, many people as a way to jump-start system building.[124] And gradually, large financial and informational networks were assembled that supported widely recognized cards like Visa, MasterCard, American Express, and Discover. Some are useful globally (e.g., Visa) while others are recognized primarily within the United States (e.g., Discover). But within the United States, the number of merchants who accepted payment cards grew from 162,000 in 1959 to 5.3 million in 2002.[125] And some industries became almost exclusively dependent on card payments (e.g., car rental agencies and airlines). Once credit cards began to play a significant role in consumer credit, they caught the attention of financial regulators. The Federal Open Market Committee meeting of July 28, 1959, noted that "the new credit card plans have made consumer borrowing even more easy and inviting" (FOMC 1959: 33).[126]

All card issuers earn their profits with the interest charged on a cardholder's monthly balance and by fees charged to both merchants (as a percentage of credit sales) and cardholders (usually an annual fee). Additionally, many cardholders are charged extra fees or higher interest rates for late payments, cash advances, balances that roll over to the next payment period, and over-limit spending.[127] Borrowers who don't fully pay their balances on time can be extremely profitable for the card issuer. Early on the banks that issued credit cards were limited by usury laws that depended on the state in which a bank was domiciled. But after a Supreme Court decision in 1978, card issuers could charge whatever interest rate was legal in the state where the issuer was chartered, rather than where its customers lived. After this decision Citibank, for example, moved its credit card operations from New York to North Dakota, where interest rate limits were less restrictive and where the small population was not a problem. Issuing banks also used credit card receivables as an underlying asset for securitization.[128] Not only could home mortgages be pooled and turned into securities, so could the payments that came from credit card holders. As with other forms of securitization, banks were able to move assets off their balance sheets and so reduce their regulatory capital.

As card systems broadened in scope, they posed serious informational challenges. It was one thing for a local department store to construct a small filing system and track the purchases and payments of customers who dwelt in the same city: vertical files, preprinted forms, carbon paper, and typewriters would suffice. But it was quite another for a national department store chain, or a credit card company, to do so for its dispersed customer base. Unsurprisingly, national card companies were very interested in information technology and had to invest heavily in order to establish and expand the networks that linked merchant locations with cardholder files on a transaction-specific basis. They took full advantage of whatever long-distance communication media were in use, starting with the postal system but soon shifting to telegraph, telephones, and teletype.[129] When a customer presented a card in order to make a purchase, there had to be some way to confirm that customer's identity and creditworthiness and quickly register the purchase. It is no surprise that the commercial adoption of mainframe computers, for example, had a big effect on credit card operations.[130] The ability to construct and analyze large databases of consumer information also enabled the development of personal credit scoring in the 1950s. And subsequent improvements in computer technology undergirded the growing sophistication of credit scoring systems. Credit cards gained particular significance because they came to serve as a kind of "gateway" credit: with a credit card, the cardholder could establish a credit record that would entitle them to other forms of credit.[131]

Payday Loans and Pawnshops

The potential abuses associated with small cash loans were very much the concern of the Russell Sage Foundation in the early twentieth century, but after World War II it moved on to other issues. However, small cash lending continued and has returned to the public policy agenda for many of the same reasons. Payday loans are typically for short periods (until someone's next paycheck), they are unsecured and involve amounts of $300 or less, and they are made to borrowers who need only establish their identity and regular employment. Often, the borrower simply gives the lender a postdated check for the amount due. The lender earns a profit by charging fees and imposing discounts, which typically constitute the equivalent of an annual interest rate between 400 and 1000 percent.[132] Today, these loans can be quickly obtained from any of a large number of conveniently located retail establishments.

Contemporary payday loans have been criticized on the grounds that they are too expensive, that they are frequently "rolled over" so that a short-term solution quickly becomes a long-term financial burden, and that lenders target unsophisticated borrowers who may not entirely understand the situation they are getting into or who may be overly optimistic about their ability to repay their debts.[133] The latter two claims imply that payday borrowers are making promises that they do not fully comprehend. Overall, researchers find that use of payday loans does not help consumers fix the kinds of problems that such loans are marketed as resolving (e.g., paying utility bills, keeping phone service, buying groceries, etc.) and note that many borrowers turn to expensive payday loans even when they could obtain cheaper credit from their credit cards.[134] Payday lenders concentrate their activities in poor, urban, and minority-dominated neighborhoods, and so they can exacerbate other forms of inequality.[135] To some, these shortcomings seem like adequate justification for protective regulatory interventions,[136] but others find that payday loan borrowers are generally realistic about their loans and how soon they will be fully repaid.[137] Overall, today's disputes recapitulate many of the arguments for and against regulation made a century ago.

For the so-called "credit invisibles," that is, people who cannot use banks or pawnshops or who do not have the steady employment required by a payday lender, there are still loan sharks and other informal lenders. In his study of the contemporary urban economy in Chicago, Venkatesh (2006) described how often small businesses, proprietorships, and individuals relied on informal lenders to finance investments, meet cash-flow problems, or simply maintain personal consumption. Even though these people seek to borrow for legitimate purposes, they cannot turn to regular banks for a variety of reasons, and so they necessarily rely on other sources. Not only do informal loans provide needed money, but they also cement social ties with other members of the local community. And in a precarious underground economy, today's lender may be tomorrow's borrower, and so informal credit relationships can also function as a kind of insurance.[138]

Student Loans

Higher education has witnessed the effects of the modern credit economy, including expansion, innovative financial engineering and risk management, securitization, and disintermediation. But it also reveals the ongoing importance of older social formations, the role of social networks for access to money and credit, and the significance of personal connections and familial obligations. Caught between rising educational costs, growing college aspirations, and enduring familial obligations to kin, many have turned to debt as the solution to the problem of paying for higher education. The result has been an expanse of indebtedness that encumbers not only students but very often their families as well, as new credit systems articulate with old systems of family support. And both the problem and its solution are deeply shaped by the government.

Thanks to federal policy, debt offers one possible solution to a financial problem. Sometimes, the government wants people to make certain kinds of promises and so some types of credit receive strong government support. Postsecondary education in the United States has become very expensive: not only do full-time students have to pay tuition and fees, purchase books and other educational materials, and meet their living expenses, but they usually forgo full-time employment.[139] Students may receive financial aid from their college, or get assistance from their families, or draw on their own savings. But today one option for students is to borrow, anticipating the additional income that a postsecondary education will help generate.[140] Since students are risky borrowers who, in the short run, lack substantial credit records or tangible assets, many financial institutions refuse to lend to them. For this reason, the U.S. federal government created a system of loans, loan subsidies, and loan guarantees to help make higher education affordable. With government backing, the promises that students made became more credible. Such a policy enabled the government to support higher education but without paying out money directly to students or to educational institutions. It also helped offset substantial cuts in public funding from state governments. Instead of direct outlays, it provided loans and subsidized loans (which students had to repay) and loan guarantees (which only mattered if a borrower defaulted).

When few people attended college and tuition was low, funding for higher education was not a major issue. As enrollment numbers and tuition increased, particularly after World War II, the demand for financing grew. Partly, this was because more postsecondary students came from middle- and working-class families, which had fewer resources to devote to their children's education. Student debt therefore became a significant part of the credit economy, and its importance increased at the end of the twentieth century as family incomes stagnated while education costs continued to rise.[141] By 2010 total student loans surpassed total credit card debt, having grown right through the financial crisis of 2008.[142] Taking on debt allows students to pay for their education, although the financial burden makes it harder for them to buy a home afterward.[143] The federal government first became involved in supporting attendance at colleges and universities with the GI Bill, which helped veterans obtain additional education after World War II. Starting with the Stafford Loan program established in 1965, the federal government began its support for student loans and with the addition and expansion of other programs the sums became substantial.[144] Students could apply for grants and loans in order to pay for postsecondary education at qualified institutions, but over time federal financial support shifted away from grants and toward loans, subsidized loans, and loan guarantees. Student loans had below-market interest rates and generous repayment schedules that could be deferred until after graduation. And although the programs initially targeted students from low-income households, eligibility criteria were relaxed and so students from middle-class backgrounds became qualified for assistance.[145] Starting in the 1990s, parents were also given the chance to borrow for their children's education via PLUS (Parent Loans for Undergraduate Students) loans, although the terms were not so generous.[146]

Broader trends of financial innovation, securitization, and disintermediation affected the student loan system. In the 1990s some private lenders began to make student loans without federal loan guarantees. Such loans were costlier for the borrower, because of the absence of guarantees, but not subject to the same eligibility restrictions. These new lenders securitized their loan receivables.[147] That is, the loans were pooled, packaged, and turned into securities that, when rated by the credit rating agencies, could be sold to investors and moved off the originator's balance sheet. This market activity was aided by the presence of "Sallie Mae" (the Student Loan Marketing Association), a government-sponsored enterprise founded in 1972 to support student loans by creating a secondary market for them. Sallie Mae started to securitize the loans it purchased from originators in the 1980s, thus setting an example for private lenders.[148]

High default rates reflected the riskiness of student loans. Most students were young adults with limited financial experience and great optimism about their future careers and earnings. Although borrowers promised to repay their loans, often they could not because of a mixture of unwillingness and inability to pay. Some for-profit universities were especially aggressive in recruiting students, who borrowed to pay the tuition, and exaggerated the benefits that their education provided. Some programs forgave loans if the student performed public service work after completing their education, but mostly student borrowers had to repay. The consequences of default became politically salient in the case of student loans, in part because of the federal loan guarantees but also because of its resonance with deeply held beliefs about the sanctity of a promise. With guaranteed loans, the cost of failure wasn't borne by the lender. Rather, it was borne by the guarantor, which, in the case of student loans, was the federal government. If the defaulting debtor filed for personal bankruptcy, he or she could discharge their debts and get a "fresh start." More will be said in chapter 8, but discharge means that after going through bankruptcy, and after handing nonexempt assets over to the bankruptcy court, the insolvent debtor is released from their pre-filing debts. Some claimed, however, that individual students were borrowing heavily and then deliberately filing for bankruptcy as a way to escape their obligations. And indeed, as student loans grew during the 1980s, the numbers of defaults grew even faster.[149] Consequently, the Higher Education Act was amended to prohibit the discharge of guaranteed or insured loans in personal bankruptcy proceedings.[150] A similar "problem" arose in the case of credit card debts, and for many years the credit card industry claimed that too many irresponsible borrowers were spending heavily with their credit cards and then deliberately filing for bankruptcy in order to escape their debts. Creditor groups argued that personal bankruptcy was being used by people to avoid keeping their promises. Thanks to political pressure from the credit card industry, the rules applicable to personal bankruptcy were changed in 2005 in order to make it harder to discharge credit card debt.[151] These changes shifted power to creditors.

The case of student loans offers a clear example of how public policy could influence the issuance and acceptance of certain types of financial promises.[152] Initially as a part of President Johnson's Great Society initiative, the federal government supported postsecondary education for less-advantaged Americans by making it easy for them to borrow, from either the government or some other lender, and pay their own way through school. In economic terms, postsecondary education led to higher personal incomes that could be used to service the debt. The program was politically popular and cheaper than direct outlays, and so the program grew to the point where the total indebtedness due from student loans eclipsed that due from credit cards. It also dovetailed with the privatization of higher education, as public funding from state government declined and costs were shifted to students and their families.[153] Students became debtors, but so did their families as parents helped shoulder the financial burden.[154] The social ties that bound a family provided new channels for the flow of educational credit and forced borrowers to undertake "relational work" with their families and partners.[155]

And the opportunities and burdens created by educational credit mirrored durable inequalities between different racial groups.[156]

Credit Scores for Individuals

As individual indebtedness grew, so did the need to gather large-scale information to determine which individuals were creditworthy. Today, Fair, Isaac & Company, inventors of the FICO score, is the best-known firm doing credit scoring for consumers.[157] This firm was established in 1956 and applied operations research techniques to credit selection. New credit card companies, like Carte Blanche, hired Fair, Isaac to help figure out which American households should be offered a card.[158] Like other creditors, credit card issuers wanted to distinguish between trustworthy and untrustworthy debtors. The solution involved calculating a numerical score for each borrower, providing a quantitative measure of creditworthiness. Unlike earlier forms of consumer credit, which were usually tied to purchases of a specific commodity or provided by a specific retailer, this credit was general: at their discretion a cardholder could use their credit when and where they pleased. The numerical score depended on a person's individual credit history, as measured by their credit record, but it could reflect other factors as well.[159] Some attributes raised credit scores (e.g., having stable employment and high income) whereas others lowered them (e.g., personal bankruptcy, having prior liens, missing payments, renting rather than owning a home).[160] Decisions about which attributes to include in the score built on previous methods of consumer credit evaluation and depended on what kinds of information were available on a mass scale. For example, an applicant's occupation was easy to determine and commonly included in credit scores, and in so doing scoring companies were simply building on prior practice.[161] FICO scores were provided to clients who then incorporated them into their own credit decisions. Very simply, a credit card company could establish a numerical threshold and issue cards to people who scored above it, while denying them to people who fell below.

Credit cards went first to higher-income wealthy households, which for obvious reasons had better credit records and higher credit scores than others. Once the rich households all had cards, however, the only place to look for market share was further down the income distribution. Improvements in credit scoring made it possible to identify "riskier" cardholders and price credit high enough to cover the increase in losses. The downward diffusion pattern was still apparent in the 1990s: in 1989, 95.5 percent of households in the highest income quintile had at least one credit card, as compared to only 29.3 percent of households in the lowest quintile. In 2001, 97.1 percent of households in the highest quintile had credit cards (a small increase from 1989), but for the lowest quintile card ownership had climbed to 42.9 percent.[162] Clearly, credit card companies learned how to make money from poorer families.

Credit scoring enabled "mechanical" or "automated" credit decision making. These new decision protocols didn't rely on the personal judgment of a loan officer, were less labor intensive, and so could be executed quickly and applied on a large scale.[163] The use of scores inaugurated a new era in the quantification of credit. Before long, millions of people were subject to an expanding calculative apparatus that made use of increasingly sophisticated statistical methods. Building on Durand's prescient analysis (1941), researchers exploited advances in computing power to refine models, analyze more data, reduce sample bias, improve measurement, and develop new statistical methods.[164] These improvements allowed lenders to extend credit more broadly and to include lower-income households that in previous decades would not have qualified. By the early 2000s, the three major credit reporting companies each had information on about 190 million individual Americans and 1.5 billion accounts.[165]

Originally designed to assist credit card companies, personal credit scores proved to be highly portable numbers, easily transplanted or aggregated into other contexts and put to "off label" uses. A poor credit score certainly made it harder to get a loan, but it could also trouble a person when it came to getting a job, purchasing car insurance, or renting an apartment.[166] A growing number of life chances are now affected by credit scores, and their fatefulness has been greatly amplified. And when home mortgage loans were pooled together and turned into asset-backed securities, the FICO scores of the borrowers played a role in the securitization process and shaped how the resulting securities were rated by the bond rating agencies. As Poon (2009) points out, the decision by key government-sponsored enterprises like "Freddie Mac" to incorporate FICO scores into automated underwriting procedures set a precedent that led to a much more widespread adoption of these scores. The quantification of individual creditworthiness spread into other realms: numbers were built out of numbers, ratings out of ratings. Simple forms of quantification multiplied into layers of quantification, and in many respects the accumulation of extensive credit records on millions of individuals, which started in the 1950s, foreshadowed the emergence of "surveillance capitalism" where consumers are very closely monitored using "big data" methods.[167]

During the 1950s and 1960s, the civil rights movement highlighted the unfair treatment of racial minorities and women in employment and housing, but also in credit markets. As women and minorities increasingly engaged the financial system, their disparate experiences became an obvious problem. In response to political pressure, the federal government enacted a number of measures in the late 1960s and 1970s. Consumer credit bureaus and consumer lenders were regulated by the Truth in Lending Act of 1968, the Fair Credit Reporting Act of 1970 (subsequently updated multiple times), and the Equal Credit Opportunity Act of 1974 (also subsequently amended).[168] One issue addressed by these laws concerned the fact that early credit scoring systems often relied on factors that discriminated against certain categories of people. For example, consideration of the race or ethnicity of the borrower was discriminatory even though this feature was statistically predictive because of durable racial differences in income and wealth. Since African American households on average had lower incomes and fewer assets, for example, on average they would find it harder to service their debts. Shifting consumer credit allocation from qualitative judgments to a formal scoring method allowed lenders to argue that the race or gender of the applicant was not a factor in calculating a credit score, if they could show that a measure of the applicant's race was not explicitly in the formula.[169] But removing discrimination wasn't so easy, for use of variables correlated with race would produce the same effect. A credit applicant's home zip code, for example, could serve as a close proxy for race even if the applicant's race was never identified, because of residential segregation. Other prohibited factors included age, religion, and marital status, but each had its own proxies, and so the problem of discrimination was not so easily solved.[170] Today, for example, fewer black and Hispanic households have credit cards, personal loans, or a line of credit as compared to white households with the same annual income.[171]

Another problem for consumer finance was that many loan contracts were hard for ordinary people to understand, and so standardized disclosures were mandated so that borrowers could understand the terms of a loan and make comparisons among competing offers to get the best deal.[172] For example, loan agreements had to calculate interest charges and state the interest rate in a standardized way, the annual percentage rate (APR), although there are many ways to calculate interest. Subsequently, however, lenders found that imposition of fees and penalties enabled them to increase profits without affecting the posted APR.[173] Finally, the accumulation of extensive personal information about tens of millions of people posed questions about privacy and whether some information should be "off limits." Were there boundaries on credit surveillance? Should credit reporting agencies have to disclose some or all of what they knew to the subjects? Did individuals have a right to learn what credit agencies knew about them? And what if credit information was factually incorrect? Who bore the responsibility to identify mistakes and fix them? Such questions have only increased in importance with the realization that detailed information about people's purchasing, payment, and other financial activities can be valuable in its own right, and not simply as a predictor of creditworthiness.[174]

Credit scores were portable, and so was the general method of credit scoring. Although small business lending traditionally depended on the judgment of bank loan officers and their connections with business owners (usually termed "relationship lending"), business credit scoring developed as a more algorithmic approach to lending. Banks began to do their own internal credit scoring, compiling the information they possessed about business customers and turning it into a number that could be used in an automated decision process.[175] These were used for various organizational purposes (tracking problem loans, determining loan officer compensation, etc.) and did not have the same general audience as Dun and Bradstreet ratings or Moody's ratings. More sophisticated versions were integrated with risk management and the development of overall risk measures like value-at-risk (which measured risk associated with an entire portfolio of assets).

Standardized Promises

Many new forms of individual credit expanded to the point where they became a type of "mass credit" suitable for a consumer society. Durable goods manufacturers gave installment loans so that their customers could buy furniture, automobiles, sewing machines, and similar items. Department stores extended credit so that their patrons could purchase goods. And credit card companies offered revolving credit to their cardholders so that they could buy almost any type of good or service. As the twentieth century unfolded, all of these forms of credit came to involve millions of consumers who, in exchange for a promise to pay in the future, were able to consume today. Mass credit fueled aggregate demand in a consumer economy. Yet these millions of people did not negotiate their own promises, nor did they set the terms of the loans they obtained. The terms were highly standardized and largely set by the seller or lender. The borrower could accept terms or reject them, but rarely could they be adjusted or renegotiated. If there was variation, it occurred for only a limited set of features, with most of the terms set in unvarying language.

The "standard form" or "adhesion" contracts used by lenders included boilerplate provisions that reflected the lender's considerable experience. After all, a national department store chain or an automobile company dealt with millions of borrowers over many years, kept detailed account records, and could draw on a deep well of experience and legal expertise to design a contract that best served its interests. By contrast, the consumer had only his or her own personal experience to draw on and was essentially presented with a take-it-or-leave-it proposition. The kind of individualized treatment that one might enjoy when dealing with a country store simply didn't apply to mass credit. Consumers often did not fully understand the terms they agreed to, and so, in a sense, the information asymmetry that ordinarily applied to credit transactions was reversed. Rather than borrowers knowing more than the lenders (about the borrower's willingness and ability to repay), the lenders knew more than the borrowers (about the nature of the transaction and the various obligations of the two parties). This asymmetry was something lenders used to their advantage.

Standard-form contracts for loans, installment loans, or credit cards meant that borrowers did not set the terms of their own promises. As more and more consumers participated in the credit economy, they did so through legal vehicles that they could not adjust to their own personal situation. Furthermore, it is clear that not everyone is financially "literate" and that the problem of not fully understanding various financial services is particularly acute for some of those using tax rebate anticipation loans, payday loans, or rent-to-own arrangements.[176] This imbalance has prompted a number of regulatory protections for vulnerable debtors. Through adoption of the Uniform Small Loan Law in the early twentieth century, for example, states regulated the contracts used for small loans in such a way as to make the transaction simpler and more transparent for the borrower.[177] At the federal level the Truth in Lending Act of 1968 mandated disclosure of standardized loan terms to make the transaction easier for the borrower to understand.[178] Today, the CFPB (the Consumer Finance Protection Bureau) implements the Credit Card Accountability Responsibility and Disclosure Act of 2009, which tried to increase the transparency of credit card agreements for cardholders. In order to redress the imbalance manifested in standard-form loan contracts, the government set some of the terms of those promises. It neither made the promises nor accepted them, but it shaped their architecture so that promisors knew better what they were promising.

The standardization of promises also facilitated their securitization.[179] Promises did not become identical, of course, but standardization reduced their variability to the point where they could be grouped together and put into pools whose overall financial properties could be estimated statistically. The standardization of home mortgages, for example, made it possible to combine them into asset pools and then calculate overall rates of return, default, prepayment, and so on. The standards were effectively determined by government-sponsored enterprises like Fannie Mae, which set guidelines for the mortgages they purchased on secondary markets, or the Federal Housing Administration (FHA), which set standards for the mortgages it insured. Similarly, the standardization of credit card contracts made it easier to securitize credit card receivables.[180] Securitization enlarged the overall volume of credit because it allowed lenders to sell their financial assets (the promises borrowers had made to them) to other investors, recover their capital, and lend again.[181] Furthermore, with securitization lenders can be less concerned about the idiosyncratic creditworthiness of individual borrowers and more about the overall financial properties of the asset pool. Investors who might be unwilling to lend to credit card holders or subprime mortgages were nevertheless willing to purchase the securities built out of those debts.

Mass Credit and Mass Indebtedness

As more forms of credit were developed, American households and families assumed more debt. They borrowed to buy houses and cars, to pay for their college education or that of their children, and to maintain a certain level of consumption. As is now well documented, median real earnings for full-time male workers stagnated in the mid-1970s, and for some it has even declined since then. Income inequality expanded after the late 1970s.[182] Household earnings could still grow as women's labor force participation increased and women's wages were added to earnings, but in general the ability of Americans to consume was tempered by their stagnant incomes. Credit helped bridge the gap between earnings and consumption. Indeed, some argue that the spread of credit helped provide domestic political stability at a time when income inequality was growing rapidly, real wages for most workers were stagnant, and redistributional public policies were being cut.[183] To meet its consumptive aspirations (as well as to stimulate demand for the macroeconomy), the middle class was enabled to borrow from its future self.

The labor force experience of women as workers was very different from that of men, and it has converged slowly as more women sought paid employment, as their qualifications rose, and as their wages increased. Women as debtors also had a distinctive experience, often bearing the brunt of discriminatory treatment in which their promises were considered less credible than those of men.[184] It was, for example, hard for married women to have their own separate credit accounts, and divorce usually meant that the credit record of the household stayed with the ex-husband, not the ex-wife. Similarly, single women who married would often have to close their accounts and reapply for credit under their new husband's name. The women's movement mobilized to address gender discrimination in credit markets, and one response was the Equal Credit Opportunity Act of 1974.[185] Initially, the act only prohibited discrimination on the basis of sex and marital status, but soon race, color, religion, national origin, and age were added.[186] While the issue of racial disparity in home mortgage loans has been studied quite extensively and has been the subject of federal legislation (see chapter 7), not so much has been learned about racial discrimination in other credit markets. Nevertheless, evidence strongly suggests that both racial minorities and women experienced discriminatory treatment.[187] In other words, consumers are not treated entirely as individuals whose features make them more or less creditworthy. Lenders acted as if the credibility of promises varied systematically from one group to another.

By the early twenty-first century, overall household indebtedness had climbed to high levels.[188] Information gathered by the Federal Reserve through its Survey of Consumer Finances showed that mortgage debt comprised the biggest proportion of total household debt.[189] However, there were other ways to borrow on the security of real estate that raised indebtedness even beyond a first mortgage (e.g., home equity loans). The average and median balances carried by families with credit cards increased.[190] And as families acquired more debts, the ratio of debt repayment to family income rose,[191] as did their leverage (the ratio of debts to assets).[192] Even though they could consume more, carrying additional debt made families financially precarious: unexpected expenses, declining asset values (especially the worth of the family home), job loss, or other interruptions to income put a family at greater risk of default. A family that dealt with financial problems by paying only the minimum required monthly payment on their credit cards soon faced ballooning debts. Thus the stage was set for a catastrophe in 2008, when the financial crisis spread to the entire economy and many over-indebted households suddenly had to deal with a succession of financial shocks. One result was the rise in delinquency rates for consumer debt, which spiked dramatically from 2006 to 2010. Many people were overwhelmed by the financial promises they had made.

Conclusion

The credit extended to individuals, families, or households went through a dramatic transformation. Initially, most people obtained informal credit from a local store or from their neighbors, but credit proliferated, expanded, and formalized. It was often tied to the purchase of tangible goods or real estate that could function as collateral.[193] And banks avoided making loans to individuals for "non-business" purposes. The meaning of indebtedness shifted: no longer a sign of social subordination, dishonesty, or ineptitude, owing money to someone became a much more common and neutral marker of adulthood. Debt was a signal of the borrower's status as a trusted and empowered individual, financially included within the credit economy. Debt did not entirely shed its moral connotations, because the personal character of the debtor remained a key determinant of creditworthiness. That famous mnemonic for credit risk, the "Three Cs," included capacity, capital, and *character*.[194] In a sense, the valence of debt had flipped: whereas before it connoted undisciplined and dependent personhood, later it reflected trustworthiness. This is one reason why those initially denied credit, women and minorities in particular, struggled politically to gain full access to it.

People received credit in order to shop, and with the emergence of large numbers of working people with regular employment and steady earnings, it became possible for them to anticipate their future income to borrow in the present. Individual credit was untied from agricultural rhythms and flowed more continuously, albeit depending on the business cycle. A big purchase didn't require personal self-discipline as it was no longer necessary to save beforehand: no more deferred gratification.[195] The invention of credit scoring formalized credit allocation and made it easier and cheaper to track and process large numbers of credit applicants. Building on methods first developed for trade credit, consumer credit decisions could be routinized and automated. Lenders also discovered how profitable it could be to extend credit to lower-income households, especially those who missed payments or didn't fully pay off their monthly balances. Credit cards provided an unusual degree of flexibility to borrowers. Within the broad constraints of the credit limit set by the card issuer, and by the extent of card acceptance, a credit card gave to its holder the ability to purchase whatever they wanted. Unlike installment loans or store credit, which were tied to specific purchases or sellers, credit cards granted discretion to the buyer, but the cost could be quite high. And the level of purchasing power was typically much greater than could be gained through a cash loan. Payday loans could be worth several hundred dollars, but credit card debts are frequently much larger. This flexibility and generality eventually proved to be extremely useful for the development of on-line commerce. People who purchase goods and services on the internet necessarily use payment cards of one form or another.

Mass credit flowed through standardized legal relationships. Among other things, standardization made it easier to securitize credit obligations, that is, to manufacture new promises out of old ones. While standardization per se can be useful, much depends on the standards and who sets them. Many of the contractual standards for consumer credit were set by lenders, on a take-it-or-leave-it basis. Given the informational imbalance between lenders and borrowers, these standards favored the lenders and sometimes prompted regulatory intervention to restore the ideal of a consensual transaction between equal parties. Such interventions mandated more disclosure and transparency for borrowers. Older forms of credit market regulation simply tried to restrict the interest rates that lenders could charge. Usury laws were intended to help make loans more affordable for borrowers, or at least protect them from "confiscatory" interest rates. However, such laws were weakly enforced and largely proved ineffectual.[196] These state laws were easily evaded by the "loan sharks" that so concerned the Russell Sage Foundation in the early twentieth century and by major credit card issuers after the Supreme Court's Marquette decision in 1978.

Mass credit conferred purchasing power on entire populations, but not everyone was treated equally. The face-to-face extension of credit gave license to lender biases and prejudices that worked against racial minorities and women. Judgment rules and formal scores tried to distinguish between the creditworthy and the unworthy, but credit decision making could also discriminate between social groups on other bases. As groups were incorporated into the credit economy, they found that they were treated differently and that some were systematically disadvantaged. Finally, although the informational apparatus that creates individual credit scores for millions of individuals has a broad reach, it is not fully panoptic in its scope. There are people whose impoverished circumstances or uneven attachment to formal employment renders them largely invisible to the rating agencies. Without the ability to establish a formal credit record, the unscored must rely on other ways to borrow or face the consequences of financial exclusion.[197]

Even as mass credit emerged, built around new information systems involving statistical calculations and fateful quantitative scores for millions of individuals, some older relationships and institutions persisted. Individuals still turned to their family if they needed to borrow money to buy a home, go to college, or establish a small business. The networks of obligations and trust built around social relationships continued to matter, even as they were embedded in larger formal structures that organized credit flows.

6

Corporate Finance and Credit Ratings

Who can make a promise? Who is bound by its terms? In thinking about promises, we generally suppose that it is a natural person who understands and commits to meet the obligations stated in their promise.[1] Furthermore, it is an individual who feels morally obliged to keep their promises, who may possess the personal character to do so, or who feels guilty afterward if they break their promises. It is therefore tempting to treat promise-making and promise-keeping as primarily psychological matters that stem from individual personalities and personal comprehension. Yet in the modern credit economy many promises are made by "fictive" individuals, not by living persons. Fictive individuals include firms, corporations, organizations, government agencies, and other types of collective actors which, thanks to the law, are able to own, buy, or sell property, sue and being sued in a court of law, enter into contracts, or borrow money. Corporations can even own other corporations, and thanks to the 2010 Citizens United decision by the U.S. Supreme Court, they can also actively participate in American politics.

Modern markets are dominated by fictive individuals, which include all the for-profit corporations that organize so much economic activity. Along with individuals, they are the entities that make and receive vast numbers of promises as both borrowers and lenders. A business might, for example, issue bonds, receive a medium-term loan from its bank, obtain short-term trade credit from its suppliers, and extend credit to its customers. Although organizations make and break promises, it is simplistic to extend the discussion of promises from persons to fictive persons without modification. Organizations don't have intentions, personalities, "moral fiber," or a sense of remorse.

Why would a corporation make a financial promise? The most obvious reason is that corporations need funds, and borrowing is one way to proceed. Many firms start out as simple proprietorships, partnerships, or family businesses, funded by family resources or money borrowed from the founder's friends. At that early stage, investors and borrowers are bound together by kinship and other close social ties, and so not only do lenders know a great deal about the ability and character of the borrowers but they may have some obligation to lend.[2] Indeed, the personal creditworthiness of the proprietor or partners and the creditworthiness of the firm are indistinguishable. But if firms succeed and grow in size, their demands for capital often outstrip the financial capacity of the founding families, and they shift from proprietorship to partnership or corporation.[3] There are many ways to raise capital, of course, and they don't all involve making promises to repay a debt. Once firms become sufficiently profitable, retained earnings can be an important internal source of financing. Instead of dispersing profits to owners, the firm keeps the money to fund further investment. Corporations can also issue shares and grant ownership rights to those who purchase the shares. But shares are different from debt in that a shareholder is a residual claimant who can enjoy a dividend only after all of a firm's financial obligations and debts have been met. In other words, only after a firm has kept all of the promises made to its creditors can it reward its owners. Dividends are an option rather than an obligation. On the investor side, bonds may be preferable to shares because they have a stronger claim on the borrowing firm's free cash flow, and their payout is more certain.

The extent to which firms raise money through borrowing poses the issue of leverage.[4] Other things being equal, greater indebtedness means higher leverage, which in turn means more fixed claims on a firm's future income. A firm that borrows is using other people's money to fund its activities but with an obligation to repay them later. Should a highly leveraged firm be profitable, there are fewer claimants on the residual profits (i.e., on the money left over after all expenses, including debt payments, have been met). And with limited liability the risk of losses shifts from owners to creditors.[5] So leverage can increase the returns to equity.[6] But it also reduces the borrowing firm's margin for error by tying up cash flow for debt service. Whereas dividend payments to shareholders are discretionary, interest payments to bondholders or other creditors are not: they are strict promises. Leverage disciplines firm managers by subjecting them to non-discretionary financial obligations. So leverage magnifies profits, but also losses. For example, British and American banks increased their leverage at the end of the twentieth century, and while this benefited shareholders when the banks were profitable, it also made them more vulnerable to economic shocks like the financial crisis of 2008.[7]

Real and fictive individuals can both make financial promises, but where do fictive individuals come from? Private corporations are creatures of the state. They exist and enjoy valuable legal powers only because some sovereign government chooses to bestow such privileges.[8] And since the early modern era, governments have granted these privileges because corporations were socially useful organizational forms: they could help advance education, encourage trade and organize economic growth, bolster public finances, or undertake specific tasks that were beyond the ability of a single individual. Fictive individuals could also, of course, serve private interests, and did so in abundance. In general, their creation serves a varying combination of public and private interests.

In the United States, the power to create a corporation is lodged at the state level.[9] At first, incorporation was a very special privilege indeed, and only a small number of corporations were created in the late eighteenth or early nineteenth century, each through a special legislative act. It took passage of a specific law to bestow a single corporate charter, so only a few corporations existed. Often they were created to achieve a particular goal: to build a canal or railroad, found and operate a bank, operate a turnpike road, and so on. With the passage of general laws of incorporation by the states, however, it became much easier to create a corporation and so their numbers grew rapidly.[10] Promoters didn't have to appeal to politicians to pass a special law; instead they could just file some paperwork, pay a fee, and thereby incorporate. A specific political act became a routine administrative procedure, and so these fictive individuals multiplied.[11] Modern corporations also possess a feature that bears directly on how the promises they issue are received: limited liability. In the event that a corporation becomes insolvent, if its liabilities exceed its assets or it can't pay its bills as they become due, the liability of the firm's owners (shareholders) to creditors is limited by the extent of their investment.[12] They may lose all that they invested, but they can lose no more even if outstanding obligations remain after all the firm's assets have been liquidated.[13] In other words, the debts of a corporation are separate from the personal obligations of its shareholders. Limited liability was established in the United States during the 1820s[14] and shifted the risk of losses from shareholders to creditors. Thereafter, assessments of promises issued by corporations were tempered by the realization that if at some point losses became sufficiently large, they would adversely affect the creditors and not just the shareholders. The burden of broken promises had shifted.

Early on in the United States the biggest corporations, with the greatest need for capital, were those concerned with the transportation projects that linked the young country together: roads, canals, and especially railroads. Infrastructural corporations were an obvious engine of economic growth and development. State governments tried to ensure their success in various ways (including generous land grants and tax concessions), although many of them did not actually become profitable.[15] Completed in 1825, the Erie Canal joined Albany, New York (on the Hudson River), to Buffalo, New York, and thereby linked the Eastern Seaboard of the United States with the newly settled Great Lakes region of the Midwest. Because shipping goods over water was so much cheaper than by land, the new canal reduced transportation costs and meant that midwestern agricultural commodities could more easily be exchanged for eastern manufactured goods.[16] Commercial barge traffic on the Erie Canal grew so quickly and profitably that it became a much-emulated success story,[17] and soon many states pursued canal and railroad projects.[18] Alas, few of these enjoyed the success of the Erie Canal, and the heavy demands they placed on state finances led to a wave of public defaults and other financial problems.[19] Collectively, however, these investments reduced transportation costs by so much that a truly national economy emerged out of previously separate regional economies: Americans living in one part of the country could readily trade with people living in an entirely different part, exchanging goods with a relatively low value-to-weight ratio.[20] The bonds of commerce reached over greater and greater distances.

The geographical expansion of exchange soon posed some fundamental problems: How to evaluate financial promises made by strangers whose social distance from the lender was amplified by physical distance? And how to ensure compliance with such promises when parties to a transaction were in different legal jurisdictions? Of course, long-distance trade has occurred for centuries throughout the world, so distance per se was not the problem. Avner Greif (2006) and Francesca Trivellato (2009) show,[21] for example, that Mediterranean trade in the Middle Ages and early modern era combined geographical dispersion with tight social coupling as socially homogeneous mercantile communities used their internal social networks to share information, circulate reputations, and reward (or sanction) good (or bad) behavior.[22] But the social heterogeneity and fluidity of the United States in the nineteenth century made this "solution" impractical because it was hard to acquire reliable information at scale, and social networks extended only so far.[23] And although domestic trade occurred within the boundaries of a single nation, it remained difficult for out-of-state creditors to enforce their claims over local debtors: an Indiana judge might not look kindly on the efforts of a New York lender to foreclose on the mortgage of a local Indianapolis business. How to determine the trustworthiness of those who were not members of the same local community or part of the same social network? As discussed in chapter 3, supply chains extended across the distances between regions, and so one answer to this question emerged in the context of business-to-business trade credit. Credit ratings provided information about debtors and so supported trade among strangers: "As long as our producers, manufacturers or merchants are satisfied to sell only to their immediate neighbors, with whose disposition and ability to pay they are perfectly conversant, so long are they independent of any outside aid in the line of business which a mercantile agency represents. . . . But as the circle of commercial transactions widens and reaches out broadly the necessity of such agency aids becomes apparent. In short, merchandise cannot be sold and distributed without the aid and acceptance of the credit system."[24] But could organizations be rated?

Corporations as fictive individuals were created through law, and the resources early corporations needed to fund their infrastructural activities frequently came from both public and private sources. Public subsidies, land grants, and other government supports funded large infrastructural projects with a contribution from the private sector. Corporations had to make promises in order to secure their private financing. For short-term credit in the nineteenth century, firms could use banks, which would "discount" the short-term promissory notes that firms issued.[25] Short-term borrowing provided working capital for day-to-day operations. In general, however, most U.S. banks were too small to be able to help firms much, and as compared to countries like Germany,[26] U.S. banks played a secondary role in financing industry.[27] A textbook on corporate finance simply noted that "bank loans are not usually to be had except on first-class securities [as collateral] and for short periods."[28] Firms could also obtain short-term financing from their suppliers, through trade credit, and thereby gain coverage by mercantile credit rating agencies like R. G. Dun. However, only the very largest firms could reliably tap the commercial paper market.

Long-term funds consisted primarily of either equity or debt.[29] Equity meant an ownership interest, but debts did not.[30] A bond was a promise, and frequently firms that issued bonds bolstered the credibility of their promises by adding collateral and pledging specific assets as security for the loan.[31] Bond indentures could include a number of provisions (termed "restrictive" or "protective" covenants) requiring the borrower to undertake specific actions and prohibiting the borrower from taking other actions, all of which were intended to enhance the borrower's creditworthiness.[32] Bonds had the additional advantage, as compared to bank loans, of being negotiable. Bonds could easily change hands if the bondholder needed cash, and for much of the late nineteenth and early twentieth centuries, more bonds were traded on the New York Stock Exchange than were stocks. By contrast, bank loans were essentially nontransferable and illiquid.

In the nineteenth century the United States was a capital-poor country, with a sparse population and much land. Domestic savers were insufficiently wealthy or numerous to provide money to borrowers, so a substantial proportion of the investment used to develop the country necessarily came from abroad, particularly from British investors.[33] The problem of whom to trust traveled right across the Atlantic Ocean. But British bond buyers had little direct knowledge of American investment opportunities, and the United States was growing so quickly that information soon became outdated: credible and timely information could not quickly travel across long distances (letters sent from New York to London could take about four weeks in a sailing ship, depending on weather and season).[34] Consider, for example, that between 1840 and 1850 the population of Chicago increased by more than 500 percent: it was impossible for foreigners to track all that occurred in the business community of such a rapidly growing and extraordinarily dynamic city. The general scarcity of information was one reason the British favored bonds over equity: investors didn't need to know as much to evaluate a bond as compared to a share.

For much of the nineteenth century, the flow of capital between American borrowers and British investors was intermediated by Anglo-American merchant banks with names like Barings, Peabody, and Rothschild.[35] Toward the end of the century, U.S. firms like J. P. Morgan & Co. and Kuhn, Loeb & Co. became more active in mediating capital flows from Europe to the United States.[36] Like today's investment banks, these merchant banks operated as "matchmakers" between borrowers and investors, using their specialized access to information to ensure that American borrowers found a ready market for their bonds and that British investors had access to good investment opportunities. The railroads were the biggest and most capital-intensive U.S. businesses and they developed stable working relationships with particular banking houses.[37] A British investor who wasn't sure about trusting an American debtor might nevertheless trust the reputation of the bank that underwrote or distributed the security issue.[38] In general, bond purchases allowed foreign investors the opportunity to benefit financially from the expansion of the U.S. economy, but in a way that promised relatively predictable rates of return and didn't require active management of the business. Furthermore, bonds had the advantage of being sellable if the bondholder needed to obtain cash before the debt fully matured.[39]

American railroads became particularly dependent on bonds as a way to raise capital.[40] To lay down new tracks and acquire the engines and rolling stock needed to move freight and passengers required unprecedented amounts of money. The railroads went through waves of expansion, and their demand for outside funding was particularly acute when, during periods like the early 1850s and 1870s, thousands of miles of new track were laid every year.[41] It is hard to get precise measures for the early years, but in the 1880s and 1890s U.S. railroads raised more money through new bond issues than through stock.[42] By using bonds, railroad promoters could obtain the financing they needed but without diluting their ownership rights, exploiting one of the advantages of leverage. Furthermore, European investors generally preferred bonds over stocks.[43] However, debt financing also raised the chances of default or insolvency: firms were contractually obligated to make fixed interest payments to bondholders whereas there was no such obligation to pay dividends to shareholders. And the importance of the entire railroad sector was such that railroads dominated stock markets as well as bond markets. Over 80 percent of the stocks traded on the New York Stock Exchange in 1885 were for railroads.[44]

During economic crises, many U.S. railroads defaulted on their bonds and ended up in receivership. Overbuilding and rate wars encumbered many railroads with too much capacity and not enough revenue to service their debts. Defaults triggered all kinds of reorganizational activity, often coordinated by financiers and bankers, in which railroad lines were merged, consolidated, and reordered. Reorganizations largely occurred outside of bankruptcy court because, until 1898, there was no permanent federal bankruptcy statute. Reorganization meant cost-cutting, including cuts to the payments owed to bondholders, in order to return the railroad to profitability. A specific federal court proceeding, known as an "equity receivership," became the main legal vehicle through which many failed railroads were reorganized, and because so many railroads failed during the 1870s and 1890s, federal judges were able to play a key role in restructuring the U.S. railroad industry.[45] Judges collaborated with railroad management and their investment bankers to reorganize the railroads into larger, robust systems, usually at the expense of the bondholders and other creditors. For example, railroads that went bankrupt in the 1890s had their fixed charges, like bond payments, reduced by 27 percent.[46] In this way, the promises that many railroads made to their investors were judicially "adjusted" after the fact so that the railroads could become economically viable again. Creditors paid the price for management mistakes and overcapacity, but also for their own over-optimism.

Over time, the U.S. economy became less dependent on foreign investors. World War I quickly changed the United States from a debtor to a creditor nation as European combatants on all sides liquidated their American assets to pay for war.[47] By the end, many of its military allies ended up owing money to the United States, a fact that played a big role in international debt negotiations during the interwar period. Domestic investors became well able to purchase the stocks and bonds that large U.S. firms used to finance their long-term growth. The appetite for securities was particularly strong among the growing numbers of domestic institutional investors that sought conservative financial returns and stable assets: insurance companies, trusts, and banks.[48] Bonds promised a steady income stream and so they were often preferred to stocks by more conservative investors.

Domestic investors had to choose from among growing numbers of alternatives, especially in the bond markets. Hundreds of railroads issued bonds, many of them multiple times, and given the dynamism of the industry and the variability among railroads it was hard for an investor to remain fully informed. As financial promises, the value of bonds depended on future railroad performance, but accurate accounting and financial information was sparse and so many investors had no adequate way to evaluate these promises. However, financial journalists like Henry Varnum Poor started to collect systematic information about railroads and to publish reference volumes (termed "manuals").[49] A subscriber could find, in one place, the kind of information that was helpful to evaluate the financial status of a listed railroad. For instance, in the 1868 manual the reader could look up the entry for the New York Central Railroad, see the names of company directors, and track mileage and equipment, earnings and income, and the various bond issues, among other things.[50] Yet in the absence of generally accepted accounting rules or standardized disclosure requirements, it was still hard for investors to interpret this complex mass of information. What was the "bottom line"? How to weigh and combine all the facts that populated Poor's heavy tomes?

In 1909, following the 1907 financial crisis,[51] John Moody went beyond Poor's format by publishing *ratings* of railroad bonds, in addition to providing descriptive information about railroads. In so doing, Moody explicitly adopted the format previously developed by rating agencies like R. G. Dun and Bradstreet's to deal with trade credit. As discussed in chapter 3, over the nineteenth century credit rating agencies educated their clients in the use of ordinal categories as a summary way to think about creditworthiness among businesses. When Dun rated a firm, it placed that firm into an ordered category system with the most creditworthy firms classified into the top category and the least creditworthy firms at the bottom. In 1905, for example, the firms with the highest level of "pecuniary strength" were rated "AA," indicating they were worth $1 million or more, and those with the best "general credit" received the "A1" rating. Alphanumerical labels reinforced the fact that the categories were ordered.[52] This method was widespread by the end of the century as agencies like R. G. Dun rated more than one million firms and provided their ratings to the business community as well as to customers like credit insurance companies and bank credit departments.[53] In the particular case of credit insurance, mercantile agencies provided the "hard evidence" used to estimate the risk of default and price an insurance contract.[54] With a growing number of overseas branch offices, Dun could even supply credit information about foreign firms to its clients. But all such rating information was cast in a highly standardized categorical format.

Thanks to the success of the mercantile agencies, ordered categories had become a familiar and taken-for-granted way for people to comprehend the trustworthiness of a business debtor: which firms were most likely to keep their financial promises? Moody's innovation was to expand the application of ordinal ratings from short-term financing to long-term debt, from unsecured trade credit to railroad bonds. Moody's initial decision to focus on railroads, rather than large industrial firms, was a wise one. It allowed him to pursue the customers who bought the older statistical compendia like that published by Poor. Railroad bonds were particularly popular investments among banks and other institutional investors, and were also commonly used to secure call-loans on the stock market, so there was a big appetite for Moody's information.[55]

The parallels between the new bond ratings and older credit ratings were made very clear to the clients that John Moody hoped to serve.[56] In one advertisement, Moody's stated that its rating book "performs the same function in respect to securities as the commercial reference books do in credit matters."[57] Elsewhere, Moody's drew a series of comparisons between different kinds of credit assessment: "Business men do not give credit to customers until they have ascertained their rating. Bankers do not discount notes or make loans until they have ascertained the applicant's rating. Investors should not buy securities until they have ascertained the 'rating' on them."[58] Yet the claim that bond ratings provided information that would improve financial decision making wasn't simply marketing hype, for Moody's very first edition was reviewed in the *Annals of the American Academy of Political and Social Science* as if it were a scholarly monograph. There, Emory R. Johnson, a business professor at the Wharton School who specialized in railroads and transportation, stated that Moody had endeavored "to demonstrate in an intelligent and scientific way the relative values of the different railroad securities."[59] Unlike the earlier reference volumes published by people like Henry Varnum Poor, Moody applied a rating system to represent what Johnson called "deductions" about railroads, and not just to compile volumes of facts.[60] The shift from description to deduction, accomplished under the aura of science, was greatly helped by the fact that after passage of the Hepburn Act of 1906, railroads were subject to accounting standards set by the Interstate Commerce Commission, which forced railroads to provide comparable financial information about their own operations.[61] Unlike Poor's earlier railroad manuals, Moody obtained more systematic financial information about railroads and used that as the basis for his bond ratings.

Moody's first bond rating manual contained an extensive discussion of the meaning of the new categories. The highest category, labeled "Aaa," was given to securities: "regarded as of the highest class, both as regards security and general convertibility."[62] Moody then described each of the rating categories, in order from "Aa," "A," "Baa," "Ba," "B," "Caa," "Ca," "C," "D," and finally "E." The latter rating was given to defaulted bond issues. Although there were some minor adjustments (including expansion of the number of categories), the basic format of the ordinal category system has persisted until today (2021) for Moody's ratings, and was quickly adopted by Moody's main competitors in the bond rating business. Inadvertently, older mercantile rating agencies like R. G. Dun had created a general "language" for evaluating financial promises. Moody also emulated the mercantile agency business model, selling information to subscribers who would then use it to guide their own investment decisions. Today, this is known as the "user pays" model.

Moody cautioned that these ratings were: "to be looked upon as indicators of values, rather than as definite and specific opinions."[63] These ratings helped summarize a large amount of detailed information that Moody gathered about each railroad. The value of a particular bond was affected by many things including the size of the populations served by the railroad, railroad location, the amount of freight and passenger traffic, average train-loads, the track mileage operated and value of the equipment, the quality of management,[64] revenues, passenger and freight rates,[65] operating expenses, fixed charges (which include interest paid on debt), gross earnings, train-mile earnings, net income on net capital, and assets and liabilities, among other things. All of these things were measured over a period of years rather than just at a single point in time. In his preface, Moody touted the use of the rating manual: "The value of the book to both the Banker and Investor is practically inestimable. . . . it presents A VAST COMPARATIVE VIEW OF RAILROAD VALUES IN THIS COUNTRY IN EVERY YEAR SINCE 1898, SHOWING THE STRENGTH OR WEAKNESS OF ALL THE VARIED SECURITY ISSUES INVOLVED [original emphasis]."[66] Putting all railroad bonds into the same category scheme invited comparative evaluation by allowing users to see whether one bond was better, worse, or about the same as another. Ratings categories provided a common metric for creditworthiness.[67]

Moody's bond rating manual was a great success. The first printing completely sold out and a revised edition was issued the very same year.[68] Such was the national demand for Moody's information that even public libraries in cities far from Wall Street subscribed to the manuals.[69] Other financial publishing firms got into the rating business, but *all* adopted some version of alphanumerically labeled ordinal categories.[70] The rating business was competitive, but a strong consensus formed within the industry about how such evaluative information should be conveyed to clients. Poor's Publishing rated bonds in all industries, beginning in 1922, and Standard Statistics and Fitch covered all industries after 1924.[71] Standard Statistics and Poor's merged in 1941, and so for most of the twentieth century bond rating was dominated by three agencies: Moody's, Standard and Poor's, and Fitch. Moody's itself expanded beyond railroad bonds into other securities, including utility and industrial bonds starting in 1914 and sovereigns (government debt) in 1918. By 1920, Moody's issued four separate manuals (for railroads, industrials, utilities, and sovereigns), rating over fifty thousand different securities.[72] And by 1924, Moody's manuals covered almost the entire bond market.[73] But the problem of how to obtain good information about non-railroad firms remained a serious one. Firms in regulated industries might have to provide some public information about their financial performance, but not until the New Deal were disclosure requirements imposed on all publicly traded firms. For those firms listed on the New York Stock Exchange, exchange rules required them to provide some information about their annual income and balance sheets, but this still left investors largely in the dark.[74] Moody's and the other rating agencies used such public financial information, in addition to developing their own sources.

Bond markets continued to grow as the issuance of debt remained an important source of financing. In 1910, the year after Moody started publishing his ratings, bonds worth $635 million were sold on the New York Stock Exchange, as compared to only $164 million worth of stock. Ten years later, $3,977 million worth of bonds were sold and only $227 million worth of stock.[75] By the mid-1920s published bond ratings were widely used by investors,[76] and the number of households investing in bonds grew rapidly during and after World War I.[77] Thus the demand for information about bonds came from both institutional investors (banks, insurance companies, trust companies, and later pension funds) and increasingly from individuals. Financial policymakers also heeded the rating agencies' information, as indicated by the fact that the Federal Reserve Board itself subscribed to Moody's manuals.[78]

The number and size of bond issues on the most important U.S. securities market, the New York Stock Exchange, grew throughout the 1920s. Bonds were bought and sold, and rated. These issuances included many domestic bonds (e.g., corporates, railroads, utilities, and municipals) but also the bonds of foreign borrowers looking to tap American sources of capital, especially sovereign and subsovereign governments.[79] European and Latin American governments were active borrowers in the New York market, forgoing London, and consequently were evaluated by the bond rating agencies.[80] Many of these foreign bond issuers went into actual default during the Great Depression, but even the foreign sovereign bonds that avoided default were downgraded substantially by the rating agencies after 1931.[81] The Great Depression was tough on bondholders and bond raters.

The use of ordered categories to rate and evaluate promises was invented in the nineteenth century by the mercantile rating agencies that focused on trade credit. Their published ratings were an informational commodity, produced by the agencies and sold to their clients. And with the commercial success of firms like Bradstreet's and R. G. Dun these categories spread throughout the business community, becoming an institutionalized and market-based means for firms to evaluate each other.[82] But the significance of ordered categories expanded even further with Moody's extension of their use from trade credit to long-term corporate finance. Just as the mercantile agencies came to encompass most small businesses within their purview, so too did the bond rating agencies eventually cover all classes of bond issuers. By the interwar period, the bond rating agencies were routinely passing judgment on sovereign governments from around the world.

Bond Ratings, Banks, and Regulators

U.S. banks were big holders of bonds, and the collapse of the economy in the early 1930s hurt corporate profits, lowered bond prices, and damaged bank balance sheets.[83] Many banks became insolvent as their assets, including both loans and financial securities, lost a great deal of value: borrowers were unable to make their loan payments and bonds went into default. On the liability side, banks were also vulnerable to bank runs, especially if they were small or had only a few branches. Without federal deposit insurance, serious doubts about the solvency of a bank could set off a rush by panicking depositors to withdraw their money. By definition, demand deposits were payable on demand, and banks couldn't fulfill all of their promises at the same time. When that happened, solvent but illiquid banks were forced to close.

Bank regulators faced an unfolding disaster that culminated in President Roosevelt's bank holiday. Traditional policy tools, like the Federal Reserve's discount window, provided little help. But some new measures began to use bond ratings in a way that, in the long run, substantially increased their significance. Following the emergency bank holiday of March 1933, 3,460 banks were suspended in the third quarter of 1933. This continued a trend that saw the total number of banks within the Federal Reserve System drop from 8,929 in 1928 to 5,606 in 1933. Over the same period, the number of non-member banks declined from 16,869 to 8,601. The collapse of bank assets, and the subsequent collapse of many banks, put tremendous pressure both on the U.S. financial system and on the regulators and politicians who oversaw it.

One response to these problems involved a change in bank examination rules. Traditionally, before the era of federal deposit insurance, it was the task of federal or state bank examiners to assess the financial status of a bank, to appraise its assets and liabilities, and to close down banks that were insolvent.[84] But by relaxing the financial standards they applied, bank regulators could make it easier for marginal banks to survive the crisis, buy a little time, and have an opportunity to recover. Before 1930, the Comptroller of the Currency (which oversaw banks with national charters) valued securities like bonds at their market value when calculating the overall worth of bank assets during a bank examination.[85] This was the equivalent of today's "mark to market" or "fair value" accounting. As market prices plummeted, the value of bank assets declined and more banks became technically insolvent (i.e., their liabilities were greater than their assets). With the collapse of the stock market, it was obvious that banks couldn't be helped by having them raise more capital from investors: no one was eager to invest in banks by purchasing bank shares. But starting in 1931, the Comptroller initiated a new regulatory policy that made use of the bond ratings produced by agencies like Moody's, Poor's Publishing, and Standard Statistics. This change built on a new valuation method devised by the Federal Reserve Bank of New York to use bond ratings as a way to estimate the overall quality of a bank's bond portfolio.[86] Gustav Osterhus, the official who invented the new procedure, styled it as a "mechanical method designed to disclose true quality of a bank's investment account."[87] According to the Comptroller's new policy, bonds rated "BBB" and higher could be valued at their *historical cost* (i.e., what the bank originally paid for them) rather than at their current market value.[88] In essence, bank examiners were given permission to ignore falling prices of highly rated bonds and to overlook the impairment of bank assets. The Federal Reserve System gave additional recognition to bond ratings when it started in 1930 to publish tables and charts that showed how current bond yields varied across different rating categories, using Moody's system of Aaa, Aa, A, and Baa for "investment grade" securities.[89] Many state bank regulators subsequently followed the Comptroller's new policy. Indeed, in 1938 the National Association of Supervisors of State Banks affirmed the use of bond ratings to group bank bond holdings into four different classes, with the highest rated bonds (i.e., given "AAA," "Aa," "A," or "Baa" ratings) being valued at their historic cost.[90] Highly rated bonds would no longer be marked to market, and so the promises that they embodied were henceforth to be treated as more credible than market prices reflected.[91] Regulators overlooked how the market valued certain promises.

New Deal bank regulations also addressed the other end of the rating spectrum: bonds with very low ratings. The Banking Act of 1935 gave to the Comptroller of the Currency the power to impose restrictions on the kinds of securities a national bank could own on its own account. In 1936, the Comptroller issued a new rule that prohibited the purchase of securities that were "distinctly or predominantly speculative," or of a lower standard.[92] The real problem with U.S. banks, the Comptroller claimed when speaking to the California Bankers Association in May 1936, lay chiefly among bank assets rather than liabilities. During the 1920s, too many banks had invested in "speculative" bonds, and it was necessary to prevent them from doing so again.[93] Speculative bonds offered the allure of high returns, so only a strict prohibition could prevent bankers from succumbing to temptation. The rule also explicitly referred to the agency rating manuals when defining terms like "speculative" or "predominantly speculative" (which, in the Moody's rating scale, meant ratings below the "Baa" level). Since bank examiners had little experience assessing financial securities, the application of ratings to bond portfolios was done quite mechanically.[94] Most state bank regulators followed the federal lead and adopted similar prohibitions.[95] Although bond ratings had been published and used by private investors since 1909, this direct incorporation of ratings into bank regulations increased and formalized their significance many-fold. Low-rated bonds were sanctioned as much as high-rated bonds were encouraged.

An additional step occurred in 1938, when the Uniform Agreement on Bank Supervisory Procedures tried to standardize bank examination procedures across multiple regulatory agencies, including the Federal Reserve, Comptroller of the Currency, and Federal Deposit Insurance Corporation (FDIC). The new common standard put bank assets into overall categories, depending on the bank examiner's judgment of the relevant level of risk or impairment. Assets in the top category were to be shown at book value, without adjustment for market depreciation.[96] In appraising assets, examiners were to consider them "in the light of inherent soundness rather than on a basis of day to day fluctuations" (Federal Reserve Board 1938a: 564). More generally, regulators affirmed that the overall solvency of the banking system "should not be measured by the precarious yardstick of current market quotations which often reflect speculative and not true appraisals of intrinsic worth" (Federal Reserve Board 1938a: 564). Here the Federal Reserve Bulletin utilized specific language to distinguish mere market prices from "intrinsic worth" or "inherent soundness" and to downplay the significance of market price. When these different measures didn't align, the agreement clearly signaled to regulators and examiners that they should overlook low valuations and emphasize instead "intrinsic worth."[97] However, the Federal Reserve Board was emphatic that ignoring market price did not mean a "relaxation of standards."[98] Many U.S. state banking authorities again followed the lead of federal regulators and henceforth the distinction between "investment grade" and "below investment grade" became enormously consequential. These policies constrained the kind of securities that banks could possess and in effect prevented them from accepting promises that were insufficiently credible. In parallel, U.S. life insurance regulators, which also operated primarily at the state level, began to use ratings in their valuation of insurance company assets. Starting in 1932, New York State began to allow bonds to be amortized (from their original purchase price) instead of being valued at market price, but only if they were highly rated by the rating agencies. Other states followed New York's lead.[99]

Bond market prices dropped at the outset of the Depression, particularly in the latter part of 1931 and into early 1932, and so these new valuation policies allowed federal and state bank and insurance regulators to overlook the collapse of asset values and to treat a regulated financial institution as if it were in better condition than it would otherwise seem. Market valuation of bank bonds was partly suspended and selectively replaced by the private evaluations of the bond rating agencies. In addition, new prudential standards for banks constrained their bond portfolios by excluding assets that were, in the judgment of the rating agencies, "below investment grade."[100] For the first time, privately generated bond ratings were given public regulatory standing in a way that deliberately protected banks from the vagaries of the bond market and forestalled insolvency. In this way, ratings didn't simply measure risk, they managed it. Such regulatory forbearance was intended to provide a "breathing space" and so keep a financial institution open until a future time when, hopefully, its assets would have recovered to their "true" value. Yet this change was not simply an ad hoc lifeline thrown to banks, for as Jones (1940: 186) explained: "bank assets have a particularly indeterminate value in periods of crisis. Current market prices cannot be accepted because markets are demoralized, and many classes of bank assets, e.g., most bank loans and real estate, cannot be sold at any price." In other words, during a crisis, previously trustworthy market signals became inaccurate measures of financial value, reflecting a "demoralized" collective sentiment rather than economic fundamentals. Since market price is the default measure of value, departure from this standard would presumably be justified only under special circumstances. Yet when the Federal Reserve Board reconsidered the Uniform Agreement in 1949, during the postwar boom, the insulation of highly rated bonds from valuation by market price was simply continued.[101] Special circumstances may have prompted the change, but there was no reversal once normality returned. As more regulatory agencies adopted ratings, the difference between "investment grade" and "below investment grade" (lower than "Baa" on Moody's rating scale) became very significant.[102]

The regulatory incorporation of ratings was not unprecedented. Even before banking regulators affirmed the significance of bond ratings, U.S. judges had already recognized them in courts of law.[103] Starting in the 1920s, U.S. judges made reference to the bond rating agencies, citing their publications as credible sources of factual information or as authoritative opinions. Ratings were useful when applying the "prudent man" rule for investment, which was particularly important in disputes involving someone in a trustee role. In part, judges were responding to the widespread adoption of bond ratings by various business groups, including unit banks, stockbrokers, and investment banks. Such widespread use helped make bond ratings seem like an integral part of normal and reasonable business practice, and thus provided a convenient benchmark for litigation about business activities. In so doing, the judiciary simply reflected the taken-for-grantedness of ratings.

What Do Ratings Signal?

The new regulatory status of bond ratings prompted more systematic investigation of their use and efficacy. For decades, until the late 1930s, producers and consumers of ratings agreed that they were useful but didn't bother to gather systematic evidence about rating performance. Because people were willing to pay for the information, and because of its widespread use, it was tempting to conclude that such information *must* be useful. Bond rating agencies publicly espoused the value of the information they sold but didn't offer empirical support. It was easy to think of many examples where highly rated corporations reliably paid interest on their bonds, and even of some instances where highly rated firms defaulted on their bonds. But there was no systematic evidence about whether highly rated bonds in general defaulted less than low-rated bonds. Following decades of unexamined usage, the first systematic investigation of bond ratings was done by a graduate student at Columbia University, subsequently published in book form. Gilbert Harold (1938) gathered a sample of 363 bonds and examined their performance from July 1929 until July 1935. The question, for Harold, was to determine the relationship between rating and performance: "Stated as a principle, the expectation of both the rating agencies and their clients is that bonds of given ratings should perform marketwise approximately in relation to bonds of other ratings as the respective ratings stand with reference to each other. Thus A+ bonds should have a market record better than those of any other rating."[104] After doing a relatively simple tabular analysis, his conclusion was that ratings indeed provided useful information about bond yields and default probabilities.[105]

At about the same time as Harold was completing his individual research, several organizations combined to undertake the much more ambitious Corporate Bond Project. This research was sponsored by the WPA (Works Progress Administration) and involved a collaboration among the NBER (National Bureau of Economic Research), the Federal Reserve System, the Comptroller of the Currency, the FDIC, the SEC, and several banks and rating agencies. The collapse of bond prices, the crisis in the banking sector, and the new involvement of the U.S. government as an insurer of bank deposits provided ample motive to gather systematic data on bond markets over a long time horizon: "On the one hand huge and steadily increasing amounts of funds were tied up in bond investment by banks, insurance companies, and other institutional investors; on the other, there was a serious lack of information regarding the behavior of the bond market by which to guide investment standards and policies."[106] So the project gathered statistical data on bonds from 1900 until 1938 so that researchers could address, among other issues, "the relative merits of market price, legal lists and investment agencies' ratings as an index of bond quality."[107] In other words: "What about the average rating performance of bond rating agencies?"[108] Work on the project began in January 1939 and data collection continued until November 1941. Analysis of the data, however, took considerably longer, and the project resulted in a series of volumes published in the 1950s.[109] Among other things, these studies finally established that overall default rates of corporate bonds varied systematically with bond ratings: higher ratings were indeed associated with lower default rates.[110] But these empirical results came after, rather than before, the widespread incorporation of bond ratings into public regulations and legal proceedings. Subsequent usage of ratings occurred in the knowledge that ratings were "predictive" when it came to corporate bonds, but they had already been widely used for decades in the total absence of such knowledge.[111]

The pace of change continued after the Great Depression, when official regulatory status was granted to credit ratings, and following World War II, with the vast expansion of U.S. industrial capacity and growth of a consumer economy. On the regulatory side, bond ratings continued to gain importance.[112] In 1951, the National Association of Insurance Commissioners (NAIC) used ratings to create uniform asset categories for insurance companies,[113] and ratings remain important in insurance regulation.[114] In 1975, the Securities and Exchange Commission began to use ratings to set net capital rules for broker-dealers and created a new official category, Nationally Recognized Statistical Rating Organizations (NRSRO), with which to designate the most important rating agencies.[115] Then, at the international level, ratings became part of the Basel II Bank Capital Standards as a way to set the "risk weights" given to bank assets. And ratings gained even more global importance when they were incorporated into the contractual language that supported the over-the-counter (OTC) financial derivatives market. Unlike the standardized derivatives traded on exchanges, OTC derivatives are customized, usually in order to "hedge" a very particular risk faced by the client (e.g., the possibility that future income denominated in a foreign currency might suddenly drop in value). Transactions are usually specified on the basis of a master agreement between a dealer-bank and its client, building on standardized contractual language designed by the International Swaps and Derivatives Association.[116] Starting in the 1990s, ratings were used to measure and mitigate "counterparty risk" for various kinds of swaps. This risk arose from the possibility that the other party to a transaction might not be able to fulfill its contractual obligation, and like the old-fashioned mortgage, risk was managed through collateral. In the "credit support annex" attached to the master agreement, credit ratings were used to estimate the magnitude of "counterparty risk," to set the amount of collateral, and to value the collateral itself.[117] So, for example, if a rating agency lowered the ratings of a party to a swap, that party would be contractually required to post more collateral. The general point is that credit ratings have been built right into the basic contractual "machinery" of the international OTC derivatives market, that they were adopted by global financial regulators, and that ratings retained their contractual and regulatory significance even after the global financial crisis of 2008.[118] As a standardized assessment of financial promises originally applied to railroads and other corporations, ratings have become pervasively important.

One striking long-term trend in corporate finance was the overall increase in leverage.[119] For many decades after 1945, U.S. corporations in unregulated industries increased their debt-to-equity ratios, borrowing more money in proportion to their equity.[120] This trend held true across many industries and among firms large and small (although in recent decades smaller firms began to deleverage). In a sense, shifting the balance of corporate finance from equity and toward debt increased the importance of the promises that firms made, if only because they were making so many more of them. When those promises took the form of bonds, their credibility was publicly assessed by the bond rating agencies. If they involved loans, then the lending bank conducted a private credit assessment. A highly leveraged firm relies on borrowed money, and the benefits of profitable performance get enjoyed by a smaller number of shareholders. But a more leveraged firm also has less margin for error as it is contractually obligated to meet its bond interest payments. To fail to do so is to default, and such an event sets off a series of unpleasant legal consequences.

Why Do Modern Firms Borrow?

Modern corporate finance is a much-studied topic, and several theories attempt to explain how and why contemporary firms raise money.[121] The obvious fact is that firms seek capital to finance investment and operations, but there are many ways to do this. The "pecking order" theory posits that firms have adopted a financing hierarchy, starting with retained earnings, then debt, and finally equity.[122] Only when the most-preferred alternative is exhausted do firms move on to the next one, so issuing stock is the measure of last resort. This approach is consistent with the fact that most investments by contemporary U.S. nonfinancial corporations are financed by internal cash flow.[123] Another approach argues that trade-offs between the costs (deadweight losses under bankruptcy) and benefits (e.g., tax advantages) of debt determine its usage, with outcomes weighted by the likelihood of their occurrence. Yet another notes that conservative investors prefer bonds, which offer less variable returns, whereas investors interested in higher gains may prefer stocks, which provide greater "upside" potential.[124] Sociological approaches stress the important of networks formed at the corporate level through board interlocks,[125] or between loan officers and business clients,[126] in shaping reliance on loans. Frank and Goyal (2009: 26) weigh different approaches and find a number of factors that raise leverage (i.e., firms with more tangible assets tend to have higher leverage, as do larger firms and firms in industries with more leverage) or lower it (i.e., firms with high profits and firms with high market-to-book ratios). But these firm-level factors do not account for the long-term trend toward greater leverage, and Graham and colleagues (2015) instead stress the importance of changes in the overall economic environment. Whatever the causes, however, it remains true that U.S. corporations increasingly used formal promises as a way to secure financial resources. And in the last several decades, U.S. corporations have borrowed less from banks and have instead issued bonds as a way to get outside funding.[127] Consequently, U.S. bond markets are relatively large as compared to those in other countries.[128]

Information is one of the keys to lending. A lender considers the promises made by a borrower in light of the lender's vulnerability but also depending on how much the lender knows about the borrower. The absence of business information certainly provided an opportunity for John Moody to gather and summarize information about bonds and then sell it to investors. Early in the twentieth century, more information was available about railroads than for industrial corporations, chiefly because the former were regulated and subject to more stringent reporting requirements.[129] Starting with Kansas in 1911, a number of states passed so-called "blue sky" laws to regulate the sale of financial securities within the given state and so prevent securities fraud, but these laws were relatively weak.[130] Credible information about large publicly traded corporations remained a problem until the 1930s. The disclosure requirements mandated by the Securities Act of 1933 and the Securities Exchange Act of 1934 required firms to publish financial statements annually and to have those statements audited by an independent accounting firm. By design, this measure expanded and standardized the amount of publicly available financial information about firms that were traded on U.S. stock exchanges.[131] The 1934 Act also established the Securities and Exchange Commission, thus ensuring a more vigorous level of enforcement. But for medium-sized or smaller firms, or for those that weren't publicly traded, credible information remained scarce and so demand continued for the services of firms like Dun and Bradstreet.[132]

Securitization

Bonds and commercial bank loans used to look like two very distinct ways for firms to raise money, but recently these two categories have become blurred from the lender side. The role of banks and bank loans in financing corporations changed, and one of its unintended effects has been to make the rating agencies even more important. U.S. banks have altered how they lend, shifting from an originate-to-hold model (where a bank kept a loan on its balance sheet until it was paid off) to the originate-to-distribute model.[133] The latter means that banks move loans off their balance sheets by securitizing them: bundling them with other similar loans, creating separate investment vehicles to receive the loan revenues, and issuing marketable securities that then can be sold to investors. For the banks, shrinking their balance sheet reduces the capital reserves they have to set aside to cover potential losses, and so bank capital isn't tied up for the full duration of the loan. In effect, securitization turned mostly illiquid loans into tradeable securities, and it allowed banks to exit their traditional role as financial intermediaries.[134] No longer would banks simply take deposits and make loans, putting the money they received from their depositors into personal, commercial, or real estate loans. Instead, disintermediation meant that banks engineered a more direct connection between savers and borrowers, using securitization as the vehicle and earning fee income by engineering deals. It also meant that when firms borrowed, they were more able to go directly to capital markets rather than rely on their bank.[135]

Securitization turns cash flows into financial instruments, and became increasingly important in the latter decades of the twentieth century.[136] Today, given how widespread securitization has become, the cash flow could arise in any number of ways: as credit card receivables (monthly payments coming from credit card holders), home mortgage payments, commercial loan payments, student loan payments, and so on. Historically, however, home mortgages were an important starting point (see chapter 7). The basic anatomy of securitization is simple. It was discovered by nineteenth-century investors in U.S. farm mortgages but then was "reinvented" in the 1970s by government-sponsored enterprises like Freddie Mac (Federal Home Loan Mortgage Corporation) as a way to support the U.S. housing market. In what is now known as a "pass through" securitization, assets are pooled together, and then new bond-like securities are issued against those assets. Each new security has a claim on a small but equal proportion of the total cash flow generated by the assets, and there is no ranking by seniority. Securitization also severs the direct link that a traditional loan establishes between a debtor and a creditor. No longer does a particular lender assess a particular borrower and hold the loan until maturity. Instead, a single investor lends to many debtors, and a single debtor borrows from many investors. Securitization helps transform illiquid loans into liquid securities. Generally, it is much easier for the investor to sell off a bond than it is for a bank to sell off a loan (partly because bonds are more standardized), and so an investor who may wish to recover their capital before a loan matures will find securitization attractive. Securitization encourages the development of secondary markets.

Modern securitizations are usually much more complicated than a "pass through" arrangement. They are based on a variety of underlying assets, including regular and "subprime" mortgages, commercial mortgages, business loans, equipment leases, credit card receivables, home equity loans, small business loans, car loan payments, and so on.[137] The assets are placed into a "special purpose vehicle" that is "bankruptcy remote" from the originator. This means that both the underlying assets and the new securities will be legally unaffected by the bankruptcy of the firm that engineered the securitization. And they involve a more complicated structure in which the securities that are issued are grouped into multiple "tranches" that vary by seniority. As payments come into the pool, the money is used first to satisfy the obligations in the top tranche, with the highest seniority, and only after do payments go to the second tranche, and then only after those obligations are fully met do payments go to the third tranche, and so on down the line. In designing complex securitizations, banks made use of the internal credit rating systems discussed in chapter 4, using them to model the riskiness of underlying assets but also the overall risk profiles of the new securities as they varied, tranche by tranche.

Today, the credit rating agencies play a central role in the success of securitizations (also known as "structured finance") because they rate the resulting securities.[138] Most investors are unable to assess the overall quality of an arrangement that puts a large pool of assets through a complex structure that involves grouping, repackaging, and tranching, plus additional credit enhancements.[139] Even if the underlying assets consist of relatively straightforward promises, the securitization process creates a new and complex compound promise that is simply opaque. So the issuer that originates a securitization (typically a commercial or investment bank, or a hedge fund) will pay one of the rating agencies to rate the securities, hoping to get as high a rating as possible. The top tranche, which has priority claim on the cash flow, will get the highest rating (typically, "AAA"), but lower-order tranches might receive only low or middling credit ratings. The lowest rating goes to the lowest tranche, termed the "equity tranche." Originators work with the rating agencies to try to get from the underlying assets the highest possible ratings for the various tranches.

Subprime mortgage securitizations became infamous in 2008, and market activity for some types of structured finance declined afterward (e.g., use of credit default swaps to create synthetic collateralized debt obligations [CDOs]). But the long-term trend was unequivocal: disintermediation in the latter part of the twentieth century meant that when corporations borrowed money from external sources, they increasingly did so by issuing bonds or by taking out loans that through a securitization process were soon turned into bonds (or bond-like instruments). Promises became the primary media of corporate finance. And whether simple (like an old-fashioned corporate bond) or complex (structured financial instruments), the credibility of those promises was evaluated by for-profit rating agencies using a schema essentially unchanged for a century.

Corporate finance is therefore linked to the growing importance of credit ratings in several ways. First of all, corporations borrow by issuing bonds, which get rated. Rating agencies evaluate the promises that corporations directly make to investors. Second, building on the legal recognition bestowed by judges, bond ratings were given regulatory standing, starting in the 1930s, because American banks were so adversely affected by the losses they sustained in their bond portfolios. A change in accounting rules incorporated ratings as an alternative to mark-to-market rules as a way to value bonds, and so banks were partially insulated from the effects of the Great Depression on corporate performance. Third, growing corporate leverage combined with securitization and disintermediation to ensure that U.S. firms increasingly financed their activities by issuing bonds or by making promises that would get turned into bonds through the securitization process. Corporate obligations constitute the underlying assets in many CDOs, including both loans and bonds.[140] As securitization grew, and to the extent that firms raised capital through debt markets rather than equity markets, the role of rating agencies increased.

The bond rating agencies borrowed their business model from the older mercantile agencies (Dun, Bradstreet's), but they first established their reputations by providing information about railroad and corporate bonds to investors. Although it was some decades before solid evidence about the accuracy of bond ratings was finally assembled, results eventually showed that ratings varied with financial outcomes in ways that made sense and demonstrated the value of ratings: higher-rated bonds were less likely to default over a range of time horizons; lower-rated bonds really were riskier.[141] And today, bond default studies done by the rating agencies themselves show that ratings are good predictors of default rates.[142] The ratings acquired new significance when they were absorbed into financial regulations and when they became central to the securitization and financial engineering activities of the late twentieth century. In a sense, they no longer just measured creditworthiness: they helped create it.

Conclusion

Corporations are among the biggest borrowers. Those operating in capital-intensive industries have a particular appetite for finance, one that seldom can be fully met through retained earnings or public offerings of shares. At the very earliest stages, founders can and do turn to family and friends, and so use their social networks, and later on startups in the tech industry can turn to venture capital, but most firms eventually rely on debt. And the development of sophisticated and predictable corporation law in the United

States, particularly in key states like New York, New Jersey, and Delaware (where many firms are now incorporated), allowed firms, as legal entities, to make credible promises. Small and medium-sized firms often look to their bank for a loan, and the firm-bank relationship is useful for exchanging information and crafting a deal. Larger firms, however, turned to capital markets for both short-term and long-term financing, selling commercial paper and issuing bonds. And banks themselves turn to capital markets as they increasingly securitize their loan portfolios.

As a matter of routine, the financial promises made by corporations are now assessed using a categorical system first proposed more than a century ago by the bond rating agencies. These assessments inform investors, as they were originally intended to do, but they also structure regulations at the state, national, and international levels, they play a role in setting legal standards in court, and they have become critical components within the contractual machinery of financial derivatives markets. Even the manifest failures of rating agencies during the 2008 global financial crisis did not displace them from their gatekeeping role within capital markets.[143] Bond raters emulated the system previously developed by the mercantile agencies to assess trade credit, down to the adoption of an ordinal category system. But for decades, until the late 1930s, no one really knew the information value of bond ratings. They were largely taken on faith.

7

Mortgages and Real Estate

People often borrow in order to purchase a home. They make a promise to repay the money, of course, but both borrower and lender understand that this money is earmarked for a very specific goal and that the purchasing power money bestows will be harnessed in a particular way. The purpose of a loan can affect how lenders judge the promises made, and in this instance that purpose receives a great deal of social and political validation. In contemporary America, homeownership is a powerful marker of adulthood and achievement, a key part of the "American dream."[1] Most people cannot purchase a home unless they also receive a loan secured by that home, that is, a home mortgage. Credit is therefore an important input for the construction industry, and new home development or rehabilitation of existing structures creates economic growth and opportunity. The connection between mortgages and residential housing makes this type of loan especially consequential. Residing in their home means that people and their families live in a specific place, in a neighborhood somewhere in a town, city, suburb, or rural area. Their location shapes all kinds of opportunities and constraints for the entire family: access to education (most children attend schools close to their home), access to jobs (most people work within commuting distance of their residence), access to transportation (public or private), exposure to risks (low-crime vs. high-crime neighborhoods), access to public amenities (parks, recreational facilities) and goods and services (stores, bars and restaurants, places of worship), and the possibility of living in a socially heterogeneous, or homogeneous, setting. For most families, their home is also the single-most valuable asset they possess, and homeownership is an important component of family wealth. Residential location is socially fateful, and so the credit that affects where people live has deeply shaped American society. Credit for housing has itself been deeply shaped by public policy, and in the twentieth century much of that policy was aimed at turning the promises contained within a mortgage into highly liquid financial commodities that could be freely bought and sold.

People usually work close to where they live, and subject to zoning rules, commercial real estate markets co-evolve with residential real estate. Credit is equally important for the construction, purchase, and sale of structures that house businesses rather than families. Whether a business owns or leases the space it uses, commercial development requires a lot of capital, much of it raised through debt. And so mortgages are as necessary for commercial real estate as they are for residential buildings, although their connection with residential segregation is not as direct. Commercial real estate differs sharply from residential real estate in that the occupants are income-generating entities. Business seeks income and profits in a way that a family does not.

Mortgages are among the oldest types of loans used to transact in one of the oldest assets: real estate (even the word "mortgage" is old).[2] And they are distinguished by a feature that enhances the attractiveness of the loan to the lender: collateral. Since this encourages the lender to make a loan, it also benefits the borrower. Yet to view a mortgage only as a bilateral device, albeit one that makes it easier for two parties to undertake a mutually advantageous transaction, is too simple. Since a mortgage grants to the lender a collateral interest in the borrower's property, mortgages will always depend on the system of property rights, enforced by the state. As we will see, governments have taken a direct interest in the vitality of particular kinds of mortgage markets, especially those that involve farms and residential homes. Encouraging the flow of credit into agriculture and housing has at times been a top political concern, and governments have intervened energetically to ensure the availability of credit. They have worked to make those particular promises more acceptable to lenders. In this way, mortgages have become multilateral affairs involving lenders, borrowers, and those trying to make loans happen.

A modern mortgage loan gives the lender the right to seize a particular asset owned by the borrower, in the event that the borrower defaults on the loan. The loan is said to be "secured" by the collateral, and the collateral is "pledged."[3] If the borrower fully repays the loan then nothing happens, but collateral means that under certain circumstances lenders can recover what is owed them by acquiring and liquidating a particular piece of the borrower's property. The market value of the collateral therefore becomes an important issue: is it enough to cover the full amount of the loan? Even in the event of bankruptcy, secured lenders are in a better position to recover their money than are ordinary unsecured creditors, for they rank ahead of unsecured creditors in access to the debtor's assets. Mortgages can themselves be ranked, with a first mortgage having priority over a second mortgage. Furthermore, the prospect of losing a valued asset motivates the borrower to repay. Thus, a mortgage is a peculiar kind of promise, for the borrower not only promises to repay the loan but also promises to give the lender a particular asset in the event that the borrower breaks her original promise. Thanks to this double-promise, lenders can reduce their vulnerability and worry less about the individual trustworthiness of the borrower.

Although many kinds of assets can "collateralize" a loan (consider so-called "chattel mortgages" and their role in installment lending, or crop liens in post-bellum Southern agriculture), loans secured by *real estate* have been particularly important in the history of American credit.[4] Land can be "improved" or left alone, but it can't be concealed or transported, and its permanence distinguishes it from almost all other economic assets. Barring a diluvian or tectonic disaster, land persists in tangible form. Furthermore, land in all its uses has been a premier economic asset, particularly when the United States had an agrarian economy. It has long served as the tax base, so governments have become expert at knowing who owns which land, and that information about property rights in land has been used by private mortgage lenders.

Farm mortgages were collateralized by farmland, the single most important asset for agricultural production. As settler populations moved west and displaced indigenous populations, with many settlers aspiring to become independent farmers, people acquired land and improved it using other people's money. Sometimes homesteaders were able to get land granted directly from the federal government, but frequently they had to purchase land privately. Off the farm, mortgage lending for residential homes has, in twentieth-century America, played a very big role in driving the residential housing market and in the spread of homeownership.[5] Entering into a mortgage agreement is one of the most important financial promises that ordinary Americans make in the course of their lives, for the home is typically the most valuable family asset. Much indeed rests upon how mortgage credit shapes real estate markets.

A mortgage poses a number of specific challenges beyond the usual issues that lending raises, including maturity and interest rate. Mortgage lenders gather information about both the borrower and the collateral. For a lender to make a loan that is "secured" by an asset, the lender must be sure that the asset exists and that the borrower actually owns it (as opposed to merely possessing or occupying it).[6] Does the borrower have clear title over the collateral? The establishment of land or property registries (often maintained by the Secretary of State's office) has helped to answer this question.[7] Some assets are easier to confirm than others (e.g., those that are tangible as opposed to intangible, or immovable instead of movable). The lender must also be certain that the property rights over the asset are freely transferable, so that the lender can claim ownership in the event of debtor default.[8] Additionally, the lender must confirm that the property isn't already "pledged," that is, already used to secure some other loan. Mortgaging the same property more than once is possible, but lenders will want to know who has the senior, and who the junior, claim.[9] And lenders also want to know the market value of the collateral in relation to the size of the loan: in case of default, will the value of the collateral cover the unpaid balance? The size of the loan has to be calibrated against the appraised value of the property (the loan-to-value ratio) and whether that value is stable. For a tangible asset, lenders worry whether it will maintain its physical integrity and value. They may insist, as a condition of lending, that the asset be protected or insured against various risks. Finally, there is the issue of who possesses the collateral while the loan is still outstanding. Sometimes collateral is kept by the lender (e.g., pawned objects are held by pawnshops), while other collateral is possessed by the borrower (e.g., homes, automobiles, and other durable goods subject to liens). These variable arrangements well illustrate the difference between ownership and possession of property.

Early Mortgages

By definition, all mortgages involve collateral. But a typical nineteenth-century home mortgage looked very different from today's mortgages. Currently, a typical new mortgage in the United States is worth between 80 and 99 percent of the value of the home, which means that a home buyer provides a 1 to 20 percent down payment and borrows the rest.[10] A standard loan is self-amortizing, and so each monthly payment covers both interest and loan principal (although the proportions change as the loan is paid down). Many mortgages have a fixed interest rate, so the monthly payments remain the same for the duration of the loan. Others have a variable interest rate that depends on some market benchmark and is reset intermittently (e.g., LIBOR plus 6 percent, or prime rate plus some fixed percentage). Sometimes mortgages with variable interest rates begin with an introductory below-market interest rate, a so-called "teaser rate," as a short-term inducement to the borrower. And the contemporary borrower can take up to thirty years to repay the loan. Together, these features made homes relatively "affordable" in the sense that buyers didn't have to save a lot to make a purchase, the monthly payments were low and predictable relative to household income, and the loan principal was fully repaid at the end. When combined with favorable tax treatment of mortgage interest payments, these mortgages made it relatively easy for someone to buy a home.

In the nineteenth century, U.S. mortgages were much less "affordable" and so less helpful in enabling people to make large purchases. Mortgages typically required a much bigger down payment (and hence had a lower loan-to-value ratio). They were also for much shorter periods of time and involved a "balloon" payment at the end (repayment of the entire loan principal as a lump sum). Consequently, a family that wanted to purchase real estate would have to accumulate more savings beforehand. Rather than "buy now, pay later" they had to "save now" in order to "buy later." Overall, this meant that people would purchase real estate later rather than sooner, and they would be carrying a lower debt load. Mortgage arrangements were largely private in the sense that there were few government programs to support or regulate mortgage markets.[11] Many states instituted homestead exemptions, which protected family property from seizure by creditors, but such measures would have given lenders pause and decreased, rather than increased, their willingness to lend.[12] Federal government intervention in support of farm mortgages didn't happen until the early twentieth century, and for home mortgages little was done until the Great Depression.

Early American mortgages were overwhelmingly person-to-person, often involving local lenders and borrowers.[13] Silsby's (1960) analysis of early nineteenth-century mortgages in western New York shows that people mostly sought mortgages to buy land, and mostly received loans from the persons selling the land (rather than from a third party). The details of these mortgages reveal little standardization, with no uniformity in maturity or number of payments required.[14] Furthermore, because of the scarcity of money a number of these mortgages accommodated payment in kind (e.g., cattle, timber, wheat) rather than in cash. In these and similar cases,[15] individual lenders could be flexible about the exact timing of payment, so long as the debtor continued to service the loan. Foreclosure proceedings were slow and costly, and to be avoided if possible. Population growth and westward expansion created huge demand for loans to purchase land and before long, certain institutional investors became involved in mortgages, particularly life insurance companies, trust companies, and mutual savings banks. For various reasons, many commercial banks did not invest in farm or home mortgages over most of the nineteenth century.[16] With long-term liabilities, insurance companies were particularly interested in safe, durable investments, and loans secured by a tangible asset like land were very attractive.[17] Thornton (2007) discusses the involvement of the Massachusetts Hospital Life Insurance Company (MHLIC) in lending to Massachusetts farmers during the 1820s and 1830s. The MHLIC relied on its staff to evaluate applications, review land titles, and assess the personal character of applicants in systematic fashion, resulting in rather less flexibility than personal lending could impart.[18] Institutional lending created greater formality and gradually reduced the importance of personal social ties between creditor and debtor.

In the postbellum Midwest, most mortgage lending was directed to farmers rather than urban homeowners and came from individual rather than institutional lenders. Mortgages were from one to five years' maturity, and over time funds came increasingly from non-local, mostly eastern, sources.[19] Frederiksen (1894) offered a useful overview of late nineteenth-century mortgages.[20] On average, mortgage interest rates were higher in the South and West than in the East, a difference that would encourage easterners to lend to people living elsewhere.[21] The average length of a mortgage was also shorter in the South (three years) and West (four years) than in the East (six years).[22] Since payments mostly consisted of interest, with a final balloon payment for the principal, many farmers had to renew their mortgages multiple times.[23] Initially, most of the banks and other financial institutions were in the Northeast, and as populations moved westward they sought credit to purchase farms and houses. Capital was scarce outside the Northeast and so interest rates were higher. At the time, these flows of capital were regarded with ambivalence, as Mappin (1889) notes. Although loans made it possible for farmers to acquire and improve their lands, the necessity to repay the debts saddled farmers with onerous obligations made worse by deflation. Debtors were perceived to be subordinate to their creditors.

According to Frederiksen (1894: 208), the main institutional sources for mortgage loans included mutual savings banks, building and loan associations, and insurance companies.[24] Insurance companies, in particular, had long-term liabilities to match against long-term assets. But, as Snowden indicates,[25] much mortgage lending still occurred on an individual basis.[26] Commercial banks were not involved either because they were prohibited from holding mortgages or because of the strictures of the "real bills" doctrine. Out-of-region investors initially relied on a network of loan agents who did much of the work of appraisal, applicant evaluation, and loan origination. Later in the nineteenth century, mortgage companies raised money from investors (largely in the eastern United States but also Europe) and loaned it out in the growing Midwest and West.[27] These companies functioned as brokers: identifying for investors a set of creditworthy (and overwhelmingly white) western and midwestern farmers who wanted to borrow money and were willing to use their farmland as security. In addition to the value of the land collateralizing the loan (which depended on acreage, fencing, and development), mortgage companies also considered the marital status and gender of the borrower.[28]

At first, mortgage companies acted like pure intermediaries and simply matched investors with individual farm mortgages. But some companies developed mortgage-backed debentures (also known as a "covered bond," akin to a modern "pass through" security) and in effect performed an elementary type of securitization. They pooled together one set of promises and transformed them into a new and very different set. Many consider securitization to be a recent invention, a financial innovation devised in the late twentieth century by Wall Street "quants" and "rocket scientists," but in fact something similar developed much earlier. These debentures pooled together groups of mortgages and used them as the basis for securities that were sold to investors. Instead of investing in a single mortgage, a purchaser of a debenture invested in a fixed proportion of multiple mortgages and in effect enjoyed the advantages of diversification.[29] This feature made farm mortgages more attractive to a broader set of investors, and so, for example, the J. B. Watkins Company was able to turn thousands of individual mortgages into debentures during the 1880s and sell these new securities to investors. By 1890 most mortgage companies were issuing debentures.[30] However, the depression of the 1890s produced very high mortgage default rates, and many of these mortgage companies simply failed and disappeared. This early form of securitization disappeared along with them.

Rural credit was a contentious political issue in the populist era of the 1880s and 1890s, along with banking and the monetary system.[31] Farmers were heavily dependent on credit, both in the short term (to get them from the spring planting to the fall harvest) and in the long term (to purchase land and equipment), and so were highly vulnerable to credit market conditions. When money was tight, or when agricultural prices were low, farmers suffered, and then mobilized politically. Yet the federal government played little direct role in credit markets during the nineteenth century.[32] The establishment of the Federal Reserve System in 1913 was an answer to banking and monetary problems (and to the financial crisis of 1907), but rural credit problems prompted their own political response. Pushed by farm groups, in 1916 the U.S. government passed the Federal Farm Loan Act, which established the Federal Farm Loan Board and twelve regional farm loan banks.[33] Working underneath the land banks were cooperative farm loan associations, which eventually numbered in the thousands and were spread throughout the country.[34] The purpose of this complex organizational apparatus was to provide credit to farmers, and so through the loan associations, the regional banks made mortgage loans to member farmers. As compared to private lenders, this system offered lower interest rates and longer maturities. Starting small, the number and value of Federal Land Bank mortgage loans grew from $156 million in 1919 to over $2.5 billion in 1935, when these loans constituted 32.3 percent of total farm loans.[35] This hybrid arrangement managed to fold cooperative arrangements into financial institutions with national, regional, and local scope. At the same time, several of the largest life insurance companies continued to invest in farm mortgages, often working through mortgage brokers but sometimes using their own agents.[36] Over the early decades of the twentieth century, the involvement of individual lenders in mortgage markets declined substantially.[37] Henceforth, most lenders were institutions of some kind. As well, the proportion of farms that were mortgaged rose in the 1910s and 1920s, and interest rates converged across regions even as overall interest rates declined and maturities lengthened.[38] But the collapse of the rural economy during the Great Depression put many farms into foreclosure, and insurance companies in particular ended up owning and managing a great deal of rural acreage.

Home Mortgages

The expanding rural population drove demand for farm mortgages, but at the end of the nineteenth century the U.S. population was rapidly urbanizing and, to a lesser extent, suburbanizing. In absolute numbers, the rural population continued to grow until well into the twentieth century, but relatively speaking it was shrinking.[39] Consequently, credit markets began to switch from rural to urban mortgages.[40] Unlike farms, however, urban residences were not units of production and so they were not intended to generate earnings. An urban house wasn't designed to cultivate the equivalent of a fall harvest, although as a tangible asset it could possess considerable value and hence could function as collateral. However, residential occupants frequently earned wages, and so home mortgages for the working and middle class became an increasingly important type of lending. Regular employment by adult household members generated cash flow to service the loan, and the loan was secured by the residence they owned and occupied. At first, home mortgages were for short maturities, with a balloon payment at the end. This simplified credit evaluation and so for many lenders it was largely a matter of setting the loan-to-value ratio.[41] As with farm mortgages, urban mortgage interest rates were marked by strong regional variations: they were lower in the Northeast and higher in the Midwest, West, and South.[42] In the early decades of the twentieth century, nonfarm homeownership rates rose until the Great Depression and then declined sharply during the economic collapse.

Building and loan societies (later known as "savings-and-loans" or "thrifts") were an important institutional source of funding for residential mortgages. They first emerged in Britain in the early nineteenth century and soon spread to the United States. In their original form, these societies embodied a moral project to encourage prudence and thrift on the part of individual workers and to institutionalize cooperative behavior among them.[43] One scholar noted their rapid growth in numbers, estimating that there were about six thousand in operation at the end of the nineteenth century.[44] These societies or associations involved cooperative financial arrangements in which a local group of working-class people saved money at an institution they created together and then borrowed from that same institution to purchase homes. Saving and lending all occurred in a geographically circumscribed region. The details of how members made payments, and how they qualified for loans, varied but basically the social and community bonds that brought the members together could be used to determine who was creditworthy, to help ensure repayment of the loan, and to facilitate valuation of the property that served as collateral.[45] Cooperative organizations proved to be particularly good at evaluating the promises made by their own members. Many early "thrifts" were based on immigrant ethnic communities, including Germans, Irish, Russians, Scottish, and Italians.[46] In addition, however, local home builders were often active in organizing building and loan associations, since they benefited directly from an active mortgage market.[47] As financial institutions, building and loan associations operated on a very local scale and were generally small and undiversified.[48] Nevertheless, by 1920 they accounted for almost 14 percent of the nonfarm mortgage market,[49] and eventually they too utilized credit reports and credit scores in making loan decisions.[50] The Great Depression hit building and loan associations hard as people defaulted on their mortgages and home values declined. Consequently, building and loan associations began to shift away from their original cooperative basis.[51] In the early twentieth century, the other major institutional investors in residential mortgages included commercial banks, mutual savings banks, and insurance companies, and together with the building and loans they provided about 60 percent of all nonfarm mortgages by 1940.[52] But many of these institutions operated on a local basis, investing in mortgages for nearby dwellers and seldom lending money in other cities or regions of the country. Assessing the trustworthiness of an individual borrower still depended heavily on local knowledge.

Community studies provide some detailed texture for some of these broader trends. In their classic study of Muncie, Indiana, the Lynds (1957: 103–4) noted the social significance of homeownership: it was a powerful signal of familial independence, respectability, and pride. Buying a home was much more than investment in an economic asset. Without readily available credit, however, homeownership was well beyond the financial reach of most working-class families. In Muncie, that credit largely came from local building and loan associations. The first was established in 1889, and by 1929 the four biggest associations together funded 75–80 percent of all local home construction. The result was a slow and steady increase in homeownership, as local savings funded local lending.

The Great Depression marked a sea change for public involvement in residential mortgage markets. New home construction stopped and homeownership rates, which had increased during the 1920s, declined in the 1930s. Mass defaults meant that many lending institutions ended up owning foreclosed real estate rather than financial assets secured by real estate, and many of these lenders themselves failed.[53] Some states tried to protect borrowers directly by making it hard for creditors to exercise their rights and, in effect, retroactively altering debt contracts in favor of debtors. In the early 1930s, twenty-five states passed legislation imposing some kind of temporary moratorium on farm mortgage foreclosures,[54] and in that same decade thirty-three states passed foreclosure moratoria on all types of mortgages.[55] State-level measures accomplished little and so of necessity, the federal government intervened to support the flow of credit into real estate markets, albeit in a largely piecemeal fashion. By using the existing Federal Land Banks to refinance mortgages, for example, federal farm mortgage loans grew from 9.9 percent of total farm mortgage debt in 1925 up to 32.3 percent in 1935.[56] In effect, the government became the "lender of last resort" for farmers, accepting their promises-to-pay and providing credit when few private institutions would do so. For nonfarmers, President Roosevelt established the Home Owners' Loan Corporation (HOLC) as an emergency measure in 1933 to deal with mass foreclosures and loan delinquencies. HOLC provided a way for homeowners to refinance their mortgages, something that helped both individual borrowers and lending institutions.[57] It developed "risk maps" of urban neighborhoods to show which areas were least risky for lenders.[58] By 1937, HOLC provided almost 14 percent of all nonfarm home mortgages in the United States, with most of the refinancing activity devoted to mortgages previously held by building and loan associations and savings banks.[59] The Title I provision in the Federal Housing Act of 1934 offered government insurance for home improvement loans, and so encouraged private banks to provide modest loans to homeowners that would raise home values and stimulate the construction industry.[60] Following Title II of the Act, the newly created Federal Housing Administration (FHA) insured home mortgages, protecting lenders from the cost of default and thus encouraging them to lend.[61] But to qualify, the mortgage had to conform to detailed standards set out by the FHA. The FHA insured over 23,000 mortgages in 1935, more than 77,000 in 1936, and over 102,000 in 1937.[62] It would only ensure mortgages that followed standards, and these were specified in underwriting manuals that explained in detail how underwriters were to value the home and assess "mortgage risk" in order to determine whether a particular mortgage was eligible for insurance. Later, the Veterans Administration (VA) created a similar mortgage insurance program so that returning military veterans could obtain credit to purchase homes,[63] and the numbers of insured mortgages quickly climbed: the VA insured 43,000 mortgages in 1945 and another 412,000 in 1946.[64]

When real estate and housing prices collapsed during the Great Depression, not only were homeowners hurt but so too were the financial institutions that had loaned them home mortgages. A homeowner's liability was the lender's asset. Many people could not keep their promises and meet their mortgage payments, and so bank assets became "nonperforming" (in banker parlance). Both those who made promises and those who had accepted them were in real trouble. Widespread defaults and foreclosures pushed many smaller banks into insolvency, and to help institutions whose lending supported the housing market the federal government took a number of emergency actions. One intervention involved a type of regulatory forbearance in which federal bank examiners from the Comptroller of the

Currency applied more "relaxed" standards to some of the assets on bank balance sheets (see the discussion in chapter 6). This of course made it easier for bank examiners to treat a troubled bank as if it were solvent and in no need of closure.

In parallel fashion, HOLC had to be creative about home valuation if it was to refinance home mortgages on a mass scale. Since the size of an individual home mortgage was determined by the value of the home (together they set the loan-to-value ratio), the collapse of housing prices made it hard for the government to lend enough new money to homeowners to pay off their old mortgages and provide adequate financial relief.[65] How to help borrowers who were "under water" (i.e., who owed more than their house was currently worth)? HOLC set a higher loan-to-value ratio than in the past (80 percent rather than 50 percent), but more importantly it was generous about the measurement of value, using an estimate of the "intrinsic worth" of the home rather than its current market value.[66] This enabled HOLC to inflate the estimated value of homes, make larger loans, and provide greater financial assistance, all the while adhering to the principle that the size of a mortgage loan was constrained by the value of the underlying collateral.[67]

Banks and other depository institutions could not function as lenders if they were themselves in trouble. Bank insolvency and expectations about insolvency worried depositors, who feared loss of their money, and set off bank runs that frequently were contagious. This problem reflected the fact that although banks are primarily considered to be lenders (who evaluate the trustworthiness of borrowers), as depository institutions and financial intermediaries they also borrowed, and so their depositors had to consider the trustworthiness of their bank. Previous state efforts had failed, so the federal government set up the Federal Deposit Insurance Corporation (FDIC) in 1933 in order to head off such financial panics and protect solvent but illiquid banks.[68] With federal deposit insurance, bank depositors could be sure that their bank's insolvency wouldn't automatically mean they would lose all their savings. Then in 1934, the federal government provided a similar measure for savings-and-loan associations (the Federal Savings and Loan Insurance Corporation [FSLIC]), as part of the Federal Housing Act. The threat of bank runs declined promptly, and failure became such a rare event that financial institutions were able to lend mortgages for many more decades. For example, from 1950 until 1960 only 32 FDIC-insured banks were closed,[69] a far cry from the financial carnage of the Great Depression when 522 banks were suspended in October 1931 alone.[70]

As an additional measure to aid troubled financial institutions, Regulation Q was imposed in 1933 and capped the interest rates depository institutions could pay on savings and checking accounts. Until it was relaxed and then abolished in 2011, it was intended to ensure that depository institutions like banks and savings-and-loans would have access to "cheap" deposits, which they could then lend out as mortgages.[71] And because many believed that instability on U.S. stock markets hurt depository banks and propagated the 1929 crash, the Glass-Steagall Act of 1933 separated commercial from investment banking. Taken together, all these measures helped create a relatively stable and regulated market environment in which money flowed from banks, savings-and-loans, and insurance companies into mortgages, and overall homeownership rates steadily rose (what Lea [1996] termed the "Wonderful Life" period).[72] The process of mortgage credit evaluation often followed methods set by the FHA, and lenders assessed the property and neighborhood as well as personal features of the borrower (e.g., current occupation, personal character and reputation, reliability, family background, etc.).[73]

The federal government intervened in many ways to provide direct help to homeowners, mortgage lenders, and the construction industry, even as many denied that government policy did anything but encourage the natural workings of the market.[74] Through new agencies like HOLC and the FHA, VA, FDIC, and FSLIC, the federal government found ways to refinance old mortgage loans, encourage new loans, stabilize lending institutions, and direct flows of credit into domestic housing markets. In the process, the typical U.S. home mortgage became more affordable to ordinary people. But in addition to encouraging credit flows, the federal government changed the basic template for a home mortgage. It *standardized* the kind of the promise that an ordinary mortgagor would make when they borrowed[75] and in so doing rendered those promises both more affordable (to the borrower) and more liquid (to investors).[76] Instead of five year interest-only balloon payment mortgages, the new standard home mortgage had a longer maturity (fifteen years, then twenty, or twenty-five), had a higher loan-to-value ceiling, and was self-amortizing (so there was no balloon payment at the end).[77] With a fixed interest rate, repayments stretching out over a longer period of time, and a smaller down payment, households could more easily afford to buy a home and then service their debt. The expansion of the personal income tax during World War II also meant that many more taxpayers could enjoy the favorable tax treatment of home mortgage interest payments, although the magnitude of the benefit depended on the tax bracket in which the homeowner found themselves.[78]

Standardization of home mortgages helped make them a more liquid asset that a lender could sell to someone else. From the lenders' standpoint, one of the disadvantages of long-maturity mortgages is that the lender isn't fully repaid for twenty or thirty years: the money is "locked up" for decades. For depository institutions like banks, this underpins part of the "maturity mismatch" between short-term liabilities (e.g., demand deposits) and long-term assets (e.g., thirty-year mortgages). If the lender has a sudden need for cash, it could try to pressure debtors to accelerate their repayments, but more realistically the lender would like to be able to sell the loan to someone else and recover its capital immediately. Unfortunately, home mortgages involve an idiosyncratic combination of home, neighborhood, and homeowner, and this makes them difficult for outsiders to judge their value or execute a quick sale.[79] Debtors, who borrowed the money, and homes, which secure the debt, vary in complicated and unclear ways. Unless the home was recently sold in a relatively stable market, its current market value has to be estimated by comparison with "similar" homes in "nearby" and "comparable" neighborhoods (the so-called "appraisal"). And if the willingness and ability of the debtor to repay the loan is hard for the lender to assess, it is even harder for a potential purchaser of the mortgage who doesn't have all the information available to the original lender. Finally, the terms of the deal that binds debtor and creditor can vary in many ways. In the United States, the law of secured transactions, including mortgages, was set at the state level (like most commercial law) and so varied across states.[80] Most mortgage lending institutions devised their own contracts, depending on where they operated. This meant that mortgage contracts would vary from state to state, and from lender to lender.[81] Standardizing mortgage contracts helps resolve some, but not all, of these informational problems and thus make mortgages more liquid.[82] The FHA also helped standardize how the underlying collateral for a mortgage loan, that is, the home itself, was to be valued. Its underwriting manuals (e.g., FHA 1936, FHA 1947, FHA 1955) provided detailed rules, personnel, and procedures for how to assess property and its location in a neighborhood, and how to rate the individual borrower, in a way that was uniform across the country.[83] They stipulated use of information provided by a private credit reporting agency about the individual mortgagor, underscoring again how thoroughly individual credit markets had been penetrated by credit ratings, scores, and reports.[84] The underwriting criteria generally favored suburban homes over those in cities, and so helped propel the postwar development of car-dependent suburbs.

The federal government also acted directly in 1938 by creating the Federal National Mortgage Association (Fannie Mae) to purchase FHA-insured mortgages from the originating lender. As Bell (1938: 513) noted at the time: "The [FHA] insured mortgage becomes a relatively liquid asset," and the development of a secondary market in individual mortgages eventually opened up many new possibilities.[85] Among other things, Fannie Mae could intervene to support housing markets by purchasing qualifying mortgages but without the need for more direct action.[86]

So long as market interest rates stayed low (i.e., below the interest rate caps), depository institutions like savings-and-loans (S&Ls) were still able to attract deposits and lend the money out as home mortgages. But in the late 1960s and into the 1970s, price inflation became a problem and reduced real interest rates. Regulation Q, which was originally intended to help depository institutions by preventing competition for deposits, now hampered them. With their funds locked up in long-term low-interest home mortgages, and fewer deposits, growing numbers of S&Ls became insolvent. Creative accounting helped some to avoid recognizing their problems, but the main policy response to these troubles was deregulation: S&Ls were allowed to engage in riskier investments (such as loans on commercial real estate) and so hopefully earn higher returns and return to solvency.[87] But such institutions were ill-equipped to be financially aggressive and so losses continued to mount, hurting both individual institutions and the FSLIC. It was politically difficult to overlook the fate of S&Ls, especially given their prominent role in domestic mortgage markets, and so the federal government acted. Eventually, a government bailout was required to save the S&Ls, costing roughly $160 billion.[88]

The experience of the S&Ls foreshadowed deregulation of the larger financial system. Many New Deal rules and regulations were repealed, starting with the Depository Institutions Deregulation and Monetary Control Act of 1980 (weakening Regulation Q and deregulating interest rates, among other things) and culminating in passage of the Financial Services Modernization Act of 1999 (which finally abolished the separation of commercial from investment banking, completely excluded over-the-counter financial derivatives from any regulation, and allowed banks to offer any kind of financial service). Not all deregulation had a direct impact on mortgage markets, but it helped unleash a period of rapid financial innovation, both within the banking system and in the so-called "shadow" banking system, that changed how mortgages were originated and distributed to investors. Fewer lenders held mortgages on their balance sheets through maturity but instead packaged them with other mortgages and sold them to investors. The traditional role of "lender" was replaced by that of "originator."

Securitization and Mortgages

In helping turn mortgages into liquid assets, standardization set the stage for modern securitization and helped broaden the number of investors willing to put money into home mortgages. Not only could standardized financial promises be more easily sold to someone else, but such promises could be pooled together to form a composite asset. And the economic value of the resulting pool wasn't dependent on the trustworthiness of a single debtor. Rather, it depended on the average (and variance) of the trustworthiness of all the individuals whose debts were put together in the securitization, features that could be estimated statistically. Securitization offered an easy pathway for investors to diversify. To be sure, some real estate companies had performed elementary securitizations in the 1880s to attract eastern capital into western farm mortgages.[89] Their efforts faded, however, during the depression of the 1890s and it wasn't until the federal government became involved in the twentieth century that the volume of mortgage securitizations became significant again. Today, many different kinds of cash flow have been securitized, arising out of credit card payments, student loan payments, car loans, home equity loans, small business loans, or lease receivables. Contemporary securitizations started in the early 1970s, when first the Government National Mortgage Association (GNMA, or "Ginnie Mae") and then the Federal Home Loan Mortgage Corporation (Freddie Mac) started to securitize home mortgages, to be joined by the Federal National Mortgage Association (Fannie Mae) in the early 1980s, with the intent of attracting new investors into residential real estate.[90] This policy enabled the federal government to encourage investment, but without directly financing real estate itself, helping preserve the appearance that policy simply enabled underlying market forces.[91] For budgetary reasons, the Johnson administration had moved Fannie Mae off the government's "balance sheet" in order to minimize the salience of its activities in creating a secondary market for home mortgages.[92] Securitization induced investors with little capacity to evaluate residential mortgages to overcome their reluctance and invest in residential mortgages.[93] It also helped overcome the local orientation that traditionally characterized mortgage lending, and so encouraged higher interregional capital flows. Securitization succeeded and the appetite for these new financial products was substantial: by 1980 there were more than

$93 billion in GMNA-guaranteed mortgage-backed securities outstanding, with another $16 billion coming from Freddie Mac.[94]

Securitization meant turning one set of promises into a different set of promises. In outline, the securitization process involved first setting aside a set of relatively homogeneous assets, for example, home mortgages, and putting them into a new legal entity that is separate from the original lender or sponsor.[95] This legal entity is called a special purpose vehicle (or special purpose entity). In so doing, the original lender moves the assets off its balance sheet. New financial securities are then issued and backed by those assets, drawing on the income they generate, and then sold to investors. For mortgage-backed securities, issuers had to make changes with respect to prepayment risk and payment frequency in order to make them more bond-like and attractive to bond investors.[96] In this manner, the securitizer creates a residential mortgage-backed security, or RMBS, from a pool of underlying home mortgages. A "pass through" is the simplest securitization, where all the mortgages are put into a single pool and a single type of financial security is issued against that pool. Instead of buying a single original mortgage, an investor in the new security is able to obtain some small proportion of a large number of the original mortgages, and so in effect to diversify. The new securities each have an equal claim on the income generated by the pool, on a pro rata basis. Rather than worry about the trustworthiness of each individual homeowner, the investor can simply estimate the average trustworthiness of the entire pool, information that is aggregate rather than granular.

For example, if 500 farm mortgages were pooled together, then the monthly payments made by the 500 farmers would constitute the relevant cash flow. If 100 bonds of equal value were issued against this pool of mortgages, then in effect each bond would have a claim on 1 percent of the monthly payments made by each of the 500 farmers, all put together. One attraction for the investor is diversification: instead of lending money to a single farmer, through securitization the investor lends to each of 500 farmers.[97] The securitized arrangement is less risky for the investor. Furthermore, rather than investigate the individual creditworthiness of 500 farmers, the investor can simply rely on the bond rating given to the resulting security as a way to gauge risk. An arrangement that is more attractive for investors attracts more investment.

More complex mortgage securitizations can involve the issuance of different classes of new securities, which vary in their seniority.[98] Organized into multiple "tranches," the most senior (or highest tranche) have first claim on the income, and only when they are fully satisfied can income then be used to pay the second tranche, and so on down the line. The bottom tranche, in other words, has the lowest priority and so is the first to feel the effects of any shortfall of income. Such a shortfall occurs, for example, when one or more of the indebted homeowners falls behind on their monthly mortgage payments. Building on the success of early securitizations, financial engineering has now produced a variety of new types of complex instruments, each with its own acronym: MBS (mortgage-backed security), RMBS (residential mortgage-backed security), CMBS (commercial mortgage-backed security), and CDO (collateralized debt obligation). And securitization continued to grow through the 1990s and 2000s as banks made it the centerpiece of their earnings.[99]

Whether the securitization is simple or complex, the direct relationship that formerly linked a debtor with a creditor disappears.[100] And when the debtor gets into trouble, this can make a critical difference. A default triggers a variety of legal actions, depending on the provisions of the loan contract. But in reality, troubled debtors often approach their lender beforehand, seeking forbearance or some kind of informal accommodation: perhaps a few late payments will be overlooked, or the repayment schedule will get stretched out, or in some manner the creditor gives the debtor some flexibility. But these renegotiations depend on whether the debtor and creditor have an ongoing relationship and if on the basis of mutual trust the creditor believes that, despite the short-term difficulties, the debtor will eventually come through. This valuable connection is lost in a securitization, where an individual debtor's obligation is partitioned and distributed across many investors, none of whom need have had any prior contact with the debtor.[101] The borrower likely deals with a "mortgage servicer," a firm that specializes in payment collection and is not a lender.[102] Furthermore, the investors in a securitization have conflicting interests, with those in senior tranches less willing to accommodate troubled borrowers than those in junior tranches.[103] There simply is no easy way to adjust the loan in the face of adversity. Evidence from the 2008 financial crisis shows that securitized home mortgages were significantly less likely to be modified to help the debtor stay current and more likely to end in foreclosure.[104] Furthermore, because the mortgage originator bundles and sells the loan to other investors, it lacks ongoing "skin in the game." The original lender no longer has a long-term interest in the solvency of the debtor and so may relax its standards when evaluating would-be borrowers and generating income from fees.

Credit rating agencies play an important role in mortgage securitizations: they rate the new financial securities by classifying them into the familiar categories originally applied to corporate bonds. When securitizations are organized into separate tranches, the senior tranches receive a higher rating than the junior tranches because they have a stronger claim on the cash flows generated by the underlying assets.[105] And the ratings matter in terms of who buys the securities. An investor who knows little or nothing about the underlying mortgage assets, and who may be unable to gather granular information about the many underlying borrowers, can nevertheless consult the ratings. Such ratings are especially important for complex securitizations, where the value of the security depends not only on the underlying assets but also on how the securitization is structured. Ratings permit easy comparison across many other types of bonds (corporates, sovereigns) and facilitate the kind of risk-return trade-off that is a staple of modern finance—a securitized mortgage becomes just another fixed income security. Through the securitization, the original borrowers can access a far broader set of lenders than they previously could and potentially can secure cheaper financing. Many institutional investors (like pension funds and insurance companies) are constrained by law to buy only the "safest" (i.e., highest-rated) securities, so in designing a securitization the securitizer tries to create as many "AAA"-rated tranches as possible. Since both the underlying assets and the resulting securities are rated, it is evident that clever financial engineering can turn assets with low ratings into highly rated assets.[106] Until the financial crisis of 2008, rating agencies were generally regarded as largely independent and credible judges,[107] but it became clear in the aftermath that various conflicts of interest had undermined their autonomy and that significant volumes of structured financial instruments had been over-rated by agencies eager to please the securitizers, who happened to be their customers.[108]

Mortgages and Racial Inequality

The mortgage system has played a significant role in producing long-standing racial disparities. Going back to 1870, the first U.S. Census where all African Americans were counted as free people, the difference in homeownership between whites and blacks was striking. The estimated rate of owner occupancy for African Americans was only 8 percent, and the corresponding rate for white Americans was 57 percent.[109] Starting from the rural South, millions of African Americans migrated north in search of jobs and opportunity.[110] DuBois's famous discussion of the "Philadelphia Negro" at the end of the nineteenth century (1996: 295–97) reveals how much rental housing surpassed homeownership among the minority residents of that northern city. And DuBois attributed the concentration of black Americans in the seventh ward to a combination of white opposition to integrated housing with their reliance on service occupations that required them to live close to downtown Philadelphia. With few options, African Americans were forced to pay dearly for substandard rental housing.[111] Black-owned banks prioritized mortgage loans to African Americans, but as noted in chapter 4 there were too few such banks to make a real difference.[112]

The innovations of the New Deal laid the groundwork for a steady long-term increase in homeownership.[113] The expansion of mortgage credit put more families in a home they could call their own, and the volume, number, and value of these distinctive promises grew. But the benefits of inclusion were not shared equally. In fact, the disparity in homeownership between black and white families proved remarkably durable, as did patterns of residential segregation. And in no small measure, those disparities were maintained through government interventions in the housing market.[114] The generous housing provisions built into the GI Bill, to enable World War II veterans to buy their own homes, overwhelmingly benefited white American men and their families.[115] And the underwriting standards set forth by the FHA, for example, privileged racially homogeneous neighborhoods and in an unobtrusive fashion helped maintain racial segregation.

Collateral is what distinguishes a secured from an unsecured loan. To reinvigorate the U.S. housing market, the FHA encouraged investment in home mortgages and therefore had to weigh carefully the value of a home, as collateral, and what determined that value. Furthermore, it sought to do this on a scale suitable for national policy applicable in all regions of the country, and so it developed detailed rules and procedures to guide its underwriters in the assessment of home values and mortgage risks. These judgments had to work over the much longer maturities that the federal government set in order to make mortgages more affordable. In its 1936 underwriting manual, the FHA observed: "Risk-rating involves forecasting and prediction. It deals with probabilities. Mortgage risk lies in the future."[116] It also stated that the value of a home depended very much on the surrounding area, and not just on the physical properties and amenities of the home itself: "Included among the elements which contribute to [mortgage] risk are the wide variety of neighborhood and location characteristics."[117] The FHA's assessment of the relevant neighborhood characteristics drew on the received wisdom of the real estate industry, and among other features the social composition of the neighborhood mattered a great deal.[118] In this regard, rules of valuation reflected developments in zoning laws and the growing ability of local governments to restrict land use.[119] Through the 1910s and 1920s, the real estate industry worked with state and local governments to develop a set of zoning principles, and these valued single-family dwellings above other residential structures (e.g., apartment buildings, rental housing, public housing, low-income housing, etc.) and land uses. They also strongly supported suburban growth at the expense of urban development and renewal and encouraged higher-density housing in African American neighborhoods.[120]

When distilling the received wisdom of the real estate industry, the FHA alerted its underwriters to be mindful of "threatening or possible infiltration of inharmonious racial groups. The possibility or imminence of such encroachments or infiltrations will always result in low ratings of some of the features in the Location category."[121] Clearly, some types of social change would, according to the FHA, hurt home values and exacerbate mortgage risk: "If a neighborhood is to retain stability it is necessary that properties shall continue to be occupied by the same social and racial classes. A change in social or racial occupancy generally leads to instability and a reduction in values."[122] Some private and public interventions could, in the judgment of the FHA, help stabilize neighborhoods and reduce mortgage risk. Their presence was therefore deemed a desirable feature: "Usually the protections against adverse influences afforded by these means [zoning and restrictive covenants] include prevention of the infiltration of business and industrial uses, lower-class occupancy, and inharmonious racial groups."[123] And more specifically, the FHA affirmed the benefit of restrictive covenants: "Recorded deed restrictions should strengthen and supplement zoning ordinances and to be really effective should include the provisions listed below . . . (g) Prohibition of the occupancy of properties except by the race for which they are intended."[124] In sum, the FHA unequivocally supported the provision of home mortgages to stable and racially homogeneous neighborhoods, and did so by insisting that segregation was the way to protect the economic value of homes.

The 1947 FHA underwriting manual provided updated guidance to underwriters for how homes were to be valued and how that value was shaped by neighborhood characteristics. FHA personnel were instructed to pay attention to likely trends, including "the probability of any change in occupancy relating to income and other characteristics of occupants which would tend to change desirability for residential purposes."[125] The language used to discuss how social heterogeneity affected home value is less explicit than before, but underwriters were still reminded: "If a mixture of user groups is found to exist it must be determined whether the mixture will render the neighborhood less desirable to present and prospective occupants. If the occupancy of the neighborhood is changing from one user group to another, or if the areas adjacent to the immediate neighborhood are occupied by a user group dissimilar to the typical occupants of the subject neighborhood or a change in occupancy is imminent or probable any degree of risk is reflected in the rating."[126] According to FHA standards, racially mixed neighborhoods undermined home value and thus discouraged investment in home mortgages.[127]

By 1955, underwriting instructions explicitly addressed the issue of race in order to protect the FHA from accusations of discrimination, or from the reality of racial animus in housing markets. "Among the most important of risk elements to be taken into consideration in determining the acceptability of a mortgage for insurance are the local real estate reactions and the attitudes of borrowers to any observable immediate or foreseeable future condition. The evaluation of these risks does not in any sense imply approval or disapproval of the market reactions or of the attitude of borrowers or an attempt to influence such reactions or attitudes. In this respect risk is never attributed solely to the fact that there is a mixture of user groups due to differences in race, color, creed, or nationality."[128] Furthermore, the FHA noted the appointment of "racial relations advisers" to help guide the chief underwriter on housing issues for minorities, including on the "appropriateness and acceptability of proposed locations to specific minority groups."[129] Nevertheless, the FHA still regarded neighborhood changes in "user groups" as a factor that could increase mortgage risk because of how it influenced home values.[130]

Even if initial FHA policy and white sentiment supported racial separation and difference, addressing durably substantial racial differences in homeownership became an unavoidable political issue.[131] Civil rights advocates and mainstream policymakers came to understand the importance of unequal access to credit as a driver of social and economic inequality, and groups affirmed the extent to which they and their constituents were excluded from beneficial public policy.[132] Homeownership was the major vehicle for wealth accumulation by families, but residence also determined where children went to school, what kinds of jobs were available to parents, and what kinds of social risks the family was exposed to (e.g., crime). And this occurred against the backdrop of a long history of racial discrimination in U.S. housing markets. In the early twentieth century, some urban housing policies were overtly discriminatory: city neighborhoods were explicitly "zoned" for specific racial groups until the Supreme Court declared such action unconstitutional in 1917.[133] However, private action using racially restrictive covenants achieved the same end of keeping different racial groups in different neighborhoods, until the Supreme Court ruled in 1948 that such covenants also were unconstitutional.[134] And, as discussed above, the appraisal criteria initially adopted by the FHA in the 1930s in its underwriting manuals strongly favored single-family housing in socially homogeneous neighborhoods over integrated communities, providing another economic justification for the maintenance of racial segregation. After World War II, it was the growing white suburbs that benefited the most from housing policy.[135]

Following the civil rights movement of the 1950s and 1960s, the prohibition of employment discrimination in the Civil Rights Act of 1964, and the prohibition of housing discrimination in the Fair Housing Act of 1968,[136] new federal laws passed in the late 1960s and early 1970s prohibiting racial or gender discrimination in lending (e.g., the Equal Credit Opportunity Act of 1974).[137] Other federal measures took aim at depository institutions, requiring them to make loans in communities where they also took deposits (e.g., the Community Reinvestment Act [CRA] of 1977)[138] or requiring them to track and report on the race of their mortgage borrowers (e.g., the Home Mortgage Disclosure Act of 1975).[139] In many respects, this period represented the high point for federal policy to address racial inequalities in mortgage and other credit markets.

As Taylor (2019) details, Great Society initiatives that originally were intended to reduce racial disparities in housing markets largely failed. The FHA-insurance program for home loans, which for decades had been used to support suburban growth, was redeployed at the end of the Johnson administration and start of the Nixon administration to benefit low-income populations, primarily African Americans.[140] Federal insurance meant that lenders wouldn't lose money if borrowers defaulted, which encouraged lenders to make FHA-compliant loans. Although the aim was to fund low-income housing in the suburbs, continued resistance to suburban desegregation confined most lending activity to urban areas where minority homeownership rose. Federal money guaranteed that lenders would profit, and some urban residents were able to transition from rental status to homeownership, but the money did little to improve the quality of urban housing stock and many new homeowners were overwhelmed by the cost of repairing or maintaining their substandard homes. A corrupt appraisal system enabled developers to overvalue properties, qualify for FHA funding, and then sell them to low-income buyers whose marginal economic status made it difficult to make needed repairs and who were therefore more likely than those with regular FHA mortgages to default on their loans.[141] At the start of the second Nixon administration, most of these initiatives were shut down and instead a voucher system ("section 8") was developed to offer housing for low-income families.

Despite new laws and various policy interventions, there is still ample evidence of discrimination in mortgage markets,[142] residential segregation continues,[143] and the racial gap in homeownership persists. In the lead-up to the 2008 financial crisis, large numbers of borrowers with poor credit records were able to obtain "subprime" (or "Alt-A") mortgages that were then packaged, securitized, rated, and sold to investors. Mortgage originators became creative in making mortgages seem "affordable" to marginal borrowers: little or no money as a down payment (i.e., extremely high loan-to-value ratios), introductory low interest rates (so-called "teaser rates") that would reset upward after a year or two, interest-only loans, negative amortization loans, and so on.[144] The typical post–New Deal mortgage, with its 20 percent down payment, thirty-year maturity, and self-amortizing fixed monthly payments, was modified to allow for adjustable interest rates, smaller down payments, and much higher loan-to-value ratios. At first, these innovations succeeded and so as families went into debt, overall homeownership rates increased, including among minorities.[145] Although highly profitable for the mortgage originators, these loans performed poorly in the 2008 financial crisis, leading to widespread homeowner defaults and foreclosures, collapsing housing prices, and sudden ratings downgrades.[146] Thanks to securitization and how it integrated capital markets, the effects of the implosion of real estate markets in places like Arizona, Nevada, Florida, and Southern California were felt around the world, not just locally. Reassured by the high ratings given to subprime mortgage-backed securities, European pension funds (and others) had been eager investors and so suffered heavy losses.[147]

Commercial Real Estate

Real estate houses businesses as well as families, and it still depends on mortgages. Business location correlates with residential location if only because people generally live within commuting distance of their work, but the forces that shaped racial residential segregation didn't apply in the same way. The value of commercial property (e.g., office, retail, industrial, recreational) depends primarily on the income it generates, not on its racial homogeneity. So when lenders decide whether to fund commercial real estate development, they are particularly interested in which businesses will serve as occupants, their tenancy, prevailing occupancy rates, tax considerations, and the future income that leasing arrangements will generate.[148] Lenders may even "look through" the leases and consider the status and credit ratings of business tenants when evaluating a commercial loan. Retail properties, for example, often combine a few big "anchor" tenants with many smaller "in-line" tenants, and the absence of the former will give a lender pause.

As compared to residential home mortgages, commercial lenders dealt with fewer borrowers and much larger loans, and contemporary borrowers tend to be corporations or single-purpose entities rather than individuals. Commercial real estate didn't have the political salience of residential housing, and so wasn't the targeted beneficiary of landmark national policies.[149] But lenders are vigilant about the value of the real estate that collateralizes their loans, and who exactly has title. For instance, a project loan to fund commercial real estate development is often dispersed in stages, contingent on progress in construction so that the amount of the loan paid out never exceeds the rising value of the property under development. In general newer buildings are more legible to lenders than older structures, so it is easier to finance new development than a rehab project.

Today, commercial banks do much of the lending, and they operate with more financial information and market data about the borrower than is the case for individual mortgages. Although they can put greater weight on quantitative measures of financial performance and risk, social networks and relationships remain important. As Garmaise and Moskowitz (2003) show, the personal ties that property brokers form with lenders, on the one hand, and commercial real estate developers, on the other, enhance the likelihood that lenders will finance developers. Even in a high-stakes situation with abundant access to volumes of quantitative information, preexisting social ties offer meaningful assurance to lenders that they can trust a particular borrower.

Like home mortgages, commercial mortgages have been securitized in recent decades,[150] enabling originators to exit their loans by selling them off to outside investors and reinforcing the ongoing importance of the rating agencies. Securitization transforms idiosyncratic and opaque real estate loans into generic bond-like instruments, and this has opened up U.S. commercial real estate to foreign investment.[151] Indeed, commercial real estate is prone to waves of activity, and the twentieth century was marked by construction booms that led to overbuilding, followed by busts.[152]

Conclusion

During the nineteenth century, the importance of credit for agriculture made the availability of farm mortgages a particularly significant economic and political issue. The United States was still a predominantly agrarian economy and credit for farms played a key role in the vitality and development of rural areas. At first, mortgage lending was done on a very local basis, like most credit in the early nineteenth century: within the community, savers transacted with borrowers. But as mortgage credit expanded beyond the bounds of local communities, it mostly flowed from the Northeast to other regions of the country. In the twentieth and twenty-first centuries, the central role that residence plays in shaping social life gave special significance to the loans that people used to buy a residential home as the country urbanized, and then suburbanized. A mortgage is more than just a simple cash loan, because it also includes collateral, a key element that reduces the lender's vulnerability. But for this feature to work, the borrower has to really own the collateral, and the collateral has to retain sufficient value, even as the borrower continues to use and occupy it. The constitution of that value has proven pivotal in mortgage markets.

Residential homes (and family farms) are large, tangible economic assets. For most contemporary American households, their residence is their single biggest asset, and so as the housing market goes, so goes the wealth of many ordinary people. Mortgage debt has enabled millions of families to acquire these assets because, for most people, the necessity to save first the purchase price of a home was too high of a hurdle. Instead, mortgages allowed them to buy now and pay later. And homeownership brought much more than just a roof over someone's head, because it located that person, and their family, in a spatial nexus of risk and opportunity across multiple social outcomes: employment, education, friendship networks, cultural amenities, transportation, exposure to crime and other dangers, and so on. Home mortgage debts are a substantial and widespread economic burden. How can so many households become so encumbered with debt, especially given the social significance of how that debt is used?[153] Why have these promises become such a common part of the adult American experience?

An elaborate organizational machinery developed to identify creditworthy borrowers, value their homes, and make loans, on a mass scale. Their common feature is that all such loans are secured by real estate, and that is why the home mortgage industry evaluates both borrowers and the collateral they offer. The estimated value of the collateral constrains the size of the loan, and use of the money is earmarked for the purchase of a specific home. The value of the mortgaged home became increasingly important as down payments shrank and as loan-to-value ratios grew: in the event of default, home foreclosure was the chief means for lenders to protect themselves against loss. However, by evaluating the value of homes in addition to the creditworthiness of homeowners, mortgage lenders could be tempted to relax their standards for creditworthiness if the value of the collateral seemed ample. During the housing bubble of the early 2000s, when the market prices of homes rose dramatically, many mortgage lenders were willing to offer new types of mortgages to borrowers with marginal or poor credit records because increasing home values assured them that in the event of default, they could simply foreclose and recover their money. It seemed that collateral would protect them from risk, and rising prices also gave homeowners an increasingly valuable asset that they could borrow against. This strategy worked well so long as housing prices rose, but when the bubble burst, its weaknesses became starkly evident.[154]

This new organizational machinery involved private and public components acting in concert. For example, private financial institutions were encouraged to lend by the public provision of mortgage insurance. It has been the focus of much public policy, as many levels of government have tried over decades to stimulate and support housing markets. The direct provision of public housing has always been only a small part of this effort, and often the most controversial. Mostly, governments worked indirectly, through loan guarantees, insurance, zoning, favorable tax treatment, and creation of secondary markets for loans. For most of the twentieth century, the benefits of all this support were unequally distributed, as racial disparities in mortgage and housing markets persisted.[155] African Americans had less access to credit, had lower rates of homeownership, and lived in segregated neighborhoods. This produced additional racial disparities because of the central role residence played in education, employment, and the formation of social networks. There were also significant gender inequalities that disadvantaged women in credit markets and prompted political action starting in the late 1960s.[156] However, because family formation continued to be predominantly heterosexual (and so the women who were disadvantaged formed families with advantaged men), the cumulative effects on inequality between households were less striking.

By design, securitization helped add liquidity to residential mortgages and encouraged broader investment in them, but it also changed the nature of home mortgage promises. Although such promises continued to encumber individual homeowners, and although pledging real estate as collateral remained a key feature, those who invested in mortgage-backed securities (MBSs) no longer emphasized the trustworthiness of an individual borrower. Instead, purchasing an MBS gave its owner an interest in a pool of mortgages, often structured in complicated ways. To the investor, the financial properties of the pool mattered much more than an individual borrower's own financial record. Indeed, as mortgage origination became a distinct market activity, the security owner most likely had no contact with the individual borrowers involved in the underlying mortgage assets. The debtor-creditor relationship was no longer direct.

Although this chapter has focused on mortgages for individual farmers and home mortgages for families, firms also borrow using mortgages, and there is both a commercial real estate mortgage market and securitization of such mortgages (to create CMBSs, or commercial mortgage-backed securities). When a firm borrows to acquire buildings or other real estate, such assets qualify as collateral for the loan. Frequently, corporate bonds were secured by the issuing firm's tangible assets, and there might be multiple mortgages in declining seniority (e.g., first, second, third, etc., mortgages). But recent changes in corporate assets make traditional funding harder: corporations have fewer fixed assets (physical property, plant, inventory) and more intangible assets,[157] and the latter do not function so well as collateral.[158]

The importance of agrarian interests in the nineteenth century gave U.S. farm mortgages particular significance. Each promise made by a farmer, and secured by farmland, was a private matter, but together all such promises were of great public consequence. As debtors, farmers formed a powerful constituency and mobilized to secure easy credit or to defy foreclosures when recessions and depressions made it hard for borrowers to pay their bills. As the country urbanized and later suburbanized, however, agrarian interests were largely replaced by homeowner interests as the main driver of mortgage politics. People who wished to buy a home could make a promise secured by that home. And because the geography of residence so profoundly affected the life chances of residents, the New Deal policies that served homeowner interests unfolded on a landscape of race and class, even as they attempted to salvage collapsing real estate markets and failing lenders. Residential segregation remained one of the most important facts about U.S. society, although the means to maintain it evolved from statutes and ordinances to restrictive covenants to appraisal standards and loans.[159]

8

Broken Promises

Most debtors are well-intentioned in making promises: they genuinely mean to repay their debts. Yet however carefully creditors try to determine who is, and who is not, trustworthy, and despite many promises made in good faith, promises get broken. A debtor sometimes cannot, or will not, fulfill their commitments. What happens then? What recourse does the creditor have? In this situation, legal rules matter a great deal, as does the formality of the original promise. And what started as a dyadic and mutually advantageous relationship between the lender and the borrower becomes triadic as other parties became involved in a conflictual scenario. A win-win situation becomes win-lose, or even lose-lose.

Historically, legal actions to collect debts were among the most common items on court dockets.[1] People used the law to enforce unkept financial promises, although going to court was usually the means of last resort. State law determined the options that creditors had when debtors failed to pay, and law varied by jurisdiction. Creditors in one state might have different rights and remedies than creditors in another state, even though they were all trying to do the same thing: collect money owed to them. Furthermore, different states regulated loans by setting maximum interest rates in usury laws, in effect constraining the kinds of legally enforceable promises people could make, and they also protected certain categories of property from seizure by creditors.[2] Keeping track of this legal variation was a challenge for creditors that operated across multiple states, and so published business, banking, and legal sources often included a summary of the relevant state laws.[3] Eventually, however, through the National Conference of Commissioners on Uniform State Laws the legal profession pushed for more standardization at the state level, and so created the Uniform Consumer Credit Code, urging its adoption by states so as to minimize legal variation and create more predictability under a federal system[4] and building on the uniformity established through the Uniform Commercial Code.[5]

Before resorting to legal action, unpaid creditors often pursued a succession of appeals, starting with polite reminders that perhaps a debtor had simply forgotten to make a payment, appealing to the debtor's sense of responsibility, or gently noting that payment would help preserve the debtor's own future creditworthiness. But if well-mannered nudges didn't work, creditors moved on to more threatening messages that laid out the dire consequences of failure to pay.[6] The idea was to motivate troubled debtors to keep their promises while offering some measure of flexibility, and the increasingly strident tone of such communication was tempered by the fact that many debtors were also customers, and held out the prospect of future business, or they could be friends and neighbors. Unvarnished aggression aimed at late-payers could be very bad for business and for one's social life.

If their own recovery efforts failed, starting in the late nineteenth century creditors might make use of a collection agency, a firm that specialized in the collection of debts.[7] Such agencies were notorious for pressuring debtors in ways that were highly unethical if not illegal. Although not as brazen as the collection methods used by loan sharks, which often included threats of physical violence, actual violence, or some kind of public shaming,[8] collection agencies would send angry letters or make repeated harassing phone calls to a debtor's home or place of work, use obscene language when communicating with debtors, threaten various kinds of legal action, misleadingly exaggerate the legal powers of the creditor, contact members of the debtor's family or their employer, or otherwise defame the debtor.[9] Such misbehavior helped justify passage of the Uniform Small Loan Law in many states during the 1910s and 1920s.[10] Although often justifiably criticized, collection agency practices were largely unregulated at the national level until passage of the Fair Debt Collection Practices Act of 1978, initially enforced by the Federal Trade Commission, which defined and proscribed various "unfair" practices.[11] Henceforth collection agencies were restricted in how, and how often, they could contact debtors, in terms of how they represented themselves, and in the nature of their communications with debtors.[12]

Despite the efforts of creditors to secure payment, and notwithstanding pressure from collection agencies, some debts remained unpaid. And against the backdrop of varied state laws that dealt piecemeal with broken promises, federal law offered its own encompassing measure: a bankruptcy proceeding. The evolution of federal rules has taken the United States from a situation where insolvent debtors were regularly thrown into prison and incarcerated until their debts were fully paid[13] to where debtors routinely surrender their assets to a court of law, have their remaining debts discharged, and then are free to enjoy a fresh start, unencumbered by their past obligations. At the outset, the chief goal was to ensure that creditors received their money but now the aim of federal law is more rehabilitative.[14] The cultural valence of bankruptcy has also shifted. Early on, bankruptcy was deeply problematic and those who failed were publicly stigmatized, their "manliness" impugned, and their reputations ruined. Business failure was considered a very personal miscarriage, and extant laws imposed punitive measures that favored creditors over debtors: as much as possible, debtors were forced to keep their promises and creditors were going to get their money back. Gradually, however, the cultural weight of failure lifted and subsequent bankruptcy rules included measures that enabled those who failed to start over again, even if they hadn't met all their obligations. Use of incorporation and the invention of limited liability separated business from personal assets and made it easier for people to "move on" after a business failure. Such measures favored debtors over creditors, and indeed the possibility of a "fresh start" undergirded the ability of dogged entrepreneurs to move past their own mistakes and on to eventual success.[15] Without the fresh start, economic failure threatened to become permanent.

Bankruptcy can only happen to someone who has borrowed money or received credit. If a person or business conducted all their transactions in cash, paying all bills fully and immediately, they would never default on their obligations for the simple reason that they wouldn't have to make any such promises. Life would be debt free and all accounts would be current. But modern economies utilize long- and short-term credit on a mass scale, and the more someone borrows, the greater the chance that they may not be able to repay a debt. In general, as the nation's credit system developed and deepened, the possibility of failure also increased. It is no coincidence that as levels of household indebtedness have increased in the United States during the last several decades, so have personal bankruptcies.[16] And yet repayment in full and on time isn't necessarily the most profitable outcome for creditors. In fact, debtors who fall behind in their payments, who carry balances month-to-month, who overdraw on their accounts, or who incur various fees and penalties can be enormously lucrative for lenders. The latter have learned to differentiate between those who are marginally creditworthy and those who are not at all creditworthy, and to profitably engage the first group while still trying to avoid the second.

A debtor who doesn't meet a financial obligation has defaulted: perhaps they promised to repay a $10,000 debt by next Friday but didn't. This may happen because the debtor is financially insolvent (i.e., has negative net worth because their total assets are less than their total liabilities) or hasn't the cash on hand to pay bills as they become due (i.e., lacks liquidity). Or perhaps the debtor has the cash and could repay but chooses not to: maybe the debtor intends to defraud the creditor or is withholding payment because of a dispute. Whatever the reason, modern legal systems offer a way for creditors to recover money owed by a defaulting debtor: they can sue the debtor in a court of law. Early modern legal systems offered harsh sanctions to spur compliance (debtors could be sent to prison until they paid up), but now the incentives are mostly monetary.

In anticipation of the possibility of a debtor's failure to repay, some creditors insisted they be given security. When loans are collateralized, the creditor can seize an asset belonging to the debtor in lieu of payment. Hence an automobile dealership might repossess a car if the owner stopped making payments on the car loan, or a bank could foreclose on a mortgaged home. And there were additional ways for creditors to reduce their vulnerability to default: some creditors purchased private credit insurance, so that if their losses were "excessive" they would receive compensation from the insurance company; others sought loan guarantors, who promised to repay the loan in the event that the original debtor failed to do so.

Debt-recovery measures can be pursued independently by creditors, but modern laws also offer collective procedures that deal with all outstanding claims on a failed debtor at the same time. These bankruptcy proceedings vary depending on whether the debtor is an individual (personal bankruptcy law) or a firm (corporate bankruptcy). One important goal is to prevent a haphazard and costly "rush to the assets" in which the debtor's assets are seized by creditors in such a piecemeal fashion that their overall value is significantly reduced.[17] Indeed, the seizure of assets can resemble an old-fashioned bank run, as panicky creditors received information (or maybe just a rumor) that others were claiming the assets of a troubled debtor and hurried to seize what they could before everything was taken.[18] Under such conditions, a solvent but illiquid debtor could be driven under by something akin to a self-fulfilling prophecy. The collective nature of bankruptcy proceedings reflected the interdependencies that emerge among creditors: when the debtor is truly insolvent then creditors are playing a zero-sum game with each other, and more for one means less for the others.

Bankruptcy is a collective process that distributes losses among the various claimants of an insolvent debtor. Since the sum total of assets is less than the total of liabilities, not all claims can be fully satisfied.[19] Someone will lose money, and the procedure distributes losses in an orderly fashion. Unfortunately, it can be a time-consuming and expensive process if stakeholders dispute the claims. Furthermore, creditors have directly competing interests in that repayment to one means less is available to repay the others. These trade-offs and potential conflicts are known in advance to creditors and so bankruptcy sets the backdrop for the negotiations that can occur when insolvency looms as an unwelcome prospect. For example, troubled debtors and their creditors often try collectively to change the terms of the original deal and avoid the delays and costs associated with a formal default. Such a process is called a "workout," "accommodation," or "restructuring" and happens outside of court. In this way, creditors can help a debtor keep their promise by agreeing to changes that make the promise easier to keep. Such renegotiations often involve stretching out payments over a longer period, lowering the interest rate, rolling over some portion of the debt, exchanging debt for equity, and maybe even including some debt forgiveness. But the new deal reflects what could happen should the debtor end up in bankruptcy court, in the "shadow of the law."

Of course, failure to keep a promise can have non-legal consequences as well. If a debtor was willing but unable to pay, through no fault of their own, they might be considered simply unlucky or unfortunate. If so, their personal reputation remained intact through the bankruptcy process and they would likely be able to borrow again in the future. However, if they were deemed culpable, a failed debtor might acquire a reputation as an unreliable individual, or worse, as an incompetent or even dishonest one. Of one failed Chicago clothing house, the newspaper recorded: "This failure, however, did not particularly astonish anybody, as the proprietor's principal business appeared to be attending horse-races and politics."[20] A well-publicized reputation for lack of business purpose made it harder to renegotiate a loan in the present or to borrow again in the future. And multiple defaults, as compared to single ones, were much more likely to hurt a person's reputation since they signaled a durable pattern of problematic behavior, either incompetence or dishonesty, or both.

Regardless of why someone failed, how they failed was carefully scrutinized. Did they treat their creditors fairly and in good faith, and try as much as possible to meet all their obligations? Debtors who failed well were singled out for praise. Consider the case of James Read & Co., which collapsed but nevertheless went to extraordinary efforts to ensure that all creditors were eventually paid 100 cents on the dollar. The *Merchants' Magazine* said of such men that "he has capital in his character, which will carry him triumphantly through the storm. We believe in his integrity—we know the generosity of his disposition, and the nobleness of his soul."[21] Did the debtor cheat creditors and misrepresent their true situation? Someone who hid assets from creditors, who favored some creditors over others (repaying a family member while stiffing others), or who attempted to escape their problems by moving to a new jurisdiction would be condemned over and above the simple fact of having failed.[22] A failed partnership of two brothers was criticized by its creditors for transferring property and cash to a third brother in order to keep assets away from the creditors.[23] Persons who acquired bad reputations could be subject to informal sanctions as well as legal ones: they were socially excluded and suffered diminished status. And likely they would be denied future opportunities to borrow.

Failure was an unwelcome but inevitable feature of capitalism. Indeed, *Bradstreet's* (January 5, 1918, p. 3) explicitly referred to a "normal" level of commercial failure, and the *Bankers' Magazine and Statistical Register* stated it to be a "notable fact" that "in the history of mercantile life, in the United States, that of the number who engage in it full seven tenths fail from one to three times" (July 1850, p. 1).[24] To expect everyone to keep all their financial promises all the time was just wildly unrealistic, and virtually everyone was at some risk.[25] At the systemic level failure couldn't be avoided in a market economy, even though individual debtors, and those who loaned to them, wished to avoid insolvency.[26] Bankruptcy provided a way to ensure that poorly performing firms, unprofitable businesses, and inefficient operations were closed down and their assets released to other uses, whether through liquidation or reorganization. It offered a procedure for the competing claims of creditors to be reconciled and paid off, as far as the debtor's assets allowed. In this way, bankruptcy undergirded the "neo-Darwinian" process that weeded out inefficiency, rewarded business success, and imparted dynamism to market economies. This "tough love" approach was represented in an article entitled "Failures Not Necessarily Calamities," which went on to say: "In every such case failure, though unfortunate for the victim, is a positive gain for the community. It is the pricking of a bubble, the dethronement of a sham, a step in the direction of putting the business of the country upon a stable footing."[27] The "hard" budget constraints of capitalism contrasted with the "soft" budget constraints characteristic of socialist economies,[28] and so from the standpoint of comparative political economy bankruptcy is a distinguishing feature.

Individuals, proprietorships, and corporations risk insolvency when they take on more debt. Greater "leverage" means greater risk of bankruptcy for a simple reason: borrowing means that the debtor has assumed a legal obligation to repay a sum of money on a specific schedule, and failure to meet that obligation entails a formal breach. The more money a debtor borrows, the higher their leverage, the greater the financial burden imposed by those legal obligations. And even when individuals don't directly borrow, if they guarantee or "endorse" the debts of others (so-called "contingent liabilities"), they indirectly make themselves more vulnerable to default. A highly indebted individual or firm has less margin for error: if the debtor can't generate enough cash to service the debt, then the debtor defaults and legal proceedings will begin. Debtors will also be at greater risk of bankruptcy depending on the kinds of assets they possess. When payments come due, it is better to have highly liquid assets, that is, ones that can easily be sold, and the cash thus generated used to make the required payments.[29] Illiquid assets, by contrast, are harder to turn into cash at short notice and if pressed, the debtor may not be able to realize their full value in a timely manner.[30]

Elements of Bankruptcy

All market economies involve some type of economic failure, but there are several features that distinguish one bankruptcy system from another.[31] In all of them, a court intervenes in the life of a troubled firm, halting individual collection proceedings on the part of creditors, identifying and taking control of the firm's assets,[32] and determining the number and magnitude of its obligations. And the same holds true for insolvent individuals. But how do bankruptcy proceedings begin? One key feature concerns the criteria upon which bankruptcy procedures are triggered, and generally there are two approaches. The first involves a balance-sheet test in which a firm's assets are compared to its liabilities, and if the total of the latter is greater than the former (i.e., the firm is worth less than zero), then the firm is declared insolvent and bankruptcy proceedings begin. However, the valuational issues can be non-trivial. Similarly, the assets and liabilities of an individual can be summed and compared, and if that person has negative net worth then off they go to bankruptcy court. Another approach depends on the firm's ability to pay its debts as they become due: when it cannot do so, regardless of the balance sheet, then bankruptcy starts. In this case, a firm that is solvent but illiquid may still end up in court. Again, there is a parallel situation for individuals. A second key feature concerns who may initiate bankruptcy proceedings. Is bankruptcy something that only creditors can trigger, or can a debtor voluntarily initiate proceedings? The latter option gives debtors more control over the timing of bankruptcy, but regardless it is clear that creditors want to be able to take action before a worsening economic situation completely dissipates the value of the assets. Bankruptcy laws also vary in their application: many early laws could only be used by merchants or traders, whereas contemporary laws generally apply to all individuals, proprietorships, partnerships, and corporations. Sometimes they can even apply to governments. Once initiated, bankruptcy laws typically impose a judicial "stay" suspending all debt collection proceedings that are underway. The stay helps prevent a disorderly and destructive "rush to the assets" that can actually reduce the value of the estate and worsen creditor losses.[33]

Bankruptcy systems produce a variety of outcomes. The traditional result of a business bankruptcy was simply liquidation: the firm's assets were gathered and distributed to the creditors (on a pro rata basis and in accordance with their seniority), and then the firm was shut down.[34] The employees lost their jobs, the firm ceased to operate, and bankruptcy resulted in organizational death. Creditors had to realize their losses and adjust their own balance sheets but could seize the remaining assets before everything disappeared. Recent laws have added a more rehabilitative approach, however, where the bankruptcy proceeding becomes a venue in which the firm is reorganized so as to return to profitable operation: operations are restructured, debts are renegotiated, costs reduced, and so on.[35] Such an approach is politically attractive because it seems to preserve jobs and bolster economic activity. There are, of course, many ways to reorganize a troubled firm, and so procedural matters make a big difference in determining how the costs will be shared: Who can propose a reorganization plan? Who must approve the plan? What standard of agreement is required for judicial approval (unanimity, majority, supermajority) and how are votes counted (does each creditor get a vote, or are votes weighted by the claim size)? And who should control an insolvent firm while it is undergoing reorganization? It could be the incumbent managers (so-called "debtors in possession"), who are most familiar with its operations but who have presided over its demise, or it could be someone new, brought in from the outside to replace current management. How much time should they be given to turn around a troubled company?

There was plenty of variation in outcomes for individual debtors as well. Early U.S. laws often put debtors in prison, where they stayed until they repaid their debts.[36] Since debtors were hard-pressed to earn income while in prison, their release often depended on the generosity of friends and family, and on the ability of debtors to mobilize their social networks. Modern laws typically offer a way for individuals to get a fresh start by offering their assets to creditors but then having the balance of their debts discharged. This basic pattern gets modified when assets can be exempted from the bankruptcy process (a feature that echoes many state laws), and some debts are non-dischargeable. For example, an insolvent debtor might be allowed to keep some of their own personal property like clothing or tools. Often, a "homestead exemption" protects the family home from seizure. But if individual debtors can keep certain assets, they may also remain stuck with certain obligations. In contemporary U.S. bankruptcy law, federal taxes, student loan payments, alimony, and child support payments are non-dischargeable.[37] Filing for individual bankruptcy does not relieve the debtor from such obligations.

Seniority matters for creditors in both individual and corporate bankruptcy, and it reconciles competing promises that a debtor has made by distributing losses unevenly. How fully a creditor can expect to be repaid depends on how they are ranked in comparison to other creditors, and so seniority creates a strict interdependence among them. The most senior claimants are paid first, and only after their debts are fully repaid does money go to more junior claimants.[38] Top-priority creditors can expect to get most of their money back, while low-priority creditors frequently receive nothing. In other words, seniority concentrates losses among the lowest-priority creditors. Seniority is determined partly by contract (secured creditors are ranked ahead of unsecured creditors) and partly by statute (current U.S. law gives priority to tax obligations, unpaid wages, etc.). These priorities determine what kind of losses a creditor can expect to endure, and how much the promises made to them will be broken.

U.S. Bankruptcy Law

Article One of the Constitution provided for a federal bankruptcy statute. But for much of the nineteenth century there was no statute in place, and legal procedures to deal with defaulting debtors had to be found among state laws. At the federal level, a cyclical pattern unfolded involving repeated passage and repeal, usually triggered by an economic crisis. Such a crisis usually meant that, all at once, many debtors faced serious financial problems and so could not make their payments or keep their promises. Insolvency suddenly became a widespread condition, and this created strong pro-debtor pressure to offer relief to debtors through a new federal bankruptcy law.[39] In a democracy, politicians are sensitive to the wishes of the electorate, especially when many voters are insolvent and seek quick help. After the law passed, and insolvent debtors used it to settle their debts, a political backlash would occur and the law would be repealed, leaving no statutory help for debtors until the next crisis.[40] Instead, creditors trying to enforce their claims would again have to rely on state law. In addition to their non-uniformity, one major problem was that state law frequently favored in-state creditors over those from out of state, a financial bias that obviously made interstate commerce difficult and generated pressure for a new federal statute.[41] State laws also offered varied ways for creditors to deal with wage earners who defaulted, via wage garnishment laws.[42] The absence of a federal bankruptcy law didn't prevent debtors from failing and didn't render creditors helpless; it simply meant that the parties involved, whether as debtors or creditors, had to proceed in state courts and without a framework for an encompassing resolution.

This cyclical pattern was established by the bankruptcy law of 1800, which was prompted by the depression of the 1790s. Although the law was set to last for five years, it was repealed after only three. The crisis of 1837 produced another federal bankruptcy law in 1841, which was on the books for only two years. And the financial panic of 1857 eventually resulted in a new bankruptcy statute passed in 1867, revised in 1874 and repealed in 1878.[43] The innovation of this law was to allow for both voluntary and involuntary bankruptcy. A permanent bankruptcy act finally passed in 1898, with major revisions made during the Great Depression and then again in 1978 and 2005.[44] Passage of other types of state law reflected the same ebb and flow of economic and political forces. In the wake of an economic crisis, for example, many states suspended creditor collections, foreclosures, or repossessions as a way to protect insolvent debtors.[45] Although politically popular, their efficacy was doubtful.

The Bankruptcy Act of 1800 offered a measure of relief and forgiveness to the debtors who took advantage of its provisions.[46] Although bankruptcy was conceived as an involuntary measure (that is, debtors couldn't initiate their own bankruptcy), many debtors were able to get at least one cooperative creditor to file suit and start the proceedings.[47] Some personal property was exempt, so after being discharged from their debts, debtors weren't completely impoverished (they might literally keep the clothes on their backs). However, the political backlash was such that the law was repealed after only three years, despite being given a five-year term of operation.[48] Before long, the United States was again a nation without a national bankruptcy statute.

For much of the nineteenth century, cultural sensibilities viewed failure to repay a debt as a kind of individual moral failing, and failure provided an opportunity to reflect on individual character.[49] Insolvency was not just a matter of misfortune, or an unfortunate situation for which the debtor bore little responsibility. Instead it revealed someone's deeply problematic character, and failure to honor debts could ruin a person's reputation and undermine their status in the community.[50] The stigma was unmistakable: "Habits and usages which have usually led to bankruptcy, have a taint of immorality."[51] This understanding clearly helped motivate the creditor's search, before making a loan, for key indicators of the debtor's personal character. Failure to keep a promise was simply an "unmanly" thing to do.[52] Furthermore, for an individual to be a debtor was in itself worrisome because of the association of debt with subordination and servitude: creditors had power over debtors so it was best to stay out of debt completely.[53] Gradually, however, the powerful stigma that had attached itself to business failure diminished, in part because indebtedness and failure were so common.[54] Instead, perceptions became more nuanced, and varied depending on the circumstances and actions of the failed individual: some disgraced themselves by behaving badly (e.g., hiding assets from creditors) while others acted with honor (repaying as much as possible and treating all creditors equally). The latter could be forgiven their failure; the former could not.

Regardless of how much the debtor was at fault, insolvency meant that the debtor's property belonged properly to the creditors. "It is a universal principle, recognized by all codes of laws, and obviously dictated by the notions of right common to all men, that the property of a debtor belongs to his creditors to the amount of their claims, and accordingly when this amount exceeds that of his property, it is the creditors, and not the debtor, who are materially interested, and who ought therefore, to have the control and disposition of the property. In such a case the debtor is commercially dead, and his estate ought to be administered upon and divided among those to whom it belongs, in the ratio of their claims."[55] Early on, there was little support for rehabilitative versions of bankruptcy, only hard budget constraints. This punitive approach for debt enforcement was particularly salient in post-Reconstruction southern states. There, the dependence of tenant farmers on their landlords for credit provided a means for white agrarian elites to maintain their dominance. Debt servitude was one way to maintain the traditional social order in the South.[56]

Those who loaned money were not the only ones paying attention to bankruptcy. The new credit rating agencies like R. G. Dun were also very interested to track both the particularity and the generality of failure. Business failure inflicted losses onto the failed firm's creditors, and consequently the debtor's failure increased the likelihood that the creditors would, in turn, fail (and potentially pull down their own creditors). In other words, failure had an unfortunate tendency to spread. In their ledgers, early credit reporting agencies were careful to record a particular individual's prior record of failure and differentiated between those who failed "well" and those who failed "badly."[57] A "bad failure" occurred when the debtor attempted to cheat the creditors, by either fleeing the scene (not uncommon in the nineteenth century), concealing assets, or wrongfully favoring some creditors over others. Those who failed "well" made an honest attempt to repay their creditors as best they could. Information about the quality of failure was considered highly indicative of a person's likelihood to fail in the future, and when signaled by a low rating could be used to warn away potential creditors. Indeed, in a New York City newspaper ad for his new service,[58] Lewis Tappan challenged potential customers to ascertain the value of his credit information using debtor default as the key test, and they would see that the Agency had anticipated which businesses would fail to repay their debts. Failure would demonstrate the success of the Agency and the quality of the information it could provide.

Counting Failures

Credit rating agencies became very interested in broader patterns of failure, and by the latter nineteenth century they had become definitive sources of information on this topic.[59] The two biggest agencies, R. G. Dun and Bradstreet's, regularly published summary tables containing commercial failure statistics,[60] showing how the total number of business failures changed over time and varied between states, or from one industry to the next.[61] Often, the accompanying text interpreted the numerical evidence so that readers could see underlying trends. Bradstreet's reminded its readers of the substantial effort that lay behind its collection of this aggregate data, as it had to "to take account of 1,013,000 changes, either in firm name, location, capital or credit, during the year just closed. This work, it is needless to say, involved the active cooperation of fully 150,000 of the company's representatives, located at 86,000 cities, towns, and post offices in the United States and Canada."[62] Their descriptive tables provided a simple analysis of failure, enabling readers to gauge the overall riskiness of extending credit in a particular location or industry. In the absence of national income statistics, aggregate measures of business failures also provided one way to gauge the overall economy and its position in the business cycle: it was easy to see that business failure rates climbed when the economy got into trouble (and vice versa). Thus R. G. Dun explained: "An accurate measure of business conditions is found by examination of the commercial death rate, just as the healthfulness of a city is measured by its proportion of deaths to total population."[63]

Bradstreet's further emphasized the value of its services by publishing numerical tables purporting to show that the incidence of failure varied with a firm's rating. Without anything resembling modern statistical rigor,[64] Bradstreet tables classified failed firms by the rating they had been given, and readers could see that most of the failed firms had previously been given a low rating.[65] And if the reader didn't get the connection, the text provided a helpful interpretation of the numerical evidence: "As to credit ratings possessed by those who failed, it might be stated that 13,698 of the 14,139, or 96.9 per cent., had Very Moderate or No Credit ratings. . . . The number failing in Good Credit, 398, was 2.8 per cent. of all, which was about the same as regards number as in 1916."[66] The clear implication was that use of Bradstreet's ratings would enable a creditor to avoid the low-rated high-risk debtors most likely to fail. By using credit ratings, a subscriber could avoid bad risks and lend to good risks. Or, as Bradstreet's put it: "liability to failure bears a close relation to the amount of capital employed, and furnish practical proof of the correctness of the credit ratings assigned by the company, based, by the way, not entirely upon the amount of capital employed, but also upon the reports as to character."[67]

These privately produced measures of failure were widely reported. Many U.S. newspapers dutifully published failure statistics obtained from a rating agency, usually Bradstreet's or Dun, in order to give their readers a sense of the national economy.[68] The *Charleston Mercury* of January 22, 1857, for example, reproduced a table obtained from the Mercantile Agency listing mercantile failures for the previous year, broken down by state. Far from the nation's commercial centers, the *Salt Lake Tribune* (April 17, 1880) reproduced failure statistics put together by R. G. Dun to shed light on general business conditions. In the South, the *Atlanta Constitution* used Dun's information to note that there had been "an enormous increase" in the number of failures over the previous year (July 13, 1878). The *Minneapolis Tribune* of May 4, 1882, even compared Dun's count of business failures in the first quarter of 1882 to that of Bradstreet's in order to judge whose published figures were more accurate. Bankers took serious note of the failure statistics assembled by the mercantile agencies (see, e.g., *Bankers' Magazine and Statistical Register*, February 1880, p. 640), as did the business community at large (see, e.g., *Merchants Magazine and Commercial Review*, February 1870, p. 97, *Commercial and Financial Chronicle* 24, no. 604 [January 20, 1877]: 52–53).[69] Even later, the *Financial Times* of London (March 31, 1891), then the premier business newspaper in the world, discussed business failure in the United States drawing on (and praising) the tabulations put together by Bradstreet's.[70] And in reporting on the Great Depression, the *New York Times* (December 2, 1930, p. 49) cited Dun's failure statistics to give an authoritative measure of the economic catastrophe. Outside of the news media, after World War I the newly established Federal Reserve System relied on statistics compiled by Dun when it discussed business failure in the United States, thus giving those numbers quasi-official status.[71]

More than any other public or private source, the rating agencies tracked business failure at the national level, compiling information from geographically dispersed sources and turning failure into a measurable and countable fact. They attended to its particularity by noting specific instances of failure and occasionally offering detailed diagnostic summaries of especially important cases.[72] These "postmortems" tried to offer valuable lessons to the reader about the causes and consequences of failure. In this regard, rating agencies joined the newspapers, which also commented on and interpreted noteworthy business failures.

Rating agencies also represented to their readers the generality of failure, providing simple analytical tables showing how failure changed over time, and how it varied across regions of the country or between different industries. As authoritative sources for failure statistics, the agencies also deemed themselves authoritative interpreters. From the tables presented in *Dun's Review* (January 7, 1911, p. 11), for example, it would be easy for a reader to see that there were many more failures among general stores than among iron manufacturers, although the liabilities involved in the latter were on average much greater. Bradstreet's also diagnosed the general causes of business failure, and who was at fault: it might be because of incompetence or inexperience, or because the firm lacked sufficient capital. Or a firm could have failed because of unforeseen disaster, or because some other firm failed.[73] Generally, it seemed to Bradstreet's, debtors were usually to blame for their own failures: "Summed up, 1917 was a year when, more than ever before in the history of Bradstreet's Causes of Failure record, the causes of the non-success of those who were unfortunate enough to fail were traced to the individuals themselves, and not credited to the influence of happenings outside of or beyond the individual's own control."[74] Dun offered its own bleak diagnosis of failures, also generally pointing the finger at those who failed: "It is well known that an army of men rush into business each year, especially in times of general prosperity, who should never have responsibility of any kind, but are only fitted to serve others. Utterly lacking in executive ability, but perhaps possessing sufficient thrift to save a little money, or inheriting a small sum, they go into business independently. It is merely a question of time when these incompetents are forced to suspend."[75]

In the late nineteenth and early twentieth centuries, there were few ways for an interested observer to get an overall sense of the U.S. economy, and how it was doing, other than through Dun's or Bradstreet's failure statistics.[76] Someone could track annual exports, steel production, cotton prices, foreign exchange rates, or railroad activity, but these were not general indicators.[77] Eventually, in the early twentieth century, a number of economic forecasting services fed the appetite for prognostication. Roger Babson and Irving Fisher, for example, both established firms that in different ways offered economic predictions about the future of the overall U.S. economy to their clients.[78] While their accuracy left much to be desired (e.g., Fisher spectacularly failed to anticipate the Depression), the demand for their services reflected a broad desire to comprehend the overall economy and its future direction. During the 1920s, the National Bureau of Economic Research studied business cycles and national income, and published its findings, but eventually, the U.S. government took over the job of generating national income statistics on a regular schedule. After considerable work in the 1930s, starting in 1947 the Commerce Department published comprehensive national income accounts and henceforth observers could use these official statistics as a kind of "barometer" of the overall economy.[79] But for many decades before that, privately created aggregate measures of failure were the only way to gauge the macroeconomy.

Bankruptcy and Big Business: Equity Receiverships

When the constitutional provision for bankruptcy law was written, business failure generally meant the insolvency of a small partnership or proprietorship, with few or no employees. In the late eighteenth century, small firms could close down without causing widespread damage to the national economy or social fabric. But the growth of businesses over the nineteenth century, and in particular the rise of large-scale railroad networks, made some business failures a much bigger problem. The simple liquidation of an insolvent railroad became a very problematic possibility, especially given how important railroads became to the nation's communications and transportation infrastructure. Railroad networks knit the nation together, and their continued operation was essential for many communities. In some respects, they were akin to today's "systemically important" financial institutions, although there was yet no conception of "too big to fail." Furthermore, large railroads typically involved such a numerous and mixed set of stakeholders (e.g., shareholders, creditors, bondholders, employees, management, and affected communities) that negotiating an informal deal to rescue a troubled railroad was extremely difficult. Just bringing all the concerned parties to the bargaining table faced serious barriers, and they had quite different and conflicting interests. In general, employees and management wished to see the troubled railroad restructured in a way that preserved their jobs. Owners or shareholders also wished to avoid a liquidation that would erase their investments. Creditors and bondholders, by contrast, wanted to recover as much of their money as possible and were less interested to save the firm as a going concern.

U.S. railroads expanded enormously over the nineteenth century and, given their capital intensity, had to raise huge sums of money. It is no coincidence that the biggest "robber barons" of the Gilded Age were involved in railroads. But railways tended to overbuild, extending track and capacity beyond what the market could sustain. When fare competition occurred and railroads slashed prices to fight for market share, all of them came under extreme financial pressure. Given their high levels of indebtedness they had substantial fixed costs and little margin for error, and so as profits fell, default on interest payments became more likely. The proportion of total railroad mileage in receivership reached 18.19 percent in 1877 and peaked again during the recession of the 1890s, reaching 19.41 percent in 1894.[80] Almost a fifth of the nation's railway system was operating under failure.

A failing railroad was certain to break its promises to its creditors, and normally this should have prompted legal action by creditors to recover their money. But railroads had become too large and important to be treated like ordinary debtors. What to do? The answer to this problem at the end of the nineteenth century was judge-led, was largely independent of federal statutes, and came to be known as an "equity receivership." U.S. federal judges shifted from protecting the sanctity of creditors' rights to preserving the viability of troubled railroads, often at the expense of creditors. It provided a model procedure that later was enshrined in statute, an instance where legal practice preceded formal law. And although bondholders should in principle have played a leading role in reorganizing insolvent railroads, thanks to the help of the federal judiciary it was frequently the railroad managers, in alliance with investment bankers, who stayed in charge of the reorganization.[81] Furthermore, the assets of an insolvent firm were supposed to be devoted to repayment of the creditors, in accordance with the seniority of their claims and on a pro rata basis, but railroads going through an equity receivership reduced their fixed costs substantially, imposed significant losses on bondholders, kept management in place, and generally maintained the operational integrity of the railroad system.[82] Judges recognized the importance of functioning railroads and so were willing to interpret the law in a creative fashion. Inadvertently, the "equity receivership" anticipated many features of the modern Chapter 11 reorganization, which is expressly intended to avoid liquidation and keep a troubled firm going.

A Permanent Bankruptcy Law

Until 1898, federal bankruptcy laws came and went. The Act of 1898, however, proved more durable than its predecessors. As with previous laws, the recession of the 1890s provided a proximate motivation for federal lawmakers to do something.[83] However, the political forces in favor of reform didn't only include debtor groups, that is, those who would gain from legal provision for a "fresh start." A century of economic development built around credit meant that the political landscape was becoming more complicated, and so groups with a general interest in a functioning credit economy, like the National Association of Credit Men, pushed hard for reform. They were particularly focused on business credit.[84] For example, in the absence of a single federal bankruptcy law, credit specialists had to master the exacting details of collection laws in each individual state.[85] One credit manager stated: "Here in Chicago we sell goods of all kinds all over the country and, of course, find it expensive and troublesome to be governed by the laws of the various states. I believe that our sales would be greater and our losses less if we had one uniform law in force."[86] Legal variation across states became increasingly problematic as credit networks expanded, with debtors borrowing from creditors in many other states and creditors lending to debtors in many states. A federal bankruptcy statute would simplify and standardize the procedures needed to deal with troubled debtors, and in this way the push for reform reflected the larger uniform law movement.[87] Writing in the *Harvard Law Review* after passage of the new law, one commentator noted: "It is cause for satisfaction that the entire country is now subject to a uniform law of bankruptcy."[88] Many state debt collection laws discriminated against out-of-state creditors, an obvious obstacle to interstate commerce that depended on the extension of credit from suppliers to customers in different locations.[89] It was also difficult within a state to discharge debts owed to out-of-state creditors.[90] Furthermore, creation of a single national legal standard for failure would help support the growth of the credit insurance industry, which offered another way for business lenders to manage their credit risks.[91] With a single legal definition of insolvency, it was easier to write an insurance contract to cover the risk of insolvency.[92] Overall, bankruptcy reform enjoyed the support of various mercantile groups, commercial associations, and boards of trade, as well as the National Association of Credit Men.[93] These proponents had to overcome sectionally based political concerns that stemmed from the fact that many creditors were in the North and East, and debtors were in the South and West.[94] The benefits of the new law were lauded vigorously: "The last decade has witnessed the growth of a new force in the credit world, the growth of various large associations of merchants, manufacturers and also of credit men, having for their common objects not only the spreading of better acquaintance and the interchange of ideas among business men of the particular cooperation among creditors in case of a debtor's failure, the promoting of frankness on the debtor's part towards his creditors, and the instituting of prosecutions of fraudulent debtors and the stamping out of fraudulent practices. . . . All this has been rendered possible, as will readily appear, solely through the existence of the Federal Bankruptcy Law."[95] And more specifically, the National Association of Manufacturers credited the 1898 Act with helping mitigate the economic damage caused by the financial crisis of 1907.[96]

Unlike its predecessors, the 1898 bankruptcy law wasn't repealed after the economy recovered.[97] It was, however, modified. In 1910, for example, amendments allowed corporations to use federal bankruptcy proceedings.[98] For bankrupt corporations, limited liability capped the losses that shareholders could endure and shifted the burden to creditors. And during the Great Depression, the Act was again substantially reformed. The extraordinary wave of business and personal failure that occurred in the 1930s generated enormous political pressure to modify the legal framework that governed bankruptcy.[99] So many businesses, households, and individuals defaulted that politicians felt compelled to act. Among other things, bankruptcy law moved further away from simple liquidation and toward business reorganization that held out more hope of saving jobs and productive capacity. Furthermore, one of the goals of reform was to protect investors more effectively from the misbehavior of corporate "insiders" who often controlled the equity receivership process and to make those charged with management of an insolvent estate more independent.[100]

The Chandler Act, passed in 1938, made a number of important changes to the federal bankruptcy code. Most of these involved the creation of new procedures to deal with corporation reorganizations (Chapter X) and insolvent small businesses (Chapter XI) but without giving too many advantages to incumbent managers in the manner characteristic of equity receiverships.[101] In practice, however, many corporations found it more advantageous to use the Chapter XI proceeding.[102] Additionally, the newly created Securities and Exchange Commission (SEC) was given a formal role in corporate reorganizations as an independent arbiter to protect the interests of small investors. The insertion of a federal administrative agency into what had previously been a judicially mediated process among private parties was a major innovation.

The next major bankruptcy reform occurred in 1978, and unlike many previous reform episodes it was not prompted by an economic crisis. Instead, a variety of factors came together to put statutory revision on the political agenda, including major studies by the Brookings Institution and a National Bankruptcy Commission and growing numbers of consumer bankruptcies.[103] The biggest change involved Chapter 11, which applied to corporations and updated the provisions of the Chandler Act. This new chapter continued the shift from liquidation to reorganization as the preferred outcome of a bankruptcy proceeding and was intended to enable incumbent management to use the law to reorganize a firm before its financial situation became completely hopeless. The measure created the possibility of "strategic bankruptcy" in which firms could reduce interest payments to creditors, reject collective bargaining agreements and leases, cap mass tort liabilities, and make other substantial operational changes even when they were currently able to meet all their financial obligations.[104] For business executives, such changes reduced the stigma attached to bankruptcy and made it part of a firm's strategic tool kit. The reform also tried to raise the status of bankruptcy judges, who presided over increasingly complex corporate reorganizations involving billions of dollars' worth of assets. This change was supported by many stakeholders but provoked opposition from the federal judiciary[105] and proved to be a major point of contention. As well, reformers proposed the creation of a new federal administrative agency to deal efficiently with large numbers of routine bankruptcies where there was nothing to dispute and no contentious issues to adjudicate, but this obvious threat to lucrative legal work was effectively opposed by the bankruptcy bar.[106]

The 1978 reforms also opened a new era in personal bankruptcy. White (2007: 175) notes that the number of personal bankruptcy filings in the United States increased more than 500 percent from 1980 to 2004. Part of this reflected the continued expansion of consumer credit: more American households were borrowing money to fund consumption. And creditors willingly loaned them that money. In fact, household indebtedness increased substantially over the same period and much of it involved "revolving credit," that is, credit card debt.[107] Families who were overwhelmed by their debts sought relief through bankruptcy.[108] This huge increase in both indebtedness and bankruptcy led to pressure from the credit card industry to modify the law and make it harder for individuals to discharge their debts in a bankruptcy filing. The industry claimed that the stigma of bankruptcy had declined to the point where people deliberately went into debt to boost consumption knowing that they could escape their obligations and start all over again. Furthermore, during the 1990s lower-income households were the ones most likely to adopt credit cards,[109] and they tended to be more economically precarious and hence likely to default. And although personal bankruptcy is often sparked by an adverse event like unemployment, unexpected health or other expenses, or divorce, high overall indebtedness made individuals and households more vulnerable to such events.[110] Whatever the true underlying causes for the rise in personal bankruptcy, the credit card industry lobbied heavily in favor of measures that would make it harder for individuals to discharge their credit card debt, and these were passed into law in 2005 in the Bankruptcy Abuse Prevention and Consumer Protection Act (BAPCPA).[111] The result was a dramatic decline in bankruptcy filings.[112] BAPCPA accomplished this partly by constraining the ability of debtors to choose between Chapter 7 and Chapter 13 when filing for bankruptcy, a choice that debtors previously had used to their advantage and bore little relation to their underlying ability to repay their debts.[113] Personal bankruptcy rates soared as the 2008 financial crisis hit, but because of the reform it was much harder for insolvent individuals to discharge their debts and get a completely fresh start: they remained bound by their promises to credit card companies.

Although the political fights surrounding passage of BAPCPA almost entirely focused on personal bankruptcy, and whether the old rules had been exploited by individuals to avoid responsibility for their debts, another important change was almost completely overlooked at the time. At the urging of the financial services industry, especially the big dealer banks, the U.S. bankruptcy code incorporated the model netting rules promulgated by the International Swaps and Derivatives Association (ISDA).[114] These rules governed the disposition of over-the-counter swaps transactions between an insolvent debtor and its counterparties. Although all other debt-collection actions are subject to the judicial stay, and hence halted by the initiation of bankruptcy proceedings, the new netting rules granted to swaps counterparties a super-priority that enabled them to escape the stay and net out their positions with respect to the debtor. In effect, they could extract economic value from the insolvent firm before any other claimant.[115] And since bankruptcy is a zero-sum game, the gains enjoyed by swaps counterparties came at someone else's expense. Roe (2011), for example, argues that the super-priority enjoyed by swaps counterparties worsened the financial crisis of 2008.

Bankruptcy rules set the balance of power between troubled debtors and their creditors as they bargain in the "shadow of the law." If the rules heavily favor creditors, then outside of bankruptcy court debtors will have to make substantial concessions when trying to negotiate an informal workout. And, obviously, if the rules change dramatically in favor of one side over the other, the bargaining also shifts. But bargaining over troubled debtors has also been affected by the rise of securitization. When a single creditor loaned money to a debtor, and kept the loan on its balance sheet, it was clear who the debtor needed to negotiate with in order to change the deal or gain forbearance.[116] And even in the case of a syndicated loan, where many banks participated, the debtor had to work with the lead bank. With securitization and disintermediation, loans may be originated by a single lender, but then multiple loans are pooled together and new securities issued against those assets. So a holder of one of these new securities, for example, a residential mortgage-backed security (RMBS), in effect possesses a small portion of a large number of different loans. And the debtor has, in effect, borrowed small sums from a large number of lenders. Furthermore, if the security is widely traded, ownership is constantly changing. This arrangement makes it much harder for debtors and creditors to reopen their agreement if the debtor has gotten into trouble.[117]

Real and Nominal Money

Credit is extended as purchasing power, and so in the United States debts are denominated in dollars. Repayment in legal tender (as opposed to in-kind payments) extinguishes those debts, both public and private, and a promise means repayment in U.S. dollars. But the real value of money can change because of inflation (when its value diminishes) or deflation (its value increases), potentially altering the value of a promise. And if price changes are substantial, the change in the value of money can be especially consequential for long-term debts. Typically, inflation is good for debtors and bad for creditors because debtors will repay their loans with dollars that are worth less than when they were borrowed. By the same logic, deflation is bad for debtors and good for creditors. Sophisticated parties can adjust their debt contracts to anticipate price changes: in a period experiencing high inflation, for example, a bank will charge a higher interest rate to cover the declining value of money.[118] It might even insist on a debt contract with adjustable interest rates or one that incorporates some kind of price index. But not all parties are equally sophisticated and sometimes price changes are unanticipated. Inflation during the 1970s put pressure on the mortgage lenders like savings-and-loans, which extended thirty-year loans that were repaid in diminished dollars. It led to vigorous action by the Federal Reserve under Paul Volcker to raise interest rates and stabilize prices. In periods of deflation, like the 1870s through the 1890s,[119] debtors had to bear the additional burden that they were obliged to repay their debts using dollars that were worth more. Deflation shifted wealth from debtors to creditors and helped motivate political action in support of debtor interests. Among other things, such action influenced political debates about the gold standard.[120] Although debtors can go into default for any number of idiosyncratic reasons, deflation makes it more difficult for debtors as a group to meet their obligations. Since it is rarely anticipated in debt contracts, it also creates political pressure for ex post adjustments (such as a moratorium on foreclosure).

Public Borrowers

The meaning of bankruptcy is clear when it comes to individuals and private firms. If their liabilities exceed their assets, or if they are unable to pay their debts as they become due, then they are insolvent and face bankruptcy. What happens if the troubled debtor is a state or municipal government? A number of states suspended or defaulted on their bond payments in the nineteenth century, but since foreign investors simply stopped lending them money, these states had to settle with their creditors before they could borrow again. No federal law has ever made provision for U.S. states to file for bankruptcy, and the 1910 amendments to the 1898 Bankruptcy Act expressly excluded municipal governments from bankruptcy procedures.[121] Many municipal governments issued bonds in the 1920s to fund infrastructural projects, and when the Great Depression struck local property tax revenues plunged and consequently many defaulted on their bond payments.[122] A law passed in 1934 created a new bankruptcy process for municipalities but was found to be unconstitutional in 1936. A modified and constitutional law was passed in 1937, and henceforth cities could go bankrupt, but in a unique manner. For starters, only the municipality itself could initiate bankruptcy proceedings: there were only voluntary bankruptcies, not involuntary ones. And since municipalities seldom have the option of liquidating assets and closing down, the bankruptcy process is intended to help them restructure their debts and finalize an agreement with creditors.[123] The legal presumption for U.S. bonds is that any change in the terms of a bond issue requires unanimous consent of all bondholders, and so the problem of bondholder holdouts is a real barrier to restructurings. The provisions of a modern Chapter 9 bankruptcy proceeding make it possible for a majority of bondholders to surmount the objections of a minority and proceed with a restructuring of municipal debts.[124]

Conclusion

Credit is based on promises, and although creditors try to predict beforehand who is more likely to keep their promises, they often mistakenly lend money to debtors who don't repay. Creditors urge debtors to repay, using a mixture of polite reminders, stern threats, pathetic begging, and everything in between. Despite their appeals, some debtors don't pay and so they break their promises. Broken promises can be enforced in courts of law, but they are also sometimes modified in light of the fact that they will not be fulfilled as originally made. There are legal vehicles for both of these options. Such proceedings recognize the interdependence that exists among promises, and so something that started out on a strictly bilateral basis (between a debtor and a creditor) becomes multilateral (between a debtor and many creditors). Creditors have informal options as well and often exploit these before turning to the courts. Social pressure, public shaming, harassment, and the suspension of future loans are all ways in which lenders have tried to get borrowers to pay up.

What happens when a debtor becomes insolvent and breaks their promises? The answer to this question, as well as who may pose it in practice, has changed over time as federal bankruptcy laws were passed and repealed in the nineteenth century, and then as a permanent federal bankruptcy law was revised through the twentieth century and later. For individuals, the legal consequences of breaking a financial promise have shifted from punitive incarceration in debtor's prison to an arrangement whereby debtors surrender their assets, creditors get paid, and the debtor is released from the remaining obligations. This creates the possibility of a fresh start and is often calibrated to judgments about the culpability of the debtor for their own failure. However, some assets are exempt and so don't have to be surrendered to creditors, and some obligations are non-dischargeable and therefore continue even after the debtor goes through the process. For firms and corporations, the consequences of failure have shifted from simple liquidation, in which repayment of creditors was given highest priority and the insolvent firm closed down, to reorganization, which aimed to salvage the troubled firm and preserve employment and productive capacity. The political incentive to shift from liquidation to reorganization was foreshadowed by the equity receiverships used to save insolvent railroads at the end of the nineteenth century. Closing a firm can be extremely disruptive to many stakeholders if the firm is particularly large or if it performs some critical economic function.

Much debt recovery activity happens in state courts, where creditors are simply trying to enforce their claims one at a time. In such settings, creditors proceed independently, each hoping to seize whatever assets their insolvent debtor still possesses. The enormous variability of these laws, however, made legal action uncertain and complicated, and the problem worsened as credit transactions increasingly crossed state boundaries. Only a federal bankruptcy law could bring order to the mad scramble that happened in state court.

Easy credit makes for economic growth. But when the overall economy experiences a broad downturn or goes into a recession or depression, businesses have to balance carefully between asserting their own claims over debtors and meeting their obligations to creditors. Then, the legal rules governing failure receive more frequent application. More debtors become insolvent, and more go through formal bankruptcy proceedings. It is easy to insist on the sanctity of contract and the necessity to fulfill promises when failure is the exception, rather than the rule. But widespread failure changes this calculation. Frequently, mass failure created political pressure to modify the rules in order to make life easier for the debtors. It is no coincidence that state governments imposed moratoria on foreclosures in order to protect resident debtors from creditors eager to seize collateral. The same considerations prompted new federal bankruptcy laws in the nineteenth century to offer relief to insolvent debtors.

What to do with broken promises is not simply a matter of principle. It very much depends on whose promises got broken. In the United States, we saw this most recently in the discussion of "too big to fail" financial institutions. A small bank that is unable to meet its obligations fails and its owners lose their money. Its assets are taken over by a receiver, and the bank itself is either closed down or, more commonly, merged into a larger, healthier institution. By contrast, a very large bank that can't meet its obligations is not simply closed down. Such a bank is too big to fail, and so it isn't allowed to do so. This is because, in the judgment of public officials, its collapse would cause financial panic, unleash a wave of insolvencies, or otherwise lead to serious problems for the financial sector as a whole. Rather, it receives a government bailout: an injection of capital, provision of guarantees, or some other commitment of public resources intended to make it solvent again. For such institutions, the normal rules of the marketplace are suspended.

9

Sovereign Borrowers

The great majority of borrowers in the United States are private individuals, organizations, and firms. Such parties are generally bound by the rules of the marketplace and the rule of law, and so are free to make promises and enter into contracts, if they so choose, but having done so must face the consequences if they fail to keep their end of the bargain. A debt contract gives both parties recourse if the other side doesn't meet their obligations. The usual problem that arises is that of debtors who don't repay, and so lenders regularly pursue them in and out of court.

There is an important class of borrowers not subject to these ordinary constraints. Indeed, the usual rules do not apply in the case of sovereign debtors. This holds true even though a substantial proportion of total indebtedness is now undertaken by governments. Sovereign powers enforce the laws that govern debt obligations, but whether they are also subject to those same laws is another matter. Sovereign immunity, for instance, sets limits on what creditors can do in relation to a sovereign debtor. In short: "there is no legal method of compelling a State to pay its debts against its will. This is on the theory that in debt matters a State is a sovereign power."[1] Such immunity doesn't prevent governments from borrowing, and in fact governments borrow heavily, but it does make the process more fraught. And this isn't just a story about the federal government, because state and municipal governments also borrow a great deal, making promises and using the money to pursue public goals.

A bankrupt corporation can be closed down, its employees fired, and its assets distributed to the creditors, but things are different when a nation or state fails to pay its bills. Government creditors can't simply seize public assets in lieu of payment. Barring a social revolution, invasion from abroad, or absorption into some other political entity, nations and states do not "shut down" in any comparable way. Polities default on their loans, to be sure, and they sometimes even disappear (witness the end of the Confederacy), but it is a rare event and lenders don't accommodate the possibility as a matter of routine. For example, commercial lenders sort out conflicts among themselves via seniority, so that some lenders have priority access to the assets of a defaulting borrower. But sovereign creditors typically all have equally strong claims on the "full faith and credit" of the borrowing government.[2]

When assessing the creditworthiness of a sovereign borrower, lenders consider similar factors as when assessing a private borrower, including the equivalent of willingness and ability to repay. Sovereign governments can tax, and so their ability to pay depends on the underlying economy, the tax base, and the future tax revenues that are not already earmarked to service other debts.[3] In other words, lenders to sovereigns consider the relative debt burden, the ratio of current debt to debt carrying capacity, where capacity depends on the size and condition of the underlying economy.[4] Their expectation is that political entities will persist into the future and will be able to use future tax revenues to repay the debt. That expectation of continuity differentiates sovereign loans from business loans, where lenders are mindful of the possibility of failure or bankruptcy, conditioned by limited liability, and followed by the actual dissolution of the borrower.

The equivalent of "willingness to pay" is harder to determine in the case of sovereign debt. A public entity isn't an individual person. Nevertheless, something like willingness was deemed to be a durable feature that could be estimated and often fell under the general rubric of "community character." As one commentator put it: "Its moral responsibility, the historical background of the community, its attitude toward debt in the past. The principal criterion is whether the municipality has defaulted at any time in the past. If it has defaulted the first thing that should be looked into is the cause of the default, because there might or might not have been mitigating circumstances. The worst possible cause of default would be bad faith, where a municipality is simply trying to take advantage of some loophole to escape paying bonds which it is perfectly capable of paying."[5] A government that previously acted in bad faith was clearly one whose bonds should be avoided.[6]

Like other entities, sovereign governments acquire resources and then deploy them. Governments raise money (via taxes and user fees, for example) and then spend it. How they spend money is a matter of public policy: budgets reflect political deals and social priorities. And in a democracy political entities are accountable to the public in a way that a for-profit borrower is not. There are times when the expenditures of a sovereign exceed its revenues and then the government will need to borrow. As compared to current taxation, borrowing offers two advantages: it pushes some of the costs of public policy into the future,[7] and it is voluntary rather than coerced. Although paying taxes is an obligation (and tax evasion is a crime), the decision to lend is subject to the lender's choice (except in the case of so-called "forced loans"). Not purchasing a government bond isn't a criminal act, even if at times it bears some stigma. And the scale of public borrowing can far exceed anything seen on the private side. National governments spend at a frightening pace when they are at war, and short of outright confiscation no democratic government is able to raise taxes fast enough, or far enough, to keep up with military expenses. Thus, major military conflicts almost always force national governments to borrow.[8] At the end of World War II, for example, outstanding U.S. federal debt exceeded the value of the entire U.S. gross domestic product. No single private individual or entity in the United States has ever borrowed on such a scale. Obviously, state and local governments do not make war and so are not burdened in the same way by military expenditures.[9] But if national government bears the responsibility for declaring, conducting, and financing war, it also has a unique appeal as a borrower: the federal government can appeal to patriotic and nationalist sentiments in a way that no county or municipal government ever could.

A government borrower will use future taxes to service its debts and so the certainty of tax revenues is an important consideration for public creditors.[10] It can also borrow and repay at the same time, simultaneously retiring old debts and issuing new ones.[11] Just as politics shapes the expenditure side of public budgets, so too does it determine the revenue side. The fiscal impositions of the state reflect political deals and priorities, as well as the structure of the underlying economy.[12] Powerful groups prove adept at lightening their own tax burdens, but effective revenue systems have to conform with underlying economic realities. Revenue authorities have to "follow the money," in other words, and so, for example, many governments shifted their tax systems to reflect the declining importance of real estate and the rising importance of intangible assets: they moved away from property taxes to wealth or income taxes. The purpose served by a public loan also matters. Borrowing money to make infrastructural investments that will eventually lead to economic growth and a larger tax base can generate the future tax revenues needed to service the debt. Such public investments may, in a sense, pay for themselves.[13] In the early nineteenth century, for example, many U.S. states borrowed in order to fund the construction of canals and roads that would lower transportation costs, increase commerce, and support economic development. Or they funded private banks to encourage investment and the provision of financial services to their citizens.[14] To ensure that future revenues will go to debt service, governments can explicitly earmark taxes for the repayment of specific debts, preventing their diversion to other purposes. Some states even resorted to constitutional amendments to bolster their creditworthiness.[15] A government borrower can also issue new debt to repay old debt, in effect "rolling over" its debts and pushing repayment off into the future.[16]

Today, the current *federal* debt is much greater than the debts accumulated by all the other levels of government. This was not the case in the past, however. In 1840, for example, most government borrowing was done by the states, and only a little was done by the federal government.[17] At the time, a great deal of public policy and expenditure was enacted at the state and local level, and if the federal government wasn't fighting a war, it could fund its ordinary operations without having to raise a lot of revenue. The Civil War massively increased the federal debt, but afterward the national government's share of outstanding government debt declined from around 72 percent in 1870 to 63 percent in 1880 and then 43 percent in 1890, as Civil War debts were retired and the United States stayed out of major wars.[18] In 1913, before World War I forced the expansion of military spending, 72 percent of all government debt was incurred at the local level, and only 21 percent was at the federal level. Proportionately, most of the public borrowing was done by county and municipal governments.[19] And local governments did most of the spending as well: in 1913, 61 percent of all government expenditures occurred at the local level, and only 30 percent came from the federal government.[20] Later, the balance shifted, and so in 1946, right after World War II, 96 percent of all government debt was owed by the federal government.[21] And although the fiscal impact of World War II eventually faded, federal spending stayed high in the postwar period because of expanded New Deal social spending as well as Cold War military activities. Relative to the size of the economy the national debt declined after World War II, but it never fully retreated back to prewar levels. It took on a new significance.

Federal indebtedness does more than enable the national government to fund deficits. Federal debts played several key roles in the nation's financial system. As mentioned in chapter 4, Civil War bonds issued by the Union government provided the foundational assets for the National Banking System. The national banks were built around government bonds, and these debts also created a financial constituency with an interest in the survival of the Union.[22] After World War I, domestic financial markets were again awash with government bonds, and the newly established Federal Reserve System discovered a new type of monetary policy. Originally, the discount window was supposed to be the Fed's key policy instrument, but Fed officials realized that by buying and selling government securities, they could influence credit markets and push interest rates up or down. In the 1930s, open market operations replaced the discount window as the premier policy instrument. And today, private financial models and algorithms all use a "risk-free" interest rate that is bench-marked by U.S. Treasury bonds.

Sovereign debt also raises important questions about democratic accountability. Who sets public policy? In a democracy, policy supposedly reflects the interests of the majority, who use elections to select their representatives. But the power embodied in debt relationships raises the possibility that lenders can wield influence over public policy, by providing or withholding financial support. Notions of creditworthiness have policy implications, and sovereign choices may be constrained if lenders are unwilling to go along with a policy they don't like. In effect, bond markets threaten to exercise veto power. As Destin Jenkins (2021) shows in the specific example of San Francisco, the need to borrow could give municipal lenders tremendous influence over city policy.

Like corporations, sovereign debtors face the problem of succession. Long-term debts encumber a sovereign government even when there has been a complete change of political leadership, policy, and financial priorities.[23] This is particularly true of democratic governments, where elections regularly produce new presidents, governors, and mayors from different and even opposing political parties. A lender has to not only judge the creditworthiness of the government leader who wishes to borrow but also assess the creditworthiness of future successors. Who is to say that a newly elected president will feel obliged to keep the promises made by his or her predecessors, especially if they were political enemies? What happens if debt funded a policy that the new leadership opposed? Perhaps the creditworthiness of a democratic government rests more on the electorate than on elected officials.[24] North and Weingast (1989) argued that the creditworthiness of the national British state strengthened during the Glorious Revolution of 1689 because power shifted from Crown to Parliament. Since the House of Commons was dominated by elected MPs, lenders could be more certain that their preference to be repaid would be respected and that they wouldn't be vulnerable to the whims of an absolutist monarch. This argument can apply to the United States: domestic lenders to U.S. governments might be reassured to know that their electoral power would make it hard for political leaders to default on a loan. As Adams observed: "when property-owners lend to the government, they lend to a corporation controlled by them-selves."[25] However, if the balance between foreign and domestic creditors shifted, or if domestic lenders lost political power, this constraint might not hold. Foreign creditors do not have the same domestic electoral leverage.

The succession issue arose most particularly in the South after the Civil War. The Confederate states borrowed to support the Southern war effort, and after the war these debts were fully repudiated. Confederate war bonds, like Confederate currency, became worthless, and Southern creditors could not enforce their claims.[26] But matters didn't stop there as the state debts incurred immediately after the war, during Reconstruc-tion, were subsequently challenged in the post-Reconstruction period by Southern Democrats who opposed Northern and Republican involvement in Southern governance and who reasserted white dominance. People sup-porting repudiation of these postwar debts argued that "carpetbagger" gov-ernments were corrupt and illegitimate, that the debts were unnecessary and mismanaged, and furthermore that the creditors were mostly from the North and were therefore responsible for the destruction of the Southern economy.[27] Undoubtedly, an important consideration was the fact that the political power of African Americans was at a high point during the Recon-struction period. As Southern Democrats returned to power, they rejected Reconstruction-era debts, and the policies they paid for, and felt unbound by the promises of their political predecessors.[28]

Setting aside debt for military purposes, most long-term state and federal government borrowing since the start of the nineteenth century has been done through issuance of bonds (called "general obligation" bonds, which are backed by the "full faith and credit" of the issuer). That is, someone who wished to lend to Illinois would purchase a financial instrument issued by the State of Illinois. Typically, investors would compare state bonds to other bonds when choosing which financial asset to acquire, and in addition to rate of return investors valued liquidity, that is, the ease with which such a bond could be bought or sold on the secondary market.[29] They often used the past record of a political entity to assess its reliability about keeping its promises. A state that had recently defaulted on its debts would find it hard to borrow again, or had to pay a high premium, but no U.S. state government, not even those reneging on their obligations, was banished forever from bond markets.[30]

Bonds are highly formalized promises and come in different varieties. One modern bond format consists of a promise by the debtor to pay a certain sum (e.g., $1,000) at a specific point in time (e.g., ten years in the future). A ten-year note is sold to investors at a discount and entitles the bondholder to be paid $1,000 in ten years. The price paid, that is, the size of the discount, will reflect market interest rates, beliefs about the solvency of the issuer, and expectations about inflation. A particularly creditworthy issuer can sell its bonds for a better price, that is, for a smaller discount (and hence lower interest), whereas more dubious issuers get lower prices and pay higher rates. And if investors completely distrust the issuer, then they simply won't buy the bond at all. Another common bond format involves coupons that entitle the bondholder to payment of interest at specified times, and at maturity the bondholder is repaid the principal. Some bonds were called "bearer bonds," in that the bond owner wasn't registered with the issuer, and payments were simply made to whoever was the bearer of the bond certificate. Such bonds were easiest to trade on the secondary market and so had more liquidity.[31] These features were often set by legislation.

Like many local governments, municipalities in Kansas became active borrowers in mid-nineteenth-century bond markets. As their populations expanded, local communities wanted to make public infrastructural investments to serve the population and support continued growth. Their ability to borrow depended on state authorization, and the enacting rules reveal extant understandings about the structure and purpose of municipal borrowing. One 1866 act authorized Kansas county and city officials to issue bonds for the purposes of building bridges or public buildings, subject to prior voter approval,[32] with a maturity between five and twenty years, and paying no more than 10 percent interest. Furthermore, county and city officials in Kansas were required to levy a tax sufficient to meet the required payments on the bonds.[33] The bonds, and the tax revenues raised to service the debt, could only be used for the stated purposes and any official diverting money to serve other ends was guilty of a misdemeanor. An 1870 act empowered Kansas municipalities to issue bonds in order to build bridges. Again, the bond issue required prior voter consent and if approved, the bonds were restricted in their maturity (to between five and thirty years) and interest rate (maximum of 10 percent). Officials had to establish a "sinking fund" so that at maturity the bonds could be fully redeemed (i.e., repay the principal to the bondholder), and the sinking fund was to invest in U.S. or Kansas bonds, or in the same bond issue the fund was established to service.[34] City and county school districts were also authorized to issue bonds in order to construct school buildings, with similar restrictions and conditions. In general, local Kansas governments could borrow money through the sale of bonds, but only for specific public purposes. They first had to gain the approval of a majority of voters, and they had to levy taxes to repay the debt. The tax revenues were explicitly earmarked for repayment.

Many state and local governments borrowed to support development. In Massachusetts, for example, the City Treasurer of Holyoke reported in the 1898 annual report that Holyoke was encumbered by almost $2.5 million in "funded debt." Some bond issues were to mature very soon: $25,000 worth of one-year bonds (paying 4 percent interest) were due December 1, 1899, and had been issued to cover the expenses of the local school system. Other issues matured far off in the future: $250,000 worth of thirty-year water bonds (also paying 4 percent) were set to mature January 1, 1927. While some of the bond issues were earmarked for specific purposes (public schools, the water system, sewers, the Holyoke and South Hadley bridge), others simply supported "general purposes."[35] The annual report also listed $119,764.17 as payment for interest, or about 8 percent of total city expenditures. Like many cities, Holyoke had borrowed money to fund its operations, and at this point the total municipal debt wasn't overly burdensome. However, by allowing public officials to push costs far into the future, some worried that the ability to borrow was being abused: "Those who vote the debt, and the councils or bodies which create it and issue the bonds, do so without much hesitation, as the burden is expected to fall principally on *posterity*. A learned justice of the Supreme Court of the United States has very fitly described the effect witnessed as a *mania* for running in debt for public improvements."[36]

It was common for state and local governments to borrow for specific purposes: expenditure in pursuit of a worthy goal could justify going into debt. And those purposes evolved over time, depending on changing conceptions of what government should do and what could be left to the private sector. At the end of the nineteenth century, Henry Adams noted: "The necessity of loans arises . . . from a determination on the part of the government to enter upon some great work of public improvement. . . . The crowding of our cities brings ever more prominently into view the necessity of adequate provision for sanitary regulations, for education, for street transportation, and the like. It is not safe to leave these matters in the hands of private corporations."[37] While public education, and hence funding school buildings, was long recognized as a responsibility of local governments, pay-ing for road construction became a more important and expensive public task after the widespread adoption of the automobile. A 1922 survey of state bonds, for example, stated: "The construction of highways and bridges is by far the leading single purpose for which the outstanding debts were incurred, over a third of the total debt of the states having been contracted for this purpose."[38] The next most important purpose was for the construction of waterways and harbors. Current tax revenues were ordinarily expected to cover the operating costs of government, but creating infrastructure rep-resented a significant way for government to support social and economic development. Infrastructure was both expensive and long-lived, conferring benefits into the future. Consequently, much public borrowing by state and local government funded infrastructure.[39] And the benefits of infrastruc-tural investments reflected political priorities, typically privileging white residents over black, and the upper and middle class over the working class and poor.[40]

The distinction between ordinary operating expenses, to be funded by tax revenues, and capital expenditures, to be funded through borrowing, seems clear in principle. But it is not so easy to operationalize the distinc-tion in practice, even when it is imperative to ensure that borrowed funds are not helping to cover a deficit in the operating budget. Fiscal rectitude sounded good in theory, but to implement it required an elaborate system of accounts, budgetary oversight, and financial information. Until the late nineteenth century, this public accounting apparatus didn't exist for most American cities, and lax stewardship of public monies created the appear-ance, and undoubtedly also the reality, of corrupt and irresponsible urban governance.[41] Adams observed: "It is not too much to say that every rule laid down by the science of finance has been disregarded by American cities. Demands have been made for unnecessary purposes; demands for neces-sary purposes have been made in excess of the requirements of economical expenditure; while the entire business has been so veiled behind municipal bonds and suppressed contracts, that the public is kept in general ignorance of what is going on."[42]

As with accounting reforms in the private sector, a premium was placed on uniformity and standardization,[43] and development of public sector accounts followed broader Progressive Era reforms in government.[44] Expert bodies like the National Municipal League played a key role in develop-ing standardized schedules and urging their adoption, and enjoyed some early successes in Ohio and New York.[45] Although imperfectly realized, more systematic governmental accounts gave citizens, rating agencies, and lenders a better sense of the financial situation of sovereign borrowers and their future ability to service debt. This additional information certainly laid bare a basic fact about local communities: some were wealthy, and others were poor. Wealthy towns had a bigger tax base and so could support more borrowing and better local services, whereas poor communities could not. Nevertheless, improved clarity and additional information also created opportunities for "off–balance sheet" strategies.

Local governments were subject to judicial oversight in terms of the purposes for which they borrowed and expended public funds. Early on, U.S. courts took a relatively narrow view of those purposes and would act to prevent local governments from becoming overly expansive about why they borrowed.[46] For example, in upstate New York in the early twentieth century, the town of Schenectady attempted to establish a municipal ice supplier to ensure that citizens without refrigeration could access low-cost ice and preserve their food in the summer heat. Such a policy engaged public health issues and food safety, but nevertheless the New York courts issued an injunction prohibiting such action.[47] And so, summer ice in Schenectady would continue to be supplied by the private sector. Gradually, however, the courts recognized a broader spectrum of public interest activities, and so state and local governments were able to borrow in pursuit of different and more ambitious types of infrastructural developments.

State and local governments were also subject to legal restrictions on their indebtedness and ability to tax, regardless of how the money was spent.[48] Their "fiscal constitutions," as Schragger (2012: 860) puts it, reflected nineteenth-century political attempts to curtail borrowing combined with twentieth-century measures to restrict taxation. Borrowing in the present allows governments to fund popular programs while pushing the costs off into the future. Debt restrictions seemed to offer a way to prevent local officials from succumbing to this temptation. Given that local public revenues depended heavily on property taxes,[49] one way to set limits was to fix a ceiling for public debt as a proportion of the assessed value of taxable property in the jurisdiction. Some states tied indebtedness to annual revenue. Other restrictions were procedural: for example, a bond issue might have to be approved by the voters (perhaps by a supermajority), and the state legislature as well, and it might even require a constitutional amendment.[50] Debt limits for local governments were often set by state government. And when state government wanted to encourage development, it could set higher debt ceilings. For instance, the State of California allowed its municipalities to borrow up to 15 percent of assessed valuation, a substantially higher level than most other states, and this funded bigger infrastructural projects and ultimately economic growth.[51] Of course, all states recognized that such restrictions could be lifted during an emergency, and although the precise definition of the latter term was necessarily left open for interpretation, it usually included wartime.[52]

As an additional defense against borrowing, issuance of municipal and state debt often required prior consent from the electorate. Voters had to approve public borrowing in a special election, where the purpose of the debt was made clear.[53] If voters turned down a bond issue, then their government could not proceed with the loan. But this hurdle could also be surmounted by politicians and political machines that effectively managed the electorate. Indeed, the basic mechanics of engineering a successful bond campaign became widely known.[54] As Erie (1992: 536–37) richly documents, in the case of elections about California municipal debt, voter turnout was often very low and so it wasn't necessary to gain the support of an actual majority of the population in order to approve a new bond issue (e.g., the special election held in April 1910 to vote on a $3,000,000 bond issue for Los Angeles generated a 15 percent voter turnout). Low-turnout elections were easier to control.[55]

Debt limits and other restrictions were supposed to curtail public spending, but they didn't always work as intended. Rather than act as simple "pre-commitment" devices, such limits also motivated organizational innovation and creative accounting to circumvent them.[56] These limits applied to "general obligation" bonds, which enjoyed the "full faith and credit" of the issuing municipality and were backed by general tax revenues. Municipalities that were up against a debt ceiling started to create new quasi-governmental entities that performed a specific public service but were not formally recognized within the municipal budget. These entities, variously named boards, administrations, authorities, districts, and so forth, issued their own "revenue bonds," backed by specific revenues but not subject to the public debt ceiling.[57] For example, the Indiana state constitution set a strict municipal debt ceiling of only 2 percent of taxable property.[58] In order to fund construction of new schools, Indiana local governments created special school-building corporations that were not subject to this debt limit.[59] Similarly, the Sanitary District of Chicago (now called the Metropolitan Water Reclamation District of Greater Chicago) was established in 1889 as an entity separate from the City of Chicago to fund and manage the water and sewer systems.[60] The city of Providence, Rhode Island, was subject to debt limits but was always able to violate those limits with the permission of the state legislature.[61] Through similar tactics, many states issued legal promises and took on large amounts of debt despite measures to constrain indebtedness.[62] In addition, governments circumvented restrictions on taxation by charging income-generating fees that applied to the users of some public service.[63] The incentive to be creative was particularly acute during the Great Depression, when tax revenues plunged and state and local governments had a hard time servicing their debts and avoiding default.[64] As a consequence, New Deal institutions like the Reconstruction Finance Corporation and the Public Works Administration loaned money or awarded grants to troubled local governments.[65]

Another period of municipal creativity was inaugurated in California with the imposition of Proposition 13 property tax caps, approved and enacted in 1978. This conservative measure led to a subsequent contraction of property tax revenues for local government, which combined with the Reagan-era decline in federal aid to cities to produce acute budgetary problems. Tax increment financing (TIF) was one way for municipalities in California, and eventually elsewhere, to regain discretionary revenues and escape politically imposed tax restrictions. TIF became popular in the 1990s and 2000s as local governments innovated to evade constraints, but other recent financial tactics included lease-back arrangements, special purpose bonds, and interest rate swaps.[66] A TIF arrangement enabled municipalities to appropriate incremental tax revenues from designated areas and escape prior earmarks, debt service commitments, and other restrictions, and represented one more move in a reciprocal pattern of political action and reaction where people try to constrain sovereign finances, and then the sovereign tries to evade those constraints. The political battle very much concerned the ability of governments to make promises and borrow.

Each of the multiple types of infrastructure had its own history of public and private provision. In all instances, however, they involved durable, capital-intensive assets and so required the investment of large sums of money up front that would generate benefits for a long time after their construction: long-term debts could fund long-term investments.[67] Roads were an early and important type of infrastructure, and at first these were supplied by the private sector via state-chartered companies.[68] Investors would fund construction of a toll road, with their debts covered by tolls charged to users of the road. But over the nineteenth century, governments increasingly took over the responsibility of building and maintaining the roads and bridges needed for ground transportation. And with the widespread adoption of automobiles, government became the primary funder of roads, bridges, and highways, often relying on gas taxes and highway tolls to generate revenue that would service the bonds issued.[69] According to Lancaster (1924: table IV), paying for streets and bridges accounted for 22 to 42 percent of total annual state and municipal security issues done in the period between 1912 and 1922. Overall, outstanding state highway debt grew from $105.4 million in 1914 to $2,114.8 million in 1934.[70]

Utility services are another significant type of infrastructure. Waterworks and sewers were particularly important in the densely populated urban areas that grew quickly in the latter nineteenth century. They also were provided privately at first but soon became the responsibility of local government.[71] Today, most of the water and sewer systems that supply potable water and treat sewage are publicly funded and maintained, especially in the big urban areas. The end of the nineteenth century also brought the widespread generation and transmission of electrical power. Electrical systems, another utility service, were initially built through a mixture of public and private investments, but with a few exceptions the electrical grid soon became a largely private matter.[72] Electrical utilities were regulated, so there was public oversight, but they were mostly private corporations that issued bonds when they needed to raise additional capital. City airports became another beneficiary of public funding for transportation infrastructure. After World War II, many large municipalities built or expanded local airports to support air transport. It is telling that most did so by selling airport revenue bonds that were secured by an income stream created by airport traffic (e.g., parking, concessions, rentals), thus avoiding the political restrictions placed on general obligation bonds.[73]

Investments in public or low-income rental housing, or in infrastructure benefiting minority neighborhoods, reflected the political limits of public borrowing.[74] Government policies favored single-family dwellings in the suburbs and provided much less financial support for housing in African American neighborhoods. Bond issues for new schools, recreational facilities, or low-rent housing in black communities were voted down.[75] Political opponents attacked the Federal Insuring Offices that provided mortgage insurance to lenders financing private low-income housing.[76] When civil rights activists fought for more equitable public social spending, bond rating agencies worried about the budgetary consequences and by lowering their ratings made borrowing even more expensive.[77] New York City's financial crisis in 1975 became a widely told morality tale about municipal fiscal rectitude, one with obvious implications for urban minority populations.

Before the Federal Reserve System started to track bond issues, it was hard to know how much state and local governments relied on the bond markets to borrow. But after 1919, it is clear that such borrowing had grown substantially.[78] Starting in the early 1920s, U.S. state and local governments issued more than $1 billion worth of new securities each year. Bond issues declined at the start of the Great Depression, as bond markets collapsed and state and local governments felt the effects of economic decline, but then rebounded at the end of the 1930s. Aggregate bond issuance declined again during World War II but surged in the late 1940s, reaching a total of over $3 billion in 1948. But these postwar sums paled by comparison with the debts of the federal government.

Ordinary investors could be as mystified by municipal bonds as by railroad bonds. The bond rating agencies' decision to get into the business of rating state and municipal bonds was a testament to the growing importance of such bonds for the investing public. How to evaluate these promises? When marginal tax rates for personal income got higher through the twentieth century, so did the advantages of tax-free municipal bonds for individual investors. With the multiplication of public and quasi-public issuers (like districts, authorities, etc.), many public issuers had no prior record to consider and were generally unknown to the investing public. Moody's started rating government and municipal securities early and made these part of its standard package of annual reports. Even in the early 1920s, Moody's was rating about thirty-five thousand government securities (domestic and foreign, federal, state, and local) using the same category system it applied to securities issued by borrowers like railroads and corporations, with "Aaa" as the highest designation, then "Aa," "A," "Baa," and so on down to the most speculative investments.[79] As noted in its Manual: "Government and Municipal securities have attracted increasing attention in the last few years. The many European and other foreign loans placed in this country since the war have created a new interest in foreign issues. At the same time, income taxes have made tax-exempt municipals exceedingly attractive and the tremendous increase in municipal bonds has added to the interest in this field."[80] By the 1950s and 1960s, there were very large numbers of municipal bonds and only a few were issued by cities or entities widely recognized by investors.[81] In addition to the City of Chicago itself, for example, Chicago-area bond issuers included numerous park districts, Cook County school districts, forest preserve districts, and a water reclamation district.[82] While Chicago, then the second biggest city in the United States, was well known, most investors knew nothing about the Ridge Avenue Park District, with the notable exception that Moody's gave its bonds the "Aaa" rating. Calvert summarized the role of ratings for municipal bonds: "Ratings have assumed considerable significance in determining eligibility of bonds for purchase by certain types of investors and in the interest rates on bonds."[83]

Who purchased municipal and other government bonds? Which creditors decided to lend to U.S. towns, cities, and states? Doubtless many individuals purchased such bonds, but starting in the middle of the nineteenth century, institutional investors played a significant role. Life insurance companies, for example, had a great fondness for bonds. Partly this was dictated by state regulation but also by the absence of good investment alternatives.[84] As sellers of life insurance, insurance companies acquired substantial long-term obligations: rising life expectancies meant that cash payouts had to be made at a point in the distant future. To meet long-term obligations, they had to invest the premiums they received in long-term assets that safely generated a positive long-term rate of return. Bonds were an obvious choice. Thus, in 1865 about 35 percent of all life insurance company assets were invested in bonds. The proportions for 1895, 1925, 1955, and 1985 were 36, 38, 53, and 51 percent, respectively.[85] For a long time insurance companies have included bonds as a significant component of their investments. Mutual savings banks were another financial institution that purchased state and local government bonds. In 1896, about 25 percent of the total assets of mutual savings banks were in such bonds.[86] The proportions for 1925 and 1955 were 9 and 2 percent, respectively, a substantial decline that reflected the growing importance of U.S. government bonds and mortgage loans on mutual savings bank balance sheets. The annual report of the Ohio Department of Banks and Banking reveals that municipal bonds were a significant asset for state-chartered banks. In 1914, more than 9 percent of assets held by Ohio state banks consisted of state, county, or municipal bonds (of course, most bank assets consisted of loans).[87] The proportions were lower for Illinois state-chartered banks in 1916, where about 3.5 percent of total bank assets were in state, county, or municipal bonds.[88] And in 1912, about 17 percent of security holdings of national banks were in state, county, or municipal bonds.[89] Later in the post–World War II era, most investment in municipal bonds came from high-income individuals (who benefited from their tax-exempt status), banks, and insurance companies.[90]

Bond purchasers varied by location as well as organizational status. A great deal of capital investment in railroad, corporate, and sovereign bonds came from Europe. In the nineteenth century, the United States was a debtor nation, and midcentury evidence on investment in Ohio state bonds bears this out. In 1857, more than 50 percent of Ohio's total state debt was held in Europe, specifically Great Britain.[91] About 13 percent of the total was held by Ohio banks, and 27 percent was held in New York City, the United States' financial capital. The United States' position changed dramatically during World War I, as European powers liquidated their American investments to pay for a war that was much more expensive than any of them expected. Eventually, the United States' European allies became debtors, as they ran out of assets and had to borrow to purchase wartime materiel. The United States went from a debtor to a creditor nation, and the inward flow of capital tapered off to become a net outflow.

Public policy affected the demand for municipal bonds. For a long time, the federal government encouraged investment in municipal bonds by exempting them from federal taxation. In the 1980s, however, this incentive shrank as Reagan-era tax reform reduced marginal tax rates for high-income investors and as Congress narrowed the qualifications for tax-exempt status.[92] States also actively encouraged investment in municipal bonds by constraining the kinds of investments that banks or insurance companies with state charters could undertake. Various prudential rules practically compelled state-chartered banks to buy bonds issued by municipalities within the same state.[93] A large number of states also followed the lead of the federal government and exempted income from municipal bonds from state taxation, and depending on state tax rates this provided an additional incentive to purchase these bonds.[94]

Federal Borrowing

Federal debt differed from state and local government debt in several important ways. First of all, the rapid growth of federal debt was closely tied to war and the need to fund the military. By contrast, expansion of state and local debt was generally driven by infrastructural investments aimed at economic development, and with the notable exception of the Civil War state debts were less affected by military spending. Second, the federal government could and did force certain private commercial entities to invest in federal debt as a condition of their operation. Such entities could choose whether they wanted to operate, of course, but it was a constrained choice with a large incentive to invest in federal bonds. State governments could do something similar but local governments, by contrast, had no such leverage. Third, after the Great Depression, the federal debt itself became an instrument of countercyclical economic policy. In a managed economy, Keynesian deficit spending helped boost aggregate demand and keep the economy growing, and the issuance of debt covered the deficit. Few of the devices used to control government spending at the state and local level (e.g., balanced budget requirements, debt ceilings, etc.) were ever enacted at the federal level and so it was easier for the national government to play a more active role in the economy, once it got past fiscal orthodoxy. Fourth, U.S. federal debt became a benchmark financial asset for investors. The development of the financial system increased options for investors and so those with capital could weigh putting their money into demand deposits, equities, bonds of various types, personal loans, mortgages, derivatives, swaps, structured financial instruments, and so on. In comparing the risks and returns associated with this growing set of alternatives, federal debt came to be the benchmark "risk-free" investment, anchoring one end of a widening spectrum of possibilities.[95] It became the embodiment of a "safe" financial bet and set the default option for other alternatives. Finally, federal debt possessed a political salience that almost no other public debt could generate. Commentators invoked a variety of political arguments associated with debt, and so at various points it represented an ill-disciplined and overspending federal government, the means for undemocratic creditor control of the nation, or the expression of highest patriotic commitment.

The most dramatic expansion of the national debt came during war. The United States was born from conflict, and the substantial debts created by the War of Independence posed an early challenge. Many states borrowed money, and these debts were consolidated and incorporated into debt obligations of the new federal government.[96] The new nation started with a national debt, worth about $75.5 million in 1791.[97] Secretary of the Treasury Alexander Hamilton's 1790 report recognized the value of public credit as well as its connection to war. Simply put, debt "was the price of liberty," and upon public credit depended "the character, security and prosperity of the nation." Good public credit enabled the United States to borrow even in foreign markets, including from the Dutch.[98] However, debt was politically controversial, and the decision to assume all state war debts seemed unfair given that some states (e.g., Virginia) had already made substantial repayments whereas others (e.g., Massachusetts) had not. Concerns about fairness also dogged the decision to fully repay both those who were original creditors and those who had purchased public notes on the secondary market, often at a substantial discount.[99]

Subsequent major wars, such as the Civil War, World War I, and World War II, put huge demands on public finance, but so did minor wars.[100] The

Mexican-American War of 1846–48, for example, forced the federal government to go to European bond markets to borrow money to cover a growing deficit.[101] The national debt grew fourfold, from $15.6 million in 1846 to $63.1 million in 1849.[102] Debts climbed as well during the War of 1812 and the Spanish-American War, at the beginning and end of the century. The increase in public indebtedness was more dramatic during the Civil War, where the national debt ballooned from $90.6 million in 1861 to $2.7 billion in 1865 (not including Confederate borrowing). And vast sums were borrowed to fund World War I, when the national debt grew from $1.2 billion in 1916 to $25.5 billion in 1919, and then World War II, when the debt expanded from $43 billion in 1940 to $269 billion in 1946. Relative to the size of the domestic economy, the national debt experienced local "peaks" during the Civil War and immediate aftermath of World War I, but the highest "peak" occurred just after World War II.[103]

Different creditors had different reasons to lend to the federal government. According to Sexton (2005: 55–60), the European investors who purchased bonds that funded the Mexican-American War had mostly financial motives and were attracted by good rates of return and the relative political stability of the United States (compared to Europe, where 1848 was a year of revolutionary ferment). European investors were not so enthusiastic about becoming financially embroiled in the Civil War, and neither the Union nor the Confederate government had great success in trying to market bonds abroad in support of military spending.[104] Of necessity, most of the borrowing was done domestically. In the North, Jay Cooke's highly successful bond campaigns played heavily on patriotic motivations and raised a great deal of money from individuals for the Union government.[105] Cooke's firm marketed directly to the general public through heavy advertising in newspapers, telling readers about the availability of bonds in denominations that ranged from $50 to $1,000 and identifying agents from whom the bonds could be purchased.[106] The small denomination bonds were intended to be affordable even for people of modest means and enabled widespread ownership. Additional demand was generated by the National Banking Acts of 1863 and 1864, which transformed the financial and monetary system and made it a condition of national bank charters to invest in federal bonds (see the discussion in chapter 4). Investors could establish federally chartered banks, to be overseen by the newly established Office of the Comptroller of the Currency, by purchasing federal bonds and using these as security for the banknotes they issued. Later, the banknotes issued by state-chartered banks were taxed, as a further way to encourage national bank charters.[107] These reforms linked the banking system directly to the national debt, shifted the financial system away from state-chartered banks and toward federally chartered banks, and helped create a more uniform national currency.[108] But most importantly, they created a big incentive for investors to lend to the federal government.

Within the nation, the regional distribution of federal creditors was highly uneven, reflecting a combination of wealth, population, and political allegiances. Less than two decades after the end of the Civil War, the 10th U.S. Census (1880) asked questions about ownership of government bonds and found that U.S. debt was held disproportionately by people in New York, Massachusetts, Pennsylvania, and Ohio, in terms of both numbers of individual holders and the value of their claims. Unsurprisingly, very little national debt was held in the states of the former Confederacy. For example, New Yorkers held over $210 million worth of U.S. bonds, whereas people from the State of Georgia held only about $181,000 worth, three orders of magnitude less.[109]

Jay Cooke's successful campaigns during the Civil War provided a model for future bond sales. During World War I, the U.S. federal government faced overwhelming financial demands that it simply could not meet by raising taxes. European investors, who had supplied a great deal of capital to the U.S. economy in the late nineteenth century, were preoccupied with their own nations' wartime expenses. Additionally, the federal government was mindful that encouraging savings, rather than consumption, would help mitigate price inflation.[110] Patriotic appeals to invest were widespread and the social pressure was unsubtle: "Every citizen of the United States who buys a Liberty Bond registers his approval of our defending ourselves against Germany. Every citizen who buys a Liberty Bond testifies to his love of country."[111] Hilt and Rahn (2016) document the importance of civil society organizations in broadcasting information about bond campaigns, enlisting support, and securing participation. Leading organizations included the Women's Christian Temperance Union, the YWCA, the National Grange, and even the Boy Scouts. But while patriotism suffused the public campaign, financial details were set to make bonds an attractive investment. For starters, the range of denominations (starting as low as $50, but going up to $100,000) made bonds affordable to almost everyone. Additionally, investors could borrow to purchase the bonds if they didn't have enough "ready money" on hand. The government emulated the private financing methods that supported the sale of durable goods by allowing individual investors to purchase bonds on an installment plan.[112] The bonds were exempt from federal taxation,[113] and bond buyers were assured of the impeccable quality of their investments: "the promise to pay a Government bond is backed by the faith and honor of the United States of America and by the taxing power of this whole country, which is the richest Nation in the world."[114] Multiple Liberty Bond campaigns were highly successful and more than 20 million people subscribed over $20 billion.[115]

The U.S. federal government faced the same problems during World War II: military spending soared and the federal government had to borrow. Based on previous experience, it was also seriously concerned about price inflation. Building on the lessons of the first world war, the government utilized all available media (newspapers, radio, movies, etc.) to broadcast its appeals in highly patriotic terms and simultaneously raise money and boost morale.[116] It made bonds even easier to purchase by reducing the minimum denomination Series E bond to only $25 (which was its value at maturity; it cost only $18.75 to purchase such a bond). For those saving in even smaller increments, there were Defense Savings Stamps, which cost as little as a dime and could be traded in for a bond. Stamps and small denomination bonds weren't going to generate a lot of money, but one goal of the program was to maximize public involvement: to make everyone part of the financial "defense effort."[117] Series F bonds were for wealthier investors, with denominations between $100 and $10,000.[118] Although there was nothing like the Civil War creation of an entire system of banks to boost institutional demand for bonds, Federal Reserve and other commercial banks financed a substantial proportion of war debt in both world wars.[119] In addition to their safety, one other key feature that helped attract investment was that government bonds could be readily bought and sold. Whether they were "bearer bonds" or "registered,"[120] someone who wanted to recover their capital before maturity could simply sell their bond on the secondary market. The promises of the federal government were liquid, and government creditors weren't "locked into" their loans.

Active management of the national debt became much more deliberate and sophisticated, in part because the federal government had the organizational means to do so, and in part because the total federal debt had become large enough to influence the macroeconomy. Although it initially relied on the discount window as a policy instrument, purchase and sale of government securities became the means through which the Federal Reserve System conducted open market operations in pursuit of economic growth and full employment after World War II. Purchasing government bonds enlarged the money supply and lowered market interest rates, while selling them had the opposite effect.[121] During the war, sovereign debt markets were also managed to avoid wartime price inflation and to keep interest rates low. The latter priority reflected the federal government's own interest as a debtor: low interest rates made it cheaper to borrow.

Sovereign borrowers typically bolster the credibility of their promises by securing additional tax revenues for debt service. It is no coincidence, for example, that the federal government imposed an income tax during the Civil War, nor that the federal income tax system was greatly expanded during the two world wars.[122] If higher taxes couldn't entirely cover current military expenses, they could at least cover future interest on the debt incurred to pay for those military expenses. Consequently, filings of federal individual income tax returns increased from 437,036 to 5,332,760 between 1916 and 1919, marginal tax rates rose, and income tax revenues grew from $345 million to more than $2 billion.[123] Similarly, the number of individual federal income tax returns grew from 7.6 million filed in 1939 to 52.8 million in 1946 as exemptions were reduced and many more middle-income and lower-income individuals were taxed.[124] Over the same period, federal individual income tax revenues increased from $1 billion to $16.1 billion.[125] Through decades of post–World War II deficit spending, and even a number of tax cuts, the federal government has continued to generate enough revenue to repay its debts as they become due and to ensure that lenders find U.S. government securities to be a good and safe investment. When there is a "flight to quality" during an economic crisis, investors love U.S. treasuries.

Politics of the National Debt

Sovereign indebtedness at low levels of government seldom prompted deep or principled reflection on the political meaning of public debt. But the national debt was different from the beginning, and many commentators believed that its import was much more than just financial. Here, beliefs about the relationship between individual debtors and creditors were projected onto the nation, where the debtor was the sovereign government. Several ideas shaped the discussion. The first was that nations, like individuals, should keep their promises and that it was beholden upon an indebted nation to honor its debts: "If the maintenance of public credit, then, be truly so important, the next enquiry which suggests itself is, by what means it is to be effected? The ready answer to which question is, by good faith, by a punctual performance of contracts. States, like individuals, who observe their engagements, are respected and trusted: while the reverse is the fate of those, who pursue an opposite conduct."[126] A good reputation was to be cherished, because once lost, it could be hard to recover. This meant that public credit was entwined with public confidence and public opinion, and discussions of credit often made reference to them.[127]

The benefits of public creditworthiness extended beyond the future ability to borrow, for a well-regarded national debt could serve a nation even in the present: "It is a well known fact, that in countries in which the national debt is properly funded, and an object of established confidence, it answers most of the purposes of money. Transfers of stock or public debt are there equivalent to payments in specie; or in other words, stock, in the principal transactions of business, passes current as specie. The same thing would, in all probability happen here, under the like circumstances. The benefits of this are various and obvious."[128] In an economy where specie or cash was in short supply, anything that could substitute for money would facilitate commerce, ease credit conditions, and help keep interest rates low. In other words, the national debt could serve as the basis for a payment system. Hamilton's original insight was given a more complex implementation when federal bonds were used as the foundation for national banks, and the passage of time has only deepened the connection between the national debt and the financial system.

The second idea posited that debtors were subordinated to their creditors: the relationship was a strictly hierarchical one where one side had power over the other. This imbalance contradicted the apparent symmetry and equality undergirding contract. By this argument, an indebted nation was not truly independent, and its weakness depended on who were the nation's creditors and therefore who exerted control. For a democracy, where voters used the electoral process to choose their nation's leaders, creditors therefore constituted a rival interest group, competing with voters for power. The national debt could be a vehicle for illegitimate and corrupting influence, and because of that, nations should avoid borrowing as much as possible. These concerns were sometimes expressed with brutal simplicity: "The public debt is the bane of liberty. . . . The debtor is the servant of the creditor—his slave, his menial—a private ownership without responsibility. . . . a national bond means national enslavement."[129] Furthermore, debt signaled that the nation was living beyond its means, and fiscal rectitude dictated that nations should therefore avoid borrowing. Nations, like people, shouldn't spend more than they earned. Both of these sentiments implied that public debts should be fully repaid as soon as possible: there should be no permanent national debt. In direct response to Hamilton, James Madison asserted: "having never been a proselyte to the doctrine, that public debts are public benefits. I consider them, on the contrary, as evils which ought to be removed as fast as honor and justice will permit, and shall heartily join in the means necessary for that purpose."[130]

A third idea recognized that debt created a new constituency with a clear financial interest in the vitality and continuity of the nation: who could want to see a nation thrive more than those to whom it owed money? Public creditors were allies rather than masters. Financial connections bolstered political support and could help solidify the foundation of a new regime: "It remains to mention one consideration which naturally occurred in the reflections upon the expediency of assuming the State Debts. This is its tendency to strengthen our infant Government by increasing the number of ligaments between the Government and the interests of Individuals."[131] A similar insight shaped policy during the Civil War, when the Treasury secretary noted that the Union debt created political allies and supporters for the North.[132] The losses suffered by Confederate creditors underscored the fact that creditors wanted their debtor to succeed, but clearly whether this alliance between a debtor and its creditors was good or not depended on the moral stature of the creditors. One commentator disparaged those who loaned money to the federal government: "So long as the principal is not paid, the debt, in its full proportions, is immortal, and the tax-payers remain forever the tributaries of the holders of the debt—be they who they may, Jew or Gentile, aliens, citizens living at home, or citizens expatriating themselves to spend their pensions in enjoying the luxuries or vices of foreign cities."[133]

A fourth and more recent idea concerned the role of debt in funding public spending. Outside of wartime, balanced budgets were fiscal orthodoxy throughout the nineteenth and into the twentieth century. But thanks to the influence of John Maynard Keynes, and the political realities of the Great Depression, policymakers came to believe that the national debt could be used to cover a budget deficit that would stimulate aggregate demand and grow the economy. All this could be done without "crowding out" private investment in the capital market and thereby offsetting whatever direct stimulus was provided.[134] Pre-Keynesian orthodoxy held that public borrowing would compete with private borrowing, to the detriment of the overall economy.[135] But with this new perspective, deficit spending went from being a problem to being a solution. Of course, if deficits were supposed to help the economy recover from a recession or depression, they were also supposed to disappear during periods of expansion. A debt-funded deficit was supposed to be a temporary feature, not a permanent one, but it could be very useful if enacted judiciously.

Today, the U.S. federal debt remains a topic of political contention, even as its economic significance has become massive. Intermittently, conservatives rail against the debt, arguing that it is a burden that threatens to crush future generations and that balanced budgets are an absolute necessity. For them, deficits should be resolved through spending cuts, not tax increases, and conservatives target social rather than military spending. For others, the federal debt has become a matter of little political concern: it shouldn't become too large (relative to GDP), but otherwise it is a fact of modern politics and finance, providing a cornerstone among safe financial assets and an important instrument for effecting economic policy. Discussions of the competitive relationship between China and the United States often note how much of the federal debt is now in Chinese hands. Thanks to many years of trade deficits, China has accumulated U.S. assets, especially U.S. Treasury notes, bills, and bonds. Does this give the Chinese government "leverage" over the United States, or is China "hostage" to its financial interest in a thriving U.S. economy?

Out of the politics of the national debt came a politics of debt restraint, prompted by an underlying concern that the government might be making too many promises. Very recently, political contention over the debt ceiling has preoccupied Congress (witness the partial federal government shutdown in the fall of 2013), but the backdrop for these battles concerns how politicians tried to control public indebtedness and, indirectly, public spending. Originally, the details of federal borrowing (their maturity, interest rate, denomination, and size of issue) were set statutorily for each bond issue. Then, starting in 1917 with the second Liberty Bond issue of World War I, Congress ceded more control to the secretary of the Treasury to work out the optimal details for a particular bond issue. But Congress continued to limit the secretary's overall borrowing authority. During the Depression, the federal government borrowed further and in 1939 Congress set an explicit limit on the overall public debt, across all types of federal securities and debt issues.[136] Since then, the debt ceiling has been raised many times, following years of budget deficits and the nominal growth of the national debt.[137] The first time the United States came close to breaching the ceiling was in the mid-1950s, when the Korean War drove up federal spending and indebtedness.[138] And very recently, passage of debt ceiling legislation has become an occasion for politicians to express their unhappiness with the expansion of federal spending and the growth of the debt or to append favored amendments to "must pass" legislation. Treasury operations become complicated as total debts approach the ceiling, so even getting close to the limit can be problematic. In general, debt ceilings have not curtailed public borrowing since almost as soon as the ceiling is in danger of being breached, it is raised. Debt ceilings have, however, created political opportunities.

Conclusion

Many of the financial promises that circulate in the U.S. economy have been made by governments. These entities borrow in pursuit of public purposes and are subject to some democratic control (depending on voter enfranchisement, electoral turnout, etc.). At the state and local level, the bulk of debt has been issued to fund economic development, provide infrastructure, or support public goods like education. These are all politically popular goals, although the ability to pursue them is uneven. Local government finances reflected the same patterns of inequality that were such a central part of U.S. residential housing markets, and racial inequalities continue to persist. More recently, state and local budgets have been increasingly burdened with pension obligations, where pensions are an important component of the post-retirement compensation of public sector workers.[139] On a larger scale, the federal government pursues similar public policy goals, but it has also borrowed extensively to fund the various wars that the United States has fought. Future tax revenues service public debt, and so the adequacy of those revenues, as well as the vitality of the economy on which they depend, helps make public promises credible. Public financial systems have developed new revenue streams as governments moved beyond property taxes and customs tariffs to tax corporate and individual income and to the imposition of various user fees. But political contention about public borrowing, and the spending that it funds, has produced various attempts to restrain or otherwise curtail public finance: balanced budget requirements, tax caps, debt limits, and so on. These encouraged various circumventions aimed at minimizing the financial impact of public policy, keeping activities off the public balance sheet.

Sovereign immunity makes sovereign borrowers unlike private borrowers. When private borrowers break their promises, they can be taken to court by their creditors. By contrast, it is hard to sue the sovereign. Nevertheless, sovereigns have been able to borrow, albeit sometimes at a high price. Democratic polities also experience regular turnover of leadership, as candidates from different political parties win and lose elections. This raises the problem of whether debts incurred under one party encumber successor regimes. Unless this issue has been firmly settled, democratic political change brings with it the possibility of debtor defaults and creditor losses. Finally, as compared to private corporate and individual borrowers, public borrowers rarely experience the equivalent of "economic death" via bankruptcy and closure. Current bankruptcy law does provide for a Chapter 9 filing, which allows municipalities to restructure their debts and settle with creditors, but it is a rarely used provision. For example, there was only 1 Chapter 9 filing in 1980 and 7 in 2010.[140] In 2018, there were 4 Chapter 9 filings; by contrast, that year there were 475,575 Chapter 7 filings (for straight liquidation), 7,095 Chapter 11 filings (for business reorganization), and 290,146 Chapter 13 filings (for individuals).[141] There have been recent high-profile municipal bankruptcies, of course, including Detroit in 2013, Jefferson County, Alabama, in 2011, and Orange County, California, in 1994, but these are quite exceptional. Overall, an insolvent government cannot be treated like an insolvent corporation or individual, and so the broken promises of the sovereign operate differently.

Despite these significant differences, the same evaluative apparatus developed for the assessment of private corporate borrowers was extended to public borrowers. Bonds issued by governments were rated by Moody's, Fitch, and Standard and Poor's, just like railroad bonds and corporate bonds, and using the same categorical system. Indeed, it wasn't long after Moody's got into the rating business that it started to rate sovereign bonds. Risk-averse investors who subscribed to a rating agency service could take comfort knowing that an "AAA"-rated government bond was as good as could be: there was no higher rating. Given that so little was known about large numbers of sovereign debt issuers, particularly local and municipal bonds, the ratings played an important role in signaling to investors that sovereign bonds could be trusted. Bond ratings were fateful evaluations that could constrain policy. Municipal bonds also played a role in how rating agencies changed their business model. Up until the late 1960s, the rating agencies compiled ratings and sold ratings to their subscribers, the so-called "user pays" business model. For several reasons, including the invention of the photocopier, the rating agencies began to charge bond issuers a fee when they rated bonds. They started with municipal bonds, but eventually charged other issuers as well, and shifted over to the "issuer pays" model.[142]

The promises of the federal government became an important benchmark for all other financial promises. In comparing various financial alternatives, investors have been able to use U.S. Treasury bonds to exemplify a "riskless" or "safe" investment. Since the market for U.S. treasuries has been highly liquid for a long time, it was always relatively easy to determine current prices and yields in a public and transparent fashion. To know the current interest rate associated with a riskless investment was useful when investors had to estimate and make trade-offs between risk and return. As finance became a more quantitatively based activity, U.S. Treasury bonds offered a convenient measure of the "risk-free" rate that could then be plugged into various formulas. For pension funds, insurance companies, and other institutional investors required to invest in very safe assets, government debt was the perfect vehicle.

The promises of the federal government also provided a foundation for the U.S. monetary and payment system, separate from gold and silver. Alexander Hamilton noted that government debt could function like money and provide an effective medium of exchange for the domestic economy. His insight was given practical effect when government debt served as the basis for the National Banking System, whose banknotes and demand deposits constituted the money supply. Not coincidentally, requiring national banks to invest in federal debt helped the Union government pay for the Civil War. This connection between federal debt and the financial system also created a new policy instrument for the Federal Reserve System: open market operations. By intervening in the market for public debt, the Federal Reserve could manipulate the money supply and either stimulate or restrain economic growth. The financial promises of government are different from private promises in a number of significant ways, but they nevertheless play an important role in the functioning of a modern market economy.

10

Conclusion

Over the last two centuries, an "economy of promises" has flourished in the United States. Today's markets are now heavily populated with promisors, promises, and promisees. Individuals, households, small businesses, big corporations, and governments are embedded in complex networks of financial obligations: borrowing money from some, lending it to others, sometimes guaranteeing someone else's promises, and operating as both debtors and creditors at the same time. Individual lives are marked by a succession of debts: school loans, car loans, mortgages, credit cards, home equity loans. Huge sums of money flow through financial markets, and financial assets constitute a large proportion of the total wealth of contemporary society. Scholars use the term "financialization" to denote the growing importance of financial institutions, markets, and relationships, recognizing that the creation and exchange of financial promises has become a central part of today's economy.[1]

At the heart of all this financial activity and development lies a specific type of social action, the promise. A financial promise encapsulates and enacts a vision of the future and expresses the promisor's commitment to create that future. It isn't a grand sweeping vision of what lies ahead but rather a specific and practical one: that the promisor will repay their debts. Nevertheless, a thriving economy emerges out of these specific and practical promises. Fundamentally, financial assets are based on promises, and the lender or investor always has to consider whether to trust the promisor. Who will keep their promises? Whom to trust? As more individuals, households, corporations, governments, and organizations make financial promises, and as these promises increase in complexity and variety, the task of evaluating promises has changed and become more challenging. Partly, this is because the overall number of promises has increased: credit abounds in the contemporary economy. But it has also changed in more fundamental ways that have to do with new kinds of information, new types of borrowers, and new and more complicated promises.

An ordinary financial promise creates a bond between debtor and creditor that only ends with full repayment of the debt. Early on, this bond was interpreted as akin to servitude, a form of bondage in which debtors were beholden to their creditors.[2] The political autonomy of Thomas Jefferson's ideal "gentleman farmer" citizen could be undermined by debt. Such perceptions stigmatized indebtedness, sometimes appropriately so. In the postbellum rural South, for example, agricultural loans were used to subordinate rural workers and protect the privileges of white landowners, even after the end of slavery. And today, "predatory" lenders make it difficult for borrowers to escape indebtedness and regain their financial independence. But indebtedness isn't always oppressive, for the ability to borrow can be extremely advantageous, even liberating. With debt, people can spend future income today. It is no wonder that following the civil rights movement of the 1950s and 1960s, women and racial minorities fought for equal access to credit. And the balance of power between debtors and creditors can shift, for as debts increase, the fate of the creditor is increasingly dependent on the debtor.

Early on, most lending occurred within small social circles. Debtors and creditors were members of the same community and so had a great deal of information about each other. They might be friends or relatives, or have some other network connection. Such communities were often geographically concentrated but they could also be spatially dispersed (when members of the same network lived far away from each other). In either case, people's personal and business reputations were known. Local stores extended credit to local households, and suppliers granted trade credit to their regular customers. To finance a new business, an entrepreneur typically turned to family and friends, borrowing from within their own social circles. Someone needing a mortgage to purchase real estate would find a local lender (who sometimes was the seller). And often, people simultaneously borrowed from some and loaned to others. They weren't simply debtors or creditors but rather both. Much of this debt was informal: loans were made without signing a formal contract or creating a legally binding obligation. Nevertheless, social networks supported non-legal sanctions that could be as effective as legal ones in encouraging a debtor to repay their debts. Such connections could also obligate the lender to exercise some measure of forbearance if a borrower was unable to repay as originally intended. The ebb and flow of credit sustained social relations and community networks.

Under these circumstances, social affiliations influenced the extension of credit. Kinship and community defined in-groups and out-groups, and people frequently trusted those with whom they shared a connection. Social ties help solve the twin problems of information and vulnerability that trust poses. Social networks are conduits for information, influence, and affiliation, and so lenders and borrowers do not meet as complete strangers. Lenders, in particular, use that information to resolve uncertainties about the debtor's future willingness and ability to repay. Furthermore, social networks and affiliations offer multiple ways for lenders to reduce their vulnerability. Embeddedness in a community creates a web of expectations and obligations that go beyond finance. Norms of reciprocity mean that those who lend can ask for help in return when they need to borrow: today's creditors become tomorrow's debtors, and a community of mutual assistance unfolds over time. And with a measure of transitivity, a friend of a friend also becomes a friend. Community norms can also broaden the considerations that inform lending decisions. Rather than narrowly focus on financial criteria, the lender may recognize a solidaristic obligation to help someone out or to weigh social and political factors. Sometimes it may only be a matter of giving someone "the benefit of the doubt." At other times, normative obligations can compel someone to lend. And these considerations apply even after the loan is made. If the debtor is unable to repay, the lender may offer some leniency. Informality helped with flexibility, for it meant that commitments weren't fixed in writing and subject to the scrutiny of legal professionals and courts. Their meaning could be reinterpreted in light of subsequent developments, their ambiguities and lacunae exploited with the benefit of hindsight. But affiliation-based lending can't escape the limits of variable wealth. Even with dense social networks that ensure the flow of information and provide multiple channels for enforcement, a poor community simply has less money to lend.

Over time, new types of debtors were able to issue promises and borrow money. The most significant of these were corporations, fictive individuals that could own property, sign contracts, and go into debt. With general laws of incorporation, it became much easier to create a corporation. Corporations grew in size and number, and could even own other corporations. Unlike the case with small proprietorships, decision making about debt wasn't tied to the personality of a single individual. Willingness-to-pay meant something different for a large organization than for a person. Nevertheless, creditors loaned money to corporations, often via long-term bonds and short-term commercial paper, and corporations in turn made loans to others. Leverage gave firms the opportunity to fund their activities with other people's money and increase profits for their owners. Corporations are now dominant players within the economy of promises.

The process of evaluation changed as well. It began as a local and largely informal process whereby lenders judged the personal character and circumstances of borrowers. With the development of mercantile agencies, credit rating agencies, and bond rating agencies, however, specialized for-profit organizations collected and sold large volumes of information about borrowers on a regional, national, and eventually international scale. There were never many of these organizations and so the business of evaluation became more concentrated. It also became quite stable: bond ratings are still dominated by Moody's, S&P, and Fitch, while Experian, TransUnion, and Equifax lead the consumer rating business, and Dun and Bradstreet remains central for business credit. The ratings they issue are pervasive and definitive, surmounting legal challenges, uneven performance, and the suspicions of many. Ratings shape the availability and cost of credit for millions of consumers and business borrowers, and even sovereign governments. Across the economy, rating agencies offered panoptic judgments.

Ratings and scores are now increasingly used in "off-label" ways that only increase their fatefulness. Starting in the early twentieth century, judges recognized credit ratings in their legal rulings. Bond ratings were inserted into national financial regulations starting in the 1930s, giving specific meaning to prudential regulations for financial institutions and insurance companies and affecting the valuation of bank assets. Later, such ratings were incorporated into global bank capital standards and the risk management techniques used within the financial OTC derivatives markets. At the time, incorporation of ratings seemed a practical solution to a very specific problem, but as ratings became "locked in," and as their use expanded, their significance amplified and the unintended consequences spread. In parallel fashion, personal credit ratings are now used to govern access to housing, insurance, and employment, as various parties use individual credit scores as a generic measure of risk. Some people even use them on dating websites and apps (where an 800+ FICO score can make someone seem especially attractive). With each new application, the biases, shortcomings, inaccuracies, and exclusions that are an inevitable part of any summary measure diffuse further to shape new decisions and restrict opportunities. And although the rapid spread of this information might be taken as proof of its value (if ratings were no good, why would anyone use them?), the predictive quality of credit information was for many decades simply taken on faith. Their widespread adoption was interpreted as proof of their accuracy. From the outset, the Mercantile Agency and its competitors touted the value of the information they sold, but without evidence. In the late 1880s, Bradstreet's published tables purportedly showing that its ratings could predict business failure, but these possessed only a veneer of science. Indeed, not until the late 1930s was there a systematic statistical study of how bond default rates varied by bond ratings, almost thirty years after Moody began publishing ratings and investors began using them.

The Proliferation of Promises and Promisors

Growing volumes of credit for growing numbers of debtors accompanied new methods of credit evaluation, and they spurred each other on. On a local scale, store owners knew that giving customers credit was a good way to generate business, since not everyone could purchase with cash. And in rural areas, dominated by the yearly cycle of planting and harvest, credit was necessary to allow farmers to operate from the spring until they realized their income in the fall. In the late nineteenth century, producers of durable consumer goods tried to sell expensive products to households and recognized that providing credit was the key to sales. Credit wasn't simply a convenience. And so installment loans were born, turning intractably large lump sum disbursements into a stream of smaller payments extending over time. With regular income from steady full-time employment of the family breadwinner, encyclopedias, pianos, sewing machines, bicycles, washing machines, and eventually automobiles became affordable to ordinary families. And if someone failed to make a payment, the lender could always repossess whatever durable good the debtor had purchased. Installment lending laid the foundation for a consumer society, and by making car ownership widely available even helped refashion the twentieth-century social landscape. With two cars in the garage and a fixed-rate thirty-year home mortgage, suburbia became a reality for many. Credit card companies further expanded the installment loan system by disengaging credit from the purchase of specific items. Instead, cardholders could use revolving credit to buy meals at any participating restaurant, or get gas for their car, or buy goods from a department store. And, eventually, they could use credit cards almost anywhere to buy almost anything, including virtual goods in cyber-space. Over time, as lenders developed their credit-assessment tools, the availability of consumer credit spread from high-income families, who were obviously well able to repay, to middle- and then lower-income families, whose circumstances were more precarious. Lenders learned they could profit handsomely from borrowers with imperfect credit records, who missed payments, carried balances, and otherwise triggered fees and pen-alties. The availability of more credit enabled more people to borrow and buy more. Household indebtedness climbed.

Alongside the mainstream lenders, a parallel world of high-risk small loans continued to operate. People who couldn't borrow from a bank, who didn't qualify for a credit card, or who hadn't established a credit record could nevertheless turn to pawnshops, payday lenders, loan sharks, salary "buyers," and other types of small loan lenders. The interest rates were often usurious, and to fail to pay could sometimes be dangerous, but poor people could turn to their own "lenders of last resort." It might require surrendering a valuable family heirloom as a pawn or signing over next week's paycheck, but this system proved that lenders could profit from people whose eco-nomic means were very modest and who didn't meet ordinary standards of creditworthiness.

The development of credit also affected firms and corporations. They sought credit from suppliers, banks, and other sources, and they gave it, typically to their customers. Occupying both roles simultaneously, firms performed a delicate balancing act, especially during periods of tight money where they might have to stall their own creditors even as they pressured their debtors for repayment. Mismanage the balance and solvent firms could run short of cash and be forced to default. To judge whether a small firm was creditworthy, it was usually enough to evaluate the owner or the partners. Their character, finances, and personal trustworthiness mostly determined the trustworthiness of the firm. But large publicly traded corporations with dispersed ownership offered no such shortcuts. Lenders had to look to a broader set of criteria, relying heavily on quantitative accounting measures of financial status and performance that were becoming increasingly avail-able. Such firms are still run by people, who have personalities, but the CEO isn't the firm.

As the U.S. population expanded, and as more people embraced modern consumerism, the number of individual debtors grew. It is rare now to find someone who is neither a borrower nor a lender. Today, there are almost 120 million households in the United States[3] participating, in one manner or another, in the credit economy. Most of them manage by making promises. At the same time, the U.S. economy shifted from its agrarian origins populated by small farms, proprietorships, and partnerships to a postindustrial economy whose leading sectors are dominated by large corporations and where most people work for someone else. Small businesses are the most numerous firms, and there were over 26 million non-employer businesses in 2018, busy making promises.[4] At the same time, there were almost 6 million employer firms in the United States in 2017, with about 20,000 of them employing 500 or more persons.[5] Today's economy of promises involves many individual debtors, whose financial obligations are relatively small and simple, a modest number of business debtors, whose obligations are more substantial and complicated, and a smaller number of very large business debtors, whose complex financial dealings dominate capital markets. All of these economic actors are knitted together in a dynamic network of credit flows that cross jurisdictional boundaries, both domestic and international, and that overlay transactions in goods, services, and employment. Operating at the center of the network are the big banks, surrounded by a penumbra of "shadow banks."[6] And at the very core lies the Federal Reserve System, which pursues its twin goals of price stability and economic growth by setting the broad conditions for all promise-makers and promise-takers, but also by intervening decisively, when needed, to support promises.

Debts directly linked debtors with creditors. The same two parties who enacted the first part of the transaction rejoined for the second and closing part. That ongoing connection made it easier to repeat transactions, as each side gained the measure of the other. And if circumstances warranted, it was also easier to renegotiate and adjust the terms of the transaction. However, these advantages came at the price of liquidity: it was often hard for the creditor to exit the relationship by transferring the debtor's obligation to someone else, and so the creditor's capital was locked up for the duration. For a two-sided institution, like a savings-and-loan association, the maturity mismatch between short-term liabilities (demand deposits) and long-term assets (mortgage loans) could be a real problem: if depositors wanted their money back, it was impossible to liquidate long-term assets fast enough to satisfy them all.[7]

Today the connections created by debt are much less durable and no longer bind the two parties who created them. Instead, debts have become more like momentary transactions than long-term marriages. If debts have been securitized, the originating bilateral obligation is turned into a multilateral arrangement involving many debtors and a changing group of creditors.

Numerous individual debts are pooled together and serve as backing for the issuance of new securities that are rated and sold to investors. Each investor has a claim on a tiny proportion of all the debts in the pool, while each debtor owes a tiny proportion of their debt to many creditors, and those creditors can exit. Securitization makes illiquid assets liquid, and hence attractive to a much bigger set of investors. As debts circulate, they are priced in a way that reflects collective judgments about the trustworthiness of the debtor. Securitization also enables investors to diversify because they are putting money into a pool of assets rather than a single loan. Because of the involvement of the bond rating agencies, investors who otherwise know little or nothing about the underlying debts can nevertheless acquire information about the risks involved, relying on ratings to tell them what is a safe bet. The originating lender can also recover their capital well before full maturity of the debt and thus manage their balance sheet and resolve any underlying maturity mismatches. Especially for big lending institutions, like banks, that are subject to capital standards and other types of regulation, the ability to move assets off the balance sheet can be very advantageous. However, if the debtor runs into trouble and cannot remain current with the loan, it is hard to renegotiate. Put simply: there is no one to talk to. Securitization means that the creditor interest has been divided and distributed among multiple parties, who keep changing as the asset-backed securities are bought and sold. Under such circumstances, renegotiation becomes highly impractical.

The traditional model of informed consent for promises is now seldom realized. The two sides are supposed to understand and consent to the agreement they reach, but no more. Particularly in consumer finance, the terms of most promises are dictated unilaterally by the promisee, and promisors enter into agreements they do not entirely grasp. Furthermore, because of developments like securitization, the two parties who initiate the offer and acceptance of a promise do not necessarily bring it to resolution, and instead obligations are sliced, diced, and distributed among an ever-changing group of investors. Even if the borrower understands their original promise, once it has been reengineered into a multitranched mortgage-backed security it becomes something mysterious.

Private Promises and Public Policy

Debtors and creditors are a numerous and heterogeneous lot, motivated by their own purposes and making their own choices. It is easy to believe that the promises debtors make, and which creditors accept, are private matters reflecting the mutual interests of two parties. But I have argued that promises are deeply shaped by public policy and that debts are not purely private affairs. Although debtors and creditors make their own choices, they do so under circumstances set by someone else. This happens in several ways. First, law is the primary means through which such promises become enforceable and binding. To make a promise is one thing, but to formalize it in a legally binding contract is a significant step further. It means that two parties can enforce their private arrangement using the coercive power of the state. The law offers a menu of possibilities from which promisors and promisees can select: some legal features and devices are timeworn and their effects are well known. To add collateral to a loan is a very old move that predictably protects the lender. Similarly, having someone cosign a loan adds their own creditworthiness to the bargain. Seniority helps reconcile the conflicting claims of multiple creditors by settling who gets first access to the assets. "Floating liens" took the idea of collateral and then applied it to dynamic assets, like inventory: the loan remains secured, even though the contents of inventory change. Various legal devices were created by rich families to protect dynastic assets from the claims of creditors, frustrating any attempts to seize collateral.[8] Current statutory and case law gives to those who wish to transact in promises a set of possibilities about how to express and enforce their intertemporal exchanges. The law offers, as Katharina Pistor terms it, a changing "code of capital."[9]

Of course, not everyone is equally fluent in this code, and the imbalance of expertise can be dramatic. Lawyers working for credit card issuers, for example, write long, complicated standard-form contracts that ordinary card users often don't even read, let alone comprehend. The card user can take it or leave it, but they can't meaningfully negotiate the terms of the deal. In situations where sophisticated lenders deal with naive consumers, policymakers sometimes try to protect the latter by insisting on simple legal language that is clear rather than opaque and that relies on standardized terms to enable comparisons. Certainly, that was part of the inspiration behind the Uniform Small Loan Law of the 1920s and the federal Truth in Lending Act of 1968. Both of these measures worked to ensure that individual borrowers could understand the legal implications of the promises they made.[10] But regulatory efforts to reimpose or bolster the traditional model founder on asymmetries of information that have reversed: borrowers supposedly knew more about their willingness and ability to repay than did lenders, but now lenders often know more than borrowers.

Beyond offering a general framework, governments actively encouraged certain kinds of promises. In the United States, state and federal governments have deliberately supported certain groups of debtors who sought to borrow for specific purposes.[11] Their political power translated into cheap credit. Farmers and homeowners have been particularly favored constituents, and whether it is via direct loans, loan guarantees, loan subsidies, valuation rules, insurance, or favorable tax treatment, governments have tried to make it easier and cheaper for these groups to borrow. Credit support has become a widespread instrument of government policy, for a number of reasons. To begin with, it is easier to minimize or disguise the apparent costs of policy. For example, direct subsidies for housing are an expense that shows up on a budget, available for public scrutiny. Loan guarantees for housing, by contrast, are contingent liabilities whose costs can be hidden from prying eyes and political opponents. Exempting interest payments from taxation is another easy way to offer targeted benefits by tweaking an already complicated tax code: support for favored borrowers becomes just another tax expenditure.[12] And the creation of secondary markets for loans through the establishment of GSEs like Fannie Mae and Freddie Mac, which supported securitization, helped attract more lenders into housing markets.

Public expenditures express political priorities. Governments spend money on issues that matter to them and their supporters, and increased spending is a very public way to signal which issues are important. But public interventions in credit markets can be equally revealing, although such activity doesn't fully register on a budget. The history of housing policy in the twentieth-century United States shows how much white suburban homeowners had their creditworthiness raised en masse, and that with public support many gained access to affordable housing and could accumulate wealth for their families. The effects of this public support ramified widely because of the importance of residence for employment, education, integration, voting, and a host of other significant social outcomes. Homeownership is part of the "American dream," and yet realization of this dream was not equally shared. And on a smaller scale, U.S. farmers continue to benefit from programs giving them access to cheap credit. There too, however, the benefits were distributed unequally.[13]

In encouraging promises, governments have sometimes intervened on the creditor side. Loan guarantees, for example, indirectly helped borrowers by reducing the risk of loss by lenders. With minimal downside risk, lenders were more willing to lend. When bank regulators changed how bank examiners valued bond portfolios in the 1930s, they were trying to help banks, as creditors, maintain their solvency by appearing to have assets that were more valuable than actual market prices indicated. Forbearance, regulators hoped, would give banks some breathing space and allow them, and their balance sheets, to recover enough to lend again. State governments sometimes acted late in the credit cycle, after a loan was made, and occasionally even after loan repayment had begun, by imposing a moratorium on foreclosures and preventing creditors from recovering their funds after debtors had defaulted. Such measures interfered with creditors' legal rights and were supposed to help debtors. On a more permanent basis, federal bankruptcy law was revised in 2005 to make it harder for individuals to discharge their credit card debts, a modification that directly benefited card issuers as creditors and was largely made at their behest. Across all these and other policy measures, governments have recurrently intervened in debtor-creditor transactions in order to encourage them, suppress them, or regulate them. In this way, private promises became instruments of public policy.

Finally, governments made their own promises. At all levels, sovereign bodies borrowed extensively by selling bonds, and in so doing escaped the limits of their own current tax revenues. During wartime, the federal government had to borrow extensively as military expenses far outpaced taxes, and its status as a debtor loomed large in shaping policy. State and local governments also borrowed to pay for investments in infrastructure like highways, sewers, schools, waterworks, and other durable public goods, although the distribution of these goods was highly uneven. Lenders have to gauge a government's willingness and ability to repay, and in the case of wartime debt some lenders may well be swayed by patriotic motives. Investment banks provided a measure of reputational assurance to the investors with whom they placed a sovereign bond issue, but starting in the early twentieth century, the bond rating agencies applied the categories they developed for corporate borrowers to sovereign debt, and so an investor could see whether a government bond was rated "AAA," "AA," or something else.

As the national debt grew, and financial markets became flooded with U.S. Treasury bonds, the Federal Reserve System discovered a new policy instrument: open market operations. By selling and purchasing government bonds, the Fed could influence financial markets in pursuit of its policy goals. The federal government inadvertently created a "gold standard" financial asset that investors craved whenever there was a crisis-driven "flight to quality."[14] And very recently the Fed supported the economy with large-scale purchases of certain classes of promises, a policy called "quantitative easing."

The sudden collapse of financial asset prices threatened collateral-based lending, and the Fed bought those assets in response.

Private Virtue and Public Vice

Debtors borrow and creditors lend for many reasons, but the simplest form of credit appears bilateral and consensual, involving only two parties. When the interests of these two align, then the transaction proceeds and both sides gain. Yet, a third party always looms in the background. The state determines which debt contracts are enforceable, and then helps enforce them. The global financial crisis of 2008 reminds us that pursuit of individual self-interest needn't serve the general interest. The paradoxical connection between private and public interests was famously posed by Adam Smith in *The Wealth of Nations* to argue that selfish action (private vice) could produce general benefits (public virtue). Smith used this irony to argue in support of a market economy, but his claim applies to finance too. If debtors and creditors are freely allowed to pursue their private interests, Smith's logic implies that society as a whole benefits. This argument, updated by neo-liberals, helped justify deregulation of the U.S. banking and financial system during the 1980s and 1990s. And yet, the pursuit of self-interest and the relaxation of regulatory oversight did not prevent calamity in 2008. In fact, deregulation contributed to the problem, as unrestrained and unmonitored risk-seeking produced an economic collapse. One observer has even questioned whether today's financial system is more efficient than the one of a hundred years ago, despite all its elaborate sophistication.[15]

In the contemporary economy of promises, the choices made by debtors and creditors affect more than just themselves. Today's complex financial system creates unintended outcomes and unanticipated dependencies. It may benefit an individual borrower to take on debt, and it can seem profitable to the willing lender, but when too many borrowers become leveraged, then the financial system as a whole becomes unstable. The insolvency of a single borrower can trigger a cascade of failures, as the losses are transmitted through a network of financial ties. A lender can manage its exposure to those who directly borrow from it, but it isn't so easy to protect oneself from those who borrowed from the debtor, and it is really tough to avoid problems stemming from a debtor's debtor. Lenders now have a variety of ways to insulate themselves from the failure of others, using credit insurance or credit default swaps. But during a serious crisis even these protections collapse, and financial actors look to the federal government for help.

Suppose that someone borrows to buy a house. A traditional mortgage means that if the borrower defaults, the lender can seize the collateral. The lender will estimate the value of the home beforehand to ensure that it is worth more than the loan. But if many people take out mortgages to buy homes, and if unemployment spikes or they are otherwise unable to make their payments, then many lenders will be foreclosing on homes, and selling them. Unfortunately, simultaneously selling so many homes lowers their market price, and lenders may not be able to recover all the money owed them. No one wants to conduct a "fire sale." These losses make it hard for lenders to be lenient toward borrowers in financial difficulty. Furthermore, even homeowners who remain current on their mortgage payments lose because the value of their homes decline along with the rest of the market. On its own each loan may have been well-calibrated to help the borrower become a homeowner and protect the lender from loss, but since each mortgage default has an adverse effect on all the others, the losses spread and eventually both the real estate market and the home loan market collapse.

Even when it is in everyone's individual interest to take on more debt, too much can collectively be harmful. High levels of leverage on the business side boost profit rates, while household leverage is useful to maintain consumption. But excessive leverage makes the financial system less robust. Levels of indebtedness in the United States grew in the late twentieth century, setting the stage for the financial crisis of 2008.[16] Many policymakers were lulled by the "Great Moderation"[17] and by their faith in self-correcting markets. At the same time, an increasingly powerful financial industry used its political connections to curtail regulatory oversight and to innovate right around regulations.[18] For these and other reasons, the dangers of accumulating indebtedness were ignored. High leverage left both businesses and households with little margin for error and not enough capital to protect themselves from an economic blow. Once the real estate bubble burst, several feedback loops amplified the problem: to maintain their capital ratios, many banks were forced to sell assets at "fire sale" prices;[19] losses from falling asset prices were more concentrated for highly leveraged financial firms; previously liquid assets suddenly became illiquid;[20] firms reliant on short-term financing were vulnerable to "bank runs" in repo markets;[21] opaque connections led to unperceived but correlated risks; as the subprime financing model collapsed, precarious households defaulted on mortgages that were larger than they could afford. And the "too big to fail" status of the largest private banks forced central bankers to rescue them at enormous expense, effectively socializing their losses. The magnitude of the resulting downturn surprised policymakers and inflicted suffering on millions of households around the world. And the recovery afterward was long, slow, and painful.

The tension between what is in the narrow self-interest of private financial actors, on the one hand, and what is in the collective interest, on the other, provided an important justification for countercyclical macroprudential regulation.[22] Financial stability was recognized as a public good. Central banks and other financial regulators have expanded how they regulate, shifting from a traditionally narrow focus on stand-alone financial organizations (is a particular bank solvent or not?) to a broader focus that considers the overall financial system (is the banking sector robust or not?). To do the latter, regulators now monitor how connections link banks with each other, and to shadow banks, in a complex and ever-evolving network of assets and liabilities.[23] As the economy of promises grew, encompassing firms and individuals, some kind of regulation became imperative. People began to appreciate how promises fit together and influenced each other, even if legally they stood on their own. These interactions could produce unpleasant and destabilizing surprises. The social, economic, and political consequences of financial collapse were too great simply to let the financial system self-regulate, and so people recognized the need to shepherd the credit economy in some fashion.

Vulnerability and Uncertainty

A promise always poses a question of trust. For promises that constitute credit, does the lender trust the borrower to repay? This trust problem has two components: the lender doesn't know what the borrower will do in the future, and the fate of the lender is in the borrower's hands. In other words, the lender is *uncertain* about the future and is *vulnerable* depending on the size and duration of the loan. Both of these challenges generated a great deal of activity over two centuries, and their practical solution created the economy of promises. To reduce uncertainty, people invented new types of information about debtors. And lenders reduced their vulnerability in a variety of ways.

In respect to *vulnerability*, the use of collateral makes a big difference. Lenders acquire an interest in some asset belonging to the debtor, and if the borrower defaults, the lender seizes the asset. It could be a house, a car, a piano, or a piece of valuable jewelry. It is only necessary that the borrower own the asset and that their interest be readily transferable to the lender. Traditionally, physical assets functioned as collateral, tangible objects like land, buildings, cattle, or machinery. But now collateralization reaches more broadly, assisted by the growing importance of intangible assets but also by the creation of more elaborate registration and tracking systems that exploit developments in information technology. These enable lienholders to monitor collateral despite its mobility and dispersion.[24] Lenders also lower their vulnerability by diversifying their lending activity across different regions, industries, and borrowers to avoid becoming too dependent on the fidelity of a single debtor. And they are able to reduce vulnerability by selling debts on secondary markets and so recover their capital from a buyer. Securitization, as a type of disintermediation that reengineers promises, enables lenders to do both things at once, in fact. And today's sophisticated lenders can also make use of financial derivatives, like credit default swaps, to protect themselves.[25]

No lenders can so reduce their vulnerability that the future doesn't matter, so they will want to know about it. There are, in other words, no perfect hedges. And the generic solution to *uncertainty* is to acquire more information. Learn more about the debtor, their current situation and future prospects, their past behavior, their obligations to other creditors, and then use all that knowledge to make a more accurate prediction about the likelihood the debtor will repay the loan. And if things don't work out, prior diligence will help deal with the repercussions. Much has changed since the early nineteenth century, in terms of the type of information, its format and provenance, and its volume. Direct knowledge of a debtor's personal character and financial dealings is possible when everyone belongs to the same small, stable social community, or if the lender and debtor have had prior dealings. Informal knowledge circulates; people have memories; reputations form. But at the same time, stereotypes circulate, people nurse grudges, lenders can discriminate, and memories can be selective. The social structure of a community is also a communication network through which information moves. And the network-based acquisition of information continues. Personal reputations still matter. But such information has been augmented, and even superseded, by new ways to discern the trustworthiness of someone who makes a promise. Today, the sheer scale of lending far surpasses what could be encompassed by personal knowledge of other individuals.

It is important to remember that information is never simply a matter of more-or-less. Quantity matters, of course, as is evident from the judgment that someone had "too little information." But the quality of information is crucial as well. How much is signal, and how much is noise? Does the information come from a reliable source, or is it just a rumor? How is it organized and formatted? Does the information provide precise measures of specific features, or does it offer only a rough classification into broad categories? Does the information enable systematic comparisons between debtors, or at different points of time? Is evidence internally consistent, or not? Is it provided in confidence or is it available to all? Is the information created by a government agency, or does it come from private sources? Does the source have an incentive to be accurate, or do they have some other agenda?

In considering these questions, one can appreciate how much the informational landscape for credit has changed. Today, there is certainly much more information about debtors than there was two centuries ago. The quantity has increased dramatically. But the quality has changed, as well, as what people knew about others became more systematic. Partly this is because the debtors have changed. In the early nineteenth century debtors were mostly individual persons or small businesses and partnerships. To evaluate a debtor was to evaluate a person, their character and situation. But fictive individuals, constituted through incorporation, were given legal personality to own property, sign contracts, sue and be sued in court. And they could borrow money. Firms, corporations, nonprofit organizations, governments, special investment vehicles, and other fictive individuals have proliferated and are very active as borrowers. Although they are staffed and run by natural persons, as debtors they do not have personal character. To judge their creditworthiness requires different kinds of information.

A first step for lending concerns authentication: Is the borrower really who they claim to be? Does an asset that is proffered as collateral really exist, and is it identifiable? In the nineteenth century, many of the documents and systems that now determine authenticity didn't exist. For personal identity, for example, there were no Social Security numbers. People didn't have passports (or driver's licenses, or even birth certificates), and frequently little was known except their name and address. Similarly, it was hard to know at a distance if a particular business actually existed, or who owned it. Again, name and address were often the only available identifiers, and these could easily be misrepresented, fabricated, or borrowed. Today, the validation of identity remains a problem, but there are multiple channels available to certify the existence and authenticity of individual and business debtors on a mass scale. Some have been created as part of a public system of documentation (e.g., Social Security numbers and government-issued identification for individuals). Other identity systems have been created privately, by some of the very same firms who invented or used credit ratings. For example, in the 1960s Dun and Bradstreet developed the D-U-N-S number, a unique

9-digit identifier for small businesses.[26] In the 1990s, real estate industry organizations created MERS, a private electronic registration and tracking system for home mortgages.[27] Secured car loans are made possible because vehicles are uniquely identified by a VIN, a vehicle identity number, so that a car note holder knows which specific automobile serves as collateral.[28] In a large-scale economy where direct knowledge is limited, decision makers necessarily rely on documents, certifications, registrations, and other informational devices to indicate which actors and claims are authentic. But this is just a first step: once authenticity is settled, lenders move on to the issues of willingness and ability to repay, an even more important informational challenge.

Creditors want timely and accurate intelligence about debtors' trustworthiness, and this guides their efforts to acquire information. But debtors and creditors have become increasingly estranged in that they mostly have no preexisting social ties and are personally unknown to each other. Consequently, creditors have to depend on information provided by someone else. Do those providers have the same interest in accuracy? The answer is not straightforward. Consider the credit information created by for-profit firms. In the nineteenth century, the mercantile agencies accumulated credit information and sold it to their customers. While the agencies repeatedly affirmed the value of their commercial intelligence, they were careful not to claim that they were making specific predictions about the future performance of debtors. Agencies didn't want to be held to such an unforgiving standard. Nevertheless, people repeatedly sued the agencies on the grounds that the ratings were "wrong." Two scenarios were common. One group of litigants included those who used high ratings to extend credit to someone who subsequently failed, and so sued the agency on the grounds that the ratings had been erroneously high. Another group consisted of those who received low ratings who asserted that they had been harmed because others, misled by the "erroneously" low ratings, had withheld credit. For much of the latter nineteenth century, the legal status of credit ratings and reports proved to be a contentious issue. But eventually, ratings came to be considered like opinions: neither right nor wrong. And who could sue a rating agency for having a "wrong" opinion? Under the original "user pays" business model, those who created and sold credit information had an interest in maximizing sales by convincing their customers that the information was useful. But "useful" was not the same as "accurate." Under the newer "issuer pays" business model, contemporary bond rating agencies are paid a fee by those they rate, and issuers have a strong preference for high ratings (which means cheaper loans). Rating agencies have an interest in keeping their customers happy, and their willingness to cut corners in order to attract business became particularly obvious during the 2008 financial crisis.[29] And the regulatory status of bond ratings ensured their significance regardless of their accuracy.[30] The incorporation of ratings into prudential regulations for banks, insurance companies, mutual funds, and pension funds guaranteed that classification of a security as "investment grade" or "below investment grade" had a big effect on demand, irrespective of its accuracy.

Different legal and political considerations have shaped privately supplied information about the creditworthiness of individuals, and these underscore the heterogeneity of credit-relevant information. Credit rating agencies like TransUnion, Equifax, and Experian dominate today's market and diligently accumulate huge volumes of information about millions of people, just as their predecessors operated at the local and state level back in the nineteenth century. Such information raised questions of privacy, about whether there were limits on how much may be recorded about an individual's personal life, and on what might be done with such information.[31] What obligation did credit rating agencies have to ensure that their information was correct and up-to-date? Did agencies have a responsibility to share credit information with those who were tracked? With the development of an extensive rating apparatus governing access to credit, and following the civil rights movement, pointed questions rose about whether all individual debtors were being treated equally when they tried to borrow. It was clear that discrimination occurred in credit markets as well as in employment and education, and that the benefits of being able to make a credible promise were not evenly shared. Could rating agencies use information about race and gender, or incorporate other features that are highly correlated with race (e.g., residential zip codes) and gender (e.g., occupation), as the basis for estimating creditworthiness? As with bond ratings, the changing legal status of individual credit information complicated progress toward greater and greater accuracy.

Broken Promises

Sometimes things just don't work out. Well-intentioned debtors may not keep their promises. And as credit expanded with population growth and economic development, so did the number of broken promises. However vigilant lenders might be in scrutinizing borrowers beforehand, inevitably some will default. Informal debts can be enforced informally: those who didn't repay faced dishonor or stigma. The legal system gave lenders recourse when loans were formalized: if the lender had insisted on security beforehand, they could seize the collateral in the event of a default. Otherwise lenders might seek a court judgment and go after the debtor's assets, hoping to force repayment. The business of U.S. courts has always included many cases brought by creditors to recover unpaid debts.

Federal law offered an encompassing framework for the resolution of an insolvent debtor's obligations. When a bankruptcy law was on the books, it provided a way to deal with all of a debtor's obligations simultaneously. In the nineteenth century, federal bankruptcy statutes were typically passed after an economic crisis, when many debtors sought relief, but then were repealed once a creditor-led backlash set it. Not until the end of the nineteenth century did the United States have a permanent statute, and the successive versions passed since then reflected the changing political demands of debtor and creditor groups as well as the evolution of the credit economy. As borrowing became more common, the stigma of debt diminished and bankruptcy became more of a rehabilitative proceeding than a simple punishment of those who violated the sanctity of contract. Insolvent debtors were given a chance to resolve their debts and then have a fresh start, unencumbered by their old obligations.[32] Even so, the moral obligation that people today feel to repay a debt can vary depending on whom they owe money to and why the debt was incurred.[33] On the corporate side, a parallel shift from liquidation proceedings to reorganization reflected the growing realization that the economy would be well served if some firms were given a second chance, particularly if closure was the alternative. The possibility of failure, and the potential for a bankruptcy proceeding, provides a backdrop for credit decision making. A diligent creditor will always wonder: what could go wrong here?

Trust in Numbers

Information helps manage uncertainty, and over time the amount of information about debtors grew dramatically. But the type of information also changed, shifting from qualitative to quantitative.[34] Today, a lender may not know anything about a borrower's personal character, but she can access their FICO score. In this way, people can lend to strangers. Similarly, investors use bond ratings to gauge the risk associated with a particular debt instrument. And everyone has much greater access to detailed financial information about both individual and business borrowers. Quantification has shaped the credit economy, just as it has affected other aspects of modern social life.[35]

Numerical information summarizes and simplifies a complex reality, and in the context of credit it allows loan terms to be more precisely calibrated to the estimated trustworthiness of a borrower. It enables broad comparisons among entire populations, critical for large-scale lending, and provides inputs into the precise formulas and algorithms of modern finance. The actuarial calculations that support modern risk management would be impossible without numerical data. Embedding numbers in decision-rules reduces the authority and discretion that experienced lenders formerly possessed, as numerical thresholds define who is, and who isn't, creditworthy. It can also protect decisions from the effects of personal bias and discriminatory animus.[36] With numbers, it is harder to include the contextual or background factors that frequently shape qualitative judgments. And numbers bring the aura of science and objectivity, which helps legitimize decisions made on their basis and enables them to supplant other types of information. The appearance of objectivity can also help conceal whatever biases and shortcomings a numerical protocol may possess.

Numbers are portable and can be applied in new situations, giving them even greater significance. FICO scores originally governed access to individual credit, but since they now also affect access to housing, insurance, and employment they are even more fateful. Their portability amplified their importance. Similarly bond ratings initially guided investors' decisions, but then became an essential component for public bank regulations and the prudential standards applied to insurance companies and pension funds. Later, they were incorporated into the private contractual language of financial derivatives. Credit insurance companies even used ratings to price their services. The older diversity of evaluations shrank as univocal scores and ratings became institutionalized.

Consequential numbers shift attention away from whatever feature the numbers are supposed to measure, to the numbers themselves.[37] When FICO scores matter, for example, people begin to worry more about how to boost their scores and lose sight of what the score reflects. In collaboration with rating agencies, bond issuers became extremely adept at manipulating ratings so as to squeeze the highest ratings out of a set of securitized assets, or at least to ensure that ratings crossed the "investment grade" threshold. The success of nineteenth-century mercantile agencies meant that agency employees who were soliciting information from businesses knew that the business owners were trying to maintain appearances and get a high rating.

"Gaming the numbers" became a viable strategy, but unfortunately such manipulations tended to degrade the value of the information.

Credit and Inequality

Debtors and creditors are obviously unequal: for starters, the creditor has money, and the debtor doesn't. This contrast has been interpreted as a form of subservience, where weak debtors are beholden to powerful creditors. Both individually and collectively, stigmatized debtors have tried to escape the shackles of indebtedness or somehow reduce their dependence on their creditors. They might try to repay their individual debts as soon as possible to regain their independence, or avoid debt altogether, but they also acted collectively and politically, pressuring creditors to get more favorable terms or seeking relief from the means of creditor enforcement. And yet these inequalities weren't static, for under some conditions debtors gained the upper hand. A creditor's influence can flip around and grant the debtor power over the creditor, particularly if debtor insolvency also threatens the creditor with ruin. A bank that has loaned too much to a single debtor has, in effect, put its own fate into the debtor's hands. Wily debtors like Eumenes can exploit their leverage over their own creditors.

Inequalities emerge among debtors, too. In one sense, lenders always discriminate when they try to differentiate between those who are creditworthy and those who are not. This ensures that access to credit will be unevenly distributed but in such a way as to ensure that a loan will be fully repaid. It leads to the oft-observed irony that bankers prefer to lend to people who don't really need the money: their wealth and income make them good credit risks. Beyond lender preferences, it is also striking how much public policy shapes credit allocation, both directly and indirectly. The government itself lends money to support activities and favor constituents, but it also strongly encourages others to lend, through subsidies, favorable tax treatment, loan guarantees, and so on. The goal was to bestow purchasing power on some groups rather than others. And because loans redistribute resources across time, they can mitigate growing economic inequality in a more unobtrusive manner.[38]

The involvement of government is no surprise when access to credit is a hot political issue. During the nineteenth century, credit and currency were scarce in many regions of the country. People who needed credit, like farmers, felt they couldn't get enough. And if they could, it was expensive and held them in thrall to their lenders. Even within the financial community, fears about the dominance of big city bankers from the Northeast, especially New York City, were widespread. And recurrent financial crises generated waves of pro-debtor public policy, followed by pro-creditor backlashes. Monetary politics peaked during the populist era with conflicts between bullionists, greenbackers, and the free silver movement, but contention about banking didn't disappear after the establishment of the Federal Reserve System.[39] In the calm periods between crises, government policy quietly directed loans toward favored constituencies. Today, growing income and wealth inequality raises the question of whether private credit can adequately resolve economic gaps or if a more muscular public policy is necessary.

Creditworthiness per se is not the only factor affecting loans, and this creates additional inequalities. Part of the problem is that true creditworthiness is hard to detect, and so lenders rely on a variety of signals to measure it.[40] Some of these combine creditworthiness with other traits, so at various points lenders believed, or acted as if, married men were more dependable than single men, that women were worse credit risks than men, or that whites were more likely to repay than blacks. Mixed signals influence individual judgments made by loan officers and credit officials, who exercise discretion in uneven ways, but they are also reflected in bureaucratic forms and organizational procedures. This produces unequal access to credit even when borrowers possess the requisite creditworthiness and goes beyond personal animus to more structural factors. FHA underwriting manuals from the 1930s reinforced residential segregation and privileged white suburbanization by shaping the valuation of real estate. Even an unbiased realtor dutifully following the manual's procedures would have reproduced racially segregated neighborhoods.

The FHA revised its manuals so that they were no longer explicitly discriminatory, and more importantly several federal laws were passed to regulate credit and mortgage markets, including the Equal Credit Opportunity Act of 1974, the Home Mortgage Disclosure Act of 1975, and the Community Reinvestment Act of 1977, but the evidence strongly suggests that these laws didn't succeed and the underlying disparities have persisted. Greater financial inclusion remains a goal as advocates recognize the importance of credit and try to ensure that all groups in the United States have equal access to financial services. Some commentators underscore the normative dimensions of credit and have developed philosophical justifications for a right to credit.[41] The issue of who can make promises, and how to ensure that promises are evaluated on an appropriate and equitable set of criteria, remains unresolved.

Perhaps the most important inequality separates those who define creditworthiness from those who are defined by it. Who determines the basic architecture of financial promises? The contrast becomes especially important when measures of individual creditworthiness are also used in non-credit contexts, like employment and housing. At first, creditworthiness was assessed locally, in a largely decentralized fashion and on the basis of personal characteristics embedded in social networks. There were no strict rules but many rules of thumb that guided lenders about whom to trust. And the heuristics that favored "insiders" equally disfavored "outsiders." Gradually, however, creditworthiness became more formulaic and centrally defined. The change wasn't uniform, because social ties remain important in certain contexts (consider the importance of family resources for business startups or college education), but the long-term trend is undeniable. Rating agencies created summary measures of creditworthiness for all borrowers, whether individual or organizational, and distributed this information on a national and then international scale. Their determinations were hard to escape, because no matter where someone moved, their ratings and reputations followed them. It privileged individuals whose regular incomes from full-time employment and residence in single-family dwellings located in segregated suburbs fit a certain profile. But not everyone was encompassed by this capacious informational apparatus. People with a weaker attachment to the formal economy couldn't easily generate a credit record and were frequently overlooked. For them, credit had to come from pawnshops, payday lenders, loan sharks, and other expensive options. Sovereign ratings produced by bond rating agencies privileged countries that embraced privatization, deregulation, liberalization, balanced budgets, and other neoliberal policies. As Tom Friedman observed: "In fact, you could almost say that we live again in a two-superpower world. There is the U.S. and there is Moody's. The U.S. can destroy a country by leveling it with bombs; Moody's can destroy a country by downgrading its bonds."[42]

Although ratings were intended to create transparency about borrowers, they were themselves enshrouded in mystery: How were they calculated? What raw evidence served as the input for a rating? How was that information sourced? How well did ratings predict whether a debtor might default? Did raters fix their mistakes afterward or try to prevent them beforehand?[43] The opacity stemmed, in part, from the for-profit status of the rating agencies: their information and calculative procedures were proprietary and undisclosed to outsiders. And the image of numerical objectivity helped keep curious skeptics at bay. Only at the end of the twentieth century did some measure of regulatory oversight get imposed, and so for most of their history the rating agencies have been largely unaccountable to anyone but their shareholders.

At the same time, creditworthiness was defined and shaped by public policy. Monetary policy has set the general conditions for creditworthiness. Central banks help determine interest rates, and borrowers who weren't creditworthy when rates were high could become creditworthy when rates moved down. They also prioritize price stability and fight inflation that could redistribute wealth from creditors to debtors. During crises, the Federal Reserve gave selective liquidity support to promises as it enacted its "lender of last resort" responsibilities and protected the value of certain financial assets.[44] The U.S. government also created a number of institutions to support securitization. The actions of government-sponsored entities like Fannie Mae and Freddie Mac encouraged a wider set of investors to appreciate that more borrowers were creditworthy. Creation of mortgage-backed securities involved a partnership between the GSEs and private rating agencies as the latter evaluated what the former created, and the net result was to create more investment in securitized loans. U.S. banks profitably and enthusiastically embraced mortgage securitization, until the bubble burst in 2008.[45]

The Future of Trust

On the basis of trust, credit reaches into the future. But what does the future of trust look like? Currently, information originally invented in the nineteenth century measures creditworthiness and shapes the allocation of credit. Their imperfections notwithstanding, formal scores, credit ratings, and credit reports provide summary measures that are recorded, tracked, processed, and transmitted. But now, ongoing developments in information technology make it possible for lenders to acquire even more information about debtors, called "alternative information" because it isn't found in a traditional credit file. Bigtech and fintech firms are busy gathering data about people's on-line shopping behavior and their social media activities. Clicks, tweets, views, downloads, and likes join paid bills in digital repositories, ready to predict payment behavior. These are not separate measures of underlying human action but rather their electronic realization. To search and shop on-line, to use various social media platforms to interact with friends and family, to post and share pictures and other digital content, is to generate rich streams of data that tech firms happily harvest, store, analyze, and monetize. These data streams are unprecedented in their variety, volume, and velocity and set the stage for what Zuboff calls "surveillance capitalism."[46] They are now being exploited by fintech startups, in partnership with traditional financial firms, to gain additional insight into the future lives of borrowers. IT firms can track individuals using "cookies," "history sniffing," and device fingerprinting across multiple pieces of equipment, including desktop computers, laptops, smartphones, and anything else connected to the internet.[47] Which operating system does a consumer use? Did they make keystroke errors when typing? What time of day were they active on their computer? The answers help predict who will default on a loan.[48] Alternative information augments regular credit information to make it even easier to automate lending, permitting high-volume, on-line loan applications with approval in seconds. Advocates claim that it could "democratize" credit because it gives people whose traditional credit records are incomplete a chance to look creditworthy. But it also tips the imbalance of information even more in favor of lenders.

In some respects, the future may look like the past. The social networks that surrounded a debtor, or which linked creditors with debtors, were important channels for credit in the early nineteenth century. People trusted others in the same or overlapping social circles, and social ties provided the basis for "insider lending." Modern credit records include lots of information about someone's income, current indebtedness, and financial history, but now social network data are being exploited. Fintech firms and social media platforms are learning that an individual's social networks can predict their creditworthiness. As people build personal on-line networks using LinkedIn, Instagram, TikTok, Twitter, and Facebook, they inadvertently create data that lenders can use and so, once again, social networks affect credit.[49]

More information about borrowers enables lenders to customize their offers and, in effect, to price discriminate. They go beyond the simple alternatives of approve vs. decline, based on the determination that an applicant was creditworthy or not. Loans have many features in addition to size, maturity, and interest rate, and these offer profitable ways for lenders to adjust their offers. An agreement that triggers fees and fines when a payment is late, or when borrowers carry an unpaid balance from one month to the next, can generate a lot of additional income for the lender over and above the interest on the loan. Introductory "teaser rates" encourage people to borrow, but when they expire the loan becomes more costly to service. Consumer lenders, including credit card companies and subprime lenders, realized they could earn a lot from marginal borrowers who maintained monthly balances, incurred fees, missed payments, and otherwise were not the most creditworthy of people. The most trustworthy borrowers didn't necessarily generate the most profits.

Economists studying information asymmetries have used credit markets as a canonical example of the "market for lemons."[50] The argument was that borrowers knew much more about their willingness and ability to repay a loan than did lenders and that it was difficult for them credibly to impart their knowledge to lenders. But this simple characterization is becoming harder to sustain as the information environment becomes much denser, and as "big data" increasingly pervades people's individual and business lives. The integration of traditional credit records with data culled from social media usage and on-line activity now provides a more intrusive and granular picture of an individual's willingness and ability. Data aggregation and data mining are now widespread and constitute the core activity of monopolistic tech firms. And unless strong privacy rules or data access restrictions come into play, and are implemented across multiple jurisdictions, this new digital panopticon is likely to become ever more pervasive. As foreshadowed by the emerging Chinese social credit systems, institutional lenders are rapidly becoming extremely knowledgeable about many aspects of a borrower's life, habits, communications, friendships, hobbies, political activities, purchasing behavior, and anything else that could potentially be relevant.[51] Even as borrowers remain personally unknown to lenders, their digital selves are becoming very familiar.[52]

Changes in information technology are also affecting how lenders manage their vulnerabilities. Lenders can take risk off their balance sheets through securitization, and the complexity and prevalence of securitizations have proceeded hand in hand with improvements in IT. Electronic registers and databases enable lenders to track the assets that can function as collateral, and the emerging "internet of things" makes it much easier to track individual items regardless of their mobility and spatial distribution. The proliferation of collateral translates into more secured lending and allows lenders to protect themselves in a tried-and-true fashion.

Traditionally, credit decisions involved personal judgments made by sellers, investors, and loan officers. Now those decisions are becoming more data-driven and rule-bound. As individuals, lenders operated within the limits of their own bounded rationality. They relied on heuristics, rules of thumb, simplifications, and prejudgments. These cognitive shortcuts made a decision easier to reach, but they could be highly discriminatory in their effects. Should a lender give an applicant the benefit of the doubt or put a thumb on the scale? Unfortunately, such discretion opened the door to unequal treatment. And in credit markets, women and minorities were long denied the benefit of the doubt.

Greater reliance on quantitative information and systematic decision protocols is hailed as a way to reduce discrimination. Someone with a FICO score above 800 has "excellent" or "exceptional" credit, regardless of whether they are male or female, black or white. But even when credit decisions minimize discretion or are driven by impersonal computer algorithms, the potential for bias remains. As a number of commentators have noted, using an algorithm is no guarantee of fairness and neutrality.[53] Bias can be "baked into" the decision protocol in ways that are not apparent to the outside and that belie the image of objectivity. For example, an artificial intelligence (AI) program that was "trained" on a particular data set can reproduce historical biases. AI can be compelled to ignore protected categories (like race and gender) even as it leverages proxies for these same categories. And long before the rise of "big data" and "machine learning," racial bias was institutionalized within the bland language of protective covenants, zoning laws, and bureaucratic devices like the risk maps used to allocate home insurance: animus wasn't needed to produce disparate outcomes. If there are doubts about neutrality, as a practical matter it is often hard to investigate potential bias given the proprietary nature of both data and algorithms.[54] Allocating or denying credit is a consequential decision, and people will want to know why their loan application was declined. Can an algorithm provide a reasonable explanation for its decision? As more credit decisions become automated, as reliance on "big data" and "black box" algorithms increases, and as model-based predictions threaten to become self-fulfilling prophesies, the need for some kind of accountability becomes acute.[55]

Intangible Values

The promises I have discussed in this book embody economic value, and they have animated the U.S. economy over the last two centuries. Intangible commitments now constitute a great deal of today's wealth, now surpassing older forms like real estate. Promises have become more numerous and more complicated. Originally, intentions begat promises, and both the person making the promise and the person receiving it had some understanding of what the promisor intended. The credibility of those intentions weighed heavily in a creditor's decision about whether to lend: was a particular borrower sincere when they promised to repay?

Today, however, many promises don't originate in an individual's clear intentions. Too many consumers, for example, do not entirely understand the promises that bind them, especially when these involve complicated contracts with lots of boilerplate language. A variety of intentions can shape whether lenders trust borrowers. What was the lender trying to accomplish? To profit from a loan, to boost sales, to bolster the housing market, or to provide financial support to a deserving person? But as lending becomes automated, and as algorithms and score-driven decision making displace personal judgments, the lenders' intentions also diminish in significance. Algorithms don't have intentions in the same way.[56] And as both sides of lending become increasingly dominated by corporate lenders and indebted firms, we are reminded of the implausibility of the idea that organizations per se have intentions. The development of composite promises further complicates the traditional role of intentions. When loans are securitized, for example, the promises of many debtors are pooled together and then dispersed widely among numerous investors. The intentions of all these parties are so heterogeneous that they cannot be discerned, nor treated summarily, even if they all flow through a single legal vehicle.

Lenders have shifted their attention away from the debtor's personal intentions to consider other types of information. A highly developed informational infrastructure now gathers, processes, and interprets data about people and firms, their current financial situations, their histories of payment, and their future prospects. Discerning personal intentions does not have the same priority as in the past, but it turns out there are many other ways to predict who will repay. And in fact, lenders are well able to evaluate promises. Consider that at the depths of the Great Recession, in the second quarter of 2009, the U.S. credit card delinquency rate peaked at 6.77 percent.[57] In other words, even when the economy was doing terribly and many households were financially distressed, 93.23 percent of credit card account holders were still meeting their obligations and keeping their accounts current. The commercial banks that offered those credit cards had done a remarkably good job assessing borrowers, and most consumers honored their promises and faithfully paid their credit card bills.

Such success, occurring during one of the worst economic crises of modern times, reminds us that however much those involved in the credit economy dwell on the possibility of failure, history reflects a remarkable achievement. Today's economy only functions because people and firms make promises and overwhelmingly keep them. Lenders mostly trust borrowers even as distrust runs rampant in politics and other areas of life.[58]

This success partly depends on individual intentions, to be sure, but it fundamentally rests upon functioning institutions. And it is one reason why financial exclusion, whether on the basis of race or gender or something else, is such a problem: the ability to participate fully and equitably in the credit economy is a real advantage. The dangers of credit bubbles show that there can be too much credit and too much leverage, so promises are not an unmitigated good. But in proper measure they knit together today's economy, constituting value, ensuring its circulation, and allowing people to live their lives.

NOTES

My thanks to John Langbein for pointing out Pound's observation.

Chapter 1

1. See Beckert 2016.

2. A "speech act" is a linguistic expression that doesn't simply provide information but also performs an action. See Austin 1975.

3. Other discussions of promises include Atiyah 1979; Fox and DeMarco 1996; Hogg 2011; Patterson 1992.

4. See Hogg 2011: 5.

5. Consider that a home mortgage gives the lender the legal right to seize the mortgaged property if the borrower defaults. However, mortgage lenders don't want to own homes, they want to receive interest payments. In modern finance, though, a sophisticated bondholder whose position is fully hedged via credit default swaps may be financially indifferent to default. In a broad historical perspective, such perfect reduction of risk is rare.

6. The classic cite is Macaulay 1963, but see also Bernstein 1992; Richman 2006.

7. According to Hunt (1856: 163): "Debts are sacred."

8. See also Ho 2021: 38.

9. See Hogg 2011: 22.

10. See Maggor 2017: 78.

11. Obviously, people have devised ways to circumvent such limits when it suits them, as any loan shark can attest.

12. I say "modern" to distinguish my analysis, which surveys roughly two hundred years of U.S. history, from the far more capacious claims of Graeber (2011), who covers five thousand years and much of the world, or Ho (2021), who surveys trust from prehistory onward. For exemplary discussions of the problems of trust in Mediterranean commerce during the Middle Ages and early modern period, see Goldberg 2012 and Trivellato 2009. Both take issue with Greif's influential analysis of trust and medieval commerce (2006).

13. See Federal Reserve System, New Security Issues, U.S. Corporations (Table 1.46), and Consumer Credit Outstanding (Levels), https://www.federalreserve.gov/data/corpsecure/current.htm and https://www.federalreserve.gov/releases/g19/current/default.htm.

14. See Beckert 2016: chap. 5.

15. See, e.g., Mann 1987, 2002; Rosen 1997; Vickers 2010. Early modern and late medieval European economies also relied on credit. See Kadens 2015; Muldrew 1998; Nightingale 2010.

16. See Quinn 2019: 39–46.

17. See Old Merchant 1873: 91, 126.

18. For example, burdensome student loans can lead to delayed marriage and lower home-ownership. See Robb, Schreiber, and Heckman 2020; Stivers and Berman 2020.

19. See, e.g., Rajan 2010; Streeck 2014.

20. See Krippner 2011.

21. These are from the Federal Reserve Flow of Funds accounts, series L103 and L218. See https://www.federalreserve.gov/releases/z1/20210311/html/l103.htm, https://www.federalreserve.gov/releases/z1/20210311/html/l218.htm, and https://www.federalreserve.gov/releases/g19/current/default.htm.

22. The idea of law as a "code of capital" is the central theme of Pistor 2019.

23. Kornai (1992) distinguished between market economies and command economies in terms of hard budget constraints and soft budget constraints. The transition from socialism to capitalism in eastern and central Europe during the 1990s involved passage of bankruptcy laws and creation of the possibility of business failure. See Carruthers and Halliday 1998.

24. See Sandage 2005.

25. Banks have to acknowledge their losses by "writing down" nonperforming loans or setting aside additional capital reserves.

26. Non-bankruptcy rules also matter, of course. For example, "limited liability" sets an upper limit on the losses sustained by shareholders of an insolvent corporation.

27. Some argue that the issuance of debt by large corporations is also a way for management to signal their devotion to shareholder value: with more leverage the margin for error shrinks and management must focus on short-term profits.

28. See, e.g., Reuben, Sapienza, and Zingales 2009; Sapienza and Zingales 2012. Even the "Ronald Reagan" solution of trust-but-verify only works on a highly selective basis. To have to verify everything would be onerous to the point of paralysis.

29. Between the extremes of giving everyone/no one credit, trade credit that is too generous means too many bad debts, but too little credit means few sales. See National Association of Credit Management 1965: 279.

30. Here I am referencing Earling's 1890 book, by the same title.

31. These figures are obtained from FRED, the Federal Reserve Economic Data website maintained by the Federal Reserve Bank of St. Louis, and from the Board of Governors of the Federal Reserve System.

32. A financial derivative is a product whose value derives from that of an underlying financial asset. For example, the value of an option to buy company shares derives from the price of those shares. In 2019 the total notional value of financial derivatives of U.S. banks numbered more than $171 trillion; see the fourth quarter report of the Office of the Comptroller of the Currency, OCC 2020.

33. For an early articulation of these complications, see Wiley 1967. For a recent one, see Fourcade and Healy 2013.

34. On the broader trend toward surveillance capitalism, see Zuboff 2019.

35. The U.S. bond rating agencies, for example, play a key role in global capital markets.

36. See Espeland and Sauder 2007; Espeland and Stevens 2008; Fourcade 2016.

37. For example, a credit card company will enjoy higher earnings from cardholders who only make the minimum required payment each month, and who therefore carry a balance from month to month.

38. See McPherson, Smith-Lovin, and Cook 2001; Rivera 2012.

39. This is termed the "flight to quality." See Gorton 2017.

40. On the general issue of government management of risk, see Moss 2002.

41. See Skeel 2001, and chapter 8 in this book.

42. See Chwieroth and Walter 2019.

43. See Hauser 1958.

44. I refer here to Karl Marx's famous formulation from *The Eighteenth Brumaire of Louis Bonaparte.*

45. The problem of legal pluralism was addressed by the legal profession in the uniform law movement, starting at the end of the nineteenth century. The idea was for legal experts to design state-of-the-art uniform laws and urge their passage in as many different states as possible. Commercial laws were among the first addressed in this way, and the movement culminated in the Uniform Commercial Code. See Guild 1920.

46. For example, if I say "I promise to be there tomorrow," the context of my utterance will often make clear what is specifically meant by "I," "there," and "tomorrow."

47. For loans, a comparable difference might be between promising that "I'll repay you as soon as I can" and "I'll repay the entire sum next Saturday."

48. See Hogg 2011: 5.

49. Obviously these are ends of a spectrum, not just a simple dichotomy.

50. Third parties needn't always be governments. In the case of the over-the-counter derivatives market, for example, the International Swaps and Derivatives Association provides standardized legal language in its Master Agreement template.

51. Consequently, unpaid wages are often given a high priority in bankruptcy proceedings.

52. See Beckett and Harris 2011; Harris, Evans, and Beckett 2010.

53. This isn't to say that involuntary legal debts are inconsequential. They can, for example, be enormously burdensome for low-income prisoner populations, played a key role in the convict lease system in the postbellum South, and are currently used to restrict civil rights in some states. See Beckett and Harris 2011: 512, 521.

54. Special purpose entities, sometimes called special purpose vehicles, are independent legal entities created to hold assets.

55. See Quinn 2019: 2–4.

56. Adrian and Shin (2010) show how accelerated disintermediation and securitization helped set the stage for the global financial crisis of 2008.

57. See Porter 1995; Espeland 1998.

58. This is in sharp contrast with social debts, which are rarely transferable. For example, if I owe a dinner invitation to my friend Carol, and she has a similar obligation to her friend Beth, it would be highly inappropriate for Carol to use my obligation to her to satisfy her obligation to Beth and, in effect, have me invite Beth to dinner.

59. As in "negotiable securities." See Freyer 1976; Whitaker 1999.

60. The ability to sell debt can certainly help institutions like banks manage the maturity mismatch between short-term liabilities, like demand deposits (e.g., savings and checking accounts), and long-term assets, like thirty-year home mortgages.

61. See Ong, Theseira, and Ng 2019.

62. See Wherry, Seefeldt, and Alvarez 2019. For a cross-national survey, see Demirgüç-Kunt and Klapper 2013.

63. Consider that the Union Iron and Steel Company of Chicago was reported to fail in the Saturday, February 3, 1883, edition of *Bradstreet's* due to a variety of factors including financial mismanagement, labor conflict, declining rail prices, and over-purchasing of supplies. Shortly after, on February 17, *Bradstreet's* reported the failure of another Chicago firm, Rogers & Co., which did a large business with the Union Iron and Steel Company. One failure led to the other. See *Bradstreet's: A Journal of Trade, Finance, and Public Economy*, February 3, 1883, p. 76, and February 17, 1883, p. 108.

64. As Calomiris and Haber (2014: 5) note, compared to other countries the United States was particularly prone to banking crises.

65. See Gorton 2010; Thiemann 2018.

66. The transitivity of social relations is often weak: the friend of a friend is more likely than not also a friend, but not always. The business partner of my business partner may also be my

partner, but not always. However, someone who is a blood relative of my blood relative is also my blood relative.

67. This is not a trivial question as it is clear that firms have developed strategies to disguise their indebtedness. See Smith 2010.

68. See Bensel 1990: 114, 163, 238. Correlatively, some postbellum Southerners criticized the national debt and claimed that it did not encumber them. See DuBois 1962: 145, 326. My thanks to Aldon Morris for calling DuBois to my attention.

69. The story of Eumenes is told in Plutarch's *Lives*, and referenced much later by Jonathan Swift in his discussion of early eighteenth-century British politics and the national debt. See Carruthers 1996.

70. Seniority is a key part of the code of capital. See Pistor 2019.

71. We will see more of Mr. Tappan in chapter 3.

72. Fitch and S&P have very similar rating categories, although the category labels differ slightly.

73. See Poon 2007.

74. Currently, China is developing a system of "social credit" scores for individuals that potentially will be even more pervasive and fateful than U.S. credit scores.

75. These are regulations intended to ensure that the regulated firms minimize risks and otherwise act in a way that is prudent.

76. See FTC 2011: 1–2, 45–49; Rona-Tas 2017.

77. Counterparty risk is the risk that the other party to a contract will not perform as stipulated in the contract, for whatever reason.

78. See *Federal Register*, vol. 84, no. 157, Wednesday, August 13, 2019, p. 41425.

79. See, e.g., John 2010, 1998.

80. See, e.g., Agrawal, Gans, and Goldfarb 2019.

81. For example, over 2,500 R. G. Dun ledgers are preserved at Harvard's Baker Library.

82. Restricted access to credit was an obvious problem for black-owned businesses in Chicago in the mid-twentieth century. See Drake and Cayton 1945: 437, 443, 453.

83. See Krippner 2017.

84. See Calomiris and Haber 2014: 61, 82 on how much housing and agriculture have been the recipients of favorable credit policy by the U.S. government.

85. See Crouch 2011; Rajan 2010; Streeck 2014. For a discussion, see Trumbull 2014: 11–12.

86. Prasad (2012: 221) terms this "mortgage Keynesianism," while Streeck (2014: 38) calls it "privatized Keynesianism." For Rajan (2010: 31, 44), private credit offered an easy way to mitigate growing economic inequality. Garon (2012: 319, 329) argues that many federal government policies favoring credit-based consumption were put in place after World War II.

87. Zaloom, for example, says: "Debts also granted the giver leverage over the receiver; debtors are subject to the demands of those who lend" (2019: 24). Benjamin Franklin proposed the same idea, discussing "debt which exposes a man to confinement and a species of slavery to his creditors" (1904: 206), and this perspective was widespread (see Sandage 2005: 53–56). In his *Genealogy of Morals*, Friedrich Nietzsche famously discussed the power of creditors over debtors.

88. On "infrastructural power," see Mann 1984.

89. One obvious hurdle is that contracts are invariably incomplete. That is, they never fully specify, ex ante, all possible contingencies.

Chapter 2

1. On these various claims in regard to trust, see Arrow 1974; Dasgupta 1988; Fukuyama 1995; Ho 2021; and Putnam 1993.

2. See Sapienza and Zingales 2012.

3. See Granovetter 2017; Schmitz 1999; Coleman 1988; Dei Ottati 1994; Misztal 1996; Uzzi 1999; Bruckmeier, Ellegård, and Piriz 2005; Sapag et al. 2008.

4. See Cook, Hardin, and Levi 2005. Guinnane (2005) suggests that we jettison the concept of trust altogether.

5. See Fukuyama 1995; Hawthorn 1988; Dasgupta 1988; Coleman 1988; Dasgupta 2009.

6. This formulation relies on Heimer 1999.

7. See Kiyonari et al. 2006.

8. In economics, this dynamic is captured with models of iterated games.

9. See Feld and Elmore 1982; Karlberg 1999.

10. For brevity's sake, I will ignore the X that A trusts B to perform.

11. There are some famous and important situations where in fact people do not trust themselves. Ulysses had himself tied to the mast of his ship because he didn't trust himself not to swim to his death upon hearing the songs of the Sirens. Distrust of oneself generates various pre-commitment devices. See Elster 1979.

12. This bias is called "homophily." See Abrahao et al. 2017; McPherson, Smith-Lovin, and Cook 2001.

13. For a good summary of the economics of information, see Stiglitz 2000.

14. See Freyer 1982; Carruthers and Halliday 1998.

15. When banks lend overseas, however, legal codes aren't always so reliable.

16. See, for example, Lepler 2013: 35, 94, 120, 129.

17. Consider the widespread use of Social Security numbers in financial matters: they are a convenient way to be sure of someone's identity.

18. Internet commerce is prompting the creation of an entirely new set of authentication practices, such as the electronic "signature."

19. In testimony before Congress, the banker J. P. Morgan also famously underscored the importance of character.

20. See, e.g., Feins and Lane 1981: 114; Munnell et al. 1996; Stuart 2003; Yinger 1995.

21. See Evans and Schmalensee 2005: 78.

22. See Prudden 1922: 2.

23. More distant social relations can also be useful in providing information. See Granovetter 1973 on the strength of weak ties.

24. See, e.g., Fontaine 2001; Lamoreaux 1994; Hanley 2004; Hunt 1996.

25. See Boyce 1995: 33; Pak 2013.

26. See also Allen and Gale 2000: 14.

27. See, e.g., Akhavenin, Goldberg, and White 2004; Uzzi 1999; Uzzi and Gillespie 2002; Uzzi and Lancaster 2003.

28. See Smith and Warner 1979.

29. On one type of state-level intervention, see Carruthers, Guinnane, and Lee 2012.

30. See Woodman 1995: 4.

31. See Lebsock 1977.

32. See Holden 1955; Freyer 1976. Negotiability in practice preceded law in some measure. See Munro 2003.

33. See, e.g., La Porta et al. 1997, 1998; Levine 1998.

34. See Macaulay 1963; Bernstein 1992.

35. See, e.g., Biggart 2001; Ham and Robinson 1923; Light and Bonacich 1988: 243–72; Light, Kwuon, and Zhong 1990; Pitt and Khandker 1998; Sanyal 2014; Tenenbaum 1993.

36. See Earling 1890. This expectation informed federal housing policy, as evidenced by the underwriting manual used by the Federal Housing Administration. When evaluating home mortgage risk, underwriters were urged to consider, among other things, the family circumstances of the (male) borrower: "The mortgagor who is married and has a family generally evidences more

stability than a mortgagor who is single because, among other things, he has responsibilities holding him to his obligations" (FHA 1947, part III, paragraph 1636(2)).

37. See Miranti 1986: 459.

38. See Cohen 2012; Sinclair 2005.

39. See White 1998.

40. See, e.g., Carruthers and Espeland 1991; Miller 1994; Porter 1995; Calavita, Pontell, and Tillman 1997; Power 1997; Mennicken and Miller 2012.

41. See Ben-Amos 2000: 328–29; Fontaine 2001: 47.

42. See, e.g., Zelizer 1994, 1996; Carruthers and Espeland 1998; Muldrew 1998; Bandelj, Wherry, and Zelizer 2017.

43. See Gelpi and Julien-Labruyère 2000.

44. See Peabody 1904: 33; National Association of Credit Management 1965: 279.

45. See Keller 1963: 127.

46. The Federal Housing Administration enjoined its underwriters to pay close attention to the motives of a mortgagor: "Consideration is given to the mortgagor's motive and need for ownership of the property and the probable strength of the mortgagor's continuing desire for the amenities or non-monetary benefits arising from ownership" (FHA 1947, part III, paragraph 1639; see also paragraph 1641(1)).

47. See American Savings and Loan Institute 1971: 79.

48. A mortgage loan, for example, can only be used by a particular borrower to purchase a particular house. The borrower cannot simply take the loan and fund a wedding or a holiday trip to Las Vegas.

49. This shifted losses from shareholders to creditors. See Moss 2002: 74.

50. See, e.g., Mann 2002.

51. See Carruthers and Halliday 1998.

52. See Delaney 1992.

53. See Sullivan, Warren, and Westbrook 2000.

54. See, e.g., Ghosh 2006; Halliday and Carruthers 2009.

55. See Clark 1999; Porter 1995; Espeland and Stevens 1998; Carruthers and Stinchcombe 1999.

56. See Morrison and Wilhelm 2007; Pak 2013.

57. See Burt 1992; Mizruchi 1996; Gulati 1995.

58. See Moss 2002: 87.

59. See Mann 2002: 172–74.

60. See Helleiner 2003; Sylla 2007: 134.

61. See Mihm 2007.

62. See Carruthers and Babb 1996.

63. See, e.g., Kavanaugh 1921: 17; Kniffen 1934: 322; Miller 1927: 9; Prendergast 1906: 220.

64. See Converse 1932.

65. See Rosen 1997: 72–73.

66. See Freyer 1982; Weinberg 1982.

67. See Olegario 2003; Sinclair 2005.

68. See Hyman 2011: 45–72.

69. See Fishback 2007: 402; Quinn 2019.

Chapter 3

1. Until the National Banking Act of 1863, individual banks issued their own unique currency and so the true value of a one-dollar bill depended on the solvency of the issuing bank. Furthermore, counterfeiting was a widespread problem (Mihm 2007).

2. One problem was that customers buying intermediate goods or raw materials would combine or transform them in such a way that a lien no longer could apply. And chattel goods had such physical mobility that it was hard for a lien holder to trace them in the event of a dispute over payment. Recently, registration systems have enabled traceability for certain products in certain industries (e.g., airplanes), but this is a recent development. See Goode 2018.

3. Although minimal, entries in a ledger could function as evidence for a debt in a court of law. As Butts says: "Original entries in shop books, or the original memoranda of charges by a party . . . are competent evidence, with the suppletory [sic] oath of the party, if living, to prove the items charged" (1849: 5).

4. See Hanna 1931.

5. See Mann 2002: 10, and discussions of reification.

6. See Balleisen 1996: 476.

7. See, e.g., Priest 1999; Clark 1990: 125–26, 166; Mann 1987: 12; Russell 1996.

8. Skeel 2001: 36.

9. See *Historical Statistics of the United States* 2006: table Df8-12.

10. *Historical Statistics of the United States* 2006: table Df17-21.

11. See also Konig 1979: 84.

12. See Vickers 2010.

13. Clark 1990: 196.

14. See Clark 1990: 71.

15. See Mann 1987: 22–23.

16. A similar seasonal ebb and flow occurred in frontier areas dominated by hunting and the fur trade rather than by settled agriculture. See Usner 1987: 178–79.

17. See Rothenberg 1985: 792.

18. See Beckert 2014: 222, 227; Clark 1996: 226.

19. See Kulikoff 1986: 118–22; Price 1980: 6, 17; Rosenblatt 1962.

20. See Kulikoff 1986: 129–30.

21. Within the tobacco-producing community, there was an "etiquette of debt," as Breen (1985: 93) terms it, in which matters of honor and personal judgment were very important.

22. See Sitterson 1944; Woodman 1966a; Beckert 2014. Of course, Southern agriculture eventually evolved away from its focus on cotton and sugar. But as Gisolfi (2006) shows in the case of Georgia, as rural areas turned from cotton production to more capital-intensive chicken production, farmers remained deeply embedded in credit networks.

23. This holds true even for "small worlds" networks, for even if virtually everyone is connected through no more than "six degrees of separation," it is extremely difficult for individuals to map out those connections, in order to exploit them (Watts 1999). For a discussion of the limitations of networks in a comparable British setting, see Hancock 2005.

24. See Jones 1936.

25. *Historical Statistics of the United States* 2006: table De1-13.

26. *Historical Statistics of the United States* 2006: table Cd378-410.

27. See Jones 1936: 139.

28. The exception was an installment loan used for the purchase of a specific durable good item. For general types of goods, it wasn't practical to collateralize the loan using mobile assets that experienced high turnover or that might be perishable. A debtor-merchant might possess inventory only until it could be sold to a customer.

29. *Atlanta Daily Constitution*, April 11, 1879, p. 3.

30. See Olegario 2006: 30.

31. The credit rating system did not arise in Europe. At the time, one commentator (Bryan 1883: 10–11) suggested that in countries like Britain and France, businesses were handed down from one family generation to the next and consequently firms developed stable long-term

relationships with each other. Furthermore, Europe was a relatively small place, making it easier to gather information about an unknown firm. Finally, other institutions played the same or similar role in gathering information (e.g., notaries in France).

32. The Agency may have been partly inspired by banknote and counterfeit detectors. These were antebellum publications that dealt with three issues: the value of banknotes depended on the solvency of the issuing bank, counterfeiting was a widespread problem, and there were many small banks operating in the United States. Banknote detectors contained information about banks, provided details about the appearance of their genuine banknotes, and identified counterfeit bills. In effect, banknote detectors sold information about the trustworthiness of banknotes, and the banks that issued them, to those who handled large volumes of cash. See Bodenhorn 1998b; Macesich 1961; Smith 1942.

33. As one newspaper article explained: "Their business is to supply to the merchants and bankers of the city, who pay them a certain yearly subscription, information in reference to the solvency and respectability of traders all through the country. For this purpose these agencies have correspondents in almost every city, town and village in the United States, who keep them notified, from time to time, of the condition and prospects of the little shopkeepers of the place" (*New York Herald*, October 26, 1857, p. 4).

34. Armstrong 1848: 31.

35. Rating agencies were usually quick to adopt any new information technology, including telegraphs, telephones, and typewriters (John 2000).

36. See Wyatt-Brown 1966: 440.

37. *New York Daily Tribune*, January 4, 1844.

38. *New York Daily Tribune*, July 3, 1844.

39. See Sandage 2005: 171.

40. See Olegario 2006: 49. According to Foulke (1941: 351), Abraham Lincoln and Ulysses S. Grant were both Agency correspondents at one point in their careers.

41. See Norris 1978: 27; Sandage 2005: 101; Wyatt-Brown 1966: 438–39. Olegario points out that Southern newspapers frequently denounced credit rating as a kind of espionage (Olegario 2006: 8).

42. Several newspaper articles on the Mercantile Agency stated explicitly that it could be used for collection work. See *New Orleans Commercial Bulletin*, September 22, 1868; *New York Times*, March 15, 1880, p. 5.

43. See Cohen 2012: 46–51.

44. See Bouk 2015: 66–67.

45. See chapter 4 in this book.

46. Since in the nineteenth century there were no Social Security numbers, driver's licenses, or passports, the issue of personal identification was not a trivial one. Nevertheless, by combining personal names with business addresses, and by utilizing local expertise, agencies were generally able to determine who was who.

47. See Carruthers and Cohen 2010: 53.

48. The two-dimensional rating system lasted a long time. In 1958, Dun and Bradstreet still classified firms in terms of their "estimated financial strength" (an updated version of "pecuniary strength") and "composite credit appraisal" (the successor to "general credit"). See Credit Research Foundation 1958.

49. No rating was sometimes interpreted as detrimental to the firm. See *New York Times*, May 27, 1887.

50. *The Independent*, April 26, 1855, p. 132.

51. Double-entry bookkeeping methods existed, of course, but this is very different from something like generally accepted accounting principles (GAAP).

52. Eventually, the imposition of income taxes forced businesses to become more systematic in measuring their own income.

53. Quoted in Foulke 1941: 349.

54. See Cohen 2012.

55. Baker Library, Harvard University, Mercantile Agency Ledger for IL, vol. 27, p. 386.

56. Baker Library, Harvard University, Mercantile Agency Ledger for IL, vol. 27, p. 386.

57. It was, of course, very difficult for free blacks to operate businesses in the antebellum period, especially in the South. But there were a number of black-owned businesses, particularly in New Orleans, and black proprietors were identified as "colored," "negro," or "mulatto" in Agency ledgers (see Schweninger 1989; Walker 1986). Postbellum residential segregation created opportunities for black-owned business to serve the black community, and they also became important in some occupational niches, like barbers (see Bristol 2004; Ingham 2003).

58. See Vose 1916: 140. There is one curious instance in which the method for deriving a credit rating is revealed. A small credit rating agency, Fouse Hershberger & Co., failed in February 1878, and its two partners were arrested. Upon investigation, it turned out they didn't independently gather their own information and derive their own ratings. Rather, they had illegally obtained the reference books of two other rating agencies, Dun, Barlow & Co., and J. M. Bradstreet's. In order to calculate a firm's capital rating, Fouse Hershberger simply summed the two other ratings together, added 10 percent, and then divided by two. The resulting rating, produced by a combination of plagiarism, fraud, and simple arithmetic, was then reported to the client. See *New York Times*, February 15, 1878, p. 8.

59. Using statistical language, ratings were like point estimates with no standard errors.

60. See Cohen 2012: 932, 935, 949. The "counterfeiting" of credit ratings ranged from issuing a ratings book that was an outright copy of another agency's book to running a business whose name could be confused with that of another agency. For example, R. G. Dun put a notice in the *St. Paul Globe* (October 21, 1900) warning readers that it should not be confused with the Dunn Commercial Collection Agency.

61. *Hunts Merchants' Magazine*, January 1851, p. 48.

62. See Vose 1916: 85, 96.

63. See Norris 1978: 110.

64. London's *Financial Times*, for example, mentioned both Bradstreet's counts of business bankruptcies (see, e.g., the March 31, 1891, issue) and those compiled by R. G. Dun (see the April 14, 1893, issue). But even newspapers in small communities far from financial centers duly reproduced Dun's failure statistics as news about general business conditions. See, e.g., *Wichita Daily Eagle*, April 8, 1904; *Vermont Phoenix*, January 11, 1907. Small-town newspapers were also careful to report the arrival of personnel from Dun or Bradstreet's, whose visits involved an evaluation of local businesses (e.g., the *Rice Belt Journal*, June 23, 1916; *North Platte Tribune*, October 4, 1910), or to report the possibility of a Dun branch office opening nearby (see *Tombstone Epitaph*, October 20, 1912).

65. Usually, refusal to provide a statement was interpreted badly. But if the firm's reputation was sufficiently sterling, a refusal might be deemed harmless or quite reasonable. Consider that the ledger entries for R. H. White & Co. of Boston are filled with praise, verging on adulation ("a complete success," "doing a splendid business," "their credit is not questioned for anything they will buy"). The firm apparently refused repeatedly to make a statement to Agency correspondents, but their resistance wasn't interpreted badly, as the entry of February 1883 makes apparent: "Are so entirely beyond question that no one here would think of seeking a statement. On best authority are worth a million $" (Baker Library, Harvard University, Mercantile Agency Ledger for MA, vol. 72, p. 201).

66. To give a sense, consider the following instructions to Dun reporters: "Numerous instances have been known where the reporter started a concern with a high rating, without a statement,

with the result that the chance of obtaining a statement in the future has been diminished, the concern being perfectly content with the rating assigned. Beware of doing this" (Dun 1918: 25). The agency here reveals that the possibility of a high rating was an inducement for rated firms to cooperate and give a statement. If a high rating had already been given, then providing a statement could only make things worse and so firms would avoid giving them to Dun staff.

67. A 1905 R. G. Dun rating book still had the two-dimensional format, pecuniary strength and general credit. Sometime before the mid-twentieth century, Dun relabeled "pecuniary strength" as "estimated financial strength," and "general credit" as "composite credit appraisal," but otherwise stuck by its rating categories.

68. Baker Library, Harvard University, Mercantile Agency Ledger for IL, vol. 30, p. 162.

69. See *New York Times*, December 22, 1883, p. 3.

70. See *Chicago Daily Tribune*, November 1, 1888, p. 7.

71. Similar cases are reported in the *St. Louis Globe-Democrat*, January 3, 1877, and the *New York Times*, January 30, 1880, p. 1.

72. See *New York Times*, May 5, 1892, p. 1.

73. See *Chicago Tribune*, July 23, 1871, p. 1.

74. See Olegario 2006: 73. Such lawsuits were common. See also *New York Times*, May 26, 1889, p. 3; *New York Times*, January 30, 1898, p. 2; *Chicago Daily Tribune*, January 17, 1885, p. 3.

75. See Cohen 2012, chaps. 4, 8; Flandreau and Geisler Mesevage 2014a, 2014b.

76. In one other common type of litigation, credit raters figured as plaintiffs rather than just defendants. To protect the value of their intellectual property, mercantile agencies sometimes sued for copyright violations. For example, Dun sued Bradstreet's in 1866, accusing it of illegally copying Dun's credit reports (*Daily Cleveland Herald*, June 27, 1867, col. C). A further legal twist is evident from a case where a printing company sued Bradstreet's on the grounds that the defendant had deliberately lowered the plaintiff's credit rating because the plaintiff had extended credit to a rival credit agency. See *San Francisco Daily Evening Bulletin*, February 7, 1874. For an academic discussion of some of the legal issues, see Greeley 1887; Brewster 1924: 105–7.

77. A newspaper advertisement for the R. G. Dun reference books stated: "The book contains near 200,000 names, embracing all that are at all likely to be found really useful to subscribers. . . . The ratings are all made upon actual data, furnished in detail by our records, the contents of which extend over a period of twenty-three years, and are two-fold in character—one indicating pecuniary resources, the other mercantile credit. . . . The utmost care has been taken to produce a work which will be both creditable to ourselves and useful to subscribers, and we confidently present it to the business community as superior in every respect to anything of the kind hitherto attempted" (*New York Times*, November 3, 1864, p. 5).

78. *New York Times*, January 27, 1870, p. 3.

79. As early as the 1850s, other publications were citing the rating agencies as authoritative sources on the matter of business failure. The January 24, 1857, edition of the *United States Economist, Dry Goods Reporter, and Bank Railroad and Commercial Chronicle* cited the Mercantile Agency in an article on bankruptcy. For another early example, see *American Railway Times*, March 6, 1858.

80. *Bradstreet's*, July 14, 1888. See also *Bradstreet's*, February 2, 1889.

81. *The Independent* (March 16, 1893, p. 23) stated: "It is but fair to add that Bradstreet states that 93% of all failures were guarded against in the reports of the mercantile agencies, the concerns failing having but moderate rating or no rating at all. This large percentage is one of which the mercantile agency system may be proud."

82. In the fourth edition of its own manual, Dun employees were instructed: "Failures or any information which is unfavorable in character must be promptly handled. To this end Reporters will blue pencil the report, in order that it will promptly reach the 'Notification Clerk.' This applies

to failures, receiverships, petitions in bankruptcy, compromises, suits, judgments, mortgages, bills of sale, fires, and to everything of unfavorable or cautionary character" (Dun 1918: 47).

83. See *Asheville Daily Citizen*, July 16, 1892, p. 1.

84. See *Chicago Tribune*, March 5, 1898, p. 11.

85. See *Atlanta Constitution*, January 28, 1893, p. 3.

86. See *Chicago Tribune*, February 15, 1883, p. 6.

87. See Flandreau and Geisler Mesevage 2014b: 233–36.

88. *Bankers' Magazine and Statistical Register*, January 1858, p. 548. Others expressed more ambivalence. For example: "it [credit rating] is no doubt worth to subscribers more than the amount of the subscription money; but . . . it is a system that is fraught with danger. In its infancy it may be harmless and comparatively accurate; but, should it grow to maturity, and be generally relied upon, the credit of the mercantile community, which is its life and soul, would be in the hands of a few men, self-constituted umpires, and their unknown and irresponsible agents, subject to the errors of ignorance and mistakes of carelessness" (Freedley 1853: 130–31).

89. *Rocky Mountain News*, January 13, 1889, p. 9.

90. Zimmerman 1904: 48.

91. Evidently, one church consulted credit ratings to help evaluate a prospective pastor. See *New York Times*, January 19, 1896, p. 17.

92. Newfang 1912: 640. One seller of alcoholic beverages, eager to affirm its stature and sober reputation in an ad, instructed potential customers to visit their local bank and inspect the Dun or Bradstreet's rating manual to assess their reliability. See *Hopkinsville Kentuckian*, November 19, 1910.

93. See, e.g., *Bankers' Magazine*, February 1902, p. 244; *Bankers' Magazine*, September 1904, p. 327; Prudden 1922: 44–45; Prendergast and Steiner 1931: 88–89.

94. See Federal Reserve Board 1922: 667–68; *The Independent*, June 23, 1904.

95. See Sinclair 2005.

96. See Seiden 1964.

97. See Bryan 1883: 10–11.

98. See Hoffman, Postel-Vinay, and Rosenthal 1998.

99. See Weinberg 1982: 572.

100. Mann 2002: 4.

101. For an argument that negotiability emerged from the early modern lex mercatoria, see Munro 2003.

102. See Dylag 2010.

103. See Horwitz 1977: chap. 7; Heckman 1973.

104. See Beutel 1940: 854, 859.

105. See Lapp 1910.

106. See Dailey 1938: 205.

107. See Meech 1923: 53.

108. See Handal 1972: 365.

109. See Hahn 1993: 54; Moody's Investors Service 2004: 3.

110. Given the importance of working capital relative to fixed capital for mercantile and manufacturing firms in the early nineteenth century, the willingness of banks to provide working capital made theirs a non-trivial contribution to economic growth (Bodenhorn 2000: 94–95).

111. See Mehrling 2002: 209. A "real bill" was a note backed by a "real transaction," i.e., the shipment of real goods from a supplier/creditor to a customer/debtor (who issued the bill).

112. Banks did not adhere to this doctrine slavishly: "Although bankers themselves were less than religious adherents to the real-bills doctrine, they nevertheless focused on the provision of short-term credit" (Bodenhorn 2000: 91).

113. See McAvoy 1922: 83.

114. See West 1976: 504.

115. See Mitchell 1923: 151–53. As an instrument of Fed policy, the discount window was eventually augmented and eclipsed by open-market operations, buying and selling government securities. The market for government securities grew very quickly soon after the establishment of the Federal Reserve System, thanks mostly to wartime government borrowing.

116. See Federal Reserve Bank of New York 1915.

117. See Moulton 1920: 827.

118. The seller was also spared the task of collecting those debts.

119. See Moulton 1920: 830.

120. Burman 1948.

121. Cavers 1935.

122. See Martin 1931: 360.

123. *Historical Statistics of the United States* 2006: table Cj1179-91.

124. The securitization of home mortgages by bank lenders at the end of the twentieth century similarly moved otherwise illiquid assets off the balance sheets of creditors.

125. Brewster 1924: chap. 20.

126. See the advertisement in the *New York Times*, June 6, 1905, p. 10, where the American Credit-Indemnity Company asks its manufacturer or wholesaler clients: "How often do you lose from bad accounts?"

127. Credit insurance developed in Britain at about the same time. In 1885, the Ocean Accident and Guarantee Corporation began to offer credit insurance on a permanent basis. See Jamieson 1991: 165.

128. More formally: "A policy of credit insurance is a contract under which an insurance company promises, in consideration of a stipulated premium and subject to specified conditions as to amount of credit and persons to whom the credit is to be extended, to indemnify the insured against the net excess over normal loss which may result from the insolvency of persons to whom the insured may sell commodities in the regular course of business and within the terms of the insurance contract" (Hanna 1931: 523–24). See also Patterson and McIntyre 1931.

129. See the ad placed in the *Minneapolis Journal* from October 3, 1905, by the American Credit-Indemnity Company of New York: "Every account on your books is a loan without security. Credit insurance is collateral upon them."

130. See Federal Reserve Board 1922: 670. Although they were invented much later, credit default swaps functioned like credit insurance, although applied to bonds rather than trade credit.

131. See Credit Research Foundation 1958: 634; Prendergast and Steiner 1931: 399.

132. See Federal Reserve Board 1922: 675.

133. See *The Independent*, February 17, 1910, p. 383.

134. *The Independent*, June 23, 1904, p. 1461.

135. "There are certain restrictions, based on capital and credit ratings, as to extending credit to customers which amount in actual practice to a kind of supplement to the systems of the mercantile agencies. That is to say, the mercantile agency furnishes certain information as to a customer's financial standing, and credit insurance indicates how great a line of credit may be extended on his rating, and pays losses that may arise because of following its guidance" (*The Independent*, June 23, 1904, p. 1461).

136. *Chicago Tribune*, April 13, 1903, p. 12.

137. See Hanna 1931: 524–25; Federal Reserve Board 1922: 673–74; Prendergast and Steiner 1931: 402–3.

138. See also the article on credit insurance published in *Bankers' Magazine*, September 1922, p. 516. It is interesting to note that as of 2007, the U.S. Export-Import Bank of the United States, a facility of the U.S. government created in 1934 to help encourage exports overseas, also offers

credit insurance, and uses credit ratings to determine eligibility and credit limits. See Ex-Im Bank Short Term Credit Standards, EIB99–09 (7/01), http://www.exim.gov/tools/eib99-09.pdf.

139. See Credit Research Foundation 1958: 640, 642; Trapp 1953: 23.

140. Note that the mercantile agencies had been publishing summary statistics about business failure since the late 1850s, but it wasn't until a permanent federal bankruptcy statute was passed, in 1898, that an unambiguous legal meaning could be given to "bankruptcy" across the entire nation.

141. The reverse order (payment first, then the goods are shipped later) occurs in situations like layaway plans, where consumers pay money to a retailer in advance of receiving the commodity they wish to acquire.

142. For a comparison with Britain, see Flandreau and Geisler Mesevage 2014a: 226–29.

143. See Flandreau and Sławatyniec 2013: 250.

144. Of course, providers of credit ratings and credit insurance depended on the legal system in order to protect intellectual property rights and enforce insurance contracts.

Chapter 4

1. See Guinnane 2001.

2. *Bankers' Magazine*, November 1905, p. 633.

3. Very recently, however, banks have become subject to KYC (know your customer) rules, instituted as part of anti-terrorism and anti-money-laundering policies, and have to become more discriminating about whom they take money from.

4. See, e.g., Bodenhorn and Cuberes 2018.

5. See Polillo 2013: 83.

6. See, generally, Ritter 1997; Shaw 2019.

7. This was part of a more general trend. See Hilt 2017.

8. See Grossman 2010: 238, 241–42. One reason to encourage the establishment of local banks is that they were an important source of state revenues. See Wright 2002: 7.

9. See Kroszner and Strahan 1999.

10. They were called "real bills" because they were issued on the basis of real commercial transactions.

11. Hammond 1957: 572.

12. Similarly, there were no general laws of incorporation for corporations either.

13. *Historical Statistics of the United States* 2006: table Cj142-48.

14. See Bodenhorn 2000: 39; Grossman 2010: 229–30.

15. See Rolnick and Weber 1983; Murphy 2017: 112–13.

16. As Bodenhorn shows (2008), worries about political patronage and corruption helped prompt the shift to free banking in New York State.

17. Jaremski 2010: 1568.

18. Atack, Jaremski, and Rousseau (2014) found that new railroads were often built to link up existing population and financial centers; once constructed, they also stimulated the establishment of new banks along the new routes.

19. Jaremski (2010) addresses directly the causes of bank failure during the free banking era.

20. See Grossman 2010: 222–25.

21. See Knodel 2010: 241; Hammond 1957: 198, 301; Murphy 2017: 1, 5.

22. See Bodenhorn 2003a: 252; and generally Polillo 2013: table 3.4.

23. Sylla 1998: 86.

24. See Bodenhorn 2003a: 48; Murphy 2017: 39, 42.

25. Banks could lose their money if both issuer and endorser defaulted on their obligation to repay the note, although if it were truly a "real bill" then there were tangible assets to help compensate creditors in case of default. Two firms might partner to deceive the banks, as when

each would issue a promissory note to the other, and then both would take their separate notes to (different) banks for rediscounting. Such a practice was called "kite-flying" (*North America and United States Gazette*, January 18, 1858). Banks sometimes tried to conceal the default of a debtor in order to avoid acknowledging loan losses. One method for this was to roll over a short-term loan into a new short-term loan whose increased value reflected the unpaid principal and interest from the first loan.

26. See Woodman 1966a, 1966b, 1968, 1995; Price 1980.

27. Insurance companies were often similarly restricted; see Wright and Kingston 2012: 474.

28. See Van Fenstermaker 1965: 27.

29. See Lamoreaux 1994; Murphy 2017: 55. Beveridge (1985) points out the substantial level of "insider lending" being done by non-commercial bank credit institutions like the New England mutual savings bank he examined in considerable detail.

30. See Lamoreaux 1994: 4.

31. See Lamoreaux 1994: 26, 79.

32. See Wright 1999: 41.

33. Wright 1999: 51.

34. See Bodenhorn 2003b: 491; Bodenhorn 1998a: 110.

35. See Gibbons 1858: 52, 61.

36. See Bodenhorn 2003a: 234, 250, 273.

37. See Calomiris and Haber 2014: 154.

38. See Van Fenstermaker 1965: 91.

39. See Skocpol, Ganz, and Munson 2000; Skocpol and Oser 2004.

40. Consider, for example, the importance of fraternal and mutual-aid societies within the African American community and for the establishment of black-owned banks. See Ammons 1996: 470–71; DuBois 1907: 109–10, 115, 121–22, 126; Garrett-Scott 2019: 6, 55; Levine 1997: 59–62.

41. See Anderson 1943.

42. See Sylla 1969: 659; Myers 1970: 163; Davis 1910: 36.

43. See the summary of the National Banking System offered in the *New York Times*, October 23, 1867, p. 1.

44. The number of state-chartered banks later rebounded as issuance of banknotes became less important as a source of bank profits, and therefore as the tax on such notes became less consequential.

45. White 1982: 34.

46. See Beckhart 1922; Sylla 1969: 660.

47. See Anderson 1936.

48. See Sylla 1969: 666.

49. Myers 1970: 125.

50. See White 1998: 19.

51. Mason 2004: 12–13.

52. See Garrett-Scott 2019: 121–22.

53. See, generally, Fleming 1927; Stein and Yannelis 2020; Levy 2012: 106.

54. Fleming 1927: 38–39.

55. Stein and Yannelis 2020: 5335. A number of white Americans used its services. See Fleming 1927: 49.

56. See Fleming 1927: 53–55, 73; Davis 2003.

57. Stein and Yannelis 2020: 5340; Fleming 1927: 85–94. Attempts to compensate the depositors failed due to the opposition of Southern Democrats. See Gilbert 1972: 141–42.

58. Gilbert 1972.

59. Stein and Yannelis 2020.

60. See Baradaran 2017: 40–43; Harris 1936: 46–47, 62; Lindsay 1929: 172.

61. See also Harris 1936: 54–55.

62. See Lindsay 1929: 179, 187, 195. The St. Luke Penny Savings Bank of Richmond, Virginia, was unusual in how much it supported the entrepreneurship of black women. See Garrett-Scott 2019: 140.

63. The number of black-owned banks in the United States grew from scarcely a handful at the end of the nineteenth century to thirty-five in the mid-1920s but then declined rapidly during the Depression. See Harris 1936: appendix IV.

64. Since networks and associations were highly segregated along racial lines, the vast majority would have overwhelmingly excluded African Americans.

65. "There should be a law passed prohibiting loans, either to [bank] officers or directors, when they are of any size, without having first passed the scrutiny and sanction of the board of directors" (*Bankers' Magazine*, March 1903, p. 376). See also Polillo 2013: 95.

66. See also Prudden 1922: 44–45; Stronck and Eigelberner 1930: 117; Rosendale 1908: 190; Wall 1919: 39; *Bankers' Magazine*, August 1898, p. 175.

67. In the early twentieth century, the newly established Federal Reserve System reinforced the importance of credit ratings by including them in the criteria that made assets eligible for rediscounting by Federal Reserve banks. See Federal Reserve Bank of New York 1915.

68. See Wall 1919: 40.

69. See Lamoreaux 1994: 105; Lamoreaux 1998: 35.

70. Kniffen 1915: 431.

71. See also Williams 1946: 2.

72. See also Hurdman 1914: 437; Prendergast 1906: 146.

73. An article on credit ratings, written for bankers, stated: "The banks to-day annually pay large sums to commercial agencies which make a business of obtaining data upon which to base the credit rating of the business community. Much capital has been invested in this kind of enterprise by the various commercial agencies. The information they furnish is generally to be relied upon, and yet from the nature of the case it can not be so accurate as to preclude all losses to the banks which accept it as a basis for judging of the value of commercial paper" (*Bankers' Magazine*, August 1898, p. 175).

74. Kavanaugh (1921: 176) claims that the first separate bank credit department was established by James G. Cannon for the Fourth National Bank of New York. Cannon went on to become the first president of the National Association of Credit Men, organized in 1896.

75. See also Prudden 1922: 3.

76. Commercial banks were spurred on by recommendations from the Federal Reserve Bank of New York to establish credit departments, if they had not already done so. See *New York Times*, May 19, 1923, p. 20.

77. Hurdman remarks: "The banker of yesterday had a much easier task than the banker of today in dispensing credit, for the reason that business was transacted on a smaller scale and the old-time banker was able to get closer to the borrower than is possible now. He lent the funds of the bank to men and concerns about whom he had close personal knowledge. Today that situation does not exist except in the small country banks" (1914: 435). See also Lamoreaux 1998: 34.

78. See also Kniffen 1915: 374.

79. See, e.g., Rosendale 1908; Wall 1919: 16–17; and consider Holt's (1917) edifying discussion of cross-reference systems for bank files.

80. Prudden (1922: 28) mentions the importance of a good filing system. Not coincidentally, permanent files are one of the hallmarks of bureaucracy according to Max Weber's famous definition (Weber 1978).

81. See Stronck and Eigelberner 1930: 48.

82. See Yates 1989.

83. This is no surprise given the asymmetries of information characteristic of credit markets. See Stiglitz 2000.

84. However, if the borrower was also a depositor, then the bank would have a record of prior financial balances and transactions.

85. See Cohen 2012: 52–53, 582, 864.

86. As Wall stated: "Only a few years ago the majority of borrowers became highly indignant if asked for a statement of their affairs" (1919: 30). Even company shareholders, i.e., owners, of large manufacturing firms were generally given very little information about the firm's finances. See Hawkins 1963: 135.

87. See White 1998: 20.

88. For example, there was little consensus on asset valuation and depreciation. On the varieties of "value," see *Harvard Business Review* (January 1927): 236–44; Brief 1966.

89. See Colley 1914; Prendergast 1906: 127.

90. See Martindale 1911: 1400. Williams (1946: 5) reproduces a financial statement given by Sears, Roebuck & Co. to Goldman Sachs, its bank, in February 1897. The statement is very simple, handwritten by Julius Rosenwald, and contains little detail.

91. See *Bankers' Magazine*, March 1898, p. 378; Steiner 1923: 444; Reihl 1906: 414.

92. A century later, a similar insight lay behind a provision within the Sarbanes-Oxley Act of 2002, which required the principal officers of a firm to certify personally the accuracy of the firm's financial reports.

93. As Meek (1914: 427) expressed it: "The signed statement is one of the most important elements in credit work." See also *Bankers' Magazine*, March 1903, p. 370.

94. Olegario 2006: 179.

95. See Meek 1914: 428. It seems that this bill was pushed by the National Association of Credit Men. See the *Atlanta Constitution*, April 26, 1914, p. B7.

96. See Hurdman 1914: 438; Colley 1914: 423.

97. Furthermore, while independent auditors add credibility to a statement, they also add cost.

98. See also Kniffen 1915: 440–41.

99. Mitchell 1916: 750.

100. See Wall 1919: 132.

101. The 2–1 ratio was deemed sufficient to absorb the tendency during a firm's insolvency for assets to shrink and for liabilities to remain the same, and even grow (Wall 1919: 132).

102. See Wall 1919: 151 for other financial ratios of interest to the banker. Wall was acknowledged as the developer of "credit barometrics," which used these ratios to forecast a firm's future (see *Harvard Business Review* 4, no. 1 [October 1925]: 79).

103. See Edwards 1958: 80. The proposal made by the Federal Reserve Board (and approved by the Federal Trade Commission) for a uniform system of accounting for manufacturing and merchandising firms was reprinted in the *Journal of Accountancy* (June 1917): 401–33. See also Conway 1915.

104. See White 1998: 21; Peple 1916.

105. See Wall 1919: 34.

106. See Yates 1989: 135. As Archambault and Archambault (2005) note, such regulation also shaped the kind of information that appeared in the annual manuals of bond rating agencies like Moody's. For the effects of government regulation on financial information about manufacturing firms, see Hawkins 1963.

107. See Powers 1914.

108. See Edwards 1958.

109. See Miranti 1986: 451–52.

110. See Hawkins 1963: 153.

111. For example, firms had to meet various disclosure requirements in order to be listed on the New York Stock Exchange. See Davis, Neal, and White 2003.

112. *New York Times*, November 8, 1896, p. 2; and see Smith 2010.

113. Cohen 2012: 52–53. See also *New York Times*, July 21, 1897, p. 8, August 22, 1897, p. 11, December 10, 1898, p. 2, October 14, 1903, p. 11; *American Lawyer* (September 1897): 458; *New York Times*, March 10, 1917, p. 15. On such issues, the NACM was often joined, and sometimes opposed, by the Commercial Law League, founded in 1895 (see *American Lawyer* [September 1895]: 404).

114. *New York Times*, March 23, 1898, p. 3.

115. See Olegario 2006: 182; Cohen 2012: 582, 864.

116. Miller 1927: 9.

117. See, e.g., *Bankers' Magazine*, November 1912, p. 541, October 1914, p. 399; Bonesteel 1919: 776; Kniffen 1934: 375; Kniffen 1911; Kavanaugh 1921: 17; Prendergast and Steiner 1931: 69; Prendergast 1906: 220; Tregoe 1921: 66. The three Cs even made it into bank advertisements; see *Washington Post*, June 23, 1913, p. 2.

118. Filsinger 1926: 830.

119. Prendergast and Steiner 1931: 71.

120. *Bankers' Magazine*, March 1903, p. 374.

121. Emory 1902: 246.

122. See Anonymous 1925.

123. Williams 1946: 20.

124. Munn 1923: 501.

125. Or, as a postwar government pamphlet on small business credit put it: "One of the principal requisites of credit to small businesses is the personal and moral character of borrowers" (Francis 1947: 3).

126. Munn 1923: 501.

127. Sometimes, collateral became a fourth "C" (see Sawyer 1940: 35). The "Cs" continued to proliferate. White (1990) discusses the five Cs of credit, including the usual suspects (character, capacity, capital) and adding two more (collateral and conditions).

128. It is worth noting that for businesses concerned with trade credit, the rating agencies offered information that was consistent with the three Cs framework, although they did not use that particular term. See Sandage 2005: 130.

129. Knight (1923: 349) describes the tipping point for a growing bank: "when its executive officers can no longer effect personal and immediate contact with all the customers whose names are on its books, those officers are subjected to daily reminders . . . that they need something to assist them to keep in touch with their valuable customers and to accumulate information that will be of value when occasion demands that they grant or refuse a request for credit accommodation. After a time they conclude that a credit department will solve their problem and they decide to install one."

130. This is one reason why the Civil War threw the Southern financial system into disarray: during the 1860s about 60 percent of Southern wealth disappeared, giving Southern borrowers far fewer assets to use as collateral (Thompson 2004: 15).

131. Wall 1919: 58.

132. Kniffen 1915: 237, 389.

133. This is why public registration of land makes such a difference for mortgages: everyone can know who really owns a specific parcel of land.

134. See Lough 1909: 113.

135. All secured creditors have higher priority than unsecured creditors, but within the class of secured creditors, senior creditors have higher priority over junior creditors. Higher-priority claims must be fully satisfied before debtor assets become available to satisfy lower-priority claims. The legal rules of secured transactions determine who has priority. On seniority more generally, see Pistor 2019.

136. Westerfield (1932: 13) notes another use for collateral: in a small bank dominated by relationship lending, insistence on collateral is a useful "excuse" for refusing a loan that would otherwise be awkward to turn down.

137. See Markowitz 1952 for an early statistical argument on why investors should care about the variance of the returns from a portfolio, not just the expected rate of return.

138. The diversification was especially difficult for black-owned banks to pursue: residential racial segregation concentrated their lending activity.

139. Some got a little too optimistic about the value of diversification. Just months before the stock market crash of 1929, Joseph Lawrence argued in the pages of the *Harvard Business Review* that "diversification eliminates the element of risk in stock investment" (Lawrence 1929: 280).

140. *Harvard Business Review* (January 1927): 207.

141. In certain situations, commercial banks could also obtain insurance for their loans (much like merchants could acquire credit insurance coverage; see chapter 3 in this book). But these situations were largely set by government policy and so were not generally an option (Quantius 1946).

142. See Murphy 2017: 125–27.

143. See Morrison and Wilhelm 2007.

144. See Pak 2013.

145. Carroll 1895: 34.

146. See also *Bankers' Magazine*, December 1914, p. 666.

147. See *Bankers' Magazine*, December 1914, p. 666.

148. See *New York Times*, May 4, 1928, p. 21, May 5, 1928, p. 19.

149. See *New York Times*, May 9, 1928, p. 37, May 30, 1928, p. 23, November 8, 1928, p. 45.

150. *New York Times*, May 13, 1928, p. 134.

151. See *New York Times*, June 8, 1928, p. 39, May 16, 1929, p. 31. These small loans were mostly used to deal with medical expenses or to settle prior debts.

152. See Haines 1932a: 585; Brown and De Lano 1938.

153. See Haines 1932b: 433.

154. See Paddi 1938.

155. See Brown and De Lano 1938: 483.

156. One article even suggested that banks consult a person's credit rating with a mercantile agency before proceeding with a personal loan (*Bankers' Magazine*, December 1914, p. 665).

157. In 1932 alone, 1,453 banks failed (Westerfield 1934: 17).

158. See Morton 1939a.

159. See Jalil 2015.

160. See White 1981: 540.

161. See Calomiris and Haber 2014: 305–7.

162. White 1981: 556.

163. Note the contrast with the failure of the Freedman's Savings Bank and the losses suffered by its depositors.

164. See Shaw 2018a, 2019.

165. Shaw (2015) points out that deposit insurance was in many respects a political alternative to branch banking.

166. See Jones 1938: 696; Golembe 1960. White (1981) explains that the way state plans were structured failed to resolve the moral hazard problem that any insurance scheme faces, and in some cases the plans were simply overwhelmed by the collapse of agricultural prices in the 1920s.

167. See Calomiris and Haber 2014: 190.

168. The annual number of FDIC-insured bank closings remained low until the early 1980s when it increased and remained high through the early 1990s. See *Historical Statistics of the United States* 2006: table Cj504-10.

169. See Shaw 2019: 166–67.

170. See Morton 1939b: 277; Harold 1938: 26; Jones 1940: 187.

171. See, e.g., *New York Times*, June 22, 1932, p. 31.

172. See Morton 1939b: 280; Jones 1940: 194.

173. This included regulations for insurance companies, pension funds, money market funds, brokerage firms, and bank capital standards. See further discussion in chapter 6.

174. See Dunkman 1949: 88.

175. Baskin and Miranti 1997: 219.

176. *Historical Statistics of the United States* 2006: table Cj251-64.

177. See Berger and Udell 1995; Petersen and Rajan 1994, 2002; Uzzi 1999; Uzzi and Lancaster 2003.

178. See Cole, Goldberg, and White 2004.

179. See Akhevein, Frame, and White 2005; Mester 1997.

180. See Berger, Frame, and Miller 2005; Frame, Srinivasan, and Woosley 2001.

181. See Mester 1997; Treacy and Carey 2000: 192–96.

182. See Bord and Santos 2012. I say more about securitization in chapters 6 and 7 in this book.

183. See Singer 2007: 37–41.

184. See Singer 2007: 47.

185. See King and Sinclair 2003: 350.

186. On the lessons learned from the Asian Financial Crisis for bank regulation, see BCBS 1999.

187. See Hirtle et al. 2001; Jones and Mingo 1998; Herring 2007.

188. See BCBS 2000, 2005; Singer 2007: 63.

189. See Brimmer 1971: 379.

190. See Brimmer 1992; Morton and Duker 1978: 32–35; Baradaran 2017: 159, 202–3, 243; GAO 2006; Price 1990.

191. For recent evidence on unequal access to banking services, see Small et al. 2021.

192. See Grossman 2010: 264–65, 269–72.

193. See Calomiris and Haber 2014: 203; Kroszner and Strahan 1999.

194. See Carruthers 2013.

195. Thiemann 2018.

196. They can also, as Turner (2016) points out, contribute too much and overextend private credit.

197. See Rockoff 2021.

198. See Cole, Goldberg, and White 2004; Petersen and Rajan 1994, 2002.

199. For a detailed discussion of how banks helped create the 2008 crisis, see Fligstein 2021.

Chapter 5

1. See Calder 1999: 90–92; Lauer 2017: 23; Mann 2002. On actual debt slavery, see Testart 2002.

2. Put another way, so that people can raise a family and have a "decent" life.

3. Before the widespread availability of health insurance, one way to finance unexpected medical expenses was to turn health care providers into involuntary creditors. That is, after receiving emergency care, the patient was slow to pay the doctor.

4. Under extreme conditions, of course, households can and do alter their composition. Dependent children might be sent away to live with relatives. The household may even dissolve.

5. This was particularly important in the era before old-age pensions ("Social Security") offered retirement-age income for the elderly, and for groups who were unlikely to inherit significant economic resources from their parents. For a general discussion, see James, Palumbo, and Thomas 2007.

6. The contemporary "gig" economy often produces unstable earnings.

7. Banks might, of course, lend to businesses that then loaned money to individual consumers.

8. Of course, the ability of a merchant to extend credit to customers often required that the merchant receive credit from suppliers (see, e.g., Plummer 1942: 389; Ransom and Sutch 1977: 120–21). In this way, complex networks of indebtedness were formed, extending from consumers back up distribution and production chains.

9. Book credit, unlike credit using a promissory note, was not transferable or negotiable. See Walker 1866: 241.

10. See Marler 2013: 95; and Suarez 1966: 195.

11. See Billings and Blee 2000: 89; Clark 1990: 65–66, 196; Friend 1997; Konig 1979: 84; Mann 1987: 26.

12. See Cornwell 2007.

13. See Lauer 2017: 20, 30, 105.

14. See English 2006.

15. See Marler 2013: 222–23, 232.

16. See Woodman 1995: 5–7, 26.

17. See Ransom and Sutch 1977: 126, 130.

18. See Beckert 2014: 285–87; Woodman 1995: 87.

19. One organization, the Farmers' Improvement Society of Texas, made the parallel explicit, calling the mortgage system "the Negro's second slavery" and attempting to develop alternative sources of credit for black farmers in Texas. See DuBois 1907: 162.

20. See Birckhead 2015; Reséndez 2017; Rosenthal 2018: 179–80; tenBroek 1951; Madley 2016: 37, 147.

21. See, e.g., Hardy 1938: 56–58; Jacobstein 1913; Kinley 1895.

22. See Knapp 1924: 169.

23. In 1880, for example, 51.5 percent of retail sales for Field, Leiter & Co. (the Chicago-based predecessor of Marshall Field & Company) were made on credit. See Twyman 1954: 129.

24. See Smalley and Sturdivant 1973: 26, 81.

25. As Plummer (1930: 3) shows, almost the entire retail sector was heavily reliant on credit sales.

26. Hanes 1915: 10–11; Lauer 2017: 57–59.

27. Initially, the Retail Credit Company charged $25 for an annual subscription to its reference book. See Flinn 1959: 70.

28. See Flinn 1959: 62; Lauer 2017: 83, 91.

29. For example, the Retail Credit Company, founded in Atlanta in 1899, branched out to other cities, expanded to cover health risks (for insurance companies) as well as credit risks, acquired other local agencies, and eventually became Equifax. See Flinn 1959: 65–67, 190, 260.

30. Mapes 1916: 22.

31. See, e.g., Hallman 1924: chap. 2; Hanes 1915: 9, 14–19.

32. See Hanes 1915: 3; Lauer 2017: 20, 30, 105, 199; Hallman 1924: 58–59; Skinner 1916: 91; Zimmerman 1916a: 41.

33. See Cole and Handcock 1960: 193–94, 210; Lauer 2017: 138–39; Phelps 1947: 3–6.

34. See Cole and Handcock 1960: 222–26; Plummer 1930: 6, 13, 19; Skinner 1916: 92–93.

35. See Lauer 2017: 201.

36. See Borges 1916: 105; Skinner 1916: 89, 95.

37. See McConnell 1916: 125; Cole and Handcock 1960: 302.

38. See Lauer 2017: 209.

39. See Parker 1938; Lynn 1957; Calder 1999: 162–63; Marron 2009: chap. 2.

40. Olney (1989) also argues that in the particular case of the automobile industry, install-ment loans helped smooth out production, reconciling seasonally fluctuating demand with the imperatives of mass production.

41. Unsurprisingly, repossessions of automobiles increased during the early years of the Great Depression, rising from 4.1 percent of new and used cars in 1928 to 10.4 percent in 1932. See Weiss 1938: 98.

42. See Foster 1935: 29.

43. See Grimes 1926: 45; Phelps 1938: 220.

44. Olney 1989: 377.

45. See Holthausen, Merriam, and Nugent 1940: table A-3.

46. Holthausen, Merriam, and Nugent 1940: table A-6.

47. See Clarke 2007: 239.

48. See Foster 1935: 41; Olney 2012: table 2.

49. At first, neither commercial banks, credit unions, nor other small loan companies were willing or available to offer car loans (Phelps 1952: 33–34), and even at the end of the 1930s the proportion of installment credit coming from these alternative sources was much smaller than from sales finance companies (Neifeld 1941: 31).

50. See Ayres 1938.

51. See Hyman 2011: 11.

52. See Burman 1948. As Moulton (1920: 830) points out, the commercial credit companies that funded business inventories and receivables made use of Dun's and Bradstreet's rating services.

53. See Nugent and Henderson 1934.

54. See generally Federal Reserve Board 2018.

55. Such specialization was also evident in the 1950s. See Federal Reserve Board 1957.

56. See, e.g., Hardy 1938: 4; Townsend 1932: 33.

57. See Degenshein 2020; Woloson 2007.

58. More recently borrowers can pawn electronic devices, brand-name luxury goods, guns, and so on. See Caskey 1991: 90; Mottershead 1938: 149; Shergold 1978: 201; Woloson 2007: 37.

59. Townsend 1932: 72.

60. See Mottershead 1938: 150.

61. Current regulations often require pawnshops to be licensed and to determine that the goods weren't stolen (i.e., that the borrower actually owned the object they wished to pawn), and so lenders had to be sure of the personal identity of the borrower.

62. See Tenenbaum 1989, 1993.

63. In 1913, the New York Hebrew Free Loan Society made over 20,000 loans (Godley 1996: table 1). Ryan (1934: 268) notes that as late as 1933 Hebrew Free Loan Societies lent out $2.5 million, in small personal loans.

64. Godley 1996.

65. See Biggart 2001; Light, Kwuon, and Zhong 1990.

66. See Light 1977.

67. See Nugent 1941.

68. For social science, see Eubank 1916, 1917; Ham 1912. For journalism, see, e.g., the article titled "Legal War Begins on Loan Sharks," *New York Times*, January 1, 1911, p. 6, or the *Chicago Tribune* article titled "Beating the Loan Shark, Whose Wake Is Strewn with Suicides, Ruined Men and Women, and Broken Homes," January 28, 1912. Other discussions of the loan shark problem and how to solve it came in the *Cincinnati Enquirer* (February 16, 1914), *Detroit Free Press* (January 10,

1913), *Boston Globe* (July 20, 1911), *Washington Post* (April 8, 1910), *Baltimore Sun* (April 2, 1912), *Atlanta Constitution* (January 25, 1914), and *Los Angeles Times* (July 13, 1918), to name but a few.

69. See Haller and Alviti 1977.

70. See, e.g., *Chicago Tribune*, January 21, 1912.

71. See Wassam 1908: 14. Technically, the loan shark was "purchasing" the borrower's salary, and as there was no explicit interest, no usury laws were violated.

72. See Anderson 2008. For news of the RSF's campaign against loan sharks, see *New York Times*, January 1, 1911, p. 6, January 5, 1911, p. 4, May 19, 1911, p. 6; *Chicago Tribune*, November 12, 1909, p. 1; *Detroit Free Press*, November 14, 1909, p. c4; *Cincinnati Enquirer*, January 8, 1911, p. 2.

73. See Carruthers, Guinnane, and Lee 2012.

74. See Easterly 2010. Foster (1938: 72) declared the USLL to be a success.

75. The term "industrial bank" came to apply to organizations like the Morris Plan.

76. See Benmelech and Moskowitz 2010: table 1.

77. This company "went public" with a stock issue in 1928, and at the time operated through 68 offices in 11 states. See *New York Times*, October 10, 1928, p. 37.

78. See Foster 1941: 155; Townsend 1932: 94.

79. See Lerch 1939: 218; Reeder 1936: 12; Schweppe 1926: 24; Townsend 1932: 9.

80. See Michelman 1966: 107.

81. Townsend 1932: 119.

82. These would be indicated by the personal appearance of the applicant, the state of their home (orderly vs. messy), their repayment history and relationship with their spouse, and so on. See Reeder 1936: 15.

83. Anderson 2008; Michelman 1966: 112–16.

84. See *New York Tribune*, February 18, 1897, p. 10.

85. Ham 1912: 112.

86. Bergengren 1937.

87. Neifeld 1931: 322.

88. Orchard 1938: 159; Shaw 2019: 214–18.

89. See Johnson 1948; McQuaid 1976.

90. Bergengren 1937: 146.

91. Neifeld 1941: 31.

92. *Historical Statistics of the United States* 2006: table Cj437-47.

93. Chapman 1940: 28.

94. See *New York Times*, May 4, 1928, p. 21; *Wall Street Journal*, May 11, 1928, p. 6; *New York Herald Tribune*, May 30, 1928, p. 24; *New York Times*, July 18, 1936, p. 19.

95. See *New York Times*, May 5, 1928, p. 19; *New York Herald Tribune*, June 8, 1928, p. 35.

96. See Hardy 1938: 45; Jennings 1939: 68.

97. See Haines 1936a: 160; Paddi 1938: 139. The *New York Times*, June 2, 1929, p. N12, reported on the National City Bank's first year of experience with personal loans, and noted that medical and dental services were the most important purpose for which borrowers sought loans.

98. See Chapman 1940: 91. Banks even turned to that oldest source of systematic credit information: the Mercantile Agency. See Chapman 1940: 92.

99. See also Hunt 2005: 10–11; Rule 1974.

100. Pagano and Jappelli 1993: 1711.

101. Chapman 1940: 80.

102. Homes would be mortgaged, and other valuable durable goods subject to liens as part of an installment loan.

103. Brown and De Lano 1938: 481–83; French 1939: 23–25; Haines 1932a: 586. And see *New York Times*, May 4, 1928, p. 21. Co-makers should also be persons of "good character"; see *New York Times*, May 13, 1928, p. 134.

104. See Converse 1932. They would also try to avoid obvious problems like a borrower who drank too much. See Kennedy 1958: 93.

105. Matherly 1944: table 1. The effects weren't uniform. Among mail-order firms, Regulation W hit Sears and Montgomery Ward much harder than it did Spiegel's (Smalley and Sturdivant 1973: 246). A number of lenders tried to evade the regulation by shifting from installment to revolving credit (Hyman 2011: 99).

106. It was reimposed to reduce consumer credit, and combat inflation, during the Korean War. See Trumbull 2014: 122–25.

107. E.g., the Truth in Lending Act (1968), the Fair Credit Billing Act (1974), and the Equal Credit Opportunity Act (1974).

108. Paddi 1938: 137. See also *New York Times*, April 27, 1930, p. 138.

109. These efforts culminated in the Truth in Lending Act of 1968, which mandated a standardized way of calculating interest (APR or annual percentage rate), but as Fleming (2018) shows this federal law was preceded by decades of effort at the state level.

110. See Evans and Schmalensee 2005: 89.

111. See Jentzsch 2007: 64; Olegario 2006: 185.

112. See *Atlanta Constitution*, July 8, 1904, p. 11.

113. *New York Times*, September 9, 1917, p. 32.

114. *New York Times*, June 10, 1924, p. 34.

115. See Credit Rating Association 1919. The volume also included a listing of Minneapolis employers, with the days of the month or week when they paid their employees.

116. Hunt 2005: 11.

117. See Truesdale 1927: 141–42; *Chicago Tribune*, September 15, 1907, p. F6.

118. See Hert 1938: 115.

119. Evans and Schmalensee 2005: 53.

120. See Plummer 1930: 6; Schweppe 1926: 22.

121. See Vanatta 2018: 355.

122. See Evans and Schmalensee 2005: 54; Wolters 2000: 321.

123. See Vanatta 2018: 359.

124. On the difficulties posed by credit card issuance, see Zumello's (2011) discussion of the failed launch of the "Everything Card" by First National City Bank of New York in the late 1960s.

125. Evans and Schmalensee 2005: 117–18.

126. The regional Federal Reserve banks also tracked the growing importance of credit cards. See Johnston 1967; Dougherty 1968.

127. Evans and Schmalensee 2005: 220–21.

128. Evans and Schmalensee 2005: 82–83.

129. Headrick 2000; John 2010.

130. Cortada 2000: 211–12; Jentzsch 2007: 66.

131. See Goodstein et al. 2021: 391.

132. Stegman 2007.

133. Campbell 2016; Zinman 2014. Payday lenders have also been criticized for targeting military personnel. See Fergus 2018: 147–50.

134. See Melzer 2011; Agarwal, Skiba, and Tobacman 2009.

135. See Brooks 2006; Pew Charitable Trust 2012; Stegman 2007.

136. See Campbell et al. 2011.

137. See Mann 2014.

138. See Venkatesh 2006: 117, 121, 135, 137, 140.

139. Goldrick-Rab 2016: 40–41.

140. Berman and Stivers 2016; Tevington, Napolitano, and Furstenberg 2017: 737–38.

141. See Goldrick-Rab 2016: 2–5.

142. Avery and Turner 2012: 165.

143. See Robb, Schreiber, and Heckman 2020.

144. Lewis 1989.

145. Somers, Hollis, and Stokes 2000: 332.

146. See Zaloom 2019: 127, 146.

147. Avery and Turner 2012: 169–70.

148. See Corder and Hoffmann 2004: 186; Berman and Stivers 2016: 135–36. Sallie Mae was a pioneer in the swaps market, being the first institution to enter into an interest rate swap. See Abken 1991: 13.

149. GAO 1990: 9.

150. Somers, Hollis, and Stokes 2000: 332.

151. Guo (2010) suggests that the changes made in 2005 also had an impact on the subprime mortgage market.

152. More generally, see Quinn 2019.

153. See Dwyer, McCloud, and Hodson 2012; Bleemer et al. 2021.

154. See Cooper 2017: 217, 249; Zaloom 2019: 119.

155. Stivers and Berman 2020.

156. See, e.g., Seamster and Charron-Chénier 2017.

157. See Marron 2009: 128–29, 163–65.

158. See Poon 2007: 288. It also developed a behavioral credit scoring method for Montgomery Ward. See Lewis 1994: 122.

159. Capon 1982.

160. There is considerable cross-national variation in what kinds of information may be collected by modern credit bureaus. In some countries, privacy laws curtail the collection of information so that only information about negative actions (e.g., defaults, insolvencies, bankruptcies, etc.) can be recorded. See Jentzsch 2007.

161. E.g., Converse 1932.

162. Johnson 2005: 475.

163. One important exception, however, concerns those whose scores are close to the cutoff threshold. When dealing with a "close call" borrower, lenders have the discretion to give someone the benefit of the doubt, or not. And the exercise of such discretion is an opportunity to favor some groups over others.

164. See Myers and Forgy 1963; Smith 1964; Weingartner 1966; Chatterjee and Barcun 1970; Hand and Henley 1997; Avery et al. 2000; Hand 2005; Crook, Edelman, and Thomas 2007.

165. Avery et al. 2003: 49.

166. See Kiviat 2019; Rona-Tas 2017. The portability of credit information isn't a new thing, as evidenced by the fact that one early credit agency, the Retail Credit Company, provided information for both retailers and life insurance companies. See Flinn 1959: 75, 86, 191, 238.

167. See Lauer 2020; Zuboff 2019.

168. See Igo 2018: 229, 259; Langer and Semmelman 1988; Lauer 2017: 235; Rohner 1979.

169. There are, of course, many ways to discriminate against a group of borrowers, beyond explicitly using group membership in a formula.

170. See Chiteji 2010.

171. See Goodstein et al. 2021: 390.

172. See Cole and Handcock 1960: 125.

173. Fergus 2018.

174. See Lauer 2020.

175. Treacy and Carey 1998, 2000.

176. See Barr 2012.

177. Carruthers, Guinnane, and Lee 2012.

178. Fleming 2018.

179. Carruthers and Stinchcombe 1999.

180. See Evans and Schmalensee 2005: 82–83; Montgomerie 2006: 312–13.

181. Hyman 2011: 254.

182. See McCall and Percheski 2010; Piketty 2014; Piketty and Saez 2003.

183. E.g., Hyman 2011: 221; Leicht 2012; Rajan 2010; Prasad 2012; Turner 2016; Streeck 2014. Trumbull agrees that credit and welfare programs were linked but notes that in the United States households went deeply into debt long before wages stagnated (Trumbull 2012: 16).

184. Hyman 2011: 191, 194; Thurston 2018: 142–82.

185. Garrison 1976; Ryan, Trumbull, and Tufano 2011: 470, 483–84.

186. Geary 1976: 1641–42.

187. Cohen 2006; Firestone 2014; Hawley and Fujii 1991; Hyman 2011: 177.

188. The flip side of this process was that U.S. household savings rates declined over many decades, starting roughly in 1980. They rebounded in 2008. See Glick and Lansing 2009.

189. Bucks, Kennickell, and Moore 2006: table 10.

190. Bucks et al. 2009: A45; White 2007: 175–76.

191. Bucks, Kennickell, and Moore 2006: table 14.

192. Bricker et al. 2012: table 12; Ryan, Trumbull, and Tufano 2011: 494.

193. Credit for very wealthy families was complicated by the legal devices, like family or marriage trusts, they used to protect assets from creditors. See Tait 2019, 2020.

194. See, e.g., Kniffen 1934: 375; Prendergast 1906: 220; Prendergast and Steiner 1931: 69; Tregoe 1921: 66.

195. Caplovitz 1968: 646.

196. Hynes and Posner 2002: 177.

197. See CFPB 2015; Puchalski 2016.

Chapter 6

1. An additional qualification is often added: that the person be of the age of maturity and that they be mentally competent. Thus, promises made by insane individuals or children are treated differently.

2. Balleisen 2001: 17.

3. Although the creditworthiness of a large corporation was clearly different from that of its management, the personal character of management was still considered an important part of credit assessment of the firm. See Anonymous 1925.

4. Roughly speaking, a firm is more leveraged to the extent that it relies on debt to finance its assets.

5. By contrast, proprietorships and partnerships often involve unlimited liability.

6. It can also offer significant tax advantages, depending on the tax treatment of interest payments.

7. I set aside the issue of overall leverage within an economy and the effects of credit cycles. See Turner 2016.

8. I set aside the case of unincorporated joint-stock companies, which obviously do not have the benefits of incorporation. See Hilt 2018: 270.

9. In the Anglo-American tradition, the earliest for-profit corporations were joint-stock companies like the East India Company, Hudson's Bay Company, Massachusetts Bay Company, and Bank of England, chartered in the seventeenth century.

10. See Hilt 2017. In the case of bank charters this was known as "free banking."

11. It is important to note that even after passage of general laws of incorporation, some restrictions remained. In several antebellum Southern states, for example, the ability to incorporate was reserved for whites. See Hilt 2017: 155–56.

12. See Djelic 2013.

13. As Blumberg put it: "The doctrine of limited liability protects the ultimate investor in the enterprise from the liabilities of the enterprise in excess of the investor's capital investment" (1986: 574–75).

14. Blumberg 1986: 591–95.

15. Goodrich 1960; Majewski 1996: 769.

16. Agricultural goods typically have a low value-to-weight ratio and are subject to spoilage; thus they are sensitive to the speed and cost of transportation.

17. Goodrich 1960: 54, 63.

18. Wallis 2007.

19. Kim and Wallis 2005: 744.

20. Goods with a very high value-to-weight ratio, e.g., luxury goods, are less affected by transportation costs and so have always been traded over long distances.

21. See also Hancock 2005; Fusaro 2012.

22. For a similar phenomenon in a contemporary setting, see Macaulay 1963; Bernstein 1992; Richman 2006.

23. "Small worlds" network structures (Watts 1999) might seem to solve the problem: if there are only "six degrees of separation" between any two random people, then surely one could use social networks to build a connection to virtually anyone, anyway. However, it is one thing to know that indirect social ties exist, it is another thing to know the exact pathway, and it is quite another thing to use indirect ties to obtain credible information about someone.

24. Bryan 1883: 11.

25. Bodenhorn 2003b.

26. Nineteenth-century laws against branch banking or interstate banking ensured that most U.S. banks were very small with little capital to lend.

27. Calomiris and Ramirez 1996: 58–59; Giedeman 2005.

28. Lough 1909: 107.

29. Later in the nineteenth century, financiers began to invent hybrid forms that possessed some of the qualities of both debt and equity. Preferred stock, for example, is senior to common stock, but junior to bonds, in its claim over a company's cash flow, and may or may not have voting rights.

30. See McDaniel 1986.

31. See Cleveland 1907. Recently, bond issuances have been affected by the shift from tangible to intangible assets, which are hard to collateralize. See Rajan and Zingales 1995: 1451, 1454.

32. See generally Smith and Warner 1979.

33. Kim and Wallis 2005; Wilkins 1991.

34. Permanent telegraphic communication across the Atlantic wasn't established until the 1860s.

35. See Chandler 1954; Flandreau and Flores 2012; Hidy and Hidy 1960.

36. See Pak 2013.

37. Churella 2013: 382.

38. Greenberg 1980: 42, 130.

39. Wilkins (1991: 14) points out that U.S. railroad securities were also actively traded in the late nineteenth century on the Amsterdam Exchange.

40. See Churella 2013: 715; Tufano 1997: 7.

41. Greenberg 1980: 40; *Historical Statistics of the United States* 2006: table Df882-85.

42. Ulmer 1960: 150.

43. See Chandler 1954; Churella 2013: 177, 381. U.S. bonds were denominated in U.S. dollars, so foreign investors faced the risk of fluctuating foreign exchange values. To counter this risk, many railroad bonds contained "gold clauses" stipulating that either interest or principal (or both) was payable in gold (Wilkins 1991: 15). Moody (1909: 118) doubted the practical efficacy of such clauses, although he acknowledged that they might offer some sentimental comfort to investors.

44. O'Sullivan 2007: 495.

45. Berk 1994: 16, 26, 36; Tufano 1997: 3–4.

46. Churella 2013: 647.

47. Wilkins 1991.

48. See O'Sullivan 2007: 532. A textbook of corporate finance noted that "banks, insurance companies, and investment companies will not ordinarily purchase stocks" (Dewing 1919: 36). Such investors preferred bonds.

49. See Chandler 1956.

50. Poor 1868: 35–38.

51. Moody was already publishing financial information about railroads but decided after the 1907 crisis that summary ratings and analyses were needed in addition to statistics. See *New York Times*, May 6, 1956, p. 163.

52. The letters of the alphabet and integer numbers are ordered, and this suggests that categories with alphanumerical labels are also ordered.

53. See, e.g., Treat 1912: 405 (on credit insurance) and MacGregor 1917: 34 (on commercial banks).

54. See Zimmerman 1916b: 69.

55. Wilson 2011: 156–57.

56. See also Harold 1938: 6–7, 9.

57. *Baltimore Sun*, July 13, 1921, p. 10.

58. *New York Times*, March 19, 1919, p. 15. And again: "You can secure credit ratings through various mercantile agencies, but this [Moody's] is the only source through which you can secure 'investment' ratings on bonds and stocks" (*Wall Street Journal*, January 29, 1919, p. 1).

59. Johnson 1909: 210.

60. Johnson 1909: 211.

61. Archambault and Archambault 2005.

62. Moody 1909: 193.

63. Moody 1909: 194. Elsewhere he stated that "the ratings themselves are, of course, to be regarded in a large degree as approximations" (129).

64. Moody stated: "As position and credit among individuals is based largely on reputation for ability and past good records, so also the credit of a railroad property, other things being equal, is better where that property is in the hands of men of acknowledged ability, integrity and financial strength than where the reverse is true" (1909: 59).

65. Consistent with how much the railroads reduced transportation costs, passenger and freight rates declined over time. Moody (1909: 76) lists the rates for the Pennsylvania Railroad, noting that passenger rates (per passenger-mile) decline from 2.25 cents in 1879 to 1.92 cents in 1907, while freight rates (per ton-mile) drop from 0.82 cents to 0.58 cents.

66. Moody 1909: 16.

67. In his first attempt at rating, Moody was quite generous: 38 percent of the railroad bonds he rated in 1909 were given "Aaa," and 85 percent were rated either "A," "Aa," or "Aaa." See Wilson 2011: 158.

68. See *Wall Street Journal*, December 1, 1909.

69. An announcement in the *Salt Lake Tribune*, August 6, 1911, p. 14, noted that the public library received its new copy of Moody's Manual. That same year, the Arizona Railway Commission paid for its own subscription to Moody's, as noted in the *Arizona Republican*, September 12, 1911, p. 8.

70. Flandreau, Gaillard, and Packer 2011: 509.

71. Cantor and Packer 1994: 2; Hickman 1958: 143.

72. As a Moody's ad claimed: "Every stock or bond you own or are thinking of purchasing is 'rated.' At a glance you can tell whether your investments are good, bad or 'indifferent.'" *Philadelphia Evening Public Ledger*, April 20, 1920, p. 20.

73. Partnoy 1999: 638–39.

74. Davis, Neal, and White 2003: 130; Sivakumar and Waymire 1993: 65. The availability of information was further complicated by the fact that a firm might list its bonds on one exchange and its shares on another.

75. See *Historical Statistics of the United States* 2006: table Cj857-58. In fact, not until the 1970s did the total annual value of stocks sold on the New York Stock Exchange regularly surpass the total value of the bonds sold. As Biais and Green (2018) show, however, U.S. bond trading shifted from organized exchanges, like the New York Stock Exchange, to over-the-counter; they suggest that this was because of the growing importance of institutional investors.

76. West 1973: 161.

77. O'Sullivan 2007: 533; Ott 2011: 2.

78. Federal Reserve Board 1920: 947.

79. Flandreau, Gaillard, and Packer 2011: 499–500.

80. The economic effects of World War I encouraged international borrowers to move from London to New York. See Rippy 1950.

81. Flandreau, Gaillard, and Packer 2011: 514.

82. Dun and Bradstreet continued to dominate the rating of commercial credit through the twentieth century, using categories remarkably like their nineteenth-century versions. See Cole and Handcock 1960: chap. 24.

83. As Morton (1939b: 273) notes, securities as a proportion of total bank assets grew from 20 percent in 1914 to 39.56 percent in 1937.

84. Jones 1940: 183.

85. Hollander (1913) documents that the growth in importance of bonds as an asset class for national banks started in the nineteenth century.

86. See Harold 1938: 160–61; Federal Reserve Board 1939: 28–30. Flandreau, Gaillard, and Packer (2011) examine the poor performance of bond rating agencies during the 1930s and wonder how ratings could have been given regulatory standing in precisely the same decade. But this move was not unprecedented for the New York Federal Reserve Bank, perhaps because of its close ties to Wall Street and familiarity with current financial practices. Issued soon after the founding of the Federal Reserve System, a New York Fed circular on the topic of eligible paper (i.e., what member bank assets could be brought to the Fed discount window for rediscounting) shows that mercantile agency credit ratings factored into the determination of eligibility (Federal Reserve Bank of New York 1915). This was done without strong evidence of the predictive accuracy of credit ratings. Furthermore, rating agencies were increasingly a point of reference in U.S. courts (Flandreau and Sławatyniec 2013).

87. Osterhus 1931: 67. He also criticized market prices as a way to value bonds on the grounds that prices simply reflect the overall judgments of investors, and most investors know little. In fact, they "do not investigate carefully" (Osterhus 1931: 110). See also Pénet 2019: 90–92.

88. Morton 1939b: 277; Harold 1938: 26; Jones 1940: 187.

89. See Federal Reserve Bank of New York 1930: 92.

90. Morton 1939b: 280; Jones 1940: 194.

91. In addition to protecting bank assets from the collapse of the bond market, this measure also put a special premium on high ratings.

92. Atkins 1938; Palyi 1938: 70; Comptroller of the Currency 1937: 21–22.

93. Federal Reserve Board 1936: 422–23.

94. Atkins 1938: 14.

95. Palyi 1938: 73.

96. Simonson and Hempel 1993: 255.

97. Bach (1949: 275–76) also notes the regulatory difference between "intrinsic soundness" and "current market value," and the importance of recognizing the former during a recessionary period. See Pénet 2019: 80.

98. Federal Reserve Board 1938b: 39.

99. O'Leary 1954: 164–65. See also Fraine 1951; Bell and Fraine 1952.

100. Fons 2004.

101. See Clayton 1949. There were some minor modifications of the labels of different groups of bonds, and group 2 ("substandard" quality) securities were to be valued at market prices rather than at an eighteenth-month moving average of market prices (Federal Reserve Board 1949). Most importantly, however, highly rated bonds were not to be valued at their market prices.

102. Fons 2004: 2–3.

103. See Flandreau and Sławatyniec 2013.

104. Harold 1938: 107.

105. See Harold 1938: 126, 145, 221.

106. NBER 1941, part 1: 1.

107. NBER 1941, part 1: 3.

108. NBER 1941, part 2: 14. It is interesting to note that in its analyses the project's researchers used the median, or mean, of the bond ratings (NBER 1941, part 3: 25). Since there were only three rating agencies, use of an aggregate measure of central tendency is somewhat odd. It may be that the purpose was to avoid "singling out" any particular rating agency or to avoid making comparisons among them.

109. See, e.g., Hickman 1953, 1957, 1958.

110. Hickman 1957: 12, 15.

111. Later on, the rating agencies themselves published large-scale quantitative analyses of how bond performance varied by rating and over a range of time horizons. For example, Moody's first corporate bond default study was published in 1989 (Fons 2004: 5).

112. Grant 1941.

113. West 1973: 162.

114. Hunt 2011.

115. SEC 1994.

116. Flanagan 2001: 223.

117. Cunningham and Werlen 1996; Gregory 2010: 65–66; ISDA 1996: 11, 20, 49–50.

118. ISDA 2010: table 4.2. For a discussion of why the rating agencies maintained their central role post-crisis, see Sinclair 2021.

119. Graham, Leary, and Roberts 2015; Stearns 1986.

120. Graham, Leary, and Roberts 2015: fig. 1.

121. Frank and Goyal 2009; Myers 2001.

122. Frank and Goyal 2003; Myers and Majluf 1984.

123. Myers 2001: 82.

124. Apkarian 2018: 88–89.

125. Mintz and Schwartz 1986; Mizruchi and Stearns 1994: 135.

126. Uzzi 1999; Uzzi and Lancaster 2003.

127. Kahle and Stulz 2017: 80.

128. Rajan and Zingales 1995: 1448.

129. Moody 1920: 78.

130. Reed 1920; Mahoney 2003.

131. Sanders 1937, 1936.

132. The information problems posed by small and medium-sized firms offers one explanation for relationship-based bank lending. See Uzzi 1999.

133. See Barth 2009: 22–28; Bord and Santos 2012; Cetorelli and Peristiani 2012; Kronovet 1997; Davis 2009.

134. Bozanic, Loumioti, and Vasvari (2018) find that securitized business loans have more standardized loan covenants, suggesting that standardization is a prerequisite for securitization.

135. Davis and Mizruchi 1999.

136. Benmelech and Dlugosz 2010: 168–69.

137. One exotic example involves the securitization of the royalty revenues from rock star David Bowie's pre-1990 recordings, resulting in so-called "Bowie bonds."

138. Benmelech and Dlugosz 2010; SEC 2012: 7–12.

139. See Comptroller of the Currency 1997: 12–23.

140. Cetorelli and Peristiani 2012: 56.

141. Harold 1938; Hickman 1957.

142. E.g., Standard and Poor's 2015.

143. See Coffee 2006: chap. 8.

Chapter 7

1. See Dickerson 2014: 1–2, 19–20.

2. The *Oxford English Dictionary* records a usage of the word "mortgage" as far back as the fourteenth century, and etymologically it derives from Anglo-Norman.

3. Furthermore, the collateral lien may have to be "perfected" to be fully enforceable, which in many states means the creditor's interest in the collateral has to be registered with some government agency.

4. In the antebellum South, slaves were another important type of security for loans to slave owners and the amount of loans secured by property in humans often exceeded that secured by real estate. See Woodman 1995: 4; Martin 2010. As valuable property, slaves were also insured by slave owners (Murphy 2005).

5. See Carruthers and Ariovich 2010: fig. 4.2.

6. For some of the history of land registration systems, see Nissenson 1939a, 1939b. Eventually, the possibility that a borrower didn't really own the property became an insurable risk, with the advent of title insurance. See Rosenberg 1977.

7. See Bogue, Cannon, and Winkle 2003: 423.

8. This issue had to worry British investors in U.S. mortgages after several states passed laws prohibiting foreign ownership of land. Under such circumstances, British creditors couldn't seize land used as collateral. See Davis and Cull 1994: 31, 51–52.

9. This is why "perfecting" a lien usually involves filing paperwork with a public agency. Once perfected, a lien becomes visible to others.

10. Recently, some contemporary mortgages didn't require any down payment (i.e., the loan-to-value ratio was 100 percent), but after 2008 this became rarer.

11. One exception concerned passage of various state-level foreclosure moratoria, usually after some financial crisis drove up loan defaults.

12. See Goodman 1993; Morantz 2006.

13. See Bogue 1976: 81. For a midcentury description of mortgages, see "History of Mortgages," *Bankers' Magazine and Statistical Register*, January 1857, pp. 513–19.

14. Silsby 1960: 13.

15. E.g., Morrison 1980: 268.

16. Snowden (2013: 11) points out that nationally chartered banks were prohibited from investment in mortgages, and state banks were strongly constrained by the real bills doctrine. Nevertheless, some state-chartered banks did make mortgage loans. See Shaw 2019: 21.

17. In the mid-1870s, for example, mortgages constituted about half of the total assets of U.S. life insurance companies. See *Historical Statistics of the United States* 2006: table Cj741-47.

18. Thornton 2007: 571–72, 589–90. See Bogue 1976: 73 for a summary of the activities of the New York Life Insurance and Trust Company.

19. See Ladin 1967; Severson 1962.

20. For a useful overview of the legalities of farm mortgages, see Robins 1916.

21. See also Snowden 1987; Bogue 1976; Holmes 1893: table 9. These regional differences are consistent with those of other interest rates and reflect, among other things, the non-integration of the domestic capital market (Davis 1965). Lending depended on geographical distance.

22. The length of mortgages was slightly lower for farms than for houses. See Snowden 1987: 675.

23. Snowden 2013: 29.

24. See also Bogue 1976: 73–74; Levy 2012: 83.

25. See Snowden 2013: 11–13.

26. See also Bogue 1955; Heller and Houdek 2004; Morrison 1980.

27. See Bogue 1953; Brewer 1976; Woodruff 1937: 3, 14.

28. Bogue 1953: 34.

29. Since there was no "tranching," mortgage debentures did not offer the advantage of seniority. See Levy 2012: 151.

30. See Bogue 1953: 46–48; Snowden 2013: 19–20.

31. See, e.g., Bensel 1990; Ritter 1997; Carruthers and Babb 1996; DeCanio 2011.

32. Of course, it chartered and oversaw national banks, and intermittently put a federal bankruptcy law in place.

33. See Palmer 1916; Shaw 2018b.

34. Engberg 1931: 133.

35. Murray 1935: 614.

36. See Black 1928: 108–9; Snowden 2013: 22–25. Their ability to do so depended on the laws of the particular state in which they were incorporated, and these varied from one state to the next.

37. Bogue 1976: 94.

38. Snowden 2013: 47.

39. *Historical Statistics of the United States* 2006: table Aa36-92.

40. Holmes 1894: 54.

41. Bryant 1956: 111.

42. Snowden 1988: 278.

43. See Mason 2004: 18, 24. Consider the claim that "the man who is striving to earn, save and pay for the home, when he has accomplished it, will be a better man, a better artisan or clerk, a better husband and a better citizen" (Dexter 1891: 144).

44. Dexter 1891: 141–42.

45. Mason 2012: 385.

46. Mason 2004: 54.

47. Snowden 1997: 229.

48. According to Snowden (1997: table 1), in the 1890s the memberships of building and loan associations usually numbered in the hundreds, and rarely exceeded one thousand.

49. Snowden 2013: 56.

50. Mason 2004: 59.

51. Mason 2012: 392.

52. See Snowden 2013: 56, 58. Through the latter nineteenth century, mortgage loans were the single biggest asset category for insurance companies (Saulnier 1950: 10).

53. Fisher 1950: 310; Saulnier 1950: 80.

54. Alston 1984.

55. See Poteat 1938. Similar measures had been put in place in the nineteenth century. For example, many states passed homestead exemption laws, which prevented the seizure of real estate in payment of debts (Goodman 1993).

56. Murray 1935: 614.

57. See Snowden 2013: 76–77; Fishback 2017: 1479. HOLC used one of the credit agencies, the Retail Credit Company (which eventually became Equifax), to get credit reports on individual homeowners. See Flinn 1959: 262.

58. These risk maps strongly favored homogeneously white neighborhoods over areas that were racially integrated or dominated by African Americans. See Aaronson, Hartley, and Mazumder 2020; Hillier 2005.

59. Bell 1938: 510, 512. See also French 1941; McDonough 1934; Tough 1951.

60. Trumbull 2014: 28–31.

61. Hyman 2011: 63–67; Weimer 1937.

62. See *Historical Statistics of the United States* 2006: table Dc1105-21.

63. Green and Wachter 2005: 96.

64. See *Historical Statistics of the United States* 2006: table Dc1105-21.

65. According to Fishback et al. 2011: 1785, housing prices dropped 30–40 percent from 1929 to 1933.

66. The term "intrinsic value" was seldom defined, but from usage it seems to refer to the pre-crisis price.

67. See Stuart 2003: 46; Fishback et al. 2011: 1788.

68. Some states set up their own deposit insurance schemes, but these were unsuccessful (White 1981; Dehejia and Lleras-Muney 2007) and undermined by adverse selection and moral hazard problems (Wheelock and Wilson 1995). See the discussion in chapter 4 in this book.

69. See *Historical Statistics of the United States* 2006: table Cj504-10.

70. See *Historical Statistics of the United States* 2006: table Cb64-70.

71. However, when inflation and interest rates were high, Regulation Q inadvertently encouraged the search for alternative investments (like NOW accounts, money market accounts, or certificates of deposit) because depositing money in a savings account was such a terrible financial option. Thus, interest rate regulations contributed to the flow of funds out of savings-and-loan institutions in the 1970s and 1980s.

72. There was, of course, a substantial and durable difference between homeownership rates among white and black families. See Collins and Margo 2011.

73. See Bryant 1956: 116–17, 121, 134.

74. See Freund 2007: 99, 148, 178, 205. On the more general pattern whereby U.S. federal policy is often kept as low profile as possible, see Mettler 2011.

75. Rose and Snowden 2013.

76. See French 1941: 62; Stuart 2003.

77. See Green and Wachter 2005: 95; Fishback et al. 2011: 1788; French 1941: 63.

78. Deductions for interest payments preceded World War II, but since very few people paid federal income taxes this measure benefited only a very few. Once the personal income tax became

a "mass tax," however, the mortgage interest deduction eventually became one of the biggest tax expenditures and a substantial government benefit for the middle class (Howard 1993, 1997).

79. Meredith 1950: 318.

80. For a discussion of the legal variations in mortgages across states and territories at the end of the nineteenth century, see Jones 1889, 1:17–37. For a survey of legal variations in the early twentieth century, see Birdseye 1924: 1629–1718.

81. As with many other standard-form contracts, the "boilerplate" provisions of the mortgage were set by the lender. The borrower might negotiate over some of the contract terms (interest rate, amount, and maturity), but a great deal of the contractual content was set on a take-it-or-leave-it basis by the lender.

82. See Carruthers and Stinchcombe 1999; Carrozzo 2005.

83. As Stuart (2003: 34, 54, 66) points out, the original valuational criteria adopted by the FHA (borrowed from the real estate industry) were highly discriminatory and, in effect, devalued homes in minority-dominated or racially mixed neighborhoods. The long-term implications for racial segregation in housing were profound. For example, the 1936 underwriting manual instructed: "The Valuator should investigate areas surrounding the location to determine whether or not incompatible racial and social groups are present, to the end that an intelligent prediction may be made regarding the possibility or probability of the location being invaded by such groups" (FHA 1936, part 2: 233).

84. See, e.g., FHA 1947, paragraphs 1602(3), 1603(1–2), 1635(2).

85. See also Meredith 1950.

86. It did so at various points in the 1960s, countering the effects of "credit crunches." See Murray 1972: 444.

87. See Downs 1991; Weber 2015: 56.

88. See generally White 1993; Pontell and Calavita 1993; Calavita, Pontell, and Tillman 1997; Calavita, Tillman, and Pontell 1997.

89. Brewer 1976. Snowden (2010) points out that the underlying assets remained on the balance sheet of the lender, unlike with modern securitizations.

90. See Black, Garbade, and Silber 1981; DiVenti 2009. For details on how these early securitizations worked, see Strine 1978.

91. See Freund 2007: 178, 205, 382.

92. Acharya et al. 2011: 17; Quinn 2017.

93. Early on, securitization was particularly aimed at institutional investors like public pension funds, which up to that point put little of their money in real estate. See Brennan 1970: 403.

94. By 1990, the totals for outstanding mortgage-backed securities were $403 billion and $316 billion, respectively, for Ginnie Mae and Freddie Mac. See *Historical Statistics of the United States* 2006: table Dc1170-91.

95. Good summaries of the basic mechanics of securitization include Hill 1997, Soukup 1996, and Shenker and Colletta 1991.

96. Vinokurova 2018: 630.

97. I have constructed this example with farm mortgages because, in fact, these formed the basis for securitization during the 1870s. See Brewer 1976; Snowden 2013.

98. See Soukup 1996; Rappaport and Wyatt 1993; Coval, Jurek, and Stafford 2009.

99. See Fligstein 2021.

100. Carrozzo 2005: 799.

101. See Agarwal et al. 2011; Piskorski, Seru, and Vig 2010.

102. On mortgage services generally, see Odinet 2019.

103. Odinet 2019: 44–45.

104. See Kruger 2018.

105. Typically raters are paid by the investment bank doing the securitization, under the "issuer pays" model. This business model replaced the older one, where users of rating information paid for it, in the early 1970s.

106. A clear example comes from the AAA-rated securities created out of subprime mortgages. The use of tranches helps make this alchemical transformation possible, but so do various other "credit enhancements," including creation of an "equity tranche" to absorb the first round of losses.

107. Admittedly there was some bad publicity for bond rating agencies following the Enron scandal.

108. See SEC 2008; MacKenzie 2011.

109. Collins and Margo 2011: 356.

110. Collins 2006: 15.

111. See Sugrue 2005: 55 on the situation in Detroit, and Drake and Cayton 1945: 61, 204, 206–7 on Chicago. DuBois also claims that blacks were suspicious of banks and building and loan associations, two institutions that could have helped encourage savings and grant access to mortgages. See DuBois 1996: 295.

112. See Garrett-Scott 2019: 140.

113. It should be noted that although the United States is distinctive for the high level of public intervention into home mortgage markets, it does not produce the highest levels of homeownership. General homeownership rates are much higher in countries like Spain, Ireland, and Chile (Acharya et al. 2011: table 7.2).

114. See Thurston 2018.

115. Freund 2007: 180–81.

116. FHA 1936, part 1, paragraph 215.

117. FHA 1936, part 1, paragraph 209.

118. A contemporary text states: "This supports the sociological truth that contentment of living is present in greater abundance in that circumstance where the inhabitants of a particular district have the same level of income, social attributes, ethnics, culture, and education. Where this ideal situation is observed in the structure of a neighborhood, there will also be found, as its product, a marked stability of realty values" (May 1942: 90). See also Rothstein 2017: 21.

119. Freund 2007: 45, 59, 230, 232; Rothstein 2017: 39–57.

120. Rothstein 2017: 65, 70; Shertzer, Twinam, and Walsh 2016.

121. FHA 1936, part 1, paragraph 323(3).

122. FHA 1936, part 2, paragraph 233. Consider the discussion in May's book on real estate valuation: "From this we may generalize that, in the city that houses a large percentage of people of foreign birth, or their children, or that contains a substantial minority percentage of people of races other than white, residential real estate values in the older districts bordering those at present inhabited by the minority peoples will exist in a state of threatened status quo" (1942: 75).

123. FHA 1936, part 2, paragraph 229.

124. FHA 1936, part 2, paragraph 284(3). Again, FHA policy mirrored industry practice. Consider another industry organization's discussion of valuation: "In addition to the zoning ordinance, there may be certain restrictions in the deed limiting use of the property. Thus a residential lot may have been sold subject to the condition that it may not be resold to anyone who is not a member of the Caucasian race, or that it may not be developed except by the erection of a dwelling of a certain design. These restrictions should not be overlooked, because they may decidedly influence the use to which the lot may be put, and the valuation placed on the lot will have to be determined subject to the uses which zoning ordinances, building codes, and deed restrictions permit" (National Association of Real Estate Boards, chap. 1, 1927: 7). See also Sugrue 2005: 43–44.

125. FHA 1947, part 3, paragraph 1104(b).

126. FHA 1947, part 3, paragraph 1320(2).

127. It should be noted that the manual also includes a detailed discussion of the importance of the mortgager's character and personal life. "Analysis of the credit characteristics of the mortgagor requires an appraisal of (a) the mortgagor's character, (b) his family life and relationship, (c) his attitude toward obligations, and (d) his ability to manage affairs. These elements relate solely to basic attitudes such as the honesty, integrity, and to some extent the judgment of the mortgagor. Consideration of these attitudes is essential to any type of credit consideration" (FHA 1947, part 3, paragraph 1634).

128. FHA 1955, part 1, paragraph 203(2).

129. FHA 1955, part 5, paragraph 2005(3).

130. FHA 1955, part 2, paragraph 1320(2). Thurston (2018: 107–12) shows how the FHA altered its underwriting rules in response to criticism from the NAACP.

131. Braasch, Miller, and Rice 1980.

132. Thurston 2018: 4, 10.

133. See Brooks 2011; Rice 1968.

134. Jones-Correa 2000.

135. Sugrue 2005: xxxix.

136. A number of states passed "fair housing" laws before federal legislation was passed. See Collins 2006: 19.

137. See Olegario 2016: 147–48; Rohner 1979; Trumbull 2014: 168–69.

138. See Krippner 2017. On the consequences of the CRA, see Bhutta 2011; Friedman and Squires 2005.

139. See Chappell 2020: 761–62; Ulrich 1991.

140. This was the aim of Section 235 of the 1968 Housing and Urban Development Act. See Chappell 2020: 750.

141. See Taylor 2019: chaps. 4 and 5.

142. See, e.g., Munnell et al. 1996; Ladd 1998; Squires and O'Connor 2001.

143. Iceland, Weinberg, and Steinmetz 2002; Massey and Denton 1993.

144. See Acharya et al. 2011: 47, 81; Dickerson 2014. As Gorton (2010) points out, these arrangements were generally sustainable so long as housing prices were rising.

145. Subprime mortgages work well in a housing boom, where the borrower can refinance after expiration of the initial teaser rate on the basis of accumulated home equity. But when the housing bubble bursts, mortgage payments quickly become unaffordable to marginal borrowers.

146. Mayer, Pence, and Sherlund 2009.

147. Quinn 2017: 75.

148. For overviews, see Brueggeman and Fisher 2018: chaps. 9, 15; Weber 2015: 42–49. For evidence that these have been long-standing factors, see Harris 1930.

149. Of course, state and municipal governments play an important role in encouraging development through the provision of local infrastructure, zoning rules, building codes, or specialized tax policies like TIFs (tax increment financing). And specific provisions of the federal tax code have played a role in steering investment into real estate; see Weiss 1989: 260.

150. These are called "commercial mortgage-backed securities." See Fabozzi, Shiller, and Tunaru 2020: 129; Gotham 2006: 262; Weber 2015: 58–60.

151. See Gotham 2006: 248–50.

152. See Weber 2015: 19, 31, 55; Sahling 1991.

153. Figure 5.1 in Acharya et al. 2011 shows well the long-term growth in U.S. mortgage debt.

154. See Acharya et al. 2011: 82.

155. Massey and Denton 1993; Thurston 2018.

156. See Krippner 2017; Thurston 2018: 142–82.

157. Kahle and Stulz 2017: 74–75.

158. If loans collateralized by real estate represent a very old type of secured lending, "repo," i.e., short-term loans collateralized by financial securities, represents a very new type of secured lending. In the last several decades, repo has become an important means for banks to finance themselves, especially as compared to deposits. See Gabor 2016; Garbade 2006.

159. See Massey and Denton 1993.

Chapter 8

1. See, e.g., Kagan et al. 1977: 133–34, 137; McIntosh 1981: 830–31; Rosen 1997; Stookey 1992: 36–37.

2. Homestead exemption laws allowed individuals to keep some of their property even if they were still indebted. For example, personal clothing, a bed and bedding, and the family Bible were exempted from seizure in many states (see Wells 1867: 288–316).

3. See, e.g., Bankers Encyclopedia Co. 1912: 1907–24; Mercantile Agency 1872: 97–110; Moses 1879; Wells 1867.

4. See Richter 1968.

5. See Gray (1986: 160) for evidence on state adoption of the Uniform Consumer Credit Code. See Llewellyn 1957 and Braucher 1958 on the rationale for the Uniform Commercial Code and its legislative history.

6. Cole and Handcock (1960: 324–42), Griffin (1927: 31–43, 97–107), and Parmalee (1914: 106–13) give a range of options for in-house collection departments.

7. If an out-of-state debtor were involved, creditors might also ask a mercantile agency to recommend an attorney to assist with debt collection, and the agency would in turn suggest the name of one of its informants or correspondents.

8. Birkhead 1941.

9. See Anonymous 1957; Eubank 1916; Krumbein 1924; Lothian 1938.

10. See the discussion in chapter 5 in this book.

11. Geltzer and Woocher 1982.

12. Rothschild 1979.

13. See Kinne 1842.

14. As reported in the *New York Times* (November 27, 1857, p. 4): "The principle has been pretty generally adopted in England, in legislating on bankruptcy, that the great, and in fact the only object to be kept in view, was the surrender of all the debtor's assets, and their fair division amongst the creditors."

15. In this way, the cultural valorization of entrepreneurship is linked to more rehabilitative versions of bankruptcy.

16. See Sullivan, Warren, and Westbrook 2006.

17. As one analyst put it: "Then would begin a mad race for precedence between executions, attachments, etc.—between the sheriff, receiver, assignee and mortgagee—to see which one would get possession of the debtor's property first. . . . Under the stern rule of the Bankruptcy Law, however, this wild scramble for precedence has ceased and cooperation among creditors has become the order of the day" (Remington 1909: 593).

18. Hansen 1998: 95.

19. As an example, business failures in New York City were reported in the newspaper, and listed by the name of the proprietor, their assets, and liabilities (*New York Times*, January 1, 1878, p. 2). In every case but one (a butcher) the assets were less than the liabilities.

20. *New York Times*, January 16, 1871, p. 2.

21. *Merchants' Magazine and Commercial Review*, November 1, 1844, p. 481. The *Massachusetts Ploughman and New England Journal of Agriculture* (October 12, 1844, p. 4) also heaped commendation on the same James Read.

22. For example, in the mid-nineteenth century insolvent married debtors could protect property from creditors by transferring title to their wives, who otherwise were used to help maintain the appearance of solvency. See Foroughi 2003: 1016.

23. *New York Times*, July 24, 1878, p. 2. In 1905, the *Times* reported an even more elaborate criminal scheme where new businesses were founded and purchased as many goods as they could on credit only to fail after transferring assets to their relatives and creating a set of false accounts to mislead unhappy creditors (*New York Times*, March 17, 1905, p. 16).

24. Similarly, *Dun's Review* asserted that "it must be realized that many failures will occur, no matter how sound the business situation, nor how bright the outlook. This may be considered the normal death rate" (*Dun's Review International Edition*, March 1903, p. 17).

25. The *Baltimore Sun* (August 6, 1860, p. 1) discussed the failure of Jacob Little, a Wall Street titan and the "shrewdest of men": "The failures of Jacob Little contain a valuable lesson for others. If ruin overtakes such a man as Jacob Little in Wall [S]treet, how should men of lesser minds hope to escape bankruptcy?"

26. Here I am setting aside situations exemplified by the Broadway comedy and movie *The Producers*, where people set out deliberately to fail.

27. *Detroit Free Press*, January 16, 1878, p. 2.

28. See Kornai 1992.

29. For example, demand deposits are highly liquid assets.

30. Examples of modern illiquid assets include some kinds of real estate, artworks, antiques, and over-the-counter derivatives.

31. See Carruthers and Halliday 1998: 35–42.

32. Which assets belong to the bankrupt firm isn't always a straightforward matter. For example, in the nineteenth century the separate property of an insolvent debtor's wife was in some danger of being swept into the bankruptcy estate and used to pay the husband's creditors. More recently, the task of identifying assets and liabilities has been complicated by the growing use of exchange-traded and over-the-counter financial derivatives, whose economic value can change on a daily basis (i.e., a particular position can switch from positive to negative very quickly).

33. As Balleisen (2001: 81) points out, state laws for the collection of debts very much favored those who acted first.

34. Limited liability capped the losses of shareholders of the insolvent corporation to the extent of their investment.

35. Of course, debtors can and do reorganize outside of the bankruptcy court. But how such a reorganization might unfold inside the court sets the backdrop for informal renegotiation of debts.

36. See Mann 2002: 79.

37. The list of non-dischargeable debts evolves over time. In the 1898 bankruptcy act, secured debts were non-dischargeable. Thanks to the 2005 revisions of federal bankruptcy law, credit card debts became more difficult to discharge. Today, student debts are presumptively non-dischargeable, and can be discharged only if the debtor demonstrates in court that the debts impose "undue hardship." On the history of the discharge, see Tabb 1991.

38. In this way, seniority among creditors resembles the seniority within the different tranches of a mortgage-backed security.

39. It probably helped that many of the creditors were overseas, in England, and that the debtors were domestic.

40. On the verge of a new bankruptcy law, the *New York Times* (November 2, 1857, p. 4) remarked: "There can be no doubt that most of the existing prejudice against a bankruptcy law is justified by the experience of the country. The act of 1841 is still fresh in people's memory, and next to its being a piece of special legislation, none of its incidents is remembered more vividly than its wholesale discharge of all the debtors who chose to avail themselves of it, and the ludicrously small dividends which came into the hands of creditors, under its operation."

41. See, e.g., Bailey 1893; Hansen 1998.

42. See Hansen and Hansen 2012. Such laws allowed a creditor to appropriate some proportion of the debtor's earnings directly at their place of employment.

43. Skeel 2001: 25. Thus, as Balleisen (2001: 69) notes: "For sixty-seven of the seventy-two years between the ratification of the Constitution and the outbreak of the civil war, American debtors and their creditors received neither guidance nor aid from a national bankruptcy system."

44. Carruthers and Halliday 1998: 254–55.

45. See Alston 1984; Balleisen 2001: 12; Poteat 1938; Skeel 2001: 25. Today, because of the Covid-19 pandemic, new political measures have been taken to provide forbearance to debtors, particularly the CARES Act of 2020.

46. It is interesting to note that the Act explicitly refers to debtors using both male and female pronouns (see Gross, Newman, and Campbell 1996).

47. Mann 2002: 223.

48. Sandage 2005: 30.

49. When the promotor and later circus manager P. T. Barnum failed, the *Chicago Tribune* (February 22, 1856, p. 2) commented: "For the parties who suffer by the failure of this prince of humbugs, we are bound, in christian kindness, to feel proper commiseration; but all the tears lie in an onion that will be shed over the pecuniary ruin of Barnum himself. . . . We are glad of his failure, and we hope its moral may not pass unheeded."

50. See Ditz 1994: 58; Mann 2002: 3, 99. In the early eighteenth century, Daniel Defoe had made clear the importance of credit: "Credit, next to real stock, is the foundation, the life and soul, of business in a private tradesman; it is his prosperity" (Defoe 1987: 233). Equally, he underscored the challenge and importance of maintaining a good reputation: "A tradesman's reputation is of the nicest nature imaginable; like a blight upon a fine flower, if it is but touched, the beauty of it, or the flavour of it, or the seed of it, is lost" (Defoe 1987: 135).

51. See Boardman 1853: 185.

52. Balleisen 2001: 77–78.

53. Sandage 2005: 55, 198.

54. Mann 2002: 59.

55. *American Jurist and Law Magazine*, April 1830, p. 201.

56. See Beckert 2015: 286–87, and the discussion in chapter 5 in this book.

57. Balleisen 2001: 173–76.

58. See the *New York Daily Tribune*, January 4, 1844.

59. Dun began publishing summary tables in the late 1850s. See, e.g., the January 1858 *Annual Circular* from the Office of the Mercantile Agency, which covered failures for 1857.

60. They were explicit about not tracking the failure of individuals or non-commercial entities.

61. By contrast, newspapers might simply list the names of people who had applied for bankruptcy relief and/or their assets. See, e.g., *Baltimore Sun*, February 11, 1842, p. 1; *New York Herald Tribune*, February 19, 1842, p. 1; *Chicago Tribune*, August 28, 1878, p. 3.

62. *Bradstreet's*, January 26, 1901, p. 50.

63. *Dun's Review*, January 5, 1901, pp. 8–9.

64. Among other things, these tables were published even before the invention of simple statistics like the correlation coefficient (1895) or the student's t (1908).

65. E.g., *Bradstreet's*, October 8, 1887, p. 662, January 21, 1905, p. 35, February 2, 1918, p. 77. Of course, Bradstreet's wasn't providing the full distribution of outcomes, and so readers couldn't find out whether most of the firms that didn't fail had also been given low ratings.

66. *Bradstreet's*, February 2, 1918, p. 78.

67. *Bradstreet's*, January 26, 1901, p. 50.

68. This was done before the invention of public national income statistics or even the descriptive work on business cycles done by the National Bureau of Economic Research, so there were few other ways for people or investors to comprehend the state of the U.S. macroeconomy.

69. Note that eighty years later, the same business publication was still discussing business failures using the figures provided by Dun and Bradstreet (see *Commercial and Financial Chronicle* 185, no. 5624 [March 28, 1957]: 1495).

70. The *Financial Times* states: "As regards the vast area covered by its operations, its data are as full as if they had been gathered together by a Government department, and the utmost reliance may be placed on the accuracy of the statistics." In the early twentieth century, another leading business publication, the *Economist*, reproduced summary failure statistics from Bradstreet's (see, e.g., the May 15, 1915 issue), as did the *Wall Street Journal* (e.g., on July 8, 1908, p. 8).

71. The example, the *Federal Reserve Bulletin* of February 1, 1919, explicitly cites R. G. Dun in a discussion of commercial failures (see p. 128). The *Bulletin* does so again in March, July, and October of that same year. The July 1, 1917, issue of the *Bulletin* combined Federal Reserve classifications with R. G. Dun failure statistics to produce a table showing the number of failures and corresponding liabilities in each Federal Reserve district (p. 520). And in 1935, during the Great Depression, the January *Bulletin* still looked to Dun to provide definitive measures of commercial failure (p. 68).

72. See, e.g., the extensive discussion in *Bradstreet's: A Journal of Trade, Finance, and Public Economy* (February 3, 1883) of the failure of the Union Iron and Steel Company of Chicago. Readers were provided details about the company's assets and liabilities, as well as the circumstances (low prices for its products combined with rising labor costs) driving it into insolvency. Two weeks later, on February 17, *Bradstreet's* recorded the collapse of Rogers and Company, another Chicago firm, which had done a large business with Union and wasn't able to survive the latter's failure. Clearly, failure was infectious.

73. See *Bradstreet's*, January 26, 1901, pp. 52–53.

74. *Bradstreet's*, February 2, 1918, p. 77.

75. *Dun's Review International Edition*, March 1903, p. 6.

76. It is telling that for measures of business failure, i.e., the numbers and liabilities of failed businesses, the official *Historical Statistics of the United States* relies on data provided by Dun and Bradstreet.

77. Dun observed that there was no way to get accurate estimates of the unemployment rate, although such a measure could, like its published failure statistics, give a measure of the overall economy (*Dun's Review International Edition*, March 1903, p. 18).

78. See Friedman 2014.

79. See Carson 1975; Kendrick 1970; Ruggles 1959.

80. See Skeel 2001: 53.

81. Berk 1994: 7, 47; Tabb 1995: 22.

82. Berk 1994: 65; Churella 2013: 647.

83. The business failure rate was at a high level in the 1890s and reached a peak in 1896. See *Historical Statistics of the United States* 2006: table Ch408-13.

84. See Smith 2010a: 10, 137–41, 151.

85. See also Prendergast 1906: 261, 300.

86. *Chicago Tribune*, April 18, 1892, p. 10.

87. See Lapp 1910; Smith and Chalmers 1916. This movement culminated in the creation of the Uniform Commercial Code and attempted to reconcile the political fact of federalism with the economic attractions of predictable and standardized commercial law.

88. Anonymous 1898.

89. Hansen 1998: 93.

90. Tabb 1995: 19.

91. See Prendergast and Steiner 1931: 399. One might think that credit ratings and credit insurance were competing ways to manage credit risk, but in fact they were complementary: credit insurance companies depended on ratings to price insurance and set limits.

92. Ackerman and Neuner 1924: 8, 52; Trapp 1953: 6. In measuring the risk of default, and in pricing their products, credit insurance companies relied on the ratings provided by the mercantile agencies like Dun's and Bradstreet's. See Ackerman and Neuner 1924: 21; Federal Reserve Board 1922: 27–30.

93. Hansen 1998.

94. Tabb 1995: 23.

95. Remington 1909: 591–92.

96. See National Association of Manufacturers 1909: 154–57.

97. As Tabb (1995: 27) notes, repeal attempts were launched in 1902, 1903, 1909, and 1910, but all failed.

98. See Smith 2010a: 174; Tabb 1995: 27. Previously, corporations were not deemed eligible because they were chartered at the state level, not the federal level (Skeel 2001: 54).

99. Business failure rates rose sharply in 1930 and reached a peak in 1932 (see *Historical Statistics of the United States* 2006: table Ch408-13), and nonfarm mortgage foreclosure rates also rose dramatically, peaking in 1933 (see *Historical Statistics of the United States* 2006: table Dc1255-70).

100. Heuston 1938. Bank failure was treated separately, and was administered by the relevant federal regulatory agency, in the case of federally chartered banks, or state agency, in the case of state-chartered banks. Eventually, with the establishment of federal deposit insurance, FDIC became the main agency that dealt with insolvent banks, just as FSLIC dealt with insolvent savings-and-loans.

101. See Douglas 1938; Rostow and Cutler 1939; Tabb 1995: 29–30. According to Rostow and Cutler (1939: 1336), the National Association of Credit Men played a large role in the design of Chapter XI.

102. Skeel 2001: 165.

103. Carruthers and Halliday 1998.

104. See Delaney 1992.

105. Including, in particular, the Chief Justice of the Supreme Court Warren Burger. See Skeel 2001: 158; Carruthers and Halliday 1998: 86, 102.

106. Carruthers and Halliday 1998: 471–74; Skeel 2001: 180.

107. See Canner and Elliehausen 2013: 7; Johnson 2005: 474. Unlike other types of debt, credit card debt is typically unsecured (i.e., there is no collateral), is not tied to the purchase of a particular good (unlike installment loans), and offers flexible repayment (the cardholder can pay off the entire balance each month, or pay only the minimum and still remain "current").

108. See Sullivan, Warren, and Westbrook 2000.

109. See Johnson 2005: 477.

110. Sullivan, Warren, and Westbrook 2006; White 2007: 177–78.

111. Certain other types of personal debt remained non-dischargeable, e.g., student loans, federal taxes, child-support payments.

112. See Federal Reserve Bank of New York 2014: 14. Of course, after the global financial crisis of 2008 personal bankruptcy filings increased sharply.

113. Under Chapter 7, the bankrupt debtor had to use their assets to repay their debts whereas under Chapter 13 the debtor had only to devote future income to the repayment of debts. In addition, more debts were dischargeable under Chapter 13. Some debtors filed first under Chapter 7 and then converted their case into a Chapter 13 proceeding. See White 2007: 183–84.

114. ISDA is an industry organization, established in the 1980s by the world's largest banks operating in the global swaps market. The market is dominated by interest rate and currency swaps,

but also includes more complex transactions like credit default swaps. On ISDA, see Flanagan 2001. On the history of "safe harbor" treatment of derivatives, see Schwarcz and Sharon 2014.

115. See Charles 2009; Edwards and Morrison 2005; Harding 2010: 406–7.

116. Bodenhorn (2003a) shows how "relationship banking" meant a greater likelihood that a bank would renegotiate its loans with its customers during a credit crunch.

117. See Odinet 2019 on the role of mortgage servicers in making renegotiations difficult.

118. For a discussion of how private contracting adapted to postbellum inflation, see Dawson and Cooper 1935.

119. See *Historical Statistics of the United States* 2006: table Cc1-2.

120. See Smith 2006: 1044. Frieden (1997) shows how Populist monetary politics were shaped by concerns about price stability and trade.

121. Lehmann 1950: 242.

122. Their financial difficulties, as well as creditor responses, are well described in Anonymous 1934.

123. For a detailed discussion of the recent bankruptcy experience of Detroit, see Hyman 2020.

124. See, e.g., Greenberg 1978: 269–70; Kevane 2011; Lehmann 1950: 244; Morrison 2002: 573–74.

Chapter 9

1. Raymond 1932: 13.

2. Very recent developments in global sovereign debt markets have centered around the import of the "pari passu" clause for bonds, the potential use of seniority and "tranches" to enhance the creditworthiness of risky sovereign borrowers, and the privileged status of lenders like the IMF and ECB, but such considerations mostly didn't matter in the United States (see Brunnermeier et al. 2017; Steinkamp and Westermann 2014). For lower levels of government, bonds might be differentiated if they were backed by different earmarked revenue streams (e.g., gas taxes vs. sales taxes).

3. See McInnes 1938; Weil 1907.

4. Bahl and Duncombe 1993; Trissell 1995: 1027.

5. Taylor 1959: 103.

6. See Raymond 1932: 48–49. For some, the racial composition of a community affected its creditworthiness. Raymond (1932: 78–79) notes that some states have a relatively large "negro population" and then asserts: "If these people were allowed to vote and have their votes counted, as they are entitled to by the Federal Constitution, they would be a serious menace to the credit of the respective States." This perceived connection between the racial makeup of a community and its economic standing mirrors that undergirding the valuation of real estate and home mortgage lending (see chapter 7 in this book).

7. One commentator called it "the policy of burdening the future" (Dillon 1876: 6).

8. See Edling 2014: 13.

9. The obvious exception concerns Civil War funding, which I discuss later. A less obvious but telling exception concerns "war debt" incurred by the State of California in the 1850s to fund military operations against indigenous civilian populations. See Madley 2016: 190, 207, 230, 253–54.

10. Obviously, states can also generate revenue to repay debts by selling off publicly owned assets, but with the exception of public land in the nineteenth century, this tends to be a once-only strategy.

11. Such public financing operations go by the quasi-religious terms of "conversion" and "redemption."

12. For example, in an economy dominated by subsistence farmers, an income tax would likely not generate very much revenue.

13. Loosely, this was one of the intuitions behind the Laffer Curve: cutting tax rates would so unleash economic growth that tax revenues would themselves grow.

14. Sylla, Legler, and Wallis 1987.

15. Wallis 2005.

16. For example, funds generated by the sale of bonds in November 1832 helped the State of Ohio pay interest due to current bondholders (Scheiber 1969: 126–27).

17. See Wallis 2000: 66.

18. United States Commerce Department 1907: 131.

19. Local school and water districts also issued bonds to pay for education and infrastructure.

20. See *Historical Statistics of the United States* 2006: table Ea10-23.

21. See *Historical Statistics of the United States* 2006: table Ea125-31.

22. See Bensel 1990: 111, 124, 161, 163.

23. Similarly, corporate bonds still encumber a corporation even if it gets a new CEO.

24. Adams (1893: 8) claimed that "it is a peculiar, and at the same time a significant, fact that borrowing has never been widely practiced except by republics or by peoples possessing some form of constitutional government."

25. Adams 1893: 9.

26. The Fourteenth Amendment to the U.S. Constitution, adopted in 1868, prohibited payment of any debt incurred in aid of "insurrection or rebellion" against the United States. See McCommas 2013: 1309–12.

27. See Bensel 2000: 94–97; Lester 2013: 419–20; Ratchford 1933: 2, 4, 8; Howland 1928: 397; Raymond 1932: 63; Sexton 2005: 231–33. On the general issue of "odious debts," see Buchheit, Gulati, and Thompson 2007. On sovereign debts in the context of decolonization, see Mallard 2021; Waibel 2021.

28. See Lester 2013: 422; McGrane 1935: 282–84.

29. Consider that, for example, the *New York Times* (March 5, 1894, p. 6) listed the bid and ask prices of municipal bonds issued by major cities such Baltimore, Boston, Chicago, Cleveland, Detroit, Louisville, Milwaukee, New York, Philadelphia, Pittsburgh, Philadelphia, St. Louis, and Toledo and traded on Wall Street. This was a sign of an active secondary market in such bonds. But even small communities gained notice: the *Cincinnati Enquirer* (January 6, 1905, p. 5) reported that Warsaw, Indiana, sold $12,000 worth of bonds in order to pave its roads. The bonds were purchased by local, midwestern firms, not by Wall Street banks.

30. English 1996.

31. Fisk and Hatch 1876: 3. Such a feature would be attractive to investors who valued liquidity. By contrast, registered bonds had to be registered with the issuer and could be transferred only with the involvement of the issuer. Such bonds were harder to buy and sell, and so were less liquid, but if they were lost or stolen the rightful owner had recourse. See Fisk and Hatch 1876: 5–6.

32. On the requirement of prior voter consent more generally, see Dillon 1876: 19.

33. Coles 1871: 3–4.

34. Coles 1871: 6–9.

35. Holyoke City Treasurer 1899: 6–7.

36. Dillon 1876: 5.

37. Adams 1893: 95–96.

38. Bank of America 1922: 7–9.

39. The 1880 Census noted that some of the most important purposes for issuances of state and local bonds included railroads, streets, waterworks, and refunding old debts. See United States Census Office 1883: 1570.

40. Jenkins (2021) details these priorities in the specific case of San Francisco over the twentieth century.

41. Moussalli 2008: 174–75.

42. Adams 1893: 24.

43. Waddell 1916.

44. Bruère 1915; Lapp 1909.

45. See Rivenbark 2005: 219; Patton and Hutchison 2013: 23–26; Potts 1978; Teaford 1981: 235, 237.

46. Nanda 2014: 556.

47. Radford 2003: 874–76.

48. Balanced budget requirements are a similar kind of measure. See Nanda 2014: 559; National Conference of State Legislatures 2010.

49. Wallis 2000: 62.

50. Ratchford (1938: 694–96) lists the different state provisions extant in the late 1930s.

51. See Erie 1992: 523. According to Radford (2003: 878), most states set local government debt ceilings at 5 percent of taxable real property. New York was more like California, and set a ceiling at 10 percent of taxable real estate (Hartwell et al. 1905: 202).

52. Ratchford 1938: 701.

53. Compton 1920: 52.

54. See Eastman 1959; Sperling 1961.

55. On bond referenda in San Francisco, see Jenkins 2021: 82–83, 131.

56. Schragger 2012: 869–70.

57. See Compton 1920; Radford 2003. By 1934, Cook County, Illinois, had over four hundred independent tax-levying bodies, in addition to the City of Chicago (Anonymous 1934: 931).

58. Nanda 2014: 557.

59. O'Donnell 1962: 262.

60. Radford 2003: 880. This district managed the heroic engineering feat of reversing the flow of the Chicago River, so that industrial waste no longer contaminated the City's drinking water. It now (2019) has roughly $3 billion in outstanding debts, rated "Aa2 stable" by Moody's.

61. Hartwell et al. 1905: 216.

62. Ratchford 1938: 706.

63. MacManus 1990: 25.

64. For a general discussion of the financial challenges faced during the 1930s, see Anonymous 1934.

65. See Fishback 2017: 1453–55.

66. See Pacewicz 2016; Bifulco et al. 2012.

67. In some cases, the maturities of municipal debt for infrastructure were extreme: in the early twentieth century, Baltimore issued a sewerage loan set to mature in 75 years, while New Orleans sold 50-year bonds to fund its sewers (Hartwell et al. 1905: 206, 212).

68. Jacobson and Tarr 1994: 5–6.

69. Higgens-Evenson 2002: 625.

70. See *Historical Statistics of the United States* 2006: table Df243-56.

71. Jacobson and Tarr 1994: 11; Schultz and McShane 1978: 393; *Historical Statistics of the United States* 2006: table Dh236-39.

72. Jacobson and Tarr 1994: 17; Masten 2011: 605.

73. Buckley 1952.

74. See Robinson 2020.

75. See Jenkins 2021: chap. 6; Robinson 2020: 1002.

76. See Robinson 2020: 992–95.

77. Jenkins 2021: 146, 148, 176.

78. See *Historical Statistics of the United States* 2006: table Cj838.

79. Moody's Investors Service 1921: vi, viii.

80. Moody's Investors Service 1926: v.

81. See Packer 1968: 94.

82. Moody's Investors Service 1921: 558–65.

83. Calvert 1959: 21.

84. Murphy 2010: 118–20.

85. See *Historical Statistics of the United States* 2006: table Cj741-47.

86. See *Historical Statistics of the United States* 2006: table Cj362-74.

87. See Ohio 1915: xiv. Most individual banks held some state, county, or municipal bonds as assets. The Peoples Banking Company of Oberlin, Ohio, for example, held $30,350 worth of such bonds, or about 11 percent of total bank assets. See Ohio 1915: 202.

88. Brady 1916: 22. The proportion of assets increases to over 10 percent if one also includes public service corporation bonds.

89. Hollander 1913: 794.

90. Calvert 1959: 21; O'Donnell 1962: 266.

91. See Bogart 1911: 395.

92. Bland and Chen 1990: 44.

93. Weil 1907: 197.

94. Raymond 1932: 366.

95. See Harries 1968: 69.

96. See Edling and Kaplanoff 2004: 736; Edling 2007.

97. See *Historical Statistics of the United States* 2006: table Ea650-51.

98. Riley 1978.

99. Herring 2016: 49.

100. See Ratchford 1947.

101. Sexton 2005: 53–57.

102. See *Historical Statistics of the United States* 2006: table Ea650-61.

103. See the IMF's Historical Public Debt Database (Abbas et al. 2011), https://www.imf.org /external/datamapper/DEBT1@DEBT/OEMDC/ADVEC/WEOWORLD/USA.

104. See Sexton 2005: 124, 132.

105. Thomson 2016.

106. See, e.g., *Chicago Tribune*, January 5, 1863, p. 3; *Cincinnati Daily Enquirer*, December 11, 1862, p. 2; *Detroit Free Press*, April 5, 1863, p. 2, where Jay Cooke & Co. announces the sale of the "Five Twenties," so named because they were "callable" after five years and matured in twenty years.

107. See Carruthers and Babb 1996; Davis 1910; Unger 1964; White 1982.

108. Ailes 1910.

109. United States Census Office 1883: 1569.

110. Leffingwell 1920.

111. United States Department of Treasury 1917: 8. See also Childs 1920: 46.

112. Hilt and Rahn 2016: 91.

113. Kang and Rockoff 2015: table 1.

114. United States Department of Treasury 1917: 5.

115. See Kang and Rockoff 2015: 57. Ott (2011) argues that the experience of purchasing a government bond set the stage for much greater popular involvement in securities markets more generally.

116. See generally Odegard and Barth 1941. And consider that the U.S. Treasury Department sponsored a radio variety show, broadcast nationally on CBS, called the *Treasury Hour—Millions for Defense*, starring famous entertainers, featuring a rendition of the Gettysburg Address, and

with its own popular theme song, composed by Irving Berlin: "Any Bonds Today?" (Odegard and Barth 1941: 406).

117. Odegard and Barth 1941: 401.

118. United States Department of Treasury 1941: 7–11.

119. Robinson 1955: 397.

120. The difference was that "bearer bonds" were assumed to be owned by whoever possessed them in good faith, whereas ownership for "registered bonds" had to be recorded with the U.S. Treasury. Title was more secure for registered bonds but transfer of title was slightly more cumbersome.

121. The current version of this is called "quantitative easing," through which central banks purchase financial assets, including government debt, in order to influence financial markets.

122. See Blakey 1914; Mehrotra 2010; Pollack 2014; Smiley and Keehn 1995. The Civil War income tax expired in 1871, and a federal income tax was reinstated after ratification of the Sixteenth Amendment in 1913.

123. See *Historical Statistics of the United States* 2006: table Ea748-57; Mehrotra 2010: 182.

124. See *Historical Statistics of the United States* 2006: tables Ea740-47, Ea748-57.

125. See *Historical Statistics of the United States* 2006: table Ea683-97.

126. Hamilton 1790.

127. Schmeller 2009.

128. Hamilton 1790.

129. Piatt 1887: 182.

130. Madison 1790. See also Kuehl 1995.

131. Hamilton 1795; see also Edling 2014: 84, 202.

132. See Davis 1910: 111–12. This connection was used by civil rights leaders to urge northern investors not to purchase the bonds of segregationist southern states. See Jenkins 2021: 225–26.

133. Hill 1886: 216.

134. In other words, there is no "Ricardian equivalence." See Seater 1993.

135. For example, Hill (1886: 214) supposed that public borrowing directly displaced private borrowing and that "the locking up of loaning-capital in public debt diminishes by so much the supply of such capital for other purposes, and thereby enhances the rate demanded and obtained upon all loans and investments of money."

136. See Austin 2015; Cooke and Katzen 1954; Hall and Sargent 2018; Kowalcky and LeLoup 1993.

137. It was even lowered, from $300 billion to $275 billion, after World War II.

138. Garbade 2016.

139. See Reilly 2013; Anenson, Slabaugh, and Lahey 2014.

140. These figures come from the administrative office of the U.S. Courts. See http://s3 .amazonaws.com/abi-org/Newsroom/Bankruptcy_Statistics/Chapter+9+Filings+1980-Current .pdf.

141. See Table F-2, U.S. Bankruptcy Courts—Business and Nonbusiness Cases Commenced, by Chapter of the Bankruptcy Code, https://www.uscourts.gov/sites/default/files/data_tables /bf_f2_1231.2018.pdf.

142. See Harries 1968.

Chapter 10

1. For a summary, see Davis and Kim 2015.

2. This remains the primary criticism of debt for Graeber (2011) and Lazzarato (2012).

3. See https://www.census.gov/quickfacts/fact/table/US/HCN010212.

4. These are businesses that do not have any employees. See https://www.census.gov/data/tables/2018/econ/nonemployer-statistics/2018-combined-report.html.

5. See https://www.census.gov/data/tables/2017/econ/susb/2017-susb-annual.html.

6. See Thiemann 2018.

7. Witness the famous bank run scene in Frank Capra's classic movie *It's a Wonderful Life*.

8. See Tait 2019, 2020 on various types of trusts.

9. See Pistor 2019.

10. Corporate clients, however, enjoy no such protection, even though they also may lack expertise. Proctor & Gamble, for example, suffered large losses in the 1990s stemming from a 5/30 swap it entered into with Bankers Trust. P&G lacked the expertise to fully understand the risks associated with financial derivatives, and successfully sued Bankers Trust in the aftermath of its sudden losses.

11. See Quinn 2019.

12. See Howard 1997; Mettler 2011.

13. See Daniel 2007; Grim 1995, 1996.

14. This term refers to investors who shift out of risky assets to safer assets during a crisis.

15. See Philippon 2019: 211–17.

16. See Turner 2016: 7, 23.

17. This was a period of decreased macroeconomic volatility, roughly from the mid-1980s till 2007. See Bean 2010: 290–93, 297; Bernanke 2013: 9–11.

18. See Philippon 2019: 207–22; Thiemann 2018.

19. See Kashyap, Berner, and Goodhart 2011: 146.

20. Or, as Gorton and Tallman (2018: 169–70) put it, debt becomes information-sensitive.

21. Turner 2016: 103.

22. See Aikman et al. 2019; Yellen 2011.

23. See Battiston et al. 2016; Bisias et al. 2012.

24. See Dubovec 2006; Goode 2018; Mooney 2018.

25. Such contracts depend on familiar elements like collateral and bond ratings. See Gregory 2010; Gullifer 2012; Gaillard and Waibel 2018.

26. See *New York Times*, May 26, 1963, p. 123.

27. See Arnold 1998; Vance and Bell 2014. On the breakdown of MERS during the global financial crisis, see Levitin 2013.

28. See, generally, Bell and Parchomovsky 2016.

29. See, e.g., SEC 2008.

30. See Partnoy 1999.

31. See Bouk 2017; Igo 2018.

32. Of course, this simple characterization sets aside complications like exempt property and non-dischargeable debts.

33. See Polletta and Tufail 2014.

34. Or in the words of Petersen and Rajan (2002), from "soft" to "hard."

35. See, e.g., Carson 2007; Chun and Sauder 2021; Didier 2020; Igo 2007; Porter 1995; Power 1997.

36. See Avery, Brevoort, and Canner 2009: 519.

37. See Espeland and Sauder 2007 on reactivity more generally.

38. See Prasad 2012; Rajan 2010; Streeck 2014.

39. See Shaw 2019.

40. The notion of "statistical discrimination" partially captures this idea.

41. See Herzog 2017; Meyer 2018.

42. *New York Times*, February 22, 1995, section A, p. 19.

43. See Smith et al. 2013.

44. See Mehrling 2011.

45. See Fligstein 2021.

46. See Zuboff 2019; FTC 2016: 1.

47. See FTC 2016: 4.

48. See Berg et al. 2020.

49. See Wei et al. 2016; De Cnudde et al. 2019; Niu, Ren, and Li 2019.

50. Along with the market for used cars, of course. See Stiglitz 2000.

51. See Liang et al. 2018; Liu 2019; Kostka 2019; Síthigh and Siems 2019.

52. See Marron 2009.

53. See, e.g., Benjamin 2019; Christin 2016; Desai and Kroll 2017; Dressel and Farid 2018; Obermeyer et al. 2019; Rhoen and Feng 2018; Vyas, Eisenstein, and Jones 2020.

54. See Pasquale 2015: 4, 25.

55. See Casey, Farhangi, and Vogl 2019; Kaminski 2019; Rudin 2019; Rona-Tas 2020.

56. Of course, they may reflect someone else's intentions, or simulate intentionality.

57. See https://www.federalreserve.gov/releases/chargeoff/delallsa.htm.

58. Generally, see Ho 2021.

BIBLIOGRAPHY

Aaronson, Daniel, Daniel Hartley, and Bhashkar Mazumder. 2020. "The Effects of the 1930s HOLC 'Redlining' Maps." Federal Reserve Bank of Chicago Working Paper 2017–12.

Abbas, S. M. Ali, Nazim Belhocine, Asmaa El-Ganainy, and Mark Horton. 2011. "Historical Patterns and Dynamics of Public Debt—Evidence from a New Database." *IMF Economic Review* 59(4): 717–42.

Abken, Peter A. 1991. "Beyond Plain Vanilla: A Taxonomy of Swaps." *Federal Reserve Bank of Atlanta Economic Review* (March/April): 12–29.

Abrahao, Bruno, Paolo Parigi, Alok Gupta, and Karen S. Cook. 2017. "Reputation Offsets Trust Judgments Based on Social Biases among Airbnb Users." *PNAS* 114(37): 9848–53.

Acharya, Viral V., Matthew Richardson, Stijn Van Nieuwerburgh, and Lawrence J. White. 2011. *Guaranteed to Fail: Fannie Mae, Freddie Mac and the Debacle of Mortgage Finance*. Princeton: Princeton University Press.

Ackerman, Saul B., and John J. Neuner. 1924. *Credit Insurance*. New York: Ronald Press.

Adams, Henry C. 1893. *Public Debts: An Essay in the Science of Finance*. New York: Appleton & Co.

Adrian, Tobias, and Hyun Song Shin. 2010. "The Changing Nature of Financial Intermediation and the Financial Crisis of 2007–2009." *Annual Review of Economics* 2: 603–18.

Agarwal, Sumit, Gene Amromin, Itzhak Ben-David, Souphala Chomsisengphet, and Douglas D. Evanoff. 2011. "The Role of Securitization in Mortgage Renegotiation." *Journal of Financial Economics* 102: 559–78.

Agarwal, Sumit, Paige Marta Skiba, and Jeremy Tobacman. 2009. "Payday Loans and Credit Cards: New Liquidity and Credit Scoring Puzzles?" *American Economic Review* 99(2): 412–17.

Agrawal, Ajay, Joshua S. Gans, and Avi Goldfarb. 2019. "Artificial Intelligence: The Ambiguous Labor Market Impact of Automating Prediction." *Journal of Economic Perspectives* 33(2): 31–50.

Aikman, David, Jonathan Bridges, Anil Kashyap, and Caspar Siegert. 2019. "Would Macroprudential Regulation Have Prevented the Last Crisis?" *Journal of Economic Perspectives* 33(1): 107–30.

Ailes, Milton E. 1910. "National Banking System and Federal Bond Issues." *Annals of the American Academy of Political and Social Science* 36(3): 114–28.

Akerlof, George A. 1970. "The Market for 'Lemons': Quality Uncertainty and the Market Mechanism." *Quarterly Journal of Economics* 84(3): 488–500.

Akhevein, Jalal, W. Scott Frame, and Lawrence J. White. 2005. "The Diffusion of Financial Innovations: An Examination of the Adoption of Small Business Credit Scoring by Large Banking Organizations." *Journal of Business* 78(2): 577–96.

Akhavein, Jalal, Lawrence G. Goldberg, and Lawrence J. White. 2004. "Small Banks, Small Business, and Relationships: An Empirical Study of Lending to Small Firms." *Journal of Financial Services Research* 26(3): 245–61.

Allen, Franklin, and Douglas Gale. 2000. *Comparing Financial Systems*. Cambridge, MA: MIT Press.

Alston, Lee J. 1984. "Farm Foreclosure Moratorium Legislation: A Lesson from the Past." *American Economic Review* 74(3): 445–57.

American Savings and Loan Institute. 1971. *Lending Principles and Practices*. Chicago: American Savings and Loan Institute Press.

Ammons, Lila. 1996. "The Evolution of Black-Owned Banks in the United States between the 1880s and 1990s." *Journal of Black Studies* 26(4): 467–89.

Anderson, Elisabeth. 2008. "Experts, Ideas, and Policy Change: The Russell Sage Foundation and Small Loan Reform, 1909–1941." *Theory and Society* 37: 271–310.

Anderson, George L. 1936. "Western Attitudes toward National Banks, 1873–74." *Mississippi Valley Historical Review* 23(2): 205–16.

———. 1943. "The South and Problems of Post–Civil War Finance." *Journal of Southern History* 9(2): 181–95.

Anenson, T. Leigh, Alex Slabaugh, and Karen Eilers Lahey. 2014. "Reforming Public Pensions." *Yale Law and Policy Review* 33(1): 1–74.

Anonymous. 1898. "The National Bankruptcy Act." *Harvard Law Review* 12(4): 272.

———. 1925. "Character of Management as a Basis for Obtaining Bank Credit." *Harvard Business Review* 3(4): 481–85.

———. 1934. "Administration of Municipal Credit." *Yale Law Journal* 43(6): 924–1006.

———. 1957. "Collection Capers: Liability for Debt Collection Practices." *University of Chicago Law Review* 24(3): 572–87.

Apkarian, Jacob. 2018. "Opposition to Shareholder Value: Bond Rating Agencies and Conflicting Logics in Corporate Finance." *Socio-Economic Review* 16(1): 85–112.

Archambault, Jeffrey J., and Marie Archambault. 2005. "The Effect of Regulation on Statement Disclosures in the 1915 Moody's Manuals." *Accounting Historians Journal* 32(1): 1–22.

Armstrong, William. 1848. *The Aristocracy of New York: Who They Are and What They Were*. New York: New York Publishing Co.

Arnold, R. K. 1998. "Real Estate Law: Yes, There Is Life on MERS." *Best of ABA Sections: General Practice, Solo & Small Firm Section* 2(1): 18–19.

Arrow, Kenneth J. 1974. *The Limits of Organization*. New York: W. W. Norton.

Atack, Jeremy, Matthew Jaremski, and Peter L. Rousseau. 2014. "American Banking and the Transportation Revolution before the Civil War." *Journal of Economic History* 74(4): 943–86.

Atiyah, P. S. 1979. "Promises and the Law of Contract." *Mind* 88(351): 410–18.

Atkins, Paul. 1938. "The Official Supervision of Bank Security Portfolios." *Bankers' Magazine* (July 1938): 13–19.

Austin, D. Andrew. 2015. "The Debt Limit: History and Recent Increases." Congressional Research Service Report RL31967. Washington, DC: CRS.

Austin, J. L. 1975. *How to Do Things with Words*. 2nd ed. Cambridge, MA: Harvard University Press.

Avery, Christopher, and Sarah Turner. 2012. "Student Loans: Do College Students Borrow Too Much—Or Not Enough?" *Journal of Economic Perspectives* 26(1): 165–92.

Avery, Robert B., Raphael W. Bostic, Paul S. Calem, and Glenn B. Canner. 2000. "Credit Scoring: Statistical Issues and Evidence from Credit-Bureau Files." *Real Estate Economics* 28(3): 523–47.

Avery, Robert B., Kenneth P. Brevoort, and Glenn B. Canner. 2009. "Credit Scoring and Its Effects on the Availability and Affordability of Credit." *Journal of Consumer Affairs* 43(3): 516–30.

Avery, Robert B., Paul S. Calem, Glenn B. Canner, and Raphael W. Bostic. 2003. "An Overview of Consumer Data and Credit Reporting." *Federal Reserve Bulletin* (February): 47–73.

Ayres, Milan V. 1938. "The Economic Function of the Sales Finance Company." *Journal of the American Statistical Association* 33(201): 59–70.

Bach, G. L. 1949. "Bank Supervision, Monetary Policy, and Governmental Reorganization." *Journal of Finance* 4(4): 269–85.

Bahl, Roy, and William Duncombe. 1993. "State and Local Debt Burdens in the 1980s: A Study in Contrast." *Public Administrative Review* 53(1): 31–40.

Bailey, Hollis R. 1893. "An Assignment in Insolvency, and Its Effect upon Property and Persons out of the State." *Harvard Law Review* 7(5): 281–99.

Balleisen, Edward J. 1996. "Vulture Capitalism in Antebellum America: The 1841 Federal Bankruptcy Act and the Exploitation of Financial Distress." *Business History Review* 70(4): 473–516.

———. 2001. *Navigating Failure: Bankruptcy and Commercial Society in Antebellum America*. Chapel Hill: University of North Carolina Press.

Bandelj, Nina, Frederick F. Wherry, and Viviana A. Zelizer, eds. 2017. *Money Talks: Explaining How Money Really Works*. Princeton: Princeton University Press.

Bank of America. 1922. *A National Survey of State Debts and Securities*. New York: Bank of America.

Bankers Encyclopedia Co. 1912. *Polk's Bank Directory*. 36th ed. New York: Bankers Encyclopedia Company.

Baradaran, Mehrsa. 2017. *The Color of Money: Black Banks and the Racial Wealth Gap*. Cambridge, MA: Harvard University Press.

Barr, Michael S. 2012. *No Slack: The Financial Lives of Low-Income Americans*. Washington, DC: Brookings Institution Press.

Barth, James R. 2009. *The Rise and Fall of the U.S. Mortgage and Credit Markets*. Hoboken, NJ: John Wiley & Sons.

Basel Committee on Banking Supervision (BCBS). 1999. "Supervisory Lessons to Be Drawn from the Asian Crisis." Basel Committee on Banking Supervision Working Paper No. 2. Basel: Bank for International Settlements.

———. 2000. "Range of Practice in Banks' Internal Ratings Systems." Basel Committee on Banking Supervision Discussion Paper. Basel: Bank for International Settlements.

———. 2005. "An Explanatory Note on the Basel II IRB Risk Weight Functions." Basel: Bank for International Settlements.

Baskin, Jonathan Barron, and Paul J. Miranti Jr. 1997. *A History of Corporate Finance*. Cambridge: Cambridge University Press.

Battiston, Stefano, Guido Caldarelli, Robert M. May, Tarik Roukny, and Joseph E. Stiglitz. 2016. "The Price of Complexity in Financial Networks." *PNAS* 113(36): 10031–36.

Bean, Charles. 2010. "The Great Moderation, the Great Panic, and the Great Contraction." *Journal of the European Economic Association* 8(2/3): 289–325.

Beckert, Jens. 2016. *Imagined Futures: Fictional Expectations and Capitalist Dynamics*. Cambridge, MA: Harvard University Press.

Beckert, Sven. 2014. *Empire of Cotton: A Global History*. New York: Knopf.

Beckett, Katherine, and Alexes Harris. 2011. "On Cash and Conviction: Monetary Sanctions as Misguided Policy." *Criminology and Public Policy* 10(3): 509–37.

Beckhart, B. H. 1922. "Outline of Banking History from the First Bank of the United States through the Panic of 1907." *Annals of the American Academy of Political and Social Science* 99: 1–16.

Bell, Abraham, and Gideon Parchomovsky. 2016. "Of Property and Information." *Columbia Law Review* 116(1): 237–86.

Bell, Haughton, and Harold G. Fraine. 1952. "Legal Framework, Trends, and Developments in Investment Practices of Life Insurance Companies." *Law and Contemporary Problems* 17(1): 45–85.

Bell, Spurgeon. 1938. "Shifts in the Sources of Funds for Home Financing, 1930–1937." *Law and Contemporary Problems* 5(4): 510–16.

Ben-Amos, Ilana Krausman. 2000. "Gifts and Favors: Informal Support in Early Modern England." *Journal of Modern History* 72: 295–338.

Benjamin, Ruha. 2019. "Assessing Risk, Automating Racism: A Health Care Algorithm Reflects Underlying Racial Bias in Society." *Science* 355(6464): 421–22.

Benmelech, Efraim, and Jennifer Dlugosz. 2010. "The Credit Rating Crisis." *NBER Macroeconomics Annual* 24(1): 161–208.

Benmelech, Efraim, and Tobias J. Moskowitz. 2010. "The Political Economy of Financial Regulation: Evidence from U.S. State Usury Laws in the 19th Century." *Journal of Finance* 65(3): 1029–73.

Bensel, Richard Franklin. 1990. *Yankee Leviathan: The Origins of Central State Authority in America, 1859–1877*. Cambridge: Cambridge University Press.

———. 2000. *The Political Economy of American Industrialization, 1877–1900*. Cambridge: Cambridge University Press.

Berg, Tobias, Valentin Burg, Ana Gombovic, and Manju Puri. 2020. "On the Rise of FinTechs: Credit Scoring Using Digital Footprints." *Review of Financial Studies* 33: 2845–97.

Bergengren, Roy F. 1937. "Cooperative Credit." *Annals of the American Academy of Political and Social Science* 191: 144–48.

Berger, Allen N., W. Scott Frame, and Nathan H. Miller. 2005. "Credit Scoring and the Availability, Price, and Risk of Small Business Credit." *Journal of Money, Credit and Banking* 37(2): 191–222.

Berger, Allen N., and Gregory F. Udell. 1995. "Relationship Lending and Lines of Credit in Small Firm Finance." *Journal of Business* 68(3): 351–81.

Berk, Gerald. 1994. *Alternative Tracks: The Constitution of American Industrial Order, 1865–1917*. Baltimore: Johns Hopkins University Press.

Berman, Elizabeth Popp, and Abby Stivers. 2016. "Student Loans as a Pressure on U.S. Higher Education." *Research in the Sociology of Organizations* 46: 129–60.

Bernanke, Ben S. 2013. "A Century of US Central Banking: Goals, Frameworks, Accountability." *Journal of Economic Perspectives* 27(4): 3–16.

Bernstein, Lisa. 1992. "Opting Out of the Legal System: Extralegal Contractual Relations in the Diamond Industry." *Journal of Legal Studies* 21: 115–57.

Beutel, Frederick K. 1940. "The Development of State Statutes on Negotiable Paper Prior to the Negotiable Instruments Law." *Columbia Law Review* 40(5): 836–65.

Beveridge, Andrew A. 1985. "Local Lending Practice: Borrowers in a Small Northeastern Industrial City, 1832–1915." *Journal of Economic History* 45(2): 393–403.

Bhutta, Neil. 2011. "The Community Reinvestment Act and Mortgage Lending to Lower Income Borrowers and Neighborhoods." *Journal of Law and Economics* 54(4): 953–83.

Biais, Bruno, and Richard Green. 2018. "The Microstructure of the Bond Market in the 20th Century." Toulouse School of Economics Working Paper TSE-960.

Bifulco, Robert, Beverly Bunch, William Duncombe, Mark Robbins, and William Simonsen. 2012. "Debt and Deception: How States Avoid Making Hard Fiscal Decisions." *Public Administration Review* 72(5): 659–67.

Biggart, Nicole Woolsey. 2001. "Banking on Each Other: The Situational Logic of Rotating Savings and Credit Associations." *Advances in Qualitative Organization Research* 3: 129–52.

Biles, Roger. 2018. "Public Policy Made by Private Enterprise: Bond Rating Agencies and Urban America." *Journal of Urban History* 44(6): 1098–1112.

Billings, Dwight B., and Kathleen M. Blee. 2000. *The Road to Poverty: The Making of Wealth and Hardship in Appalachia*. Cambridge: Cambridge University Press.

Birdseye, Clarence F. 1924. *Encyclopedia of General Business and Legal Forms*. New York: Baker, Voorhis and Co.

Birckhead, Tamar R. 2015. "The New Peonage." *Washington & Lee Law Review* 72: 1595–1678.

Birkhead, Joe B. 1941. "Collection Tactics of Illegal Lenders." *Law and Contemporary Problems* 8(1): 78–87.

Bisias, Dimitrios, Mark Flood, Andrew W. Lo, and Stavros Valavanis. 2012. "A Survey of Systemic Risk Analytics." *Annual Review of Financial Economics* 4: 255–96.

Black, A. G. 1928. "The Provision for Agricultural Credit in the United States." *Quarterly Journal of Economics* 43(1): 94–131.

Black, Deborah G., Kenneth D. Garbade, and William L. Silber. 1981. "The Impact of the GNMA Pass-Through Program on FHA Mortgage Costs." *Journal of Finance* 36(2): 457–69.

Blakey, Roy G. 1914. "The New Income Tax." *American Economic Review* 4(1): 25–46.

Bland, Robert L., and Li-Khan Chen. 1990. "Taxable Municipal Bonds: State and Local Governments Confront the Tax-Exempt Limitation Movement." *Public Administration Review* 50(1): 42–48.

Bleemer, Zachary, Meta Brown, Donghoon Lee, Katherine Strair, and Wilbert van der Klaauw. 2021. "Echoes of Rising Tuition in Students' Borrowing, Educational Attainment, and Homeownership in Post-recession America." *Journal of Urban Economics* 122: 1–24.

Blumberg, Phillip I. 1986. "Limited Liability and Corporate Groups." *Journal of Corporate Law* 11: 573–631.

Boardman, H. A. 1853. *The Bible in the Counting House: A Course of Lectures to Merchants*. Philadelphia: Lippincott, Grambo & Co.

Bodenhorn, Howard. 1998a. "Free Banking and Financial Entrepreneurship in Nineteenth Century New York: The Black River Bank of Watertown." *Business and Economic History* 27(1): 102–14.

———. 1998b. "Quis Custodiet Ipsos Custodes?" *Eastern Economic Journal* 24(1): 7–24.

———. 2000. *A History of Banking in Antebellum America: Financial Markets and Economic Development in an Era of Nation-Building*. New York: Cambridge University Press.

———. 2003a. *State Banking in Early America: A New Economic History*. New York: Oxford University Press.

———. 2003b. "Short-Term Loans and Long-Term Relationships: Relationship Lending in Early America." *Journal of Money, Credit, and Banking* 35(4): 485–505.

———. 2008. "Free Banking and Bank Entry in Nineteenth-Century New York." *Financial History Review* 15(2): 175–201.

Bodenhorn, Howard, and David Cuberes. 2018. "Finance and Urbanization in Early Nineteenth-Century New York." *Journal of Urban Economics* 104: 47–58.

Bodfish, Morton. 1935. "Government and Private Mortgage Loans on Real Estate." *Journal of Land and Public Utility Economics* 11(4): 402–9.

Bogart, Ernest L. 1911. "History of the State Debt of Ohio: II." *Journal of Political Economy* 19(5): 385–403.

Bogue, Allan G. 1953. "The Administrative and Policy Problems of the J. B. Watkins Land Mortgage Company, 1873–1894." *Bulletin of the Business Historical Society* 27(1): 26–59.

———. 1955. *Money at Interest: The Farm Mortgage on the Middle Border*. Ithaca, NY: Cornell University Press.

———. 1976. "Land Credit for Northern Farmers, 1789–1940." *Agricultural History* 50(1): 68–100.

Bogue, Allan G., Brian Q. Cannon, and Kenneth J. Winkle. 2003. "Oxen to Organs: Chattel Credit in Springdale Town, 1849–1900." *Agricultural History* 77(3): 420–52.

Bonesteel, Verne C. 1919. "Banks as Custodians of Credit." *Bankers' Magazine* (December): 776–78.

Bord, Vitaly M., and João A. C. Santos. 2012. "The Rise of the Originate-to-Distribute Model and the Role of Banks in Financial Intermediation." *Federal Reserve Bank of New York Economic Policy Review* (July 2012): 21–34.

Borges, Berthold E. 1916. "Credits and Collections in a Manufacturing House." In *Credits and Collections: Organizing the Work, Correct Policies and Methods, Five Credit and Collection Systems*, 102–23. Chicago: W. A. Shaw.

Botsman, Rachel. 2017. *Who Can You Trust? How Technology Brought Us Together and Why It Might Drive Us Apart*. New York: Public Affairs.

Bouk, Dan. 2015. *How Our Days Became Numbered: Risk and the Rise of the Statistical Individual*. Chicago: University of Chicago Press.

———. 2017. "The History and Political Economy of Personal Data over the Last Two Centuries in Three Acts." *Osiris* 32: 85–106.

Boyce, Gordon H. 1995. *Information, Mediation and Institutional Development: The Rise of Large-Scale Enterprise in British Shipping, 1870–1919*. Manchester: Manchester University Press.

Bozanic, Zahn, Maria Loumioti, and Florin Vasvari. 2018. "Corporate Loan Securitization and the Standardization of Financial Covenants." *Journal of Accounting Research* 56(1): 45–83.

Braasch, George H., Fred H. Miller, and James N. Rice. 1980. "Equal Credit Opportunity." *Business Lawyer* 35(3): 1237–58.

Brady, James J. 1916. *Statement Showing the Condition of Illinois State Banks*. Springfield: State of Illinois Auditor of Public Accounts.

Braucher, Robert. 1958. "The Legislative History of the Uniform Commercial Code." *Columbia Law Review* 58(6): 798–814.

Breen, T. H. 1985. *Tobacco Culture: The Mentality of the Great Tidewater Planters on the Eve of Revolution*. Princeton: Princeton University Press.

Brennan, J. William. 1970. "Securities Backed by Loan Packaging." *Business Lawyer* 26(2): 401–9.

Brewer, H. Peers. 1976. "Eastern Money and Western Mortgages in the 1870s." *Business History Review* 50(3): 356–80.

Brewster, Stanley F. 1924. *Legal Aspects of Credit*. New York: Ronald Press Co.

Bricker, Jesse, Arthur B. Kennickell, Kevin B. Moore, and John Sabelhaus. 2012. "Changes in U.S. Family Finances from 2007 to 2010: Evidence from the Survey of Consumer Finances." *Federal Reserve Bulletin* 98(2): 1–80.

Brief, Richard P. 1966. "The Origin and Evolution of Nineteenth-Century Asset Accounting." *Business History Review* 40(1): 1–23.

Brimmer, Andrew F. 1971. "The Black Banks: An Assessment of Performance and Prospects." *Journal of Finance* 26(2): 379–405.

———. 1992. "The Dilemma of Black Banking: Lending Risks vs. Community Service." *Review of Black Political Economy* 20: 5–29.

Bristol, Douglas, Jr. 2004. "From Outposts to Enclaves: A Social History of Black Barbers from 1750 to 1915." *Enterprise and Society* 5(4): 594–606.

Brooks, Richard R. W. 2006. "Credit Past Due." *Columbia Law Review* 106(4): 994–1028.

———. 2011. "Covenants without Courts: Enforcing Residential Segregation with Legally Unenforceable Agreements." *American Economic Review* 101(3): 360–65.

Brown, Jonathan A., and James E. De Lano. 1938. "Commercial Banks and Small Loans." *Harvard Business Review* 16(4): 481–90.

Bruckmeier, Karl, Anders Ellegård, and Laura Piriz. 2005. "Fishermen's Interests and Cooperation: Preconditions for Joint Management of Swedish Coastal Fisheries." *Ambio* 34(2): 101–10.

Bruckner, Matthew Adam. 2018. "The Promise and Perils of Algorithmic Lenders' Use of Big Data." *Chicago-Kent Law Review* 93(1): 3–60.

Brueggeman, William B., and Jeffrey D. Fisher. 2018. *Real Estate Finance and Investments*. 16th ed. New York: McGraw-Hill.

Bruère, Henry. 1915. "Development of Standards in Municipal Government." *Annals of the American Academy of Political and Social Science* 61: 199–207.

Brunnermeier, Markus K., Sam Langfield, Marco Pagano, Ricardo Reis, Stijn Van Nieuwerburgh, and Dimitri Vayanos. 2017. "ESBies: Safety in the Tranches." *Economy Policy* 32(90): 175–219.

Bryan, Clark W. 1883. *Credit: Its Meaning and Moment*. New York: Bradstreet Press.

Bryant, Willis R. 1956. *Mortgage Lending: Fundamentals and Practices*. New York: McGraw-Hill.

Buchheit, Lee C., G. Mitu Gulati, and Robert B. Thompson. 2007. "The Dilemma of Odious Debts." *Duke Law Journal* 56(5): 1201–62.

Buckley, James C. 1952. "Revenue Bond Financing for Airport Improvements." *Analysts Journal* 8(5): 85–91.

Bucks, Brian K., Arthur B. Kennickell, Traci L. Mach, and Kevin B. Moore. 2009. "Changes in U.S. Family Finances from 2004 to 2007: Evidence from the Survey of Consumer Finances." *Federal Reserve Bulletin* (February 2009): A1–A56.

Bucks, Brian K., Arthur B. Kennickell, and Kevin B. Moore. 2006. "Recent Changes in U.S. Family Finances: Evidence from the 2001 and 2004 Survey of Consumer Finances." *Federal Reserve Bulletin* (March 2006): A1–A38.

Burman, Raymond W. 1948. "Practical Aspects of Inventory and Receivables Financing." *Law and Contemporary Problems* 13(4): 555–65.

Burt, Ronald S. 1992. *Structural Holes: The Social Structure of Competition*. Cambridge, MA: Harvard University Press.

Butts, I. R. 1849. *The Creditor's and Debtor's Assistant, or the Mode of Collecting Debts*. Boston: I. R. Butts.

Calavita, Kitty, Henry Pontell, and Robert Tillman. 1997. *Big Money Crime: Fraud and Politics in the Savings and Loan Crisis*. Berkeley: University of California Press.

Calavita, K., R. Tillman, and H. N. Pontell. 1997. "The Savings and Loan Debacle, Financial Crime, and the State." *Annual Review of Sociology* 23: 19–38.

Calder, Lendol. 1999. *Financing the American Dream: A Cultural History of Consumer Credit*. Princeton: Princeton University Press.

Calomiris, Charles W., and Stephen H. Haber. 2014. *Fragile by Design: The Political Origins of Banking Crises and Scarce Credit*. Princeton: Princeton University Press.

Calomiris, Charles W., and Carlos D. Ramirez. 1996. "The Role of Financial Relationships in the History of American Corporate Finance." *Journal of Applied Corporate Finance* 9(2): 52–73.

Calvert, Gordon L. 1959. "Development, Volume, Purchasers and Ratings." In *Fundamentals of Municipal Bonds*, 15–28. Washington, DC: Investment Bankers Association of America.

Campbell, John Y. 2016. "Restoring Rational Choice: The Challenge of Consumer Financial Regulation." *American Economic Review* 106(5): 1–30.

Campbell, John Y., Howell E. Jackson, Brigitte C. Madrian, and Peter Tufano. 2011. "Consumer Financial Protection." *Journal of Economic Perspectives* 25(1): 91–133.

Canner, Glenn B., and Gregory Elliehausen. 2013. "Consumer Experiences with Credit Cards." *Federal Reserve Bulletin* 99(5): 1–36.

Cannon, James G. 1893. "Bank Credits." *Bankers' Magazine and Statistical Register* (January): 535–36.

Cantor, Richard, and Frank Packer. 1994. "The Credit Rating Industry." *Federal Reserve Bank of New York Quarterly Review* 19(2): 1–26.

Caplovitz, David. 1968. "Consumer Credit in the Affluent Society." *Law and Contemporary Problems* 33(4): 641–55.

Capon, Neal. 1982. "Credit Scoring Systems: A Critical Analysis." *Journal of Marketing* 46(2): 82–91.

Carroll, Edward, Jr. 1895. *Principles and Practice of Finance*. New York: G. P. Putnam's Sons.

Carrozzo, Peter M. 2005. "Marketing the American Mortgage: The Emergency Home Finance Act of 1970, Standardization and the Secondary Market Revolution." *Real Property, Probate and Trust Journal* 39(4): 765–805.

Carruthers, Bruce G. 1996. *City of Capital: Politics and Markets in the English Financial Revolution*. Princeton: Princeton University Press.

———. 2013. "Diverging Derivatives: Law, Governance and Modern Financial Markets." *Journal of Comparative Economics* 41: 386–400.

Carruthers, Bruce G., and Laura Ariovich. 2010. *Money and Credit: A Sociological Approach.* Cambridge: Polity Press.

Carruthers, Bruce G., and Sarah Babb. 1996. "The Color of Money and the Nature of Value: Greenbacks and Gold in Postbellum America." *American Journal of Sociology* 101(6): 1556–91.

Carruthers, Bruce G., and Barry Cohen. 2010. "Noter le crédit: Classification et cognition aux États-Unis." *Genèses* 79: 48–73.

Carruthers, Bruce G., and Wendy Nelson Espeland. 1991. "Accounting for Rationality: Double-Entry Bookkeeping and the Rhetoric of Economic Rationality." *American Journal of Sociology* 97(1): 31–69.

———. 1998. "Money, Meaning and Morality." *American Behavioral Scientist* 41(10): 1384–1408.

Carruthers, Bruce G., Timothy W. Guinnane, and Yoonseok Lee. 2012. "Bringing 'Honest Capital' to Poor Borrowers: The Passage of the U.S. Uniform Small Loan Law, 1907–1930." *Journal of Interdisciplinary History* 42(3): 393–418.

Carruthers, Bruce G., and Terence C. Halliday. 1998. *Rescuing Business: The Making of Corporate Bankruptcy Law in England and the United States.* Oxford: Oxford University Press.

Carruthers, Bruce G., and Arthur L. Stinchcombe. 1999. "The Social Structure of Liquidity: Flexibility in Markets and States." *Theory and Society* 28(3): 353–82.

Carson, Carol S. 1975. "The History of the United States National Income and Product Accounts: The Development of an Analytical Tool." *Review of Income and Wealth* 21(2): 153–81.

Carson, John. 2007. *The Measure of Merit: Talents, Intelligence, and Inequality in the French and American Republics, 1750–1940.* Princeton: Princeton University Press.

Casey, Bryan, Ashkon Farhangi, and Roland Vogl. 2019. "Rethinking Explainable Machines: The GDPR's 'Right to Explanation' Debate and the Rise of Algorithmic Audits in Enterprise." *Berkeley Technology Law Journal* 34(1): 143–88.

Caskey, John P. 1991. "Pawnbroking in America: The Economics of a Forgotten Credit Market." *Journal of Money, Credit and Banking* 23(1): 85–99.

Cavers, David F. 1935. "The Consumer's Stake in the Finance Company Code Controversy." *Law and Contemporary Problems* 2(2): 200–217.

Cetorelli, Nicola, and Stavros Peristiani. 2012. "The Role of Banks in Asset Securitization." *Federal Reserve Bank of New York Economic Policy Review* (July): 47–63.

Chandler, Alfred D. 1954. "Patterns of American Railroad Finance, 1830–1850." *Business History Review* 28(3): 248–63.

———. 1956. *Henry Varnum Poor: Business Editor, Analyst, and Reformer.* Cambridge, MA: Harvard University Press.

Chapman, John M. 1940. *Commercial Banks and Consumer Instalment Credit.* New York: National Bureau of Economic Research.

Chappell, Marisa. 2020. "The Strange Career of Urban Homesteading: Low-Income Homeownership and the Transformation of American Housing Policy in the Late Twentieth Century." *Journal of Urban History* 46(4): 747–74.

Charles, GuyLaine. 2009. "OTC Derivative Contracts in Bankruptcy: The Lehman Experience." *New York Business Law Journal* 13(1): 14–17.

Chatterjee, Samprit, and Seymour Barcun. 1970. "A Nonparametric Approach to Credit Screening." *Journal of the American Statistical Association* 65(329): 150–54.

Childs, C. Frederick. 1920. "United States Government Bonds." *Annals of the American Academy of Political and Social Science* 88: 43–50.

Chiteji, N. S. 2010. "The Racial Wealth Gap and the Borrower's Dilemma." *Journal of Black Studies* 41(2): 351–66.

Christin, Angele. 2016. "From Daguerreotypes to Algorithms: Machines, Expertise, and Three Forms of Objectivity." *ACM Computers & Society* 46(1): 27–32.

Chun, Hyunsik, and Michael Sauder. 2021. "The Logic of Quantification: Institutionalizing Numerical Thinking." *Theory and Society.* https://doi.org/10.1007/s11186-021-09453-1.

Churella, Albert J. 2013. *The Pennsylvania Railroad,* vol. 1: *Building an Empire, 1846–1917.* Philadelphia: University of Pennsylvania Press.

Chwieroth, Jeffrey M., and Andrew Walter. 2019. *The Wealth Effect: How the Great Expectations of the Middle Class Have Changed the Politics of Banking Crises.* Cambridge: Cambridge University Press.

Clark, Christopher. 1990. *The Roots of Rural Capitalism: Western Massachusetts, 1780–1860.* Ithaca: Cornell University Press.

———. 1996. "Rural America and the Transition to Capitalism." *Journal of the Early Republic* 16(2): 223–36.

Clark, Geoffrey W. 1999. *Betting on Lives: The Culture of Life Insurance in England, 1695–1775.* New York: Manchester University Press.

Clark, Horace F., and Frank A. Chase. 1934. *Elements of a Modern Building and Loan Association.* New York: Macmillan.

Clarke, Sally H. 2007. *Trust and Power: Consumers, the Modern Corporation, and the Making of the United States Automobile Market.* New York: Cambridge University Press.

Clayton, Lawrence. 1949. *Memorandum to Board of Governors.* The Marriner S. Eccles document collection. http://fraser.stlouisfed.org/docs/historical/eccles/046_20_0002.pdf.

Cleveland, Frederick A. 1907. "Bonds in Their Relation to Corporate Finance." *Annals of the American Academy of Political and Social Science* 30: 220–35.

Coffee, John C., Jr. 2006. *Gatekeepers: The Professions and Corporate Governance.* Oxford: Oxford University Press.

Cohen, Barry. 2012. "Constructing an Uncertain Economy: Credit Reporting and Credit Rating in the Nineteenth Century United States." PhD thesis, Northwestern University.

Cohen, Edward E. 1992. *Athenian Economy and Society: A Banking Perspective.* Princeton: Princeton University Press.

Cohen, Mark A. 2006. "Imperfect Competition in Auto Lending: Subjective Markup, Racial Disparity, and Class Action Litigation." Vanderbilt University Law School Law and Economics Working Paper 07-01. Nashville: Vanderbilt University.

Cohen-Cole, Ethan. 2011. "Credit Card Redlining." *Review of Economics and Statistics* 93(2): 700–713.

Cole, Rebel A., Lawrence G. Goldberg, and Lawrence J. White. 2004. "Cookie Cutter vs. Character: The Micro Structure of Small Business Lending by Large and Small Banks." *Journal of Financial and Quantitative Analysis* 39(2): 227–51.

Cole, Robert H., and Robert S. Handcock. 1960. *Consumer and Commercial Credit Management.* Homewood, IL: Richard Dorsey.

Coleman, James S. 1988. "Social Capital in the Creation of Human Capital." *American Journal of Sociology* 94 (Supplement): S95–S120.

Coles, W. N. 1871. *Laws of Kansas Authorizing the Issue of Municipal Bonds, and Opinion of Attorney-General.* New York: W. N. Coles & Co.

Colley, F. G. 1914. "Bank Loans under the New Conditions." *Journal of Accountancy* (December): 418–26.

Collins, William J. 2006. "The Political Economy of State Fair Housing Laws before 1968." *Social Science History* 30(1): 15–49.

Collins, William J., and Robert A. Margo. 2011. "Race and Home Ownership from the End of the Civil War to the Present." *American Economic Review* 101(3): 355–59.

Coman, E. T. 1904. "Some of the Elements of a Good Loan." *Bankers' Magazine* (September): 326–33.

Compton, William R. 1920. "Municipal Bonds." *Annals of the American Academy of Political and Social Science* 88: 51–56.

Comptroller of the Currency. 1937. *Seventy-Fifth Annual Report of the Comptroller of the Currency.* Washington, DC: U.S. Government Printing Office.

———. 1997. *Asset Securitization: Comptroller's Handbook.* Washington, DC: Comptroller of the Currency.

Consumer Financial Protection Bureau (CFPB). 2015. *Data Point: Credit Invisibles.* Washington, DC: CFPB Office of Research.

Converse, Paul. D. 1932. "Occupation and Credit." *Bankers' Magazine* (October): 339–42.

Conway, Thomas, Jr. 1915. "The Influence of the Federal Reserve Act upon Commercial Borrowing." *Annals of the American Academy of Political and Social Science* 59: 226–35.

Cook, Karen S., Russell Hardin, and Margaret Levi. 2005. *Cooperation without Trust?* New York: Russell Sage Foundation.

Cooke, H. J., and M. Katzen. 1954. "The Public Debt Limit." *Journal of Finance* 9(3): 298–303.

Cooper, Melinda. 2017. *Family Values: Between Neoliberalism and the New Social Conservatism.* New York: Zone Books.

Corder, J. Kevin, and Susan M. Hoffmann. 2004. "Privatizing Federal Credit Programs: Why Sallie Mae?" *Public Administration Review* 64(2): 180–91.

Cornwell, Benjamin. 2007. "The Protestant Sect Credit Machine: Social Capital and the Rise of Capitalism." *Journal of Classical Sociology* 7(3): 267–90.

Cortada, James W. 2000. "Progenitors of the Information Age: The Development of Chips and Computers." In *A Nation Transformed by Information: How Information Has Shaped the United States from Colonial Times to the Present*, ed. Alfred D. Chandler Jr. and James W. Cortada, 177–216. New York: Oxford University Press.

Coval, Joshua, Jakub Jurek, and Erik Stafford. 2009. "The Economics of Structured Finance." *Journal of Economic Perspectives* 23(1): 3–25.

Credit Rating Association. 1919. *Credit Guide: Tells How They Pay.* Minneapolis: Credit Rating Association.

Credit Research Foundation. 1958. *Credit Management Handbook.* Homewood, IL: Richard Irwin, Inc.

Crook, Jonathan N., David B. Edelman, and Lyn C. Thomas. 2007. "Recent Developments in Consumer Credit Risk Assessment." *European Journal of Operational Research* 183: 1447–65.

Crouch, Colin. 2011. *The Strange Non-Death of Neoliberalism.* Cambridge: Polity Press.

Cunningham, Daniel, and Thomas Werlen. 1996. "Derivatives and the Reduction of Credit Risk." *International Financial Law Review* 15: 35–36.

Dailey, Don M. 1938. "The Early Development of the Note-Brokerage Business in Chicago." *Journal of Political Economy* 46(2): 202–17.

Daniel, Pete. 2007. "African American Farmers and Civil Rights." *Journal of Southern History* 73(1): 3–38.

Dasgupta, Partha. 1988. "Trust as a Commodity." In *Trust: Making and Breaking Cooperative Relations*, ed. Diego Gambetta. Oxford: Basil Blackwell.

———. 2009. "Trust and Cooperation among Economic Agents." *Philosophical Transactions: Biological Sciences* 364(1533): 3301–9.

Davis, Andrew McFarland. 1910. *The Origin of the National Banking System.* 61st Cong., 2nd sess., Senate Document no. 582. Washington, DC: National Monetary Commission.

Davis, Gerald F. 2009. *Managed by the Markets: How Finance Re-Shaped America.* New York: Oxford University Press.

Davis, Gerald F., and Suntae Kim. 2015. "Financialization of the Economy." *Annual Review of Sociology* 41: 203–21.

Davis, Gerald F., and Mark S. Mizruchi. 1999. "The Money Center Cannot Hold: Commercial Banks in the U.S. System of Corporate Governance." *Administrative Science Quarterly* 44(2): 215–39.

Davis, John Martin, Jr. 2003. "Bankless in Beaufort: A Reexamination of the 1873 Failure of the Freedmans Savings Branch in Beaufort, South Carolina." *South Carolina Historical Magazine* 104(1): 25–55.

Davis, Lance E. 1965. "The Investment Market, 1870–1914: The Evolution of a National Market." *Journal of Economic History* 25(3): 355–99.

Davis, Lance E., and Robert J. Cull. 1994. *International Capital Markets and American Economic Growth, 1820–1914.* Cambridge: Cambridge University Press.

Davis, Lance, Larry Neal, and Eugene N. White. 2003. "How It All Began: The Rise of Listing Requirements on the London, Berlin, Paris, and New York Stock Exchanges." *International Journal of Accounting* 38: 117–43.

Dawson, John P., and Frank E. Cooper. 1935. "The Effect of Inflation on Private Contracts: United States, 1861–1879." *Michigan Law Review* 33(6): 852–922.

DeCanio, Samuel. 2011. "Populism, Paranoia, and the Politics of Free Silver." *Studies in American Political Development* 25: 1–26.

De Cnudde, Sofie, Julie Moeyersoms, Marija Stankova, Ellen Tobback, Vinayak Javaly, and David Martens. 2019. "What Does Your Facebook Profile Reveal about Your Creditworthiness? Using Alternative Data for Microfinance." *Journal of the Operational Research Society* 70(3): 353–63.

Defoe, Daniel. 1987 [1726]. *The Complete English Tradesman.* Gloucester: Alan Sutton.

Degenshein, Anya. 2020. "The Object Economy: 'Alternative' Banking in Chicago." *Contexts* 19(1): 18–23.

Dehejia, Rajeev, and Adriana Lleras-Muney. 2007. "Financial Development and Pathways of Growth: State Branching and Deposit Insurance Laws in the United States, 1900–1940." *Journal of Law and Economics* 50(2): 239–72.

Dei Ottati, Gabi. 1994. "Trust, Interlinking Transactions and Credit in the Industrial District." *Cambridge Journal of Economics* 18: 529–46.

Delaney, Kevin J. 1992. *Strategic Bankruptcy: How Corporations and Creditors Use Chapter 11 to Their Advantage.* Berkeley: University of California Press.

Demirgüç-Kunt, Asli, and Leora Klapper. 2013. "Measuring Financial Inclusion: Explaining Variation in Use of Financial Services across and within Countries." *Brookings Papers on Economic Activity* (Spring 2013): 279–321.

Desai, Deven R., and Joshua A. Kroll. 2017. "Trust but Verify: A Guide to Algorithms and the Law." *Harvard Journal of Law & Technology* 31(1): 1–64.

Dewing, Arthur Stone. 1919. *The Financial Policy of Corporations.* New York: Ronald Press.

Dexter, Seymour. 1891. "The Growth and Economic Value of Building and Loan Associations." *Publications of the American Economic Association* 6(1/2): 141–44.

Dickerson, Mechele. 2014. *Home Ownership and America's Financial Underclass: Flawed Premises, Broken Promises, New Prescriptions.* New York: Cambridge University Press.

Didier, Emmanuel. 2020. *America by the Numbers: Quantification, Democracy, and the Birth of National Statistics.* Trans. Priya Var Sen. Cambridge, MA: MIT Press.

Dillon, John F. 1876. *The Law of Municipal Bonds.* St. Louis: G. I. Jones & Co.

Ditz, Toby L. 1994. "Shipwrecked: or, Masculinity Imperiled: Mercantile Representations of Failure and the Gendered Self in Eighteenth-Century Philadelphia." *Journal of American History* 81(1): 51–80.

DiVenti, Theresa R. 2009. "Fannie Mae and Freddie Mac: Past, Present, and Future." *Cityscape* 11(3): 231–42.

Djelic, Marie-Laure. 2013. "When Limited Liability Was (Still) an Issue: Mobilization and Politics of Signification in 19th-Century England." *Organizational Studies* 34(5–6): 595–621.

Dougherty, Eunice R. 1968. "Charge Accounting Banking." *Federal Reserve Bank of Richmond Monthly Review* (March): 10–12.

Douglas, William O. 1938. "Improvement in Federal Procedure for Corporate Reorganizations." *American Bar Association Journal* 24(11): 875–79.

Downs, Anthony. 1991. "From Flood to Drought: The 1990s Shift in Real Estate Finance." *Brookings Review* 9(3): 48–53.

Drake, St. Clair, and Horace R. Cayton. 1945. *Black Metropolis: A Study of Negro Life in a Northern City*. Chicago: University of Chicago Press.

Dressel, Julia, and Hany Farid. 2018. "The Accuracy, Fairness, and Limits of Predicting Recidivism." *Science Advances* 4: 1–5.

DuBois, W.E.B., ed. 1907. *Economic Cooperation among Negro Americans*. Atlanta: Atlanta University Press.

———. 1962. *Black Reconstruction in America, 1860–1880*. New York: Free Press.

———. 1996 [1899]. *The Philadelphia Negro*. Philadelphia: University of Pennsylvania Press.

Dubovec, Marek. 2006. "The Problems and Possibilities for Using Electronic Bills of Lading as Collateral." *Arizona Journal of International and Comparative Law* 23(2): 437–66.

Dun, R. G. 1916. *The Strategic Trade Centers of the World*. New York: R. G. Dun & Co.

———. 1918. *The Mercantile Agency Reports' Manual*. 4th ed. New York: R. G. Dun & Co.

Dunkman, William E. 1949. "Postwar Commercial Bank Lending Policies." *Journal of Finance* 4(2): 87–100.

DuPont, Brandon. 2017. "Bank Networks and Suspensions in the 1893 Panic: Evidence from the State Banks and Their Correspondents in Kansas." *Financial History Review* 24(3): 265–82.

Durand, David. 1941. *Risk Elements in Consumer Instalment Financing*. New York: National Bureau of Economic Research.

Dwyer, Rachel E., Laura McCloud, and Randy Hodson. 2012. "Debt and Graduation from American Universities." *Social Forces* 90(4): 1133–55.

Dylag, Matthew. 2010. "The Negotiability of Promissory Notes and Bills of Exchange in the Time of Chief Justice Holt." *Journal of Legal History* 32(2): 149–75.

Earling, P. R. 1890. *Whom to Trust: A Practical Treatise on Mercantile Credits*. Chicago: Rand, McNally.

Easterly, Michael E. 2008. "Your Job Is Your Credit: Creating a Market for Loans to Salaried Employees in New York City, 1885–1920." PhD diss., University of California, Los Angeles.

———. 2010. "Your Job Is Your Credit: Creating a Market for Loans to Salaried Employees in New York City, 1885–1920." *Journal of Economic History* 70(2): 463–68.

Eastman, F. H. 1959. "Mechanics of Bond Issue Campaigns." *Journal of the American Water Works Association* 51(9): 1079–94.

Edling, Max M. 2007. "'So Immense a Power in the Affairs of War': Alexander Hamilton and the Restoration of Public Credit." *William and Mary Quarterly* 64(2): 287–326.

———. 2014. *A Hercules in the Cradle: War, Money, and the American State, 1783–1867*. Chicago: University of Chicago Press.

Edling, Max M., and Mark D. Kaplanoff. 2004. "Alexander Hamilton's Fiscal Reform: Transforming the Structure of Taxation in the Early Republic." *William and Mary Quarterly* 61(4): 713–44.

Edwards, Franklin R., and Edward R. Morrison. 2005. "Derivatives and the Bankruptcy Code: Why the Special Treatment?" *Yale Journal on Regulation* 22: 91–122.

Edwards, James Don. 1958. "Public Accounting in the United States from 1913 to 1928." *Business History Review* 32(1): 74–101.

Elliott, William S. 1941. "Federal Lending Agencies." *Bankers' Magazine* (January): 26–34.

Elster, Jon. 1979. *Ulysses and the Sirens: Studies in Rationality and Irrationality*. Cambridge: Cambridge University Press.

Emory, J. C. 1902. "The Credit Department of a Bank." *Bankers' Magazine* (February): 244–47.

Engberg, R. C. 1931. "The Functioning of the Federal Land Banks." *Journal of Farm Economics* 13(1): 133–45.

English, Linda. 2006. "Recording Race: General Stores and Race in the Late Nineteenth-Century Southwest." *Southwestern Historical Quarterly* 110(2): 192–217.

English, William B. 1996. "Understanding the Costs of Sovereign Default: American State Debts in the 1840s." *American Economic Review* 86(1): 259–75.

Erie, Steven P. 1992. "How the Urban West Was Won: The Local State and Economic Growth in Los Angeles, 1880–1932." *Urban Affairs Quarterly* 27(4): 519–54.

Espeland, Wendy Nelson. 1998. *The Struggle for Water: Politics, Rationality, and Identity in the American Southwest*. Chicago: University of Chicago Press.

Espeland, Wendy Nelson, and Michael Sauder. 2007. "Rankings and Reactivity: How Public Measures Recreate Social Worlds." *American Journal of Sociology* 113(1): 1–40.

Espeland, Wendy Nelson, and Mitchell L. Stevens. 2008. "A Sociology of Quantification." *European Journal of Sociology* 49(3): 401–36.

Eubank, Earle Edward. 1916. *The Loan Shark in Chicago*. Bulletin of the Department of Public Welfare City of Chicago. Vol. 1, no. 4.

———. 1917. "Loan Sharks and Loan Shark Legislation in Illinois." *Journal of the American Institute of Criminal Law and Criminology* 8(1): 69–81.

Evans, David S., and Richard Schmalensee. 2005. *Paying with Plastic: The Digital Revolution in Buying and Borrowing*. 2nd ed. Cambridge, MA: MIT Press.

Fabozzi, Frank J., Robert J. Shiller, and Radu S. Tunaru. 2020. "A 30-Year Perspective on Property Derivatives." *Journal of Economic Perspectives* 34(4): 121–45.

Federal Housing Administration (FHA). 1936. *Underwriting Manual: Underwriting and Valuation Procedure under Title II of the National Housing Act*. Washington, DC: FHA.

———. 1947. *Underwriting Manual: Underwriting Analysis under Title II, Section 203 of the National Housing Act*. Washington, DC: FHA.

———. 1955. *Underwriting Manual: Underwriting Analysis under Title II, Section 203 of the National Housing Act*. Washington, DC: FHA.

Federal Open Market Committee (FOMC). 1959. July 28 Meeting Minutes. Washington, DC: Federal Reserve Board.

Federal Reserve Bank of New York. 1915. "Eligible Paper." Circular No. 25, June 19. New York: Federal Reserve Bank of New York.

———. 1930. *Monthly Review of Business and Credit Conditions*. December 1: 89–97.

———. 2014. *Quarterly Report on Household Debt and Credit*. New York: Federal Reserve Bank of New York.

Federal Reserve Board. 1920. *Federal Reserve Bulletin September 1920*. Washington, DC: U.S. Government Printing Office.

———. 1922. "Credit Insurance." *Federal Reserve Bulletin* (June): 667–78.

———. 1936. "Law Department." *Federal Reserve Bulletin* (June): 419–26.

———. 1938a. "Revision in Bank Examination Procedure and in the Investment Securities Regulation of the Comptroller of the Currency." *Federal Reserve Bulletin* (July): 563–66.

———. 1938b. *Twenty-Fifth Annual Report of the Board of Governors of the Federal Reserve System*. Washington, DC.

———. 1939. *Problems of Banking and Bank Supervision: Excerpts from 1938 Annual Report of the Board of Governors of the Federal Reserve System.*

———. 1949. "Revision in Bank Examination Procedure." *Federal Reserve Bulletin* (July): 776–77.

———. 1957. "Survey of Finance Companies, Mid-1955." *Federal Reserve Bulletin* (April): 392–408.

———. 2018. "Survey of Finance Companies, 2015." *Federal Reserve Bulletin* 104(3): 1–19.

Federal Trade Commission (FTC). 2011. *Forty Years of Experience with the Fair Credit Reporting Act: An FTC Staff Report with Summary of Interpretations.* Washington, DC: FTC.

———. 2016. *Big Data: A Tool for Inclusion or Exclusion?* Washington, DC: FTC.

Feins, Judith D., and Terry Saunders Lane. 1981. *How Much for Housing? New Perspectives on Affordability and Risk.* Cambridge, MA: Abt Books.

Feld, Scott L., and Richard Elmore. 1982. "Patterns of Sociometric Choices: Transitivity Reconsidered." *Social Psychology Quarterly* 45(2): 77–85.

Fergus, Devin. 2018. *Land of the Fee: Hidden Costs and the Decline of the American Middle Class.* New York: Oxford University Press.

Filsinger, E. B. 1926. "Is Credit Needed in Export Trade?" *Bankers' Magazine* (June): 830–32.

Firestone, Simon. 2014. "Race, Ethnicity, and Credit Card Marketing." *Journal of Money, Credit and Banking* 46(6): 1205–24.

Fishback, Price. 2007. "The New Deal." In *Government and the American Economy: A New History*, ed. Price Fishback et al., 384–430. Chicago: University of Chicago Press.

———. 2017. "How Successful Was the New Deal? The Microeconomic Impact of New Deal Spending and Lending Policies in the 1930s." *Journal of Economic Literature* 55(4): 1435–85.

Fishback, Price V., Alfonso Flores-Lagunes, William C. Horrace, Shawn Kantor, and Jaret Treber. 2011. "The Influence of the Home Owners' Loan Corporation on Housing Markets during the 1930s." *Review of Financial Studies* 24(6): 1782–1813.

Fisher, Ernest M. 1950. "Changing Institutional Patterns of Mortgage Lending." *Journal of Finance* 5(4): 307–15.

Fisk and Hatch. 1876. *Memoranda Concerning Government Bonds, For the Information of Investors.* New York: Fisk and Hatch.

Flanagan, Sean M. 2001. "The Rise of a Trade Association: Group Interactions within the International Swaps and Derivatives Association." *Harvard Negotiation Law Review* 6: 211–63.

Flandreau, Marc, and Juan H. Flores. 2012. "The Peaceful Conspiracy: Bond Markets and International Relations during the Pax Britannica." *International Organization* 66: 211–241.

Flandreau, Marc, Norbert Gaillard, and Frank Packer. 2011. "To Err Is Human: U.S. Rating Agencies and the Interwar Foreign Government Debt Crisis." *European Review of Economic History* 15: 495–538.

Flandreau, Marc, and Gabriel Geisler Mesevage. 2014a. "The Separation of Information and Lending and the Rise of Rating Agencies in the USA (1841–1907)." *Scandinavian Economic History Review* 62(3): 213–42.

———. 2014b. "The Untold History of Transparency: Mercantile Agencies, the Law, and the Lawyers (1851–1916)." *Enterprise and Society* 15(2): 213–51.

Flandreau, Marc, and Joanna Kinga Sławatyniec. 2013. "Understanding Rating Addition: US Courts and the Origins of Rating Agencies' Regulatory Licence (1900–1940)." *Financial History Review* 20(3): 237–57.

Fleming, Anne. 2018. "The Long History of 'Truth in Lending.'" *Journal of Policy History* 30(2): 236–71.

Fleming, Walter L. 1927. *The Freedman's Savings Bank: A Chapter in the Economic History of the Negro Race.* Chapel Hill: University of North Carolina Press.

Fligstein, Neil. 2021. *The Banks Did It: An Anatomy of the Financial Crisis.* Cambridge: Harvard University Press.

Flinn, William Adams. 1959. "History of Retail Credit Company: A Study in the Marketing of Information about Individuals." PhD diss., Ohio State University.

Fons, Jerome S. 2004. "Tracing the Origins of 'Investment Grade.'" *Special Comment*. New York: Moody's Investors Service.

Fontaine, Laurence. 2001. "Antonio and Shylock: Credit and Trust in France, c. 1680–c. 1780." *Economic History Review* 54: 39–57.

Foroughi, Andrea R. 2003. "Vine and Oak: Wives and Husbands Cope with the Financial Panic of 1857." *Journal of Social History* 36(4): 1009–32.

Foster, LeBaron R. 1935. "Instalment Credit Costs and the Consumer." *Journal of Business* 8(1): 27–45.

Foster, William Trufant. 1938. "Public Supervision of Consumer Credit." *Journal of the American Statistical Association* 33(201): 71–80.

———. 1941. "The Personal Finance Business under Regulation." *Law and Contemporary Problems* 8(1): 154–72.

Foulke, Roy A. 1941. *The Sinews of American Commerce*. New York: Dun & Bradstreet.

Fourcade, Marion. 2016. "Ordinalization." *Sociological Theory* 34(3): 175–95.

Fourcade, Marion, and Kieran Healy. 2013. "Classification Situation: Life-Chances in the Neoliberal Era." *Accounting, Organizations and Society* 38: 559–72.

Fox, Richard M., and Joseph P. DeMarco. 1996. "On Making and Keeping Promises." *Journal of Applied Philosophy* 13(2): 199–208.

Fraine, H. G. 1951. "The Valuation of Security Holdings of Life Insurance Companies." *Journal of Finance* 6(2): 124–38.

Frame, W. Scott, Aruna Srinivasan, and Lynn Woosley. 2001. "The Effect of Credit Scoring on Small-Business Lending." *Journal of Money, Credit and Banking* 33(3): 813–25.

Francis, Gerald M. 1947. *The Small Businessman and His Bank*. Economic (Small Business) Series No. 64. Washington, DC: U.S. Department of Commerce.

Frank, Murray Z., and Vidhan K. Goyal. 2003. "Testing the Pecking Order Theory of Capital Structure." *Journal of Financial Economics* 67(2): 217–48.

———. 2009. "Capital Structure Decisions: Which Factors Are Reliably Important?" *Financial Management* (Spring): 1–37.

Franklin, Benjamin. 1904. *The Works of Benjamin Franklin, including the Private as well as the Official and Scientific Correspondence, together with the Unmutilated and Correct Version of the Autobiography*. The Federal Edition in 12 vols. Vol. 1: *Autobiography, Letters and Misc. Writings, 1725–1734*, compiled and edited by John Bigelow. New York: G. P. Putnam's Sons.

Frederiksen, D. M. 1894. "Mortgage Banking in America." *Journal of Political Economy* 2(2): 203–34.

Freedley, Edwin T. 1853. *A Practical Treatise on Business: Or How to Get, Save, Spend, Give, Lend, and Bequeath Money*. Philadelphia: Lippincott, Grambo & Co.

French, David M. 1941. "The Contest for a National System of Home-Mortgage Finance." *American Political Science Review* 35(1): 53–69.

French, Walter B. 1939. *Small Loans: An Investment for Banks*. Cambridge, MA: Bankers Publishing.

Freund, David M. P. 2007. *Colored Property: State Policy and White Racial Politics in Suburban America*. Chicago: University of Chicago Press.

Freyer, Tony A. 1976. "Negotiable Instruments and the Federal Courts in Antebellum American Business." *Business History Review* 50(4): 435–55.

———. 1979. *Forums of Order: The Federal Courts and Business in American History*. Greenwich, CT: JAI Press.

———. 1982. "Antebellum Commercial Law: Common Law Approaches to Secured Transactions." *Kentucky Law Journal* 70: 593–608.

Frieden, Jeffry. 1997. "Monetary Populism in Nineteenth-Century America: An Open Economy Interpretation." *Journal of Economic History* 57(2): 367–95.

Friedman, Samantha, and Gregory D. Squires. 2005. "Does the Community Reinvestment Act Help Minorities Access Traditionally Inaccessible Neighborhoods." *Social Problems* 52(2): 209–31.

Friedman, Walter A. 2014. *Fortune Tellers: The Story of America's First Economic Forecasters.* Princeton: Princeton University Press.

Friend, Craig T. 1997. "Merchants and Markethouses: Reflections on Moral Economy in Early Kentucky." *Journal of the Early Republic* 17(4): 553–74.

Froman, Lewis A. 1935. "Credit Unions." *Journal of Business* 8(3): 284–96.

Frost, John. 1841. *The Young Merchant.* Boston: George W. Light.

Fukuyama, Francis. 1995. *Trust: The Social Virtues and the Creation of Prosperity.* New York: Free Press.

Fusaro, Maria. 2012. "Cooperating Mercantile Networks in the Early Modern Mediterranean." *Economic History Review* 65(2): 701–18.

Gabor, Daniela. 2016. "The (Impossible) Repo Trinity: The Political Economy of Repo Markets." *Review of Radical Political Economy* 23(6): 967–1000.

Gaillard, Norbert J., and Michael Waibel. 2018. "The Icarus Syndrome: How Credit Rating Agencies Lost Their Quasi Immunity." *SMU Law Review* 71: 1077–1116.

Gambetta, Diego. 1993. *The Sicilian Mafia: The Business of Private Protection.* Cambridge, MA: Harvard University Press.

Garbade, Kenneth D. 2006. "The Evolution of Repo Contracting Conventions in the 1980s." *Federal Reserve Bank of New York Economic Policy Review* 12(1): 27–42.

———. 2016. "The First Debt Ceiling Crisis." Federal Reserve Bank of New York Staff Report No. 783. https://www.newyorkfed.org/research/staff_reports/sr783.html.

Garmaise, Mark J., and Tobias J. Moskowitz. 2003. "Informal Financial Networks: Theory and Evidence." *Review of Financial Studies* 16(4): 1007–40.

Garon, Sheldon. 2012. *Beyond Our Means: Why America Spends while the World Saves.* Princeton: Princeton University Press.

Garrett-Scott, Shennette. 2019. *Banking on Freedom: Black Women in U.S. Finance before the New Deal.* New York: Columbia University Press.

Garrison, Martha L. 1976. "Credit-Ability for Women." *Family Coordinator* 25(3): 241–48.

Geary, Anne J. 1976. "Equal Credit Opportunity—An Analysis of Regulation B." *Business Lawyer* 31(3): 1641–58.

Gehrken, George A. 1922. "Credit and Its Development." *Bankers' Magazine* (August): 260–63.

Gelpi, Rosa-Maria, and François Julien-Labruyère. 2000. *The History of Consumer Credit: Doctrines and Practices.* Trans. Mn Liam Gavin. London: Macmillan Press.

Geltzer, Robert L., and Lois Woocher. 1982. "Debt Collection Regulation: Its Development and Direction for the 1980s." *Business Lawyer* 37(4): 1401–13.

General Accounting Office (GAO). 2006. *Minority Banks: Regulators Need to Better Assess Effectiveness of Support Efforts.* Washington, DC: GAO-07-6.

Ghosh, Swati R. 2006. *East Asian Finance: The Road to Robust Markets.* Washington, DC: World Bank.

Gibbons, J. S. 1858. *The Banks of New-York, Their Dealers, and the Panic of 1857.* New York: D. Appleton & Co.

Giedeman, Daniel C. 2005. "Branch Banking Restrictions and Finance Constraints in Early Twentieth-Century America." *Journal of Economic History* 65(1): 129–51.

Gilbert, Abby L. 1972. "The Comptroller of the Currency and the Freedman's Savings Bank." *Journal of Negro History* 57(2): 125–43.

Gisolfi, Monica Richmond. 2006. "From Crop Lien to Contract Farming: The Roots of Agribusiness in the American South, 1929–1939." *Agricultural History* 80(2): 167–89.

Glick, Reuven, and Kevin J. Lansing. 2009. "U.S. Household Deleveraging and Future Consumption Growth." *FRBSF Economic Letter* 2009-16. San Francisco: Federal Reserve Bank of San Francisco.

Godley, Andrew. 1996. "Jewish Soft Loan Societies in New York and London and Immigrant Entrepreneurship, 1880–1914." *Business History* 38(3): 101–16.

Goldberg, Jessica L. 2012. *Trade and Institutions in the Medieval Mediterranean: The Geniza Merchants and Their Business World*. Cambridge: Cambridge University Press.

Goldrick-Rab, Sara. 2016. *Paying the Price: College Costs, Financial Aid, and the Betrayal of the American Dream*. Chicago: University of Chicago Press.

Golembe, Carter H. 1960. "The Deposit Insurance Legislation of 1933: An Examination of Its Antecedents and Its Purposes." *Political Science Quarterly* 75(2): 181–200.

Goode, Roy. 2018. "Asset Identification under the Cape Town Convention and Protocols." *Law and Contemporary Problems* 81(1): 135–54.

Goodman, Paul. 1993. "The Emergence of Homestead Exemption in the United States: Accommodation and Resistance to the Market Revolution, 1840–1880." *Journal of American History* 80(2): 470–98.

Goodrich, Carter. 1960. *Government Promotion of American Canals and Railroads, 1800–1860*. New York: Columbia University Press.

Goodstein, Ryan M., Alicia Lloro, Sherrie L. W. Rhine, and Jeffrey M. Weinstein. 2021. "What Accounts for Racial and Ethnic Differences in Credit Use?" *Journal of Consumer Affairs* 55: 389–416.

Gorton, Gary B. 2010. *Slapped by the Invisible Hand: The Panic of 2007*. New York: Oxford University Press.

———. 2017. "The History and Economics of Safe Assets." *Annual Review of Economics* 9: 547–86.

Gorton, Gary B., and Ellis W. Tallman. 2018. *Fighting Financial Crises: Learning from the Past*. Chicago: University of Chicago Press.

Gotham, Kevin Fox. 2006. "The Secondary Circuit of Capital Reconsidered: Globalization and the U.S. Real Estate Sector." *American Journal of Sociology* 112(1): 231–75.

Graeber, David. 2011. *Debt: The First 5000 Years*. Brooklyn: Melville House Publishing.

Graham, John R., Mark T. Leary, and Michael R. Roberts. 2015. "A Century of Capital Structure: The Leveraging of Corporate America." *Journal of Financial Economics* 118: 658–83.

Granovetter, Mark. 1973. "The Strength of Weak Ties." *American Journal of Sociology* 78(6): 1360–80.

———. 1985. "Economic Action and Social Structure: The Problem of Embeddedness." *American Journal of Sociology* 91(3): 481–510.

———. 2017. *Society and Economy: Framework and Principles*. Cambridge, MA: Harvard University Press.

Grant, Daniel L. 1941. "The Problem of Security Ratings." *Bankers' Magazine* (May): 378–82.

Gray, Whitmore. 1986. "E pluribus unum? A Bicentennial Report on Unification of Law in the United States." *Rabel Journal of Comparative and International Private Law* 50(1/2): 111–65.

Grebler, Leo. 1940. "The Home Mortgage Structure in Transition." *Harvard Business Review* 18(3): 357–71.

Greeley, Louis M. 1887. "What Publications of Commercial Agencies Are Privileged." *American Law Register* 35(11): 681–93.

Green, Richard K., and Susan M. Wachter. 2005. "The American Mortgage in Historical and International Context." *Journal of Economic Perspectives* 19(4): 93–114.

Greenberg, Dolores. 1980. *Financiers and Railroads, 1869–1889: A Study of Morton, Bliss & Company*. Newark: University of Delaware Press.

Greenberg, Ronald David. 1978. "Municipal Bankruptcy: Some Basic Aspects." *Urban Lawyer* 10(2): 266–88.

Gregory, Jon. 2010. *Counterparty Credit Risk: The New Challenge for Global Financial Markets.* New York: Wiley.

Greif, Avner. 2006. *Institutions and the Path to the Modern Economy: Lessons from Medieval Trade.* New York: Cambridge University Press.

Griffin, Bryant W. 1927. *Installment Sales and Collections.* New York: Prentice-Hall.

Grim, Valerie. 1995. "The Politics of Inclusion: Black Farmers and the Quest for Agribusiness Participation, 1945–1990s." *Agricultural History* 69(2): 257–71.

———. 1996. "Black Participation in the Farmers Home Administration and Agricultural Stabilization and Conservation Service, 1964–1990." *Agricultural History* 70(2): 321–36.

Grimes, William A. 1926. *Financing Automobile Sales by the Time-Payment Plan.* Chicago: A. W. Shaw.

Gross, Karen, Marie Stefanini Newman, and Denise Campbell. 1996. "Ladies in Red: Learning from America's First Female Bankrupts." *American Journal of Legal History* 40(1): 1–40.

Grossman, Richard S. 2010. *Unsettled Account: The Evolution of Banking in the Industrialized World since 1800.* Princeton: Princeton University Press.

Guild, Frederic H. 1920. "Uniform Legislation." *American Political Science Review* 14(3): 458–60.

Guinnane, Timothy W. 2001. "Cooperatives as Information Machines: German Rural Credit Cooperatives, 1883–1914." *Journal of Economic History* 61(2): 366–89.

———. 2005. "Trust: A Concept Too Many." *Jahrbuch für Wirtschaftsgeschichte* 46(1): 77–92.

Gulati, Ranjay. 1995. "Social Structure and Alliance Formation Patterns: A Longitudinal Analysis." *Administrative Science Quarterly* 40: 619–52.

Gullifer, Louise. 2012. "What Should We Do about Financial Collateral?" *Current Legal Problems* 65: 377–410.

Guo, Jiequn. 2010. "The Impact of the 2005 Bankruptcy Law on Subprime Mortgage Performance." *Journal of Structured Finance* (Spring): 33–38.

Hahn, Thomas K. 1993. "Commercial Paper." *Federal Reserve Bank of Richmond Economic Quarterly* 79(2): 45–67.

Haines, Howard Wright. 1932a. "Costs of Small Loan Department." *Bankers' Magazine* (December): 585–89.

———. 1932b. "Late Trends in Personal Loans." *Bankers' Magazine* (November): 433–36.

———. 1936a. "Small Loan Technique." *Bankers' Magazine* (August): 151–77.

———. 1936b. "Small Loan Technique." *Bankers' Magazine* (June): 533–41.

Hall, George J., and Thomas J. Sargent. 2018. "Brief History of US Debt Limits before 1939." *PNAS* 115(12): 2942–45.

Haller, Mark H., and John V. Alviti. 1977. "Loansharking in American Cities: Historical Analysis of a Marginal Enterprise." *American Journal of Legal History* 21(2): 125–56.

Halliday, Terence C., and Bruce G. Carruthers. 2009. *Bankrupt: Global Lawmaking and Systemic Financial Crisis.* Stanford: Stanford University Press.

Hallman, J. W. 1924. *Organizing the Credit Department.* New York: Ronald Press.

Ham, Arthur H. 1912. "Remedial Loans: A Constructive Program." *Proceedings of the Academy of Political Science in the City of New York* 2(2): 109–17.

Ham, Arthur H., and Leonard G. Robinson. 1923. *A Credit Union Primer.* New York: Russell Sage Foundation.

Hamilton, Alexander. 1790. "Report Relative to a Provision for the Support of Public Credit, [9 January 1790]." *Founders Online, National Archives*, version of January 18, 2019, https://founders.archives.gov/documents/Hamilton/01-06-02-0076-0002-0001. Original source: *The Papers of Alexander Hamilton*, vol. 6, December 1789–August 1790, ed. Harold C. Syrett, 65–110. New York: Columbia University Press, 1962.

———. 1795. "The Defence of the Funding System, [July 1795]." *Founders Online, National Archives*, version of January 18, 2019, https://founders.archives.gov/documents/Hamilton /01-19-02-0001. Original source: *The Papers of Alexander Hamilton*, vol. 19, July 1795–December 1795, ed. Harold C. Syrett, 1–73. New York: Columbia University Press, 1973.

Hammond, Bray. 1957. *Banks and Politics in America: From the Revolution to the Civil War*. Princeton: Princeton University Press.

Hancock, David. 2005. "The Trouble with Networks: Managing the Scots' Early-Modern Madeira Trade." *Business History Review* 79: 467–91.

Hand, D. J. 2005. "Good Practice in Retail Credit Scorecard Assessment." *Journal of the Operational Research Society* 56(9): 1109–17.

Hand, D. J., and W. E. Henley. 1997. "Statistical Classification Methods in Consumer Credit Scoring: A Review." *Journal of the Royal Statistical Society*, ser. A, 160(3): 523–41.

Handal, Kenneth V. 1972. "The Commercial Paper Market and the Securities Acts." *University of Chicago Law Review* 39(2): 362–402.

Hanes, C. O. 1915. *The Retail Credit and Adjustment Bureaus: Their Organization and Conduct*. Columbia, MO: Retail Merchants' Association.

Hanley, Anne. 2004. "Is It Who You Know? Entrepreneurs and Bankers in São Paulo, Brazil, at the Turn of the Twentieth Century." *Enterprise and Society* 5(2): 187–225.

Hanna, John. 1931. "Credit Insurance." *University of Pennsylvania Law Review and American Law Register* 79(5): 521–48.

Hansen, Bradley. 1998. "Commercial Associations and the Creation of a National Economy: The Demand for Federal Bankruptcy Law." *Business History Review* 72(1): 86–113.

Hansen, Mary Eschelbach, and Bradley A. Hansen. 2012. "Crisis and Bankruptcy: The Mediating Role of State Law, 1920–1932." *Journal of Economic History* 72(2): 448–68.

Harding, P. C. 2010. *Mastering the ISDA Master Agreements (1992 and 2002)*. 3rd ed. Harlow: Financial Times Prentice-Hall.

Hardy, Charles O. 1938. *Consumer Credit and Its Uses*. New York: Prentice-Hall.

Harold, Gilbert. 1938. *Bond Ratings as an Investment Guide: An Appraisal of Their Effectiveness*. New York: Ronald Press.

Harries, Brenton W. 1968. "Standard and Poor's Corporation New Policy on Rating Municipal Bonds." *Financial Analysts Journal* 24(3): 68–71.

Harris, Abram L. 1936. *The Negro as Capitalist: A Study of Banking and Business among American Negroes*. Philadelphia: American Academy of Political and Social Science.

Harris, Alexes, Heather Evans, and Katherine Beckett. 2010. "Drawing Blood from Stones: Legal Debt and Social Inequality in the Contemporary United States." *American Journal of Sociology* 115(6): 1753–99.

Harris, W. Carlton. 1930. "Real Estate and Real Estate Problems." *Annals of the American Academy of Political and Social Science* 148: 1–6.

Hartwell, Edward M., Solomon Blum, F. E. Stevens, Max B. May, Edwin Z. Smith, James J. McLoughlin, John A. Butler, George S. Wilson, Sidney A. Sherman, Delos F. Wilcox, J. Allen Smith, and W. G. Joerns. 1905. "Notes on Municipal Government. Municipal Indebtedness: A Symposium." *Annals of the American Academy of Political and Social Science* 25: 201–21.

Hauser, Rita E. 1958. "The Use of Index Clauses in Private Loans: A Comparative Study." *American Journal of Comparative Law* 7(3): 350–65.

Hawkins, David F. 1963. "The Development of Modern Financial Reporting Practices among American Manufacturing Corporations." *Business History Review* 37(3): 135–68.

Hawley, Clifford B., and Edwin T. Fujii. 1991. "Discrimination in Consumer Credit Markets." *Eastern Economic Journal* 17(1): 21–30.

Hawthorn, Geoffrey. 1988. "Three Ironies in Trust." In *Trust: Making and Breaking Cooperative Relations*, ed. Diego Gambetta. Oxford: Basil Blackwell.

Headrick, Daniel R. 2000. *When Information Came of Age: Technologies of Knowledge in the Age of Reason and Revolution, 1700–1850*. New York: Oxford University Press.

Heckman, Charles A. 1973. "The Relationship of Swift v. Tyson to the Status of Commercial Law in the Nineteenth Century and the Federal System." *American Journal of Legal History* 17(3): 246–55.

Heimer, Carol A. 1999. "Solving the Problem of Trust." In *Social Structure and Trust*, ed. Karen S. Cook, Margaret Levi, and Russell Hardin. New York: Russell Sage Foundation.

Helleiner, Eric. 2003. *The Making of National Money: Territorial Currencies in Historical Perspective*. Ithaca: Cornell University Press.

Heller, Charles F., Jr., and John T. Houdek. 2004. "Women Lenders as Sources of Land Credit in Nineteenth-Century Michigan." *Journal of Interdisciplinary History* 35(1): 37–67.

Henderson, Leon. 1931. "State Regulation of Small Loan Businesses." *Journal of Business of the University of Chicago* 4(3): 217–26.

Herring, Richard J. 2007. "The Rocky Road to Implementation of Basel II in the United States." *Atlantic Economic Journal* 35: 411–29.

Herring, William Rodney. 2016. "The Rhetoric of Credit, the Rhetoric of Debt: Economic Arguments in Early America and Beyond." *Rhetoric and Public Affairs* 19(1): 45–82.

Hert, Arthur H. 1938. "Charge Accounts of Retail Merchants." *Annals of the American Academy of Political and Social Science* 196: 111–20.

Herzog, Lisa. 2017. "What Could Be Wrong with a Mortgage? Private Debt Markets from a Perspective of Structural Injustice." *Journal of Political Philosophy* 25(4): 411–34.

Heuston, Alfred N. 1938. "Corporate Reorganizations under the Chandler Act." *Columbia Law Review* 38(7): 1199–1241.

Hickman, W. Braddock. 1953. *The Volume of Corporate Bond Financing since 1900*. Princeton: NBER and Princeton University Press.

———. 1957. *Corporate Bonds: Quality and Investment Performance*. NBER Occasional Paper 59. New York: National Bureau of Economic Research.

———. 1958. *Corporate Bond Quality and Investor Experience*. Princeton: NBER and Princeton University Press.

Hidy, Ralph W., and Muriel E. Hidy. 1960. "Anglo-American Merchant Bankers and the Railroads of the Old Northwest, 1848–1860." *Business History Review* 34(2): 150–69.

Higgens-Evenson, R. Rudy. 2002. "Financing a Second Era of Internal Improvements: Transportation and Tax Reform, 1890–1929." *Social Science History* 26(4): 623–51.

Hill, Claire A. 1997. "Securitization: A Low-Cost Sweetener for Lemons." *Journal of Applied Corporate Finance* 10(1): 64–71.

Hill, N. P. 1886. "Payment of the National Debt." *North American Review* 143(358): 209–18.

Hillier, Amy E. 2005. "Residential Security Maps and Neighborhood Appraisals: The Home Owners' Loan Corporation and the Case of Philadelphia." *Social Science History* 29(2): 207–33.

Hilt, Eric. 2017. "Corporation Law and the Shift toward Open Access in the Antebellum United States." In *Organizations, Civil Society, and the Roots of Development*, ed. Naomi R. Lamoreaux and John Joseph Wallis, 147–77. Chicago: University of Chicago Press.

———. 2018. "Business Organization in American Economic History." In *The Oxford Handbook of American Economic History*, ed. Louis P. Cain, Price V. Fishback, and Paul W. Rhode, 1:261–88. Oxford: Oxford University Press.

Hilt, Eric, and Wendy M. Rahn. 2016. "Turning Citizens into Investors: Promoting Savings with Liberty Bonds during World War I." *RSF: Russell Sage Foundation Journal of the Social Sciences* 2(6): 86–108.

Hirtle, Beverly J., Mark Levonian, Marc Saidenberg, Stefan Walter, and David Wright. 2001. "Using Credit Risk Models for Regulatory Capital: Issues and Options." *Federal Reserve Bank of New York Policy Review* (March): 19–36.

Ho, Benjamin. 2021. *Why Trust Matters: An Economist's Guide to the Ties That Bind Us*. New York: Columbia University Press.

Hoffman, Philip T., Gilles Postel-Vinay, and Jean-Laurent Rosenthal. 1998. "What Do Notaries Do? Overcoming Asymmetric Information in Financial Markets: The Case of Paris, 1751." *Journal of Institutional and Theoretical Economics* 154(3): 499–530.

Hogg, Martin. 2011. *Promises and Contract Law: Comparative Perspectives*. Cambridge: Cambridge University Press.

Holden, J. Milnes. 1955. *The History of Negotiable Instruments in English Law*. London: Athlone Press.

Hollander, Jacob H. 1913. "The Security Holdings of National Banks." *American Economic Review* 3(4): 793–814.

———. 1914. "The Probable Effects of the New Currency Act on Bank Investments." *Journal of Political Economy* 22(5): 444–52.

Holmes, George K. 1893. "Investigations of Mortgages and Farm and Home Proprietorship in the United States." *Journal of the Royal Statistical Society* 56(3): 443–81.

———. 1894. "A Decade of Mortgages." *Annals of the American Academy of Political and Social Science* 4: 48–62.

Holt, Harry Milton. 1917. "Keeping Track of Credit Information: The Cross Reference System for the Filing of Information and as a Method for Investigating." *Bankers' Magazine* (May): 532–33.

Holthausen, Duncan McC., Malcolm L. Merriam, and Rolf Nugent. 1940. *The Volume of Consumer Instalment Credit, 1929–38*. New York: National Bureau of Economic Research.

Holyoke City Treasurer. 1899. *Annual Report of the City Treasurer of Holyoke, Mass. for the Year 1898*. Holyoke, MA.

Hoppit, Julian. 1987. *Risk and Failure in English Business, 1700–1800*. Cambridge: Cambridge University Press.

Horwitz, Morton J. 1977. *The Transformation of American Law, 1780–1860*. Cambridge, MA: Harvard University Press.

Howard, Christopher. 1993. "The Hidden Side of the American Welfare State." *Political Science Quarterly* 108(3): 403–36.

———. 1997. *The Hidden Welfare State: Tax Expenditures and Social Policy in the United States*. Princeton: Princeton University Press.

Howland, Charles P. 1928. "Our Repudiated State Debts." *Foreign Affairs* 6(3): 395–407.

Hoyt, Wm. Henry. 1920. "Municipal Bonds." *Bulletin of the National Tax Association* 5(4): 104–9.

Hunt, Freeman. 1856. *Worth and Wealth: A Collection of Maxims, Morals and Miscellanies for Merchants and Men of Business*. New York: Stringer & Townsend.

Hunt, John Patrick. 2011. "Credit Ratings in Insurance Regulation: The Missing Piece of Financial Reform." *Washington and Lee Law Review* 68(4): 1667–97.

Hunt, Margaret R. 1996. *The Middling Sort: Commerce, Gender, and the Family in England, 1680–1780*. Berkeley: University of California Press.

Hunt, Robert M. 2005. "A Century of Consumer Credit Reporting in America." Working Paper No. 05-13. Philadelphia: Federal Reserve Bank of Philadelphia.

Hunter, Joel. 1914. "The Public Accountant and the Credit Man." *Journal of Accountancy* (December): 1–12.

Hurdman, Frederick H. 1914. "Credits from the Viewpoint of a Certified Public Accountant." *Journal of Accountancy* (December): 435–54.

Hyman, Louis. 2011. *Debtor Nation: The History of America in Red Ink*. Princeton: Princeton University Press.

Hyman, Mikell. 2020. "When Policy Feedback Fails: 'Collective Cooling' in Detroit's Municipal Bankruptcy." *Theory and Society* 49: 633–68.

Hynes, Richard, and Eric A. Posner. 2002. "The Law and Economics of Consumer Finance." *American Law and Economics Review* 4(1): 168–207.

Iceland, John, Daniel H. Weinberg, and Erika Steinmetz. 2002. *Racial and Ethnic Residential Segregation in the United States: 1980–2000*. Washington, DC: U.S. Census Bureau.

Igo, Sarah E. 2007. *The Averaged American: Surveys, Citizens, and the Making of a Mass Public*. Cambridge, MA: Harvard University Press.

———. 2018. *The Known Citizen: A History of Privacy in Modern America*. Cambridge, MA: Harvard University Press.

Ingham, John N. 2003. "Building Businesses, Creating Communities: Residential Segregation and the Growth of African American Business in Southern Cities, 1880–1915." *Business History Review* 77(4): 639–65.

International Swaps and Derivatives Association (ISDA). 1996. *Guidelines for Collateral Practitioners*. New York: ISDA.

———. 2010. *ISDA Margin Survey 2010*. New York: ISDA.

Jackson, Kenneth T. 1985. *Crabgrass Frontier: The Suburbanization of the United States*. New York: Oxford University Press.

Jacobson, Charles D., and Joel A. Tarr. 1994. "Ownership and Financing of Infrastructure: Historical Perspectives." Policy Research Working Paper 1466. Washington, DC: World Bank.

Jacobstein, Meyer. 1913. "Farm Credit in a Northwestern State." *American Economic Review* 3(3): 598–605.

Jalil, Andrew J. 2015. "A New History of Banking Panics in the United States, 1825–1929: Construction and Implications." *American Economic Journal: Macroeconomics* 7(3): 295–330.

James, John A., Michael G. Palumbo, and Mark Thomas. 2007. "Consumption Smoothing among Working-Class American Families before Social Insurance." *Oxford Economic Papers* 59(4): 606–40.

Jamieson, Alan G. 1991. "Credit Insurance and Trade Expansion in Britain, 1820–1980." *Accounting, Business and Financial History* 1(2): 163–76.

Jaremski, Matthew. 2010. "Free Bank Failures: Risky Bonds versus Undiversified Portfolios." *Journal of Money, Credit and Banking* 42(8): 1565–87.

Jeacle, Ingrid, and Eamonn J. Walsh. 2002. "From Moral Evaluation to Rationalization: Accounting and the Shifting Technologies of Credit." *Accounting, Organizations and Society* 27: 737–61.

Jenkins, Destin. 2021. *The Bonds of Inequality: Debt and the Making of the American City*. Chicago: University of Chicago Press.

Jennings, Henrietta Cooper. 1939. *The Consumer in Commercial Banking*. New York: Consumer Credit Institute.

Jentzsch, Nicola. 2007. *Financial Privacy: An International Comparison of Credit Reporting Systems*. 2nd ed. Berlin: Springer-Verlag.

J.F.C. 1924. "The Mercantile Use of the Chattel Mortgage on an Open Stock." *Yale Law Journal* 34(2): 175–83.

John, Richard R. 1998. "The Politics of Innovation." *Daedalus* 127(4): 187–214.

———. 2000. "Recasting the Information Infrastructure for the Industrial Age." In *A Nation Transformed by Information: How Information Has Shaped the United States from Colonial Times to the Present*, ed. Alfred D. Chandler Jr. and James W. Cortada, 55–105. New York: Oxford University Press.

———. 2010. *Network Nation: Inventing American Telecommunications*. Cambridge, MA: Harvard University Press.

Johnson, Emory R. 1909. "Review of Moody's Analyses of Railroad Investments." *Annals of the American Academy of Political and Social Science* 34(1): 210–11.

Johnson, Gerald W. 1948. *Liberal's Progress*. New York: Coward-McCann.

Johnson, Kathleen W. 2005. "Recent Developments in the Credit Card Market and the Financial Obligations Ratio." *Federal Reserve Bulletin* 91: 473–86.

Johnston, Robert. 1967. "Credit—and Credit Cards." *Federal Reserve Bank of San Francisco Monthly Review* (September): 171–77.

Jones, David, and John Mingo. 1998. "Industry Practices in Credit Risk Modeling and Internal Capital Allocations: Implications for a Models-Based Regulatory Capital Standard." *Federal Reserve Bank of New York Economic Policy Review* (October): 53–60.

Jones, Fred Mitchell. 1936. "Retail Stores in the United States, 1800–1860." *Journal of Marketing* 1(2): 134–42.

Jones, Homer. 1938. "Insurance of Bank Deposits in the United States of America." *Economic Journal* 48(192): 695–706.

———. 1940. "An Appraisal of the Rules and Procedures of Bank Supervision, 1929–39." *Journal of Political Economy* 48(2): 183–98.

Jones, Leonard A. 1889. *A Treatise on the Law of Mortgages of Real Property*. 2 vols. 4th ed. Boston: Houghton, Mifflin.

Jones-Correa, Michael. 2000. "The Origins and Diffusion of Racial Restrictive Covenants." *Political Science Quarterly* 115(4): 541–68.

Kadens, Emily. 2015. "Pre-Modern Credit Networks and the Limits of Reputation." *Iowa Law Review* 100: 2429–55.

Kagan, Robert A., Bliss Cartwright, Lawrence M. Friedman, and Stanton Wheeler. 1977. "The Business of State Supreme Courts, 1870–1970." *Stanford Law Review* 30(1): 121–56.

Kahle, Kathleen M., and René M. Stulz. 2017. "Is the US Public Corporation in Trouble?" *Journal of Economic Perspectives* 31(3): 67–88.

Kahn, C. Harry. 1960. *Personal Deductions in the Federal Income Tax*. Princeton: Princeton University Press.

Kali, Raja. 2001. "Business Networks in Transition Economies: Norms, Contracts, and Legal Institutions." In *Assessing the Value of Law in Transition Economies*, ed. Peter Murrell. Ann Arbor: University of Michigan Press.

Kaminski, Margot E. 2019. "The Right to Explanation, Explained." *Berkeley Technology Law Journal* 34(1): 189–218.

Kang, Sung Won, and Hugh Rockoff. 2015. "Capitalizing Patriotism: The Liberty Loans of World War I." *Financial History Review* 22(1): 45–78.

Karlberg, Martin. 1999. "Testing Transitivity in Digraphs." *Sociological Methodology* 29: 225–51.

Kashyap, Anil K., Richard Berner, and Charles A. E. Goodhart. 2011. "The Macroprudential Toolkit." *IMF Economic Review* 59(2): 145–61.

Kavanaugh, Thomas J. 1921. *Bank Credit Methods and Practice*. New York: Bankers Publishing.

Keehn, Richard H., and Gene Smiley. 1977. "Mortgage Lending by National Banks." *Business History Review* 51(4): 474–91.

Keller, Morton. 1963. *The Life Insurance Enterprise, 1885–1910: A Study in the Limits of Corporate Power*. Cambridge, MA: Harvard University Press.

Kendrick, John W. 1970. "The Historical Development of National-Income Accounts." *History of Political Economy* 2(2): 284–315.

Kennedy, Walter. 1958. *Bank Management*. Boston: Bankers Publishing.

Kerr, W. G. 1963. "Scotland and the Texas Mortgage Business." *Economic History Review* 16(1): 91–103.

———. 1976. *Scottish Capital on the American Credit Frontier*. Austin: Texas State Historical Association.

Kerwer, Dieter. 2001. "Standardising as Governance: The Case of Credit Rating Agencies." Bonn: Max-Planck-Projektgruppe Recht der Gemeinschaftsgüter.

Kevane, Henry C. 2011. "Chapter 9 Municipal Bankruptcy: The New 'New Thing'? Part I." *Business Law Today* (May): 1–3.

Kilborne, R. D. 1925. "A Review of the Operations of the Federal Farm Loan System." *Bankers' Magazine* (November): 697–700.

Kim, Namsuk, and John Joseph Wallis. 2005. "The Market for American State Government Bonds in Britain and the United States, 1830–43." *Economic History Review* 58(4): 736–64.

King, Michael R., and Timothy J. Sinclair. 2003. "Private Actors and Public Policy: A Requiem for the New Basel Capital Accord." *International Political Science Review* 24(3): 345–62.

Kinley, David. 1895. "Credit Instruments in Retail Trade." *Journal of Political Economy* 3(2): 203–16.

Kinne, Asa. 1842. *The Laws of the Different States and Territories of the United States on Imprisonment for Debt*. New York: Gould, Banks & Co.

Kiviat, Barbara. 2019. "The Art of Deciding with Data: Evidence from How Employers Translate Credit Reports into Hiring Decisions." *Socio-Economic Review* 17(2): 283–309.

Kiyonari, Toko, Toshio Yamagishi, Karen S. Cook, and Coye Cheshire. 2006. "Does Trust Beget Trustworthiness? Trust and Trustworthiness in Two Games and Two Cultures: A Research Note." *Social Psychology Quarterly* 69(3): 270–83.

Klaman, Saul B. 1957. "Mortgage Companies in the Postwar Mortgage Market." *Journal of Finance* 12(2): 148–59.

Knapp, Joseph G. 1924. "Credit Costs in Nebraska Retail Stores." *Journal of Business* 2(2): 169–72.

Kniffen, William. 1911. "The Essentials in Granting Credit." *Bankers' Magazine* (October): 419–22.

———. 1915. *The Practical Work of a Bank*. New York: Bankers Publishing.

———. 1934. *The Practical Work of a Bank: A Treatise on Practical Banking*. 8th ed. New York: Bankers Publishing.

Knight, M. A. 1923. "The Organization and Operation of the Credit Department." *Bankers' Magazine* (September): 348–58.

Knodel, Jane. 2010. "The Role of Private Bankers in the US Payments System, 1835–1865." *Financial History Review* 17(2): 239–62.

Konig, David Thomas. 1979. *Law and Society in Puritan Massachusetts, Essex County, 1629–1692*. Chapel Hill: University of North Carolina Press.

Kornai, Janos. 1992. *The Socialist System: The Political Economy of Communism*. Princeton: Princeton University Press.

Kostka, Genia. 2019. "China's Social Credit Systems and Public Opinion: Explaining High Levels of Approval." *New Media & Society* 21(7): 1565–93.

Kowalcky, Linda K., and Lance T. LeLoup. 1993. "Congress and the Politics of Statutory Debt Limitation." *Public Administration Review* 53(1): 14–27.

Krippner, Greta. 2011. *Capitalizing on Crisis: The Political Origins of the Rise of Finance*. Cambridge, MA: Harvard University Press.

———. 2017. "Democracy of Credit: Ownership and the Politics of Credit Access in Late Twentieth-Century America." *American Journal of Sociology* 123(1): 1–47.

Kronovet, Alan. 1997. "An Overview of Commercial Mortgage Backed Securitization: The Devil Is in the Details." *North Carolina Banking Institute* 1(1): 288–321.

Kroszner, Randall S., and Philip E. Strahan. 1999. "What Drives Deregulation? Economics and Politics of the Relaxation of Branch Banking Restrictions." *Quarterly Journal of Economics* 114(4): 1437–67.

Kruger, Samuel. 2018. "The Effect of Mortgage Securitization on Foreclosure and Modification." *Journal of Financial Economics* 129: 586–607.

Krumbein, William C. 1924. "Collection Agencies." *University Journal of Business* 3(1): 48–67.

Kuehl, John W. 1995. "Justice, Republican Energy, and the Search for Middle Ground: James Madison and the Assumption of State Debts." *Virginia Magazine of History and Biography* 103(3): 321–38.

Kulikoff, Allan. 1986. *Tobacco and Slaves: The Development of Southern Cultures in the Chesapeake, 1680–1800*. Chapel Hill: University of North Carolina Press.

Ladd, Helen F. 1998. "Evidence on Discrimination in Mortgage Lending." *Journal of Economic Perspectives* 12(2): 41–62.

Ladin, Jay. 1967. "Mortgage Credit in Tippecanoe County, Indiana, 1865–1880." *Agricultural History* 41(1): 37–44.

Lamoreaux, Naomi. 1994. *Insider Lending: Banks, Personal Connections, and Economic Development in New England*. Cambridge: Cambridge University Press.

———. 1998. "Commentary." *Federal Reserve Bank of St. Louis Review* (May/June): 33–36.

Lancaster, Lane W. 1924. "The Trend in City Expenditures." *Annals of the American Academy of Political and Social Science* 113: 15–22.

Langer, Jeffrey I., and Andrew T. Semmelman. 1988. "Creditor List Screening Practices: Certain Implications under the Fair Credit Reporting Act." *Business Lawyer* 43(3): 1123–41.

La Porta, Raphael, Florencio Lopez-de-Silanes, Andrei Shleifer, and Robert W. Vishny. 1997. "Legal Determinants of External Finance." *Journal of Finance* 52(3): 1131–50.

———. 1998. "Law and Finance." *Journal of Political Economy* 106(6): 1113–55.

Lapp, John A. 1909. "Uniform Public Accounting and State Supervision of Accounts." *American Political Science Review* 3(2): 205–8.

———. 1910. "Uniform State Legislation." *American Political Science Review* 4: 576–81.

Lauer, Josh. 2017. *Creditworthy: A History of Consumer Surveillance and Financial Identity in America*. New York: Columbia University Press.

———. 2020. "Plastic Surveillance: Payment Cards and the History of Transactional Data, 1888 to Present." *Big Data and Society* (January–June): 1–14.

Lawrence, Joseph Stagg. 1929. "Is Investment Hedging Possible?" *Harvard Business Review* 7(3): 280–87.

Lazzarato, Maurizio. 2012. *The Making of the Indebted Man*. Trans. Joshua David Jordan. Los Angeles: Semiotext(e).

Lea, Michael J. 1996. "Innovation and the Cost of Mortgage Credit: A Historical Perspective." *Housing Policy Debate* 7(1): 147–74.

Lebsock, Suzanne. 1977. "Radical Reconstruction and the Property Rights of Southern Women." *Journal of Southern History* 43(2): 195–216.

Leffingwell, R. C. 1920. "Treasury Methods of Financing the War in Relation to Inflation." *Proceedings of the Academy of Political Science in the City of New York* 9(1): 16–41.

Lehmann, Henry W. 1950. "The Federal Municipal Bankruptcy Act." *Journal of Finance* 5(3): 241–56.

Leicht, Kevin T. 2012. "Borrowing to the Brink: Consumer Debt in America." In *Broke: How Debt Bankrupts the Middle Class*, ed. Katherine Porter, 195–217. Stanford: Stanford University Press.

Lepler, Jessica M. 2013. *The Many Panics of 1837: People, Politics, and the Creation of a Transatlantic Financial Crisis*. New York: Cambridge University Press.

Lerch, Marlin E. 1939. "Small Loan Lessons." *Bankers' Magazine* (September): 216–18.

Lester, V. Markham. 2013. "The Effect of Southern State Bond Repudiation and British Debt Collection Efforts on Anglo-American Relations, 1840–1940." *Journal of British Studies* 52(2): 415–40.

Levine, Daniel. 1997. "A Single Standard of Civilization: Black Private Social Welfare Institutions in the South, 1880s–1920s." *Georgia Historical Quarterly* 81(1): 52–77.

Levine, Ross. 1998. "The Legal Environment, Banks, and Long-Run Economic Growth." *Journal of Money, Credit, and Banking* 30(3): 596–613.

Levitin, Adam J. 2013. "The Paper Chase: Securitization, Foreclosure, and the Uncertainty of Mortgage Title." *Duke Law Journal* 63(3): 637–734.

Levy, Jonathan. 2012. *Freaks of Fortune: The Emerging World of Capitalism and Risk in America*. Cambridge, MA: Harvard University Press.

Lewis, Edward M. 1994. *An Introduction to Credit Scoring*. San Rafael, CA: Athena Press.

Lewis, Gwendolyn L. 1989. "Trends in Student Aid: 1963–4 to 1988–89." *Research in Higher Education* 30(6): 547–61.

Liang, Fan, Vischupriya Das, Nadiya Kostyuk, and Muzammil M. Hussain. 2018. "Constructing a Data-Driven Society: China's Social Credit System as a State Surveillance Infrastructure." *Policy & Internet* 10(4): 415–53.

Light, Ivan. 1977. "Numbers Gambling among Blacks: A Financial Institution." *American Sociological Review* 42(6): 892–904.

Light, Ivan, and Edna Bonacich. 1988. *Immigrant Entrepreneurs: Koreans in Los Angeles, 1965–1982*. Berkeley: University of California Press.

Light, Ivan, Im Jung Kwuon, and Deng Zhong. 1990. "Korean Rotating Credit Associations in Los Angeles." *Amerasia* 16: 35–54.

Lindsay, Arnett G. 1929. "The Negro in Banking." *Journal of Negro History* 14(2): 156–201.

Lipartito, Kenneth. 2013. "Mediating Reputation: Credit Reporting Systems in American History." *Business History Review* 87: 655–77.

Liu, Chencheng. 2019. "Multiple Social Credit Systems in China." *Economic Sociology: The European Electronic Newsletter* 21(1): 22–32.

Llewellyn, Karl N. 1957. "Why We Need the Uniform Commercial Code." *University of Florida Law Review* 10(4): 367–81.

Lord, Eleazar. 1834. *On Credit, Currency and Banking*. New York: G & C & H Carvill.

Lothian, E. H. 1938. "Collection Agency Activities: The Problem from the Standpoint of the Agencies." *Law and Contemporary Problems* 5(1): 29–34.

Lough, William H., Jr. 1909. *Corporation Finance*. Chicago: De Bower-Elliott Company.

Lynd, Robert S., and Helen Merrell Lynd. 1957. *Middletown: A Study in Modern American Culture*. New York: Harcourt Brace.

Lynn, Robert A. 1957. "Installment Credit before 1870." *Business History Review* 31(4): 414–24.

Macaulay, Stuart. 1963. "Non-Contractual Relations in Business." *American Sociological Review* 28: 55–69.

Macesich, George. 1961. "Counterfeit Detectors and Pre-1860 Monetary Statistics." *Journal of Southern History* 27(2): 229–32.

MacGregor, T. D. 1917. *The New Business Department: Its Organization and Operation in a Modern Bank*. New York: Bankers Publishing.

MacKenzie, Donald. 2003. "An Equation and Its Worlds: Bricolage, Exemplars, Disunity and Performativity in Financial Economics." *Social Studies of Science* 33(6): 831–68.

———. 2011. "The Credit Crisis as a Problem in the Sociology of Knowledge." *American Journal of Sociology* 116(6): 1778–1841.

MacManus, Susan A. 1990. "Financing Federal, State, and Local Governments in the 1990s." *Annals of the American Academy of Political and Social Science* 509: 22–35.

Madison, James H. 1974. "The Evolution of Commercial Credit Reporting in Nineteenth-Century America." *Business History Review* 48: 164–86.

Madison, James. 1790. "Discrimination between Present and Original Holders of the Public Debt, [11 February] 1790." *Founders Online, National Archives*, version of January 18, 2019, https://founders.archives.gov/documents/Madison/01-13-02-0030. Original source: *The Papers of James Madison*, vol. 13, 20 January 1790–31 March 1791, ed. Charles F. Hobson and Robert A. Rutland, 34–39. Charlottesville: University Press of Virginia, 1981.

Madley, Benjamin. 2016. *An American Genocide: The United States and the California Indian Catastrophe*. New Haven: Yale University Press.

Maggor, Noam. 2017. "To Coddle and Caress These Great Capitalists: Eastern Money, Frontier Populism, and the Politics of Market-Making in the American West." *American Historical Review* (February): 55–84.

Mahoney, Paul G. 2003. "The Origins of the Blue-Sky Laws: A Test of Competing Hypotheses." *Journal of Law and Economics* 46: 229–51.

Majewski, John. 1996. "Who Financed the Transportation Revolution? Regional Divergence and Internal Improvements in Antebellum Pennsylvania and Virginia." *Journal of Economic History* 56(4): 763–88.

Mallard, Grégoire. 2021. "We Owe You Nothing: Decolonization and Sovereign Debt Obligations in International Public Law." In *Sovereign Debt Diplomacies: Rethinking Sovereign Debt from Colonial Empires to Hegemony*, ed. Pierre Pénet and Juan Flores Zendejas, 189–212. Oxford: Oxford University Press.

Mann, Bruce H. 1987. *Neighbors and Strangers: Law and Community in Early Connecticut*. Chapel Hill: University of North Carolina Press.

———. 2002. *Republic of Debtors: Bankruptcy in the Age of American Independence*. Cambridge, MA: Harvard University Press.

Mann, Michael. 1984. "The Autonomous Power of the State: Its Origins, Mechanisms and Results." *European Journal of Sociology* 25(2): 185–213.

Mann, Ronald. 2014. "Assessing the Optimism of Payday Loan Borrowers." *Supreme Court Economic Review* 21(1): 105–32.

Mapes, Dorchester. 1916. "The Organization and Management of a Credit Department." In *Credits and Collections: Organizing the Work, Correct Policies and Methods, Five Credit and Collection Systems*, 19–27. Chicago: W. A. Shaw.

Mappin, W. F. 1889. "Farm Mortgages and the Small Farmer." *Political Science Quarterly* 4(3): 433–51.

Markowitz, Harry. 1952. "Portfolio Selection." *Journal of Finance* 7(1): 77–91.

Marler, Scott P. 2013. *The Merchants' Capital: New Orleans and the Political Economy of the Nineteenth-Century South*. New York: Cambridge University Press.

Marron, Donncha. 2009. *Consumer Credit in the United States: A Sociological Perspective from the 19th Century to the Present*. New York: Palgrave Macmillan.

Martin, Bonnie. 2010. "Slavery's Invisible Engine: Mortgaging Human Property." *Journal of Southern History* 76(4): 817–66.

Martin, Boyce F. 1931. "Recent Movements in the Commercial Paper Market." *Harvard Business Review* 9(3): 360–70.

Martindale, Joseph B. 1911. "The Business of a Commercial Bank." *The Independent* (December 21): 1399–1402.

Mason, David L. 2004. *From Buildings and Loans to Bail-Outs: A History of the American Savings and Loan Industry, 1831–1995*. Cambridge: Cambridge University Press.

———. 2012. "The Rise and Fall of the Cooperative Spirit: The Evolution of Organisational Structures in American Thrifts, 1831–1939." *Business History* 54(3): 381–98.

Massey, Douglas S., and Nancy A. Denton. 1993. *American Apartheid: Segregation and the Making of the Underclass*. Cambridge, MA: Harvard University Press.

Masten, Scott E. 2011. "Public Utility Ownership in 19th-Century America: The 'Aberrant' Case of Water." *Journal of Law, Economics, and Organization* 27(3): 604–54.

Matherly, Walter J. 1944. "The Regulation of Consumer Credit." *Southern Economic Journal* 11(1): 34–44.

May, Arthur A. 1942. *The Valuation of Residential Real Estate*. New York: Prentice-Hall.

Mayer, Christopher, Karen Pence, and Shane M. Sherlund. 2009. "The Rise in Mortgage Defaults." *Journal of Economic Perspectives* 23(1): 27–50.

McAvoy, Walter. 1922. "The Economic Importance of the Commercial Paper House." *Journal of Political Economy* 30(1): 78–87.

McCall, Leslie, and Christine Percheski. 2010. "Income Inequality: New Trends and Research Directions." *Annual Review of Sociology* 36: 327–47.

McCommas, Stuart. 2013. "Forgotten But Not Lost: The Original Public Meaning of Section 4 of the Fourteenth Amendment." *Virginia Law Review* 99(6): 1291–1326.

McConnell, J. W. 1916. "Credits and Collections in a Retail House." In *Credits and Collections: Organizing the Work, Correct Policies and Methods, Five Credit and Collection Systems*, 124–34. Chicago: W. A. Shaw.

McDaniel, Morey W. 1986. "Bondholders and Corporate Governance." *Business Lawyer* 41(2): 413–60.

McDonough, J. E. 1934. "The Federal Home Loan Bank System." *American Economic Review* 24(4): 668–85.

McFarlane, Larry A. 1983. "British Investment and the Land: Nebraska, 1877–1946." *Business History Review* 57(2): 258–72.

McGrane, Reginald C. 1935. *Foreign Bondholders and American State Debts*. New York: Macmillan.

McInnes, Russell. 1938. "The Investment Analyst Looks at Municipal Securities." *Annals of the American Academy of Political and Social Science* 199: 39–42.

McIntosh, Wayne. 1981. "150 Years of Litigation and Dispute Settlement: A Court Tale." *Law and Society Review* 15(3/4): 823–48.

McPherson, Miller, Lynn Smith-Lovin, and James M. Cook. 2001. "Birds of a Feather: Homophily in Social Networks." *Annual Review of Sociology* 27: 415–44.

McQuaid, Kim. 1976. "An American Owenite: Edward A. Filene and the Parameters of Industrial Reform, 1890–1937." *American Journal of Economics and Sociology* 35(1): 77–94.

Meech, S. P. 1923. "Recent Tendencies in Credit Relations between Commercial Paper Houses and Business Concerns." *University Journal of Business* 2(1): 52–71.

Meek, Charles E. 1914. "Credit Granting." *Journal of Accountancy* (December): 427–34.

Mehrling, Perry. 2002. "Economists and the Fed: Beginnings." *Journal of Economic Perspectives* 16(4): 207–18.

———. 2011. *The New Lombard Street: How the Fed Became the Dealer of Last Resort*. Princeton: Princeton University Press.

Mehrotra, Ajay K. 2010. "Lawyers, Guns, and Public Moneys: The U.S. Treasury, World War I, and the Administration of the Modern Fiscal State." *Law and History Review* 28(1): 173–225.

Melzer, Brian T. 2011. "The Real Costs of Credit Access: Evidence from the Payday Lending Market." *Quarterly Journal of Economics* 126(1): 517–55.

Mennicken, Andrea, and Peter Miller. 2012. "Accounting, Territorialization and Power." *Foucault Studies* 12: 4–24.

Mercantile Agency. 1872. *The Mercantile Agency Annual for 1872*. New York: Dunn, Barlow & Co.

Meredith, L. Douglas. 1950. "Liquidity: A Growing Attribute of Mortgage Loan Portfolios." *Journal of Finance* 5(4): 316–23.

Mester, Loretta J. 1997. "What's the Point of Credit Scoring?" *Federal Reserve Bank of Philadelphia Business Review* (September/October): 3–16.

Mettler, Suzanne. 2011. *The Submerged State: How Invisible Government Policies Undermine American Democracy*. Chicago: University of Chicago Press.

Meyer, Marco. 2018. "The Right to Credit." *Journal of Political Philosophy* 26(3): 304–26.

Michelman, Irving S. 1966. *Consumer Finance: A Case History in American Business*. New York: Frederick Fell.

Mihm, Stephen. 2007. *A Nation of Counterfeiters: Capitalists, Con Men, and the Making of the United States*. Cambridge, MA: Harvard University Press.

Miller, Glenn H., Jr. 1958. "The Hawkes Papers: A Case Study of a Kansas Mortgage Brokerage Business, 1871–1888." *Business History Review* 32(3): 293–310.

Miller, Mahlon D. 1927. *Bank Loans on Statement and Character*. New York: Ronald Press.

Miller, Matthew T. 1846. *Bicknell's Counterfeit Detector and Bank Note List*. Vol. 15, no. 8. Philadelphia.

Miller, Peter. 1994. "Accounting as Social and Institutional Practice: An Introduction." In *Accounting as Social and Institutional Practice*, ed. Anthony Hopwood and Peter Miller. Cambridge: Cambridge University Press.

Mintz, Beth, and Michael Schwartz. 1985. *The Power Structure of American Business*. Chicago: University of Chicago Press.

———. 1986. "Capital Flows and the Process of Financial Hegemony." *Theory and Society* 15(1/2): 77–101.

Miranti, Paul J., Jr. 1986. "Associationalism, Statism, and Professional Regulation: Public Accountants and the Reform of the Financial Markets, 1896–1940." *Business History Review* 60(3): 438–68.

Misztal, Barbara. 1996. *Trust in Modern Societies: The Search for the Bases of Social Order*. Cambridge: Polity Press.

Mitchell, S. Roger. 1916. "What Does an Accountant's Certified Statement Represent? What Value Should Be Given It by a Banker in Connection with the Extension of Credit?" *Bankers' Magazine* (June): 749–56.

Mitchell, Waldo F. 1923. "Credit Statements and Supervisory Influence of Banks over Business." *University Journal of Business* 1(2): 150–68.

Mizruchi, Mark S. 1996. "What Do Interlocks Do? An Analysis, Critique and Assessment of Research on Interlocking Directorates." *Annual Review of Sociology* 22: 271–98.

Mizruchi, Mark S., and Linda Brewster Stearns. 1994. "A Longitudinal Study of Borrowing by Large American Corporations." *Administrative Science Quarterly* 39(1): 118–40.

Montgomerie, Johnna. 2006. "The Financialization of the American Credit Card Industry." *Competition and Change* 10(3): 301–19.

Moody, John. 1909. *Moody's Analyses of Railroad Investments*. New York: Analyses Publishing.

———. 1920. "Industrial Bonds." *Annals of the American Academy of Political and Social Science* 88: 73–78.

Moody's Investors Service. 1921. *Moody's Analyses of Investments and Security Rating Books, Part IV, Government and Municipal Securities*. New York: Moody's Investors Service.

———. 1926. *Moody's Manual of Investments and Security Rating Service: Foreign and American Government Securities*. New York: Moody's Investors Service.

———. 2004. "Special Comment: Short-term Rating Performance and Corporate Commercial Paper Defaults, 1972–2004." New York: Moody's Investors Service.

Mooney, Charles W., Jr. 2018. "Fintech and Secured Transactions Systems of the Future." *Law and Contemporary Problems* 81(1): 1–20.

Moore, William H. 1949. "State Experiments in Mortgage Lending." *Journal of Business* 22(3): 169–77.

Morantz, Alison D. 2006. "There's No Place Like Home: Homestead Exemption and Judicial Constructions of Family in Nineteenth-Century America." *Law and History Review* 24(2): 245–95.

Morman, James B. 1920. "Cooperative Credit Institutions in the United States." *Annals of the American Academy of Political and Social Science* 87: 172–82.

Morrison, Alan D., and William J. Wilhelm Jr. 2007. *Investment Banking: Institutions, Politics, and Law*. Oxford: Oxford University Press.

Morrison, Fred L. 2002. "The Insolvency of Public Entities in the United States." *American Journal of Comparative Law* 50: 567–79.

Morrison, Grant. 1980. "A New York City Creditor and His Upstate Debtors: Isaac Bronson's Moneylending, 1819–1836." *New York History* 61(3): 255–76.

Morton, T. Gregory, and Jacob M. Duker. 1978. "Black Financial Institutions: An Appraisal." *Financial Management* 7(2): 28–36.

Morton, Walter A. 1939a. "The Country Bank." *Harvard Business Review* 17(4): 402–13.

———. 1939b. "Liquidity and Solvency." *American Economic Review* 29(2): 272–85.

Moses, Raphael J., Jr. 1879. *State Insolvent Laws: A Compilation of the Laws on Insolvency of the States and Territories of the United States and Canada, in force November 1, 1878*. New York: Baker, Voorhees & Co.

Moss, David A. 2002. *When All Else Fails: Government as the Ultimate Risk Manager*. Cambridge, MA: Harvard University Press.

Mottershead, Edmund. 1938. "Pawn Shops." *Annals of the American Academy of Political and Social Science* 196: 149–54.

Moulton, H. G. 1920. "Commercial Credit or Discount Companies." *Journal of Political Economy* 28(10): 827–39.

Moulton, Lynne. 2007. "Divining Value with Relational Proxies: How Moneylenders Balance Risk and Trust in the Quest for Good Borrowers." *Sociological Forum* 22(3): 300–330.

Moussalli, Stephanie D. 2008. "State and Local Government Accounting in 19th Century America: A Review of the Literature." *Accounting Historians Journal* 35(1): 167–95.

Muldrew, Craig. 1998. *The Economy of Obligation: The Culture of Credit and Social Relations in Early Modern England*. Houndmills: Macmillan Press.

Munn, Glenn G. 1923. "Granting Credit—The Credit Department." *Bankers' Magazine* (October): 500–503.

Munnell, Alicia H., Geoffrey M. B. Tootell, Lynn E. Browne, and James McEneaney. 1996. "Mortgage Lending in Boston: Interpreting HMDA Data." *American Economic Review* 86(1): 25–53.

Munro, John H. 2003. "The Medieval Origins of the Financial Revolution: Usury, *Rentes*, and Negotiability." *International History Review* 25(3): 505–52.

Murphy, Sharon Ann. 2005. "Securing Human Property: Slavery, Life Insurance, and Industrialization in the Upper South." *Journal of the Early Republic* 25(4): 615–52.

———. 2010. *Investing in Life: Insurance in Antebellum America*. Baltimore: Johns Hopkins University Press.

———. 2017. *Other People's Money: How Banking Worked in the Early American Republic*. Baltimore: Johns Hopkins University Press.

Murray, James E. 1972. "The Developing National Mortgage Market: Some Reflections and Projections." *Real Property, Probate and Trust Journal* 7(3): 441–50.

Murray, William G. 1935. "Farm Mortgages and the Government." *Journal of Farm Economics* 17(4): 613–24.

Myers, James H., and Edward W. Forgy. 1963. "The Development of Numerical Credit Evaluation Systems." *Journal of the American Statistical Association* 58(303): 799–806.

Myers, Margaret G. 1970. *A Financial History of the United States*. New York: Columbia University Press.

Myers, Stewart C. 2001. "Capital Structure." *Journal of Economic Perspectives* 15(2): 81–102.

Myers, Stewart C., and Nicolas S. Majluf. 1984. "Corporate Financing and Investment Decisions When Firms Have Information That Investors Do Not Have." *Journal of Financial Economics* 13(2): 187–221.

Nanda, Ved P. 2014. "Limitations on Government Debt and Deficits in the United States." *American Journal of Comparative Law* 62: 539–60.

National Association of Credit Management. 1965. *Credit Management Handbook*. Homewood, IL: Richard D. Irwin.

National Association of Manufacturers. 1909. *Proceedings of the Fourteenth Annual Convention of the National Association of Manufacturers of the United States of America*. New York.

National Association of Real Estate Boards. 1927. *Real Estate Appraising: Chapter 1, Appraising Vacant Residential Lots*. Chicago: National Association of Real Estate Boards.

National Bureau of Economic Research (NBER). 1941. *The Corporate Bond Project*. New York: NBER.

National Conference of State Legislatures. 2010. *NCSL Fiscal Brief: State Balanced Budget Provisions.* Washington, DC: National Conference of State Legislatures.

Neifeld, M. R. 1931. "Credit Unions in the United States." *Journal of Business* 4(4): 320–45.

———. 1941. "Institutional Organization of Consumer Credit." *Law and Contemporary Problems* 8(1): 23–35.

Newburgh, Conrad. 1991. "Character Assessment in the Lending Process." *Journal of Commercial Bank Lending* (April): 34–39.

Newfang, Oscar. 1912. "The Essentials of Commercial Credit." *Bankers' Magazine* 84(5): 639–46.

Nightingale, Pamela. 2010. "Gold, Credit, and Mortality: Distinguishing Deflationary Pressures on the Late Medieval English Economy." *Economic History Review* 63(4): 1081–1104.

Nissenson, S. G. 1939a. "The Development of a Land Registration System in New York." *New York History* 20(1): 16–42.

———. 1939b. "The Development of a Land Registration System in New York (II)." *New York History* 20(2): 161–88.

Niu, Beibei, Jinzheng Ren, and Xiaotao Li. 2019. "Credit Scoring Using Machine Learning by Combing Social Network Information: Evidence from Peer-to-Peer Lending." *Information* 10: 397–411.

Nolan, J. Bennett. 1944. "Ben Franklin's Mortgage on the Daniel Boone Farm." *Proceedings of the American Philosophical Society* 87(5): 394–97.

Norris, James D. 1978. *R. G. Dun & Co., 1841–1900: The Development of Credit-Reporting in the Nineteenth-Century.* Westport, CT: Greenwood Press.

North, Douglass C., and Barry R. Weingast. 1989. "Constitutions and Commitment: The Evolution of Institutions Governing Public Choice in Seventeenth-Century England." *Journal of Economic History* 49(4): 803–32.

Nugent, Rolf. 1941. "The Loan-Shark Problem." *Law and Contemporary Problems* 8(1): 3–13.

Nugent, Rolf, and Leon Henderson. 1934. "Installment Selling and the Consumer: A Brief for Regulation." *Annals of the American Academy of Political and Social Science* 173: 93–103.

Obermeyer, Ziad, Brian Powers, Christine Vogeli, and Sendhil Mullainathan. 2019. "Dissecting Racial Bias in an Algorithm Used to Manage the Health of Populations." *Science* 366: 447–53.

Odegard, Peter H., and Alan Barth. 1941. "Millions for Defense." *Public Opinion Quarterly* 5(3): 399–411.

Odinet, Christopher K. 2019. *Foreclosed: Mortgage Servicing and the Hidden Architecture of Homeownership in America.* New York: Cambridge University Press.

O'Donnell, John L. 1962. "Some Postwar Trends in Municipal Bond Financing." *Journal of Finance* 17(2): 259–68.

Office of the Comptroller of the Currency (OCC). 2016. *Quarterly Report on Bank Trading and Derivatives Activity: First Quarter 2016.* Washington, DC: Office of the Comptroller of the Currency.

Ohio. 1915. *Department of Banks and Banking Eighth Annual Report for the Period Nov. 16, 1914–June 30, 1915.* Columbus, OH: F. J. Heer.

Old Merchant. 1873. *Mercantile Failures: Their Causes and Preventions.* St. Louis: Mercantile Publishing Company.

O'Leary, James J. 1954. "Valuation of Life Insurance Company Holdings of Corporate Bonds and Stocks—Some Recent Developments." *Journal of Finance* 9(2): 160–77.

Olegario, Rowena. 2003. "Credit Reporting Agencies: A Historical Perspective." In *Credit Reporting Systems and the International Economy*, ed. Margaret J. Miller. Cambridge, MA: MIT Press.

———. 2006. *A Culture of Credit: Embedding Trust and Transparency in American Business.* Cambridge, MA: Harvard University Press.

———. 2016. *The Engine of Enterprise: Credit in America*. Cambridge, MA: Harvard University Press.

Olmstead, Alan L. 1972. "Investment Constraints and New York City Mutual Savings Bank Financing of Antebellum Development." *Journal of Economic History* 32(4): 811–40.

———. 1976. *New York City Mutual Savings Banks, 1819–1861*. Chapel Hill: University of North Carolina Press.

Olney, Martha L. 1989. "Credit as a Production-Smoothing Device: The Case of Automobiles, 1913–1938." *Journal of Economic History* 49(2): 377–91.

———. 2012. "From Skip to Hapless Victim: Interwar Changes in the Cost of Default." Unpublished manuscript, Department of Economics, University of California, Berkeley.

Ong, Qiyan, Walter Theseira, and Irene Y. H. Ng. 2019. "Reducing Debt Improves Psychological Functioning and Changes Decision-Making in the Poor." *PNAS* 116(15): 7244–49.

Orchard, C. R. 1938. "Cooperative Consumer Credit." *Annals of the American Academy of Political and Social Science* 196: 155–61.

Osterhus, Gustav. 1931. "Flaw-Tester for Bond Lists." *American Bankers Association Journal* (August): 67–110.

O'Sullivan, Mary. 2007. "The Expansion of the U.S. Stock Market, 1885–1930: Historical Facts and Theoretical Fashions." *Enterprise and Society* 8(3): 489–542.

Ott, Julia C. 2011. *When Wall Street Met Main Street: The Quest for an Investors' Democracy*. Cambridge, MA: Harvard University Press.

Ott, Julia, and Louis Hyman. 2013. "The Politics of Debt: How Labor Should Think about the Debt Question." *New Labor Forum* 22(2): 28–38.

Pacewicz, Josh. 2016. "The City as a Fiscal Derivative: Financialization, Urban Development, and the Politics of Earmarking." *City and Community* 15(3): 264–88.

Packer, Stephen B. 1968. "Municipal Bond Ratings." *Financial Analysts Journal* 24(4): 93–97.

Paddi, John B. 1938. "The Personal Loan Department of a Large Commercial Bank." *Annals of the American Academy of Political and Social Science* 196: 135–41.

Pagano, Marco, and Tullio Jappelli. 1993. "Information Sharing in Credit Markets." *Journal of Finance* 48(5): 1693–1718.

Pak, Susie J. 2013. *Gentlemen Bankers: The World of J. P. Morgan*. Cambridge, MA: Harvard University Press.

Palmer, Walter B. 1916. "The Federal Farm Loan Act." *Publications of the American Statistical Association* 15(115): 292–312.

Palyi, Melchior. 1938. "Bank Portfolios and the Control of the Capital Market." *Journal of Business* 11(1): 70–111.

Parker, Frank. 1938. "The Pay-as-You-Use Idea." *Annals of the American Academy of Political and Social Science* 196: 57–62.

Parmalee, C. A. 1914. "Credits and Collections." In *Mercantile Credits: A Series of Practical Lectures Delivered before the Young Men's Christian Association of Los Angeles, California*, ed. M. Martin Kallman et al., 102–17. New York: Ronald Press.

Partnoy, Frank. 1999. "The Siskel and Ebert of Financial Markets?: Two Thumbs Down for the Credit Rating Agencies." *Washington University Law Quarterly* 77(3): 620–715.

Pasquale, Frank. 2015. *The Black Box Society: The Secret Algorithms That Control Money and Information*. Cambridge, MA: Harvard University Press.

Patterson, Dennis M. 1992. "The Value of a Promise." *Law and Philosophy* 11(4): 385–402.

Patterson, Edwin W., and Harry J. McIntyre. 1931. "Unsecured Creditor's Insurance." *Columbia Law Review* 31(2): 212–37.

Patton, Terry K., and Paul D. Hutchison. 2013. "Historical Development of the Financial Reporting Model for State and Local Governments in the United States from Late 1800s to 1999." *Accounting Historians Journal* 40(2): 21–53.

Paul, Randolph E. 1954. *Taxation in the United States*. Boston: Little, Brown.

Paxton, Pamela. 2005. "Trust in Decline?" *Contexts* 4(1): 40–46.

Peabody, F. F. 1904. "The Characteristics of a Good Credit Man." In *Credit and Collections: The Factors Involved and the Methods Pursued in Credit Operations: A Practical Treatise by Eminent Credit Men*, ed. T. J. Zimmerman, 28–37. Chicago: System Company.

Pénet, Pierre. 2019. "Rhetorical Metrics: Building Securities Regulation in America's Era of Booms and Busts, 1890–1940." *European Journal of Sociology* 60(1): 69–107.

Peple, Charles A. 1916. "Statements of Borrowers from the Viewpoint of the Federal Reserve Bank." *Journal of Accountancy* (June): 410–23.

Petersen, Mitchell A., and Raghuram G. Rajan. 1994. "The Benefits of Lending Relationships: Evidence from Small Business Data." *Journal of Finance* 49(1): 3–37.

———. 2002. "Does Distance Still Matter? The Information Revolution in Small Business Lending." *Journal of Finance* 57(6): 2533–70.

Pew Charitable Trust. 2012. *Payday Lending in America: Who Borrows, Where They Borrow, and Why*. Washington, DC: Pew Charitable Trust.

Phelps, Clyde William. 1938. "Installment Credit Principles Reconsidered." *Journal of Marketing* 2(3): 219–25.

———. 1947. *Important Steps in Retail Credit Operation: Official Handbook of the National Retail Credit Association*. St. Louis: NRCA.

———. 1952. *The Role of the Sales Finance Companies in the American Economy*. Baltimore: Commercial Credit Company.

Philippon, Thomas. 2019. *The Great Reversal: How America Gave Up on Free Markets*. Cambridge, MA: Harvard University Press.

Piatt, A. Sanders. 1887. "Payment of the National Debt." *North American Review* 145(369): 180–86.

Piketty, Thomas. 2014. *Capital in the Twenty-First Century*. Trans. Arthur Goldhammer. Cambridge, MA: Harvard University Press.

Piketty, Thomas, and Emmanuel Saez. 2003. "Income Inequality in the United States, 1913–1998." *Quarterly Journal of Economics* 118(1): 1–39.

Piskorski, Tomasz, Amit Seru, and Vikrant Vig. 2010. "Securitization and Distressed Loan Renegotiation: Evidence from the Subprime Mortgage Crisis." *Journal of Financial Economics* 97: 369–97.

Pistor, Katharina. 2019. *The Code of Capital: How the Law Creates Wealth and Inequality*. Princeton: Princeton University Press.

Pistor, Katharina, and Philip A. Wellons. 1998. *The Role of Law and Legal Institutions in Asian Economic Development, 1960–1995*. Oxford: Oxford University Press.

Pitt, Mark M., and Shahidur R. Khandker. 1998. "The Impact of Group-Based Credit Programs on Poor Households in Bangladesh: Does the Gender of Participants Matter?" *Journal of Political Economy* 106: 958–96.

Plummer, Wilbur C. 1930. *National Retail Credit Survey*. Washington, DC: U.S. Government Printing Office.

———. 1942. "Consumer Credit in Colonial Philadelphia." *Pennsylvania Magazine of History and Biography* 66(4): 385–409.

Plummer, Wilbur C., and Ralph A. Young. 1940. *Sales Finance Companies and Their Credit Practices*. New York: National Bureau of Economic Research.

Polillo, Simone. 2013. *Conservatives versus Wildcats: A Sociology of Financial Conflict*. Stanford: Stanford University Press.

Pollack, Sheldon D. 2014. "The First National Income Tax, 1861–1872." *Tax Lawyer* 67(2): 311–30.

Polletta, Francesca, and Zaibu Tufail. 2014. "The Moral Obligations of Some Debts." *Sociological Forum* 29(1): 1–28.

Pontell, Henry N., and Kitty Calavita. 1993. "The Savings and Loan Industry." *Crime and Justice* 18: 203–46.

Poon, Martha. 2007. "Scorecards as Devices for Consumer Credit: The Case of Fair, Isaac & Co.." *Sociological Review* 55: 284–306.

———. 2009. "From New Deal Institutions to Capital Markets: Commercial Consumer Risk Scores and the Making of Subprime Mortgage Finance." *Accounting, Organizations and Society* 34(5): 654–74.

Poor, Henry Varnum. 1868. *Railroad Manual of the United States, for 1868–69*. New York: H. V. & H. W. Poor.

Pope, Jesse E. 1914. "Agricultural Credit in the United States." *Quarterly Journal of Economics* 28(4): 701–46.

Porter, Theodore. 1995. *Trust in Numbers: The Pursuit of Objectivity in Science and Public Life*. Princeton: Princeton University Press.

Poteat, J. Douglass. 1938. "State Legislative Relief for the Mortgage Debtor during the Depression." *Law and Contemporary Problems* 5(4): 517–44.

Potts, James H. 1978. "The Evolution of Municipal Accounting in the United States: 1900–1935." *Business History Review* 52(4): 518–36.

Power, Michael. 1997. *The Audit Society: Rituals of Verification*. Oxford: Oxford University Press.

Powers, L. G. 1914. "Governmental Regulation of Accounting Procedure." *Annals of the American Academy of Political and Social Science* 53: 119–27.

Prasad, Monica. 2012. *The Land of Too Much: American Abundance and the Paradox of Poverty*. Cambridge, MA: Harvard University Press.

Prendergast, William A. 1906. *Credit and Its Uses*. New York: D. Appleton & Co.

Prendergast, William A., and William H. Steiner. 1931. *Credit and Its Uses*. New York: D. Appleton.

Price, Douglas A. 1990. "Minority-Owned Banks: History and Trends." Federal Reserve Bank of Cleveland. *Economic Commentary*, July 1.

Price, Jacob M. 1980. *Capital and Credit in British Overseas Trade: The View from the Chesapeake, 1700–1776*. Cambridge, MA: Harvard University Press.

———. 1989. "What Did Merchants Do? Reflections on British Overseas Trade, 1660–1790." *Journal of Economic History* 49(2): 267–84.

Priest, Claire. 1999. "Colonial Courts and Secured Credit: Early American Commercial Litigation and Shays' Rebellion." *Yale Law Journal* 108(8): 2413–50.

Prudden, Russell F. 1922. *The Bank Credit Investigator*. New York: Bankers Publishing.

Puchalski, Vance Alan. 2016. "Credit at the Corner Store: An Analysis of Resource Exchange among Detroit-Area Urban Poor." *Sociological Forum* 31(4): 1040–62.

Putnam, Robert D. 1993. *Making Democracy Work: Civic Traditions in Modern Italy*. Princeton: Princeton University Press.

Puyans, Michel E. 1936. "Making the Most of the Credit Department." *Bankers' Magazine* (June): 497–500.

Quantius, Frances. 1946. "The Insurance of Bank Loans and Its Implications." *Journal of Business of the University of Chicago* 19(3): 133–44.

Quinn, Sarah. 2017. "'The Miracles of Bookkeeping': How Budget Politics Link Fiscal Policies and Financial Markets." *American Journal of Sociology* 123(1): 48–85.

———. 2019. *American Bonds: How Credit Markets Shaped a Nation*. Princeton: Princeton University Press.

Radford, Gail. 2003. "From Municipal Socialism to Public Authorities: Institutional Factors in the Shaping of American Public Enterprise." *Journal of American History* 90(3): 863–90.

Rajan, Raghuram. 2010. *Faultlines: How Hidden Fractures Still Threaten the World Economy*. Princeton: Princeton University Press.

Rajan, Raghuram, and Luigi Zingales. 1995. "What Do We Know about Capital Structure? Some Evidence from International Data." *Journal of Finance* 50(5): 1421–60.

Ransom, Roger L., and Richard Sutch. 1977. *One Kind of Freedom: The Economic Consequences of Emancipation*. Cambridge: Cambridge University Press.

Rappaport, A., and R. W. Wyatt. 1993. "An Overview of the Securitization of SBA Guaranteed Loans Originated by Commercial Banks." *Small Business Economics* 5(3): 215–20.

Ratchford, Benjamin U. 1933. "The North Carolina Public Debt, 1870–1878." *North Carolina Historical Review* 10(1): 1–20.

———. 1938. "American Government and Politics: Constitutional Provisions Governing State Borrowing." *American Political Science Review* 32(4): 694–707.

———. 1947. "History of the Federal Debt in the United States." *American Economic Review* 37(2): 131–41.

Raymond, William L. 1932. *State and Municipal Bonds*. 2nd ed. Boston: Financial Publishing.

Reed, Robert R. 1920. "'Blue Sky' Laws." *Annals of the American Academy of Political and Social Science* 88: 177–87.

Reeder, Nell M. 1936. *Consumer Credit*. Rev. ed. New York: New York Association of Personal Finance Companies.

Reihl, Charles W. 1906. "Credit Department of a Bank: Its Use, How to Conduct It, and Its Forms." *Bankers' Magazine* (March): 408–17.

Reilly, Thom. 2013. "Reforming Public Pay and Benefits." *State and Local Government Review* 45(1): 57–64.

Remington, Harold. 1909. "Bankruptcy Law and Peaceable Settlements of Business Failure." *Yale Law Journal* 18(8): 590–95.

Reséndez, Andrés. 2017. "North American Peonage." *Journal of the Civil War Era* 7(4): 597–619.

Reuben, Ernesto, Paola Sapienza, and Luigi Zingales. 2009. "Is Mistrust Self-fulfilling?" *Economic Letters* 104: 89–91.

Rhoen, Michiel, and Qing Yi Feng. 2018. "Why the 'Computer Says No': Illustrating Big Data's Discrimination Risk through Complex Systems Science." *International Data Privacy Law* 8(2): 140–59.

Rice, Roger L. 1968. "Residential Segregation by Law, 1910–1917." *Journal of Southern History* 34(2): 179–99.

Richman, Barak D. 2006. "Ethnic Networks, Extralegal Certainty, and Globalisation: Peering into the Diamond Industry." In *Contractual Certainty in International Trade*, ed. Volkmar Gessner. Oxford: Hart Publishing.

Richter, George R., Jr. 1968. "The Uniform Consumer Credit Code of the National Conference of Commissioners on Uniform State Laws." *Business Lawyer* 24(1): 183–97.

Riley, James C. 1978. "Foreign Credit and Fiscal Stability: Dutch Investment in the United States, 1781–1794." *Journal of American History* 65(3): 654–78.

Rippy, J. Fred. 1950. "A Bond-Selling Extravaganza of the 1920s." *Journal of Business* 23(4): 238–47.

Ritter, Gretchen. 1997. *Goldbugs and Greenbacks: The Antimonopoly Tradition and the Politics of Finance in America, 1865–1896*. New York: Cambridge University Press.

Rivenbark, William C. 2005. "A Historical Overview of Cost Accounting in Local Government." *State & Local Government Review* 37(3): 217–27.

Rivera, Lauren A. 2012. "Hiring as Cultural Matching: The Case of Elite Professional Service Firms." *American Sociological Review* 77(6): 999–1022.

Robb, Cliff A., Samantha L. Schreiber, and Stuart J. Heckman. 2020. "The Role of Federal and Private Student Loans in Homeownership Decisions." *Journal of Consumer Affairs* 54(1): 43–69.

Robins, Kingman Nott. 1916. *The Farm Mortgage Handbook: A Book of Facts Regarding the Methods by Which the Farmers of the United States and Canada Are Financed*. Garden City, NY: Doubleday, Page.

Robinson, John N., III. 2020. "Making Markets on the Margins: Housing Finance Agencies and the Racial Politics of Credit Expansion." *American Journal of Sociology* 125(4): 974–1029.

Robinson, Marshall A. 1955. "Federal Debt Management: Civil War, World War I, and World War II." *American Economic Review* 45(2): 388–401.

Rockoff, Hugh. 2021. "Oh, How the Mighty Have Fallen: The Bank Failures and Near Failures That Started America's Greatest Financial Panics." *Journal of Economic History* 81(2): 331–58.

Roe, Mark J. 2011. "The Derivatives Market's Payment Priorities as Financial Crisis Accelerator." *Stanford Law Review* 63: 539–90.

Rohner, Ralph J. 1979. "Equal Credit Opportunity Act." *Business Lawyer* 34(3): 1423–33.

Rolnick, Arthur J., and Warren E. Weber. 1983. "New Evidence on the Free Banking Era." *American Economic Review* 73(5): 1080–91.

Rona-Tas, Akos. 2017. "The Off-Label Use of Consumer Credit Ratings." *Historical Social Research* 42(1): 52–76.

———. 2020. "Predicting the Future: Art and Algorithms." *Socio-Economic Review* 18(3): 893–911.

Rose, Jonathan D., and Kenneth A. Snowden. 2013. "The New Deal and the Origins of the Modern American Real Estate Loan Contract." *Explorations in Economic History* 50: 548–66.

Rosen, Deborah A. 1997. *Courts and Commerce: Gender, Law, and the Market Economy in Colonial New York.* Columbus: Ohio State University Press.

Rosenberg, Moses K. 1977. "Historical Perspective of the Development of Rate Regulation of Title Insurance." *Journal of Risk and Insurance* 44(2): 193–209.

Rosenblatt, Samuel M. 1962. "The Significance of Credit in the Tobacco Consignment Trade: A Study of John Norton and Sons, 1768–1775." *William and Mary Quarterly* 19(3): 383–99.

Rosendale, William M. 1908. "Credit Department Methods." *Bankers' Magazine* (February): 183–94.

Rosenthal, Caitlin. 2018. *Accounting for Slavery: Masters and Management.* Cambridge, MA: Harvard University Press.

Rostow, Eugene V., and Lloyd N. Cutler. 1939. "Competing Systems of Corporate Reorganization: Chapters X and XI of the Bankruptcy Act." *Yale Law Journal* 48(8): 1334–76.

Rothenberg, Winifred B. 1985. "The Emergence of a Capital Market in Rural Massachusetts, 1730–1838." *Journal of Economic History* 45(4): 781–808.

Rothschild, Toby J. 1979. "Debt Collection." *Business Lawyer* 34(3): 1459–66.

Rothstein, Richard. 2017. *The Color of Law: A Forgotten History of How Our Government Segregated America.* New York: Liveright Publishing.

Rozman, David. 1927. "Land Credit in the Town of Newton, Manitowoc County, Wisconsin, 1848–1926." *Journal of Land and Public Utility Economics* 3(4): 371–84.

Rudin, Cynthia. 2019. "Stop Explaining Black Box Machine Learning Models for High Stakes Decisions and Use Interpretable Models Instead." *Nature Machine Intelligence* 1: 106–215.

Ruggles, Richard. 1959. "The U.S. National Accounts and Their Development." *American Economic Review* 49(1): 85–95.

Rule, James B. 1974. *Private Lives and Public Surveillance: Social Control in the Computer Age.* New York: Schocken Books.

Russell, Thomas D. 1996. "The Antebellum Courthouse as Creditors' Domain: Trial-Court Activity in South Carolina and the Concomitance of Lending and Litigation." *American Journal of Legal History* 40(3): 331–64.

Ryan, Andrea, Gunnar Trumbull, and Peter Tufano. 2011. "A Brief Postwar History of U.S. Consumer Finance." *Business History Review* 85: 461–98.

Ryan, Franklin W. 1934. "Short Term Loans in the United States during 1932 and 1933." *Journal of Business* 7(3): 266–69.

Sahling, Leonard G. 1991. "Real Estate Markets in the 1990s." *Challenge* 34(4): 43–52.

Sandage, Scott A. 2005. *Born Losers: A History of Failure in America*. Cambridge, MA: Harvard University Press.

Sanders, T. H. 1936. "Influence of the Securities and Exchange Commission upon Accounting Principles." *Accounting Review* 11(1): 66–74.

———. 1937. "Accounting Aspects of the Securities Act." *Law and Contemporary Problems* 4(2): 191–217.

Sanyal, Paromita. 2014. *Credit to Capabilities: A Sociological Study of Microcredit Groups in India*. New York: Cambridge University Press.

Sapag, J. C., M. Aracena, L. Villarroel, F. Poblete, C. Berrocal, R. Hoyos, M. Martínez, and I. Kawachi. 2008. "Social Capital and Self-Rated Health in Urban Low Income Neighbourhoods in Chile." *Journal of Epidemiology and Community Health* 62(9): 790–92.

Sapienza, Paola, and Luigi Zingales. 2012. "A Trust Crisis." *International Review of Finance* 12(2): 123–31.

Saulnier, R. J. 1950. *Urban Mortgage Lending by Life Insurance Companies*. New York: National Bureau of Economic Research.

Sawyer, E. W. 1940. "The Bank's Insurance Problems." *Bankers' Magazine* (July): 35–37.

Scheiber, Harry N. 1969. "Public Canal Finance and State Banking in Ohio, 1825–1837." *Indiana Magazine of History* 65(2): 119–32.

Schmeller, Mark. 2009. "The Political Economy of Opinion: Public Credit and Concepts of Public Opinion in the Age of Federalism." *Journal of the Early Republic* 29(1): 35–61.

Schmitz, Hubert. 1999. "From Ascribed to Earned Trust in Exporting Clusters." *Journal of International Economics* 48: 139–50.

Schragger, Richard C. 2012. "Democracy and Debt." *Yale Law Journal* 121(4): 860–86.

Schultz, Stanley K., and Clay McShane. 1978. "To Engineer the Metropolis: Sewers, Sanitation, and City Planning in Late-Nineteenth-Century America." *Journal of American History* 65(2): 389–411.

Schwarcz, Steven L., and Ori Sharon. 2014. "The Bankruptcy-Law Safe Harbor for Derivatives: A Path-Dependence Analysis." *Washington and Lee Law Review* 71(3): 1715–56.

Schweninger, Loren. 1989. "Black-Owned Businesses in the South, 1790–1880." *Business History Review* 63(1): 22–60.

Schweppe, George A. 1926. *Instalment Selling in Department Stores*. New York: Dry Goods Economist.

Seamster, Louise, and Raphaël Charron-Chénier. 2017. "Predatory Inclusion and Educational Debt: Rethinking the Racial Wealth Gap." *Social Currents* 4(3): 199–207.

Searle, John R. 1976. "A Classification of Illocutionary Acts." *Language in Society* 5(1): 1–23.

Seater, John J. 1993. "Ricardian Equivalence." *Journal of Economic Literature* 31(1): 142–90.

Securities and Exchange Commission (SEC). 1994. *Nationally Recognized Statistical Rating Organizations, Concept Release 34-34616*. Washington, DC: SEC.

———. 2008. *Summary Report of Issues Identified in the Commission Staff's Examinations of Select Credit Rating Agencies*. Washington, DC: SEC.

———. 2012. *Report to Congress on Assigned Credit Ratings*. Washington, DC: SEC Division of Trading and Markets.

Seiden, Martin H. 1964. *The Quality of Trade Credit*. New York: National Bureau of Economic Research.

Several Tradesmen. 1819. *The London Tradesman; A Familiar Treatise on the Rationale of Trade and Commerce*. London: Simpkin and Marshall.

Severson, Robert F. 1962. "The Source of Mortgage Credit for Champaign County, 1865–1880." *Agricultural History* 36(3): 150–55.

Severson, Robert F., James F. Niss, and Richard D. Winkelman. 1966. "Mortgage Borrowing as a Frontier Developed: A Study of Mortgages in Champaign County, Illinois, 1836–1895." *Journal of Economic History* 26(2): 147–68.

Sexton, Jay. 2005. *Debtor Diplomacy: Finance and American Foreign Relations in the Civil War Era, 1837–1873*. New York: Oxford University Press.

Shaw, Christopher W. 2015. "'The Man in the Street Is for It': The Road to the FDIC." *Journal of Policy History* 27(1): 36–60.

———. 2018a. "'Banks of the People': The Life and Death of the U.S. Postal Savings System." *Journal of Social History* 52(1): 121–52.

———. 2018b. "'Tired of Being Exploited': The Grassroots Origin of the Federal Farm Loan Act of 1916." *Agricultural History* 92(4): 512–40.

———. 2019. *Money, Power, and the People: The American Struggle to Make Banking Democratic*. Chicago: University of Chicago Press.

Shenker, Joseph C., and Anthony J. Colletta. 1991. "Asset Securitization: Evolution, Current Issues and New Frontiers." *Texas Law Review* 69: 1369–1429.

Shergold, Peter R. 1978. "The Loan Shark: The Small Loan Business in Early Twentieth-Century Pittsburgh." *Pennsylvania History* 45(3): 195–223.

Shertzer, Allison, Tate Twinam, and Randall P. Walsh. 2016. "Race, Ethnicity, and Discriminatory Zoning." *American Economic Journal: Applied Economics* 8(3): 217–46.

Silsby, Robert W. 1960. "Mortgage Credit in the Phelps-Gorham Purchase." *New York History* 41(1): 3–34.

Simonson, Donald G., and George H. Hempel. 1993. "Banking Lessons from the Past: The 1938 Regulatory Agreement Interpreted." *Journal of Financial Services Research* 7: 249–67.

Sinclair, Timothy J. 2005. *The New Masters of Capital: American Bond Rating Agencies and the Politics of Creditworthiness*. Ithaca, NY: Cornell University Press.

———. 2021. *To the Brink of Destruction: America's Rating Agencies and Financial Crisis*. Ithaca: Cornell University Press.

Singer, David Andrew. 2007. *Regulating Capital: Setting Standards for the International Financial System*. Ithaca, NY: Cornell University Press.

Síthigh, Daithí Mac, and Mathias Siems. 2019. "The Chinese Social Credit System: A Model for Other Countries?" *Modern Law Review* 82(6): 1034–71.

Sitterson, J. Carlyle. 1944. "Financing and Marketing the Sugar Crop of the Old South." *Journal of Southern History* 10(2): 188–99.

Sivakumar, Kumar N., and Gregory Waymire. 1993. "The Information Content of Earnings in a Discretionary Reporting Environment: Evidence NYSE Industrials, 1905–10." *Journal of Accounting Research* 31(1): 62–91.

Skeel, David A., Jr. 2001. *Debt's Dominion: A History of Bankruptcy Law in America*. Princeton: Princeton University Press.

Skinner, Edward M. 1904. "Credits and Collections in a Wholesale House." In *Credit and Collections: The Factors Involved and the Methods Pursued in Credit Operations: A Practical Treatise by Eminent Credit Men*, ed. T. J. Zimmerman, 85–101. Chicago: System Company.

———. 1916. "Credits and Collections in a Wholesale House." In *Credits and Collections: Organizing the Work, Correct Policies and Methods, Five Credit and Collection Systems*, 85–101. Chicago: W. A. Shaw.

Skocpol, Theda, Marshall Ganz, and Ziad Munson. 2000. "A Nation of Organizers: The Institutional Origins of Civil Voluntarism in the United States." *American Political Science Review* 94(3): 527–46.

Skocpol, Theda, and Jennifer Lynn Oser. 2004. "Organization despite Adversity: The Origins and Development of African American Fraternal Associations." *Social Science History* 28(3): 367–437.

Small, Mario L., Armin Akhavan, Mo Torres, and Qi Wang. 2021. "Banks, Alternative Institutions and the Spatial-Temporal Ecology of Racial Inequality in U.S. Cities." *Nature Human Behaviour*. https://doi.org/10.1038/s41562-021-01153-1.

Smalley, Orange A., and Frederick D. Sturdivant. 1973. *The Credit Merchants: A History of Spiegel, Inc.* Carbondale: Southern Illinois University Press.

Smiley, Gene, and Richard H. Keehn. 1995. "Federal Personal Income Tax Policy in the 1920s." *Journal of Economic History* 55(2): 285–303.

Smith, Arthur A. 1942. "Bank Note Detecting in the Era of State Banks." *Mississippi Valley Historical Review* 29(3): 371–86.

Smith, Clifford W., Jr., and Jerold B. Warner. 1979. "On Financial Contracting: An Analysis of Bond Covenants." *Journal of Financial Economics* 7: 117–61.

Smith, David Sellers. 2010a. "Business Moralists: Credit Men and the Rise of Corporate America, 1893–1929." PhD diss., Northwestern University.

———. 2010b. "The Elimination of the Unworthy: Credit Men and Small Retailers in Progressive Era Capitalism." *Journal of the Gilded Age and the Progressive Era* 9(2): 197–220.

Smith, Donald J. 2010. "Hidden Debt: From Enron's Commodity Prepays to Lehman's Repo 105s." *Financial Analysts Journal* 67(5): 15–22.

Smith, Gregor W. 2006. "The Spectre of Deflation: A Review of Empirical Evidence." *Canadian Journal of Economics* 39(4): 1041–72.

Smith, L. Douglas, Michael Staten, Thomas Eyssell, Maureen Karig, Beth A. Freeborn, and Andrea Golden. 2013. "Accuracy of Information Maintained by U.S. Credit Bureaus: Frequency of Errors and Effects on Consumers' Credit Scores." *Journal of Consumer Affairs* 47(3): 588–601.

Smith, Paul F. 1964. "Measuring Risk on Consumer Instalment Credit." *Management Science* 11(2): 327–40.

Smith, Walter George, and M. D. Chalmers. 1916. "National Conference of Commissioners on Uniform State Laws in the United States." *Journal of the Society of Comparative Legislation* 16(2): 154–69.

Snowden, Kenneth A. 1987. "Mortgage Rates and American Capital Market Development in the Late Nineteenth Century." *Journal of Economic History* 47(3): 671–91.

———. 1988. "Mortgage Lending and American Urbanization, 1880–1890." *Journal of Economic History* 48(2): 273–85.

———. 1997. "Building and Loan Associations in the U.S., 1880–1893: The Origins of Localization in the Residential Mortgage Market." *Research in Economics* 51: 227–50.

———. 2010. "Covered Farm Mortgage Bonds in the United States during the Late Nineteenth Century." *Journal of Economic History* 70(4): 783–812.

———. 2013. *Mortgage Banking in the United States, 1870–1940.* Washington, DC: Research Institute for Housing America.

Somers, Patricia, James M. Hollis, and Tim Stokes. 2000. "The Federal Government as First Creditor on Student Loans: Politics and Policy." *Educational Evaluation and Policy Analysis* 22(4): 331–39.

Soukup, Lynn A. 1996. "When Assets Become Securities: The ABCs of Asset Securitization." *Business Law Today* 6(2): 20–23.

Sperling, Ted. 1961. "Public Relations Aspects of Promoting a Bond Issue." *Journal of the Water Pollution Control Federation* 33(6): 585–92.

Squires, Gregory D., and Sally O'Connor. 2001. *Color and Money: Politics and Prospects for Community Reinvestment in Urban America.* Albany: State University of New York Press.

Standard and Poor's. 2015. *2014 Annual Global Corporate Default Study and Rating Transitions.* New York: Standard & Poor's.

Stearns, Linda Brewster. 1986. "Capital Market Effects on External Control of Corporations." *Theory and Society* 15(1/2): 47–75.

Stegman, Michael A. 2007. "Payday Lending." *Journal of Economic Perspectives* 21(1): 169–90.

Steil, Justin P., Len Albright, Jacob S. Rugh, and Douglas S. Massey. 2018. "The Social Structure of Mortgage Discrimination." *Housing Studies* 33(5): 759–76.

Stein, Luke C. D., and Constantine Yannelis. 2020. "Financial Inclusion, Human Capital, and Wealth Accumulation: Evidence from the Freedman's Savings Bank." *Review of Financial Studies* 33: 5333–77.

Steiner, W. H. 1923. "Development of American Bank Credit Methods." *University Journal of Business* 1(4): 441–50.

———. 1924. "Bank versus Mercantile Credits." *Bankers' Magazine* (May): 712–14.

Steinkamp, Sven, and Frank Westermann. 2014. "The Role of Creditor Seniority in Europe's Sovereign Debt Crisis." *Economic Policy* 29(79): 495–552.

Stevens, Albert C. 1891. "The Commercial Death Rate." *Publications of the American Statistical Association* 2(13): 186–94.

Stiglitz, Joseph. 2000. "The Contributions of the Economics of Information to Twentieth Century Economics." *Quarterly Journal of Economics* 115: 1441–78.

Stivers, Abby, and Elizabeth Popp Berman. 2020. "Parents, Partners, Plans, and Promises: The Relational Work of Student Loan Borrowing." *Socius* 6: 1–13.

Stoner, Paul Matthew. 1943. "The Mortgage Market: Today and after World War I." *Journal of Land and Public Utility Economics* 19(2): 224–30.

Stookey, John A. 1992. "Trying Times: A Sociopolitical History of Litigation during the First Half of the Twentieth Century." *Social Science History* 16(1): 23–61.

Streeck, Wolfgang. 2014. *Buying Time: The Delayed Crisis of Democratic Capitalism*. Trans. Patrick Camiller. London: Verso.

Strine, Walter M., Jr. 1978. "New Commercial Devices—Mortgage-Backed Securities." *Real Property, Probate and Trust Journal* 13(4): 1011–54.

Stronck, H. N., and J. Eigelberner. 1930. *Bank Loan Management*. New York: Rand McNally.

Stuart, Guy. 2003. *Discriminating Risk: The U.S. Mortgage Lending Industry in the Twentieth Century*. Ithaca, NY: Cornell University Press.

Suarez, Raleigh A. 1966. "Bargains, Bills, and Bankruptcies: Business Activity in Rural Antebellum Louisiana." *Louisiana History* 7(3): 189–206.

Sugrue, Thomas J. 2005. *The Origins of the Urban Crisis: Race and Inequality in Postwar Detroit*. Princeton: Princeton University Press.

Sullivan, Teresa A., Elizabeth Warren, and Jay Lawrence Westbrook. 2000. *The Fragile Middle Class: Americans in Debt*. New Haven: Yale University Press.

———. 2006. "Less Stigma or More Financial Distress: An Empirical Analysis of the Extraordinary Increase in Bankruptcy Filings." *Stanford Law Review* 59(2): 213–56.

Sylla, Richard. 1969. "Federal Policy, Banking Market Structure, and Capital Mobilization in the United States, 1863–1913." *Journal of Economic History* 29(4): 657–86.

———. 1998. "U.S. Securities Markets and the Banking System, 1790–1840." *Federal Reserve Bank of St. Louis Review* (May/June): 83–98.

———. 2007. "Reversing Financial Reversals: Government and the Financial System since 1789." In *Government and the American Economy: A New History*, ed. Price Fishback et al., 115–47. Chicago: University of Chicago Press.

Sylla, Richard, John B. Legler, and John J. Wallis. 1987. "Banks and State Public Finance in the New Republic: The United States, 1790–1860." *Journal of Economic History* 47(2): 391–403.

Tabb, Charles Jordan. 1991. "The Historical Evolution of the Bankruptcy Discharge." *American Bankruptcy Law Journal* 65: 325–71.

———. 1995. "The History of the Bankruptcy Laws in the United States." *American Bankruptcy Institute Law Review* 3: 5–51.

Tait, Allison Anna. 2019. "Trusting Marriage." *University of California Irvine Law Review* 10: 199–250.

———. 2020. "The Law of High Wealth Exceptionalism." *Alabama Law Review* 71(4): 981–1037.

Taylor, H. C. 1959. "Analyzing Municipal Credit—General Obligations." In *Fundamentals of Municipal Bonds*, 103–16. Washington, DC: Investment Bankers Association of America.

Taylor, Keeanga-Yamahtta. 2019. *Race for Profit: How Banks and the Real Estate Industry Undermined Black Homeownership*. Chapel Hill: University of North Carolina Press.

Teaford, Jon C. 1981. "State Administrative Agencies and the Cities, 1890–1920." *American Journal of Legal History* 25(3): 225–48.

tenBroek, Jacobus. 1951. "Thirteenth Amendment to the Constitution of the United States: Consummation to Abolition and Key to the Fourteenth Amendment." *California Law Review* 39(2): 171–203.

Tenenbaum, Shelly. 1989. "Culture and Context: The Emergence of Hebrew Free Loan Societies in the United States." *Social Science History* 13(3): 211–36.

———. 1993. *A Credit to Their Community: Jewish Loan Societies in the United States, 1880–1945*. Detroit: Wayne State University Press.

Testart, Alain. 2002. "The Extent and Significance of Debt Slavery." *Revue française de sociologie* 43: 173–204.

Tevington, Patricia, Laura Napolitano, and Frank F. Furstenberg. 2017. "Financing Children's Futures: Economic Strategies for Postsecondary Education among Middle-Income Families." *Sociological Forum* 32(4): 726–47.

Thiemann, Matthias. 2018. *The Growth of Shadow Banking: A Comparative Institutional Analysis*. Cambridge: Cambridge University Press.

Thompson, Elizabeth Lee. 2004. *The Reconstruction of Southern Debtors: Bankruptcy after the Civil War*. Athens: University of Georgia Press.

Thomson, David K. 2016. "'Like a Cord through the Whole Country': Union Bonds and Financial Mobilization for Victory." *Journal of the Civil War Era* 6(3): 347–75.

Thornton, Tamara Plakins. 2007. "'A Great Machine' or a 'Beast of Prey': A Boston Corporation and Its Rural Debtors in an Age of Capitalist Transformation." *Journal of the Early Republic* 27(4): 567–97.

Thurston, Chloe N. 2018. *At the Boundaries of Homeownership: Credit, Discrimination, and the American State*. New York: Cambridge University Press.

Tobey, Ronald, Charles Wetherell, and Jay Brigham. 1990. "Moving Out and Settling In: Residential Mobility, Home Owning, and the Public Enframing of Citizenship, 1921–1950." *American Historical Review* 95(5): 1395–1422.

Tootell, Geoffrey M. B. 1993. "Defaults, Denials, and Discrimination in Mortgage Lending." *New England Economic Review* (September/October): 45–51.

Tough, Rosalind. 1951. "The Life Cycle of the Home Owners' Loan Corporation." *Land Economics* 27(4): 324–31.

Townsend, Genevieve. 1932. *Consumer Loans in Wisconsin*. Madison, WI: Straus.

Trapp, Joseph T. 1953. *Credit Insurance: A Factor in Bank Lending*. Baltimore: American Credit Indemnity Company of New York.

Treacy, William F., and Mark S. Carey. 1998. "Credit Risk Rating at Large U.S. Banks." *Federal Reserve Bulletin* 84: 897–921.

———. 2000. "Credit Risk Rating Systems at Large US Banks." *Journal of Banking and Finance* 24: 167–201.

Treat, E. M. 1912. "Credit Insurance." In *The Business of Insurance*, vol. 2, ed. Howard P. Dunham, 401–10. New York: Ronald Press.

Tregoe, J. H. 1921. "Standards for Granting Credit." *Annals of the American Academy of Political and Social Science* 97: 63–66.

Trissell, Teresa Dondlinger. 1995. "Derivative Use in Tax-Exempt Financing." *Tax Lawyer* 48(4): 1021–41.

Trivellato, Francesca. 2009. *The Familiarity of Strangers: The Sephardic Diaspora, Livorno, and Cross-Cultural Trade in the Early Modern Period*. New Haven: Yale University Press.

Truesdale, J. R. 1927. *Credit Bureau Management*. New York: Prentice-Hall.

Trumbull, Gunnar. 2012. "Credit Access and Social Welfare: The Rise of Consumer Lending in the United States and France." *Politics and Society* 40(1): 9–34.

———. 2014. *Consumer Lending in France and America: Credit and Welfare*. New York: Cambridge University Press.

Tufano, Peter. 1997. "Business Failure, Judicial Intervention, and Financial Innovation: Restructuring U.S. Railroads in the Nineteenth Century." *Business History Review* 71(1): 1–40.

Turner, Adair. 2016. *Between Debt and the Devil: Money, Credit, and Fixing Global Finance*. Princeton: Princeton University Press.

Twyman, Robert W. 1954. *History of Marshall Field & Co., 1852–1906*. Philadelphia: University of Pennsylvania Press.

Ulmer, Melville J. 1960. *Capital in Transportation, Communications, and Public Utilities: Its Formation and Financing*. Princeton: Princeton University Press.

Ulrich, Craig. 1991. "Home Mortgage Disclosure Act Developments." *Business Lawyer* 46(3): 1077–82.

Unger, Irwin. 1964. *The Greenback Era*. Princeton: Princeton University Press.

United States Census Office. 1883. *Compendium of the Tenth Census (June 1, 1880), Part II*. Washington, DC: Department of the Interior.

United States Department of Commerce. 1907. *Wealth, Debt, and Taxation: Special Report of the Census Office*. Washington, DC: U.S. Government Printing Office.

United States Department of Treasury. 1917. *United States Government Bonds of the Second Liberty Loan: What They Are and How to Buy Them*. Washington, DC: U.S. Government Printing Office.

———. 1941. *Defense Savings Bonds and Stamps . . . What They Are and the Part They Play in the Defense Program*. Washington, DC: U.S. Government Printing Office.

United States General Accounting Office (GAO). 1990. "Financial Problems in the Stafford Student Loan Program." Testimony of Franklin Frazer before the Committee on Banking, Housing and Urban Affairs, United States Senate, July 27. GAO: GAO/T-HRD-90-52.

Usner, Daniel H. 1987. "The Frontier Exchange Economy of the Lower Mississippi Valley in the Eighteenth Century." *William and Mary Quarterly* 44(2): 165–92.

Uzzi, Brian. 1999. "Embeddedness in the Making of Financial Capital: How Social Relations and Networks Benefit Firms Seeking Financing." *American Sociological Review* 64: 481–505.

Uzzi, Brian, and James Gillespie. 2002. "Knowledge Spillover in Corporate Financing Networks: Embeddedness, Network Transitivity, and Trade Credit Performance." *Strategic Management Journal* 23: 595–618.

Uzzi, Brian, and Ryon Lancaster. 2003. "Relational Embeddedness and Learning: The Case of Bank Loan Managers and Their Clients." *Management Science* 49(4): 383–99.

Vanatta, Sean H. 2018. "Charge Account Banking: A Study of Financial Innovation in the 1950s." *Enterprise and Society* 19(2): 352–90.

Vance, Richard A., and Katherine A. Bell. 2014. "MERS Litigation in 2012 and 2013: A Survey of Claims by Borrowers and Others." *Business Lawyer* 69(2): 657–69.

Van Deusen, Edgar. 1907. "Farm Mortgage Loans as Investments." *Bankers' Magazine* (February): 183–94.

Van Fenstermaker, J. 1965. *The Development of American Commercial Banking: 1782–1837*. Kent, OH: Kent State University Press.

Venkatesh, Sudhir Alladi. 2006. *Off the Books: The Underground Economy of the Urban Poor*. Cambridge, MA: Harvard University Press.

Vickers, Daniel. 2010. "Errors Expected: The Culture of Credit in Rural New England, 1750–1800." *Economic History Review* 63(4): 1032–57.

———. 2011. "Credit and Misunderstanding: On Nantucket Island, Massachusetts (1683–1763)." *Quaderni Storici* 46(137): 415–40.

Vinokurova, Natalya. 2018. "How Mortgage-Backed Securities Became Bonds: The Emergence, Evolution, and Acceptance of Mortgage-Backed Securities in the United States, 1960–1987." *Enterprise and Society* 19(3): 610–60.

Vose, Edward Neville. 1916. *Seventy-Five Years of the Mercantile Agency R. G. Dun & Co., 1841–1916.* Brooklyn: R. G. Dun.

Vyas, Darshali A., Leo G. Eisenstein, and David S. Jones. 2020. "Hidden in Plain Sight: Reconsidering the Use of Race Correction in Clinical Algorithms." *New England Journal of Medicine* 383: 874–82.

Waddell, Theodore C. 1916. "Uniform Municipal Accounting." *Bulletin of the National Tax Association* 2(3): 65–68.

Wadhwani, R. Daniel. 2006. "Protecting Small Savers: The Political Economy of Economic Security." *Journal of Policy History* 18(1): 126–45.

Waibel, Michael. 2021. "Decolonization and Sovereign Debt: A Quagmire." In *Sovereign Debt Diplomacies: Rethinking Sovereign Debt from Colonial Empires to Hegemony*, ed. Pierre Pénet and Juan Flores Zendejas, 213–31. Oxford: Oxford University Press.

Walker, Amasa. 1866. *The Science of Wealth: A Manual of Political Economy*. Boston: Little, Brown.

Walker, Juliet E. K. 1986. "Racism, Slavery, and Free Enterprise: Black Entrepreneurship in the United States before the Civil War." *Business History Review* 60(3): 343–82.

Wall, Alexander. 1919. *The Banker's Credit Manual*. Indianapolis: Bobbs-Merrill.

Wallis, John Joseph. 2000. "American Government Finance in the Long Run: 1790–1990." *Journal of Economic Perspectives* 14(1): 61–82.

———. 2005. "Constitutions, Corporations, and Corruption: American States and Constitutional Change, 1842–1852." *Journal of Economic History* 65(1): 211–56.

———. 2007. "The National Era." In *Government and the American Economy: A New History*, ed. Price Fishback et al., 148–87. Chicago: University of Chicago Press.

Wassam, Clarence W. 1908. *Salary Loan Business in New York City*. New York: Charity Organization Society.

Watts, Duncan J. 1999. *Small Worlds: The Dynamics of Networks between Order and Randomness*. Princeton: Princeton University Press.

Weber, Max. 1978. *Economy and Society*. Ed. Guenther Roth and Claus Wittich. Berkeley: University of California Press.

Weber, Rachel. 2015. *From Boom to Bubble: How Finance Built the New Chicago*. Chicago: University of Chicago Press.

Wei, Yanhao, Pinar Yildirim, Christophe Van den Bulte, and Chrysanthos Dellarocas. 2016. "Credit Scoring with Social Network Data." *Marketing Science* 35(2): 234–58.

Weil, Harry E. 1907. "Municipal Bond Issues Explained." *Annals of the American Academy of Political and Social Science* 30: 197–203.

Weimer, Arthur M. 1937. "The Work of the Federal Housing Administration." *Journal of Political Economy* 45(4): 466–83.

Weinberg, Harold R. 1982. "Commercial Paper in Economic Theory and Legal History." *Kentucky Law Journal* 70: 567–92.

Weingartner, H. Martin. 1966. "Concepts and Utilization of Credit Scoring Techniques." *Banking* (February): 51–53.

Weiss, Julian D. 1938. "Installment Selling: A Critical View." *Harvard Business Review* 17(1): 96–104.

Weiss, Marc A. 1989. "Real Estate History: An Overview and Research Agenda." *Business History Review* 63(2): 241–82.

Wells, John G. 1867. *Every Man His Own Lawyer and Business Form Book*. New York: Benj. W. Hitchcock.

West, Richard R. 1973. "Bond Ratings, Bond Yield and Financial Regulation: Some Findings." *Journal of Law and Economics* 16(1): 159–68.

West, Robert Craig. 1976. "Real Bills, the Gold Standard, and Central Bank Policy." *Business History Review* 50(4): 503–13.

Westerfield, Ray B. 1932. "The Trend to Secured Loans." *Journal of Business of the University of Chicago* 5(1): 1–18.

———. 1934. "National versus State Banks." *Annals of the American Academy of Political and Social Science* 171: 17–34.

Wheelock, David C., and Paul W. Wilson. 1995. "Explaining Bank Failures: Deposit Insurance, Regulation, and Efficiency." *Review of Economics and Statistics* 77(4): 689–700.

Wherry, Frederick F., Kristin S. Seefeldt, and Anthony S. Alvarez. 2019. *Credit Where It's Due: Rethinking Financial Citizenship*. New York: Russell Sage Foundation.

Whitaker, R. David. 1999. "Rules under the Uniform Electronic Transactions Act for an Electronic Equivalent to a Negotiable Promissory Note." *Business Lawyer* 55(1): 437–53.

White, Edward. 1909. "Farm Lands as Security for Investment." *Bankers' Magazine* (October): 592–94.

White, Eugene N. 1981. "State-Sponsored Insurance of Bank Deposits in the United States, 1907–1929." *Journal of Economic History* 41(3): 537–57.

———. 1982. "The Political Economy of Banking Regulation, 1864–1933." *Journal of Economic History* 42(1): 33–40.

———. 1998. "Were Banks Special Intermediaries in Late Nineteenth Century America?" *Federal Reserve Bank of St. Louis Review* (May/June): 13–32.

White, Larry R. 1990. "Credit Analysis: Two More C's of Credit." *Journal of Commercial Bank Lending* (October): 11–15.

White, Lawrence J. 1993. "A Cautionary Tale of Deregulation Gone Awry: The S&L Debacle." *Southern Economic Journal* 59(3): 496–514.

White, Michele J. 2007. "Bankruptcy Reform and Credit Cards." *Journal of Economic Perspectives* 21(4): 175–200.

Wiley, Norbert. 1967. "America's Unique Class Politics: The Interplay of the Labor, Credit and Commodity Markets." *American Sociological Review* 32(4): 529–41.

Wilkins, Mira. 1991. "Foreign Investment in the U.S. Economy before 1914." *Annals of the American Academy of Political and Social Science* 516: 9–21.

Williams, Charles W. 1946. *The Credit Department: A Training Ground for the Loan Officer*. Philadelphia: Robert Morris Associates.

Williamson, Harold F., and Orange A. Smalley. 1957. *Northwestern Mutual Life: A Century of Trusteeship*. Evanston, IL: Northwestern University Press.

Wilson, Berry K. 2011. "On the Informational Content of Ratings: An Analysis of the Origin of Moody's Stock and Bond Ratings." *Financial History Review* 18(2): 155–90.

Woloson, Wendy A. 2007. "In Hock: Pawning in Early America." *Journal of the Early Republic* 27: 35–81.

Wolters, Timothy. 2000. "Carry Your Credit in Your Pocket: The Early History of the Credit Card at Bank of America and Chase Manhattan." *Enterprise and Society* 1(2): 315–54.

Woo, Jung-En. 1991. *Race to the Swift: State and Finance in Korean Industrialization*. New York: Columbia University Press.

Woodman, Harold D. 1966a. "The Decline of Cotton Factorage after the Civil War." *American Historical Review* 71(4): 1219–36.

———. 1966b. "Itinerant Cotton Merchants of the Antebellum South." *Agricultural History* 40(2): 79–90.

———. 1968. *King Cotton and His Retainers: Financing and Marketing the Cotton Crop of the South, 1800–1925.* Lexington: University of Kentucky Press.

———. 1995. *New South—New Law: The Legal Foundations of Credit and Labor Relations in the Postbellum Agricultural South.* Baton Rouge: Louisiana State University Press.

Woodruff, Archibald M., Jr. 1937. *Farm Mortgage Loans of Life Insurance Companies.* New Haven: Yale University Press.

Wright, Robert E. 1999. "Bank Ownership and Lending Patterns in New York and Pennsylvania, 1781–1831." *Business History Review* 73(1): 40–60.

———. 2002. *The Wealth of Nations Rediscovered: Integration and Expansion in American Financial Markets, 1780–1850.* New York: Cambridge University Press.

Wright, Robert E., and Christopher Kingston. 2012. "Corporate Insurers in Antebellum America." *Business History Review* 86(3): 447–76.

Wyatt-Brown, Bertram. 1966. "God and Dun & Bradstreet, 1841–1851." *Business History Review* 40(4): 432–50.

Yates, JoAnne. 1989. *Control through Communication: The Rise of System in American Management.* Baltimore: Johns Hopkins University Press.

Yellen, Janet L. 2011. "Macroprudential Supervision and Monetary Policy in the Post-Crisis World." *Business Economics* 46(1): 3–12.

Yinger, John. 1995. *Closed Doors, Opportunities Lost: The Continuing Costs of Housing Discrimination.* New York: Russell Sage Foundation.

Zaloom, Caitlin. 2019. *Indebted: How Families Make College Work at Any Cost.* Princeton: Princeton University Press.

Zelizer, Viviana A. 1994. *The Social Meaning of Money: Pin Money, Paychecks, Poor Relief and Other Currencies.* New York: Basic Books.

———. 1996. "Payments and Social Ties." *Sociological Forum* 11: 481–95.

Zimmerman, T. J. 1904. "The Function and Work of the Commercial Agency." In *Credit and Collections: The Factors Involved and the Methods Pursued in Credit Operations. A Practical Treatise by Eminent Credit Men,* ed. T. J. Zimmerman, 38–48. Chicago: System Company.

———. 1916a. "The Function and Work of a Commercial Agency." In *Credits and Collections: Organizing the Work, Correct Policies and Methods, Five Credit and Collection Systems,* 38–49. Chicago: W. A. Shaw.

———. 1916b. "Credit Insurance—Its Object and Worth." In *Credits and Collections: Organizing the Work, Correct Policies and Methods, Five Credit and Collection Systems,* 65–76. Chicago: W. A. Shaw.

Zinman, Jonathan. 2014. "Consumer Credit: Too Much or Too Little (or Just Right)?" *Journal of Legal Studies* 43(S2): S209–S237.

Zuboff, Shoshana. 2019. *The Age of Surveillance Capitalism: The Fight for a Human Future at the New Frontier of Power.* New York: Public Affairs.

Zumello, Christine. 2011. "The 'Everything Card' and Consumer Credit in the United States in the 1960s." *Business History Review* 85: 551–75.

A NOTE ON THE TYPE

This book has been composed in Adobe Text and Gotham.
Adobe Text, designed by Robert Slimbach for Adobe,
bridges the gap between fifteenth- and sixteenth-century
calligraphic and eighteenth-century Modern styles.
Gotham, inspired by New York street signs, was designed
by Tobias Frere-Jones for Hoefler & Co.